INSIDE TERRORIST ORGANIZATIONS

D0048104

CASS SERIES ON POLITICAL VIOLENCE
ISSN 1365-0580

Series Editors: David C. Rapoport, University of California, Los Angeles
Paul Wilkinson, University of St Andrews, Scotland

1. *Terror from the Extreme Right*, edited by Tore Bjørgo

2. *Millennialism and Violence*, edited by Michael Barkun

3. *Religious Radicalism in the Greater Middle East*, edited by Bruce Maddy-Weitzman and Efraim Inbar

4. *The Revival of Right-Wing Extremism in the Nineties*, edited by Peter H. Merkl and Leonard Weinberg

5. *Violence in Southern Africa*, edited by William Gutteridge and J.E. Spence

6. *Aviation Terrorism and Security*, edited by Paul Wilkinson and Brian M. Jenkins

7. *Terrorism Today*, Christopher C. Harmon

8. *The IRA, 1968–2000: An Analysis of a Secret Army*, J. Bowyer Bell

9. *Terrorism Versus Democracy: The Liberal State Response*, Paul Wilkinson

10. *Inside Terrorist Organizations*, edited by David C. Rapoport

INSIDE TERRORIST ORGANIZATIONS

Edited by
DAVID C. RAPOPORT

FRANK CASS
LONDON • PORTLAND, OR

First published in 2001 in Great Britain by
FRANK CASS PUBLISHERS
Crown House, 47 Chase Side
Southgate, London N14 5BP, England

and in the United States of America by
FRANK CASS PUBLISHERS
c/o ISBS, 5824 N.E. Hassalo Street
Portland, Oregon 97213-3644

Website: www.frankcass.com

British Library Cataloguing in Publication Data

A catalogue record for this book is available from the British Library

ISBN 0-7146-8179-2 (paper)

Library of Congress Cataloging-in-Publication Data

Inside terrorist organizations / edited by David C. Rapoport.– 2nd ed.
  p.cm.
  Includes bibliographical references.
  ISBN 0-7146-8179-2
  1. Terrorism. 2. Terrorists–Psychology. I. Rapoport, David C.
HV6431 .I48 2001
303.6'25–dc21

00-065926

This group of studies first appeared in a Special Issue:
Inside Terrorist Organizations, *The Journal of Strategic Studies*
(ISSN 0140-2390) Vol.10, No.4 (Dec. 1987) published by Frank Cass.
The Kaplan chapter is from the journal *Terrorism and
Political Violence* (ISSN 0954-6553) Vol.9, No.3
(Autumn 1997) published by Frank Cass.

Printed in Great Britain by
Antony Rowe Ltd, Chippenham, Wilts

Contents

Preface to the 2nd Edition   **David C. Rapoport**   xi

Introduction   **David C. Rapoport**   1

I. INTERNAL STRUCTURE AND CONFLICT

Theories of Terrorism: Instrumental and
Organizational Approaches   **Martha Crenshaw**   13

The International World As Some Terrorists
Have Seen It: A Look at a
Century of Memoirs   **David C. Rapoport**   32

The Internal Dynamics of the FLQ
During the October Crisis of 1970   **Ronald D. Crelinsten**   59

A Battlegroup Divided:
The Palestinian Fedayeen   **David Th. Schiller**   90

The Shining Path and Peruvian
Terrorism   **Gordon H. McCormick**   109

II. MOTIVATIONS AND JUSTIFICATIONS

The Terrorist Revolution: Roots of Modern
Terrorist   **Zeev Ivianski**   129

When Terrorists Do the Talking:
Reflections on Terrorist Literature   **Bonnie Cordes**   150

The Logic of Religious Violence   **Mark Juergensmeyer**   172

From Messianic Pioneering to Vigilante Terrorism:
The Case of the Gush Emunim Underground   **Ehud Sprinzak**   194

Cultural Narrative and the Motivation
of the Terrorist   **Khachig Tololyan**   217

III. CONCLUDING SEQUEL

Terror as an Instrument of Foreign Policy   **Grant Wardlaw**   237

'Leaderless Resistance'   **Jeffrey Kaplan**   260

Notes on the Contributors

David C. Rapoport, Professor of Political Science, UCLA is the Founding and current Co-Editor of the Journal of *Terrorism and Political Violence*. At UCLA he was Founding Director of the Center for the Study of Religion. His early work was in political theory, and he published essays on praetorianism, corruption, and on the political dimensions of religion. His books include *Assassination and Terrorism* (1971) and four edited and co-edited volumes, including *The Democratic Experience and Violence* (Frank Cass, 2001).

Martha Crenshaw is John E. Andrus Professor of Government at Wesleyan University, in Middletown, Connecticut. Her edited book, *Terrorism in Context*, was published by the Pennsylvania State University Press in 1995. She also contributed the entry on terrorism for the 2001 edition of the *International Encyclopedia of the Social Sciences*.

Ronald D. Crelinsten is Professor of Criminology at the University of Ottawa, Canada. He is a founder member of the editorial board of *Terrorism and Political Violence* and has been studying the problem of combating terrorism in liberal democracies for more than 20 years. His publications include *The Politics of Pain: Torturers and Their Masters* (Westview Press, 1995), *Western Responses to Terrorism* (Frank Cass, 1993), *Hostage-Taking* (Lexington Books, 1979), and *Terrorism and Criminal Justice* (Lexington Books, 1978). He is currently Visiting Professor in the Department of International Relations and the Department of Political Science and Public Administration at the Middle East Technical University in Ankara, Turkey.

David Th. Schiller, a citizen of both Germany and Israel, received his PhD at the Free University of Berlin in 1982 with a thesis on the development of the Palestinian paramilitary nationalism. He was a consultant for the RAND Corporation and other research institutes as well as government and law enforcement agencies. An associate editor with TVI magazine, he has worked and published extensively in the field of European and Middle Eastern terrorism.

Gordon H. McCormick is currently an Associate Professor and Chairman of the Program in Defense Analysis, US Naval Postgraduate School, Monterey, California. Prior to this he was a member of the Senior Research Staff of the RAND Corporation and held teaching positions at the University of Pennsylvania and the Johns Hopkins University, School of Advanced International Studies. His publications on political violence in Peru include, 'From the Sierra to the Cities: the

Urban Campaign of the Shining Path', 'Sharp Dressed Men: Peru's Tupac Amaru Revolutionary Movement', and 'Peruvian Maoism: The Shining Path and the Theory of "People's War"'.

Zeev Ivianski, former lecturer at the Department of General History and Russian Studies of the Hebrew University, is the author of *Individual Terror, Theory and Practice* (1977) and numerous articles including 'Individual Terror: Concept and Typology' (*Contemporary History*, 1977); 'Provocation at the Center: A Study in the History of Counter-Terror' (*Terrorism*, 1980); 'The Blow at the Center: The Concept and its History' (*Proceedings of the Conference on Terrorism*, Tel Aviv, 1979); 'The Moral Issue – Some Aspects of Individual Terror' (*The Morality of Terrorism*, 1982). He has also done extensive work on *1905 – Revolution and Terror* (1988 in Hebrew).

Bonnie Cordes was a staff member of the Security and Subnational Conflict Research Program at the RAND Corporation, Santa Monica, California. With the Program from 1980, she participated in several major research projects dealing with international terrorism, the potential for nuclear terrorism, and the computerization of terrorism data bases. She has conducted extensive research on ethnocultural terrorism, specifically the Armenian terrorist movement; and, European terrorism, particularly terrorism in France and Belgium. Her articles on Armenian and French terrorism have appeared in issues of *TVI Journal: Terrorism, Violence, and Insurgency*, and she is the author of several RAND reports.

Mark Juergensmeyer, Professor of Sociology and Director of Global and International Studies at the University of California, Santa Barbara, has authored or edited 11 books, including *Terror in the Mind of God: The Global Rise of Religious Violence* (University of California Press, 2000) and *The New Cold War? Religious Nationalism Confronts the Secular State* (University of California Press, 1993).

Ehud Sprinzak, Hebrew University Professor of Political Science, has retired recently to become the Founding Dean of the Lauder School of Government, Policy and Diplomacy at the Interdisciplinary Center in Herzliya, Israel's first private university. He is the author of five books and over 60 articles. His book *Ascendance of Israel's Radical Right* (Oxford University Press, 1991) won Israel's 1992 Michael Landau Prize for the best political science book on Israel and the Middle East. Sprinzak's most recent book, *Brother against Brother: Violence and Extremism in Israeli Politics from Altalena to the Rabin Assassination* (The Free Press, 1999) was a finalist for the Jewish National Book Award in the category of Israel.

Khachig Tololyan is Professor of English at Wesleyan University in Middletown, Connecticut, a co-founder and co-editor of *Pynchon Notes* (1977–), a journal devoted to the study of the fiction of Thomas Pynchon, and founding and continuing editor of *Diaspora: A Journal of Transitional Studies* (1991–). He is the author of many articles, among them 'National Self-Determination and the Limits of Sovereignty: Armenia, Azerbaijan and the secession of Nagorno-Karabagh', *Nationalism and Ethnic Politics* 1/1 (1994); 'Terrorism in Modern Armenian Political Culture', *Terrorism and Political Violence* 4/4 (1992). He is the author of a book, *Spyurki Mech* [In the Diaspora] in Armenian (Paris: Haratch Press, 1980) and of some 200 articles and reviews in English and Armenian.

Grant Wardlaw is Managing Director of Wardlaw Consulting Pty Ltd, a Canberra, Australia-based strategy and management consulting firm. He has worked in the intelligence, law enforcement and criminology fields and is a specialist on terrorism trends, strategy and policy. Most recently he was the inaugural Director of the Australian Government's Office of Strategic Crime Assessments (OSCA), which provides over-the-horizon (i.e., five years ahead) strategic assessments of significant crime trends and emerging criminal threats to the national interest. Dr Wardlaw has lectured at universities and police and military academies in several countries and is the author of *Political Terrorism: Theories, Tactics and Countermeasures* (Cambridge University Press) and numerous other books and articles.

Jeffrey Kaplan is the author of *Encyclopedia of White Power: A Sourcebook on the Radical Racist Right* (AltaMira Press, 2000); *Radical Religion in America: Millenarian Movements from the Far Right to the Children of Noah* (Syracuse University Press, 1997); *The Emergence of an Euro-American Radical Right* [co-authored with Leonard Weinberg] (Rutgers University Press, 1998); *Beyond The Mainstream: The Emergence of Religious Pluralism in Finland, Estonia and Russia* (Suomalaisen Kirjallisuuden Seura, 2000); and is co-editing with Bron Taylor *Encyclopedia of Religion and Nature* (Cassell/Continuum, forthcoming 2002). He has published as well several anthologies as well as articles on the far right and other millenarian movements in *Terrorism and Political Violence, Syzygy, Christian Century* and *Nova Religio*. He is currently teaching at the University of Alaska Anchorage and is working with the Stockholm International Forum on Conscience and Humanity: Combating Intolerance for the government of Sweden.

Preface to the 2nd Edition

David C. Rapoport

When Frank Cass asked for a second edition of *Inside Terrorist Organizations*, I was delighted for this was the second time the volume had produced good fortune. It had received favorable reviews as the first set of truly scholarly essays on terrorist organization, and that reception induced the publisher to establish an academic journal dedicated to the subject. Thus, the Journal of *Terrorism and Political Violence* was born, and several contributors to the book became associated in various ways with the Journal.

The original introduction complained that studies of terrorism focused on counter terrorist policies and we produced the volume to address that problem by focusing on organization and context, and subsequently the Journal helped to close that gap even further. But the articles in the first edition are still very timely. We have added a new one by Jeff Kaplan 'Leaderless Resistance' dealing with a form of terrorist activity popularized in recent years. Since he wrote the piece without this collection in mind, it will be useful to supplement our original Introduction with a brief note here in the Preface showing how his piece relates to our collection.

The first edition ignored Anarchist activity, a dominant feature of the 'first wave' of modern terror (1870s to 1914). The Anarchists, of course, refused to establish permanent organizational structures on principle, certain that any structure would compromise their ultimate ideal. But they failed miserably, and while we knew their position was historically important, we thought it would never be resuscitated in our lifetime and did not give it much attention. So much for trying to visualize the future as always a continuation and enhancement of present trends, perhaps THE original sin of social scientists.

In the fourth wave of modern terror (1979–?), American right-wing religious racist elements began championing 'lone actor' activity again, though this time operations by tiny wholly-autonomous cells were recommended too. 'Leaderless Resistance' became conspicuous, Kaplan shows, in the context of the Randy Weaver, Waco, and Oklahoma City tragedies, and the term itself was popularized (not created) in a 1992 essay by Louis Beam, a former KKK leader with close ties to the Christian Identity movement.

Early and recent advocates of leaderless resistance have significant differences which Kaplan helps us understand, though he does not compare the groups. Anarchists believed that only one form of struggle could realize their ultimate aim, a society without formal organization, and their enthusiasm dissipated as they finally understood that effective terror required organization. The form most appropriate to terror was constructed from cells composed of three or four persons. Each cell was linked only to one above and another below it. The structure resembled a pyramid culminating in a headquarters cell defining and directing strategy. This form, suggested first in imperial Russia, became a model both for the anti-colonial uprisings dominating the second wave of modern terror and for the Viet Cong and 'New Left' uprisings in the third wave drenching us in the 1960s.

The new doctrine of leaderless resistance has another ethos or source. Its supporters, unlike the Anarchists, do not believe it has value in itself. It is only a 'second best choice', because no other organizational structure seems to work for them. Their groups fragment too easily, and the police are always infiltrating. This is why Kaplan says that the idea of leaderless resistance signified 'more a mark of despair than a revolutionary strategy… [it] sought to make a virtue of weakness and and political isolation'. No wonder that Louis Beam's essay ends with 'limited hopes of success'. Kaplan indicates there is no evidence that supporters of the doctrine have become more enthusiastic, and I might add it is very unlikely that they will furnish that seemingly endless supply of advocates that the Anarchists did during their heyday.

Ironically, especially after the 1995 Oklahoma City bombing, government authorities do display deep anxieties about the doctrine and emphasize how much more difficult it is to protect against lone individuals than to deal with the actions of groups. And they remind us also that the weapons now at the disposal of individuals have greater destructive potential than ever before. This argument is familiar to those who know the history of terrorism; police officials in many countries during the late nineteenth century made the same complaint, that it was impossible to defend against lone individuals able to employ that century's new weapon – dynamite. Will the replay end in a similar conclusion?

Introduction

David C. Rapoport

In 1969 when I began to prepare a series of lectures for the Canadian Broadcasting Corporation, entitled *Assassination and Terrorism*,[1] I struggled to find appropriate materials but could only discover a handful of items. Seventeen years later, Amos Lakos published a bibliography on the same subjects which contained 5,622 items in English alone![2] Has any academic enterprise ever grown so much in so short a time?

Although the literature on terrorism is abundant now, it is very unevenly distributed. No subject commands more attention than counter-terrorist policies does and this is no surprise. One would think that this interest should lead inevitably to studies in terrorist organization too. But that does not seem to be the case.

There is no clear explanation for the discrepancy. The most obvious one is the difficulty academics have in observing underground groups. But the materials on terrorist psychology and on terrorist tactics are quite voluminous; and one would have thought that in some respects the same barrier existed there.[3] Indeed, interviews with captured terrorists by academics seem to focus on motivation; virtually no questions are asked about organizational details and issues. It is also clear that public materials like pamphlets and especially terrorist memoirs − terrorists seem almost compelled to write memoirs − which contain much information on these matters have not drawn much attention.[4] Useful but ignored materials are contained in some able studies of particular groups, like J. Bowyer Bell, *The Secret Army*, Helena Cobban, *The Palestinian Liberation Organization* and Arturo Porzecanski, *Uruguay's Tupamoros; The Urban Guerrilla*. There is a similar indifference to the accounts of those who have participated in specific campaigns, that is, Roger Trinquer, *Modern Warfare* and Abraham Guillen, *Philosophy of the Urban Guerrilla*.

Whatever the reason, the plain fact is that we have not used the opportunities available; and a principal aim of this collection is to fill a very small portion of that gap. In making internal conflicts the focus of the volume, especially in its first half, our contributors highlight a feature present in virtually all human organizations. We would not emphasize the obvious so much here if the academic and popular literature did not picture terrorist organizations as composed of persons who agree on all essential matters. Of course, there are organizational patterns peculiar to terrorists deriving from their special purposes and means, and in the latter portion of the volume some contributors explicitly recognize the issue, though for a variety of reasons they could not give it as much attention as its importance warrants.

Those struggling against the greater society and employing peculiarly repulsive means inevitably stimulate others to ask about their reasons, and therefore motivation and justification, our second theme, has received more attention in the literature than internal conflict has. But psychologists and psychiatrists have dominated this discussion; and they tend to focus on what seems unusual about the terrorist's 'personality' and whether or not we can talk about psychological types. Our contributors have gone about their task in a different way concentrating on the context in which the terrorist operates, namely the role of revolutionary traditions and various cultural milieux in shaping self-perceptions and expectations. This sociological account of motivation and justification responds to Alex Schmidt's invitation to 'repair the greatest deficiency' in terrorist studies, the tendency to perceive the subject in isolation or shorn of its appropriate context.[5] The consequence, whether intended or not, makes the contemporary terrorist a less unique figure than he is usually described as being. Indeed, in many respects several concluding essays argue, he acts out very ancient and sometimes venerated roles.

The most fundamental kind of conflict in any organization is that waged over the organization's purpose. In his fascinating play, 'The Just Assassins', which explores the internal dynamics of a Russian terrorist cell in 1905, Albert Camus personifies that conflict in the struggle of his two principal characters Stephan and Yanek. To Stephan the organization is an instrument of a larger political purpose, the destruction of Russian monarchy; and neither the organization nor its members can have value in themselves. To Yanek the organization represents 'brotherhood', and exhibits the kind of concern and care for each particpant which the Revolution ultimately was supposed to produce everywhere. The difference represented by these two views is the basic theoretical distinction of Martha Crenshaw's 'Theories of Terrorism: Instrumental and Organizational Approaches' though one must hasten to add that she develops it in directions not visualized by Camus, and goes on to discuss implications of the distinction for counter-terrorist policies.

If we assume that the members of an organization share a reasonably clear political goal (for example, revolution) which they pursue in a calculated fashion by devising the most suitable organizational structure and decreasing organizational strikes when the costs are too high for the rewards gained while increasing activity when circumstances are more favorable, then terrorist behaviour may be best understood by means of the 'instrumental' model which incorporates strategic theory. The terrorist and his adversary act in ways to change each other's behaviour; and if a terrorist group fails, it is because the government has virtually eliminated any possibility that its actions will be rewarded. One might note that this view, which emphasizes the ability to capitalize opportunities available, helps explain why terrorists flourish in relatively open or democratic societies but seem to have such formidable obstacles in the Marxist and/or authoritarian world.

To the extent that this picture of terrorist activity is appropriate, internal conflicts must appear as disagreements over purpose, strategies, and tactics. Changes in organizational structures and tactics are most likely to reflect new opportunities available (which technology may create) and the ability of terrorists to effect surprise which is the only way they believe they can cope with the government's enormous advantage in coercive capabilities. Classical conceptions of deterrence and denial policies inform responses of government to terrorist problems.

But a quite different picture emerges when Crenshaw's 'organizational' model is appropriate. From this perspective what an organization does stems from its own internal problems or needs and not from the necessity to realize a broader political purpose. Belonging to an underground organization may provide those feelings of worth and love which Yanek found so essential. But there are other rewards too which Crenshaw specifies, opportunities for action, social status (especially when the terrorists are from ethnic communities with a long history of struggle) and material rewards.[6] The will to persist in such a life where rewards are so real may become so strong that the terrorists continue year after year even though the group becomes less and less able to achieve its stated purposes. 'In fact, the organization's leaders may be reluctant to see its purpose accomplished and the organization's utility ended. They are likely to seek incremental gains sufficient to sustain group morale but not to end the members' dependence on the organization.' Sometimes this concern for organizational rewards leads the group to escalate the struggle against government, even when escalation appears to be inappropriate or irrational, from the perspective of the instrumental model.

The remaining essays are case studies of particular groups or special issues. And it should be noted that virtually all the contributors are concerned with the history of their subject, a dimension normally ignored in terrorist studies.

My own essay 'The International World as Some Terrorists Have Seen It: A Look at a Century of Memoirs' illustrates Crenshaw's 'instrumental view', for it attempts to explain why terrorists have believed that their political purpose was better served by entering the international arena and what costs those decisions imposed. The memoirs, which represent the history of modern terror, reveal three waves of terrorism, an initial one in the late nineteenth and early twentieth centuries, a colonial one from 1921 to the present day, and a contemporary one beginning in the 1960s. Four major variables are decisive in shaping the three different contexts; terrorist commitments to international revolution, the willingness of foreign publics and governments to help, the availability of émigré or diaspora populations, and the political changes in the international system which had occurred prior to the onset of the particular period in question.

While there are some obvious advantages in going abroad, the disadvantages are significant too, sometimes producing catastrophic consequences. To get the broadest possible foreign support, an organization may have to conceal its true aims, a ploy which disconcerts and divides members. Soliciting foreign support may induce one to ignore more important local bases. Most of all, to depend upon foreign support is to depend upon the undependable, upon more powerful bodies and states whose interests are distinctly different from those of the terrorists.

Today the international activities of contemporary terrorist groups are much more conspicuous than they have ever been, but ironically the most successful exploitation of international forces occurred during the colonial period when terrorists had more secure local bases and a cause which more foreign states could identify with. On the whole, terrorists become international to remedy conspicuous domestic weaknesses, but the decision often seems to compound rather than alleviate those particular inadequacies.

Ronald Crelinsten's study illustrates Crenshaw's second view, the organizational one which explains action directed towards the external world as more likely to be inspired by the need to protect or enhance internal advantages. Crelinsten demonstrates the point by focusing on a single incident, the most dramatic and important episode in the life of the *Front de liberation du Quebec* (FLQ) in 1970 when the Canadian government assumed the War Measure Powers. His extraordinarily detailed sensitive account shows that contrary to popular and academic impressions – one fostered by the terrorists themselves, a trait which Zeev Ivianski's essay sees as a common theme in the history of terrorism – the FLQ was not really an organization at all. It consisted of two cells with different domestic and international concerns, different strategies, and no common leaders. The members of each cell knew each other, shared a common name, maintained a sense of mutual solidarity, and were committed to an independent Quebec. But that was all.

The desire of one cell to gain immediate publicity by kidnapping British Trade Commissioner, James Cross, had the unintended effect of forcing the second cell to abandon its plans to remain underground until it built a coherent organization with an appropriate infrastructure. Instead, the second cell, in order to compete with the other, seized the first available political personality, Quebec Minister Pierre La Porte (competition between elements is a pervasive theme in the history of terrorism, and the logic of this action in particular illustrates a point made by Crenshaw and others that when terrorists compete they become more militant). Negotiations for La Porte's release were dictated by the very different political concerns and intransigence of the second cell which undermined the gains achieved by the first, bringing both to ruin.

Beyond the conflicts which emerge directly out of elements within the group, Crelinsten notes there are tensions between terrorists and their supporters who are not underground; and there are decisions which result from the government's ability to manipulate internal frictions especially through *agents provocateur* who are so prominent in terrorist history, especially that of the FLQ. The Canadian experience, finally, reminds us, although one wonders why we must be reminded, that internal pressures which keep a terrorist group from pursuing publicly announced purposes in a consistent calculated manner also characterize government counterterrorist policy.

The subject of David Schiller's essay is the PLO; no contemporary organization, three of our other contributors note, has been so divided, and a large proportion of its terror against *non-Palestinians* is dictated more by the desire to gain internal political leverage than by true strategic considerations. These frictions lead again and again to considerable intraorganizational bloodshed throughout the Middle East and Europe. Although the geographical locus and some peculiar characteristics of the conflict have changed since the Palestinian diaspora began and the PLO formed, Schiller's review of the historical phases of Palestinian resistance in the last 50 years shows that violent internal strife is such a constant feature, it would be a serious error to see this problem primarily as a consequence of PLO leadership or structure.

Schiller points to the relevance of the external environment (the Palestinian community and the Arab world) in explaining these conflicts. Palestinian politics is characterized by hostile rivalries of notables rooted in deeply suspicious clan and confessional groups, a pattern which penetrates PLO organizational dynamics. A second permanent factor since the 1930s has been a dependence on forces outside the Palestinians which has complicated and intensified PLO divisions because foreigners find those divisions so easy to manipulate for their own national purposes. Continual failure, partly due to the extraordinary internal conflicts, leads to the 'repeated emergence of rebels from the lieutenant level of the fedayeens', a process which Schiller details. Each new faction seeks to demonstrate superior militancy (this is, as Crenshaw and Crelinsten suggest, the normal result of terrorist competition) and the completion forces the organization against the will of its major faction into conflict which have resulted in monumental disasters – the civil wars in Jordan and Lebanon. The struggles within the organization prevented some groups, or so those groups claim, from having operating room on the Israeli border, thereby 'forcing' them to go to Europe to hijack Western aircraft. These tactics provided a publicity bonanza, but in the long run they have hurt the Palestinian cause. Most important of all, the militancy mystique made it impossible to seize fleeting opportunities for political settlements.

It would be hard to find a terrorist organization more unlike the PLO than the *Sendero Luminoso* (Shining Path) in Peru. Despite great casualties, its cohesion and morale are high and its discipline remains exemplary; there have been no breakaway factions – a commonplace phenomenon in terrorist history. There are few defectors, and the government has had virtually no success in penetrating a large, by terrorist standards, organization. The picture Gordon McCormick draws is incomplete not only because procuring terrorist organizational details is always difficult but also for another quite startling reason. The Shining Path avoids all publicity though publicity supposedly is the oxygen, to borrow Mrs Thatcher's metaphor, of terrorist movements. It was six years before its leader permitted a press interview; it rarely claims credit for attacks and has produced so far only two short texts! In spite of this distaste for publicity (or maybe because of it) the organization has been extremely destructive, carrying out probably 12,000 operations in six years, resulting in 10,000 deaths. If these statistics are accurate, the Shining Path may well be the most destructive rebel terrorist group in the contemporary world, comparable in this respect to the early sacred terror groups.[7]

A most striking feature of this self-proclaimed Maorist movement is the unusual overwhelming domination of a single person, its founder, Abimael Guzman. No one in the organizations discussed in this volume occupies such a significant position, though Grivas, I point out below, the founder of EOKA in Cyprus, tells us that the organization would have collapsed without him. Guzman spent at least five years carefully laying the ideological and organizational groundwork. (The normal time for putting a terrorist group together is two years.) He apparently has reserved all significant decisions for himself, even though the movement operates through the well-known traditional terrorist network of autonomous cells. Unlike the PLO, it has a secure isolated rural base to sustain its cohesion. It has cut itself off from other groups and has virtually no competitors; were either condition reversed its unity might be impaired. It uses a technology which makes it independent of outside influences. For most groups, several contributors suggest, international activity is a source of division; and, unlike other Latin American groups, Sendero has resisted such connections. Clearly, the death of Guzman could destroy Sendero's linchpin and set in motion a series of decisions which could disrupt the physical and political conditions of its cohesion.

In the second part of the volume – Motivations and Justifications – Zeev Ivianski treats the development of the tradition of professional revolutionaries, an unintended legacy of the French Revolution. Successive generations of reflections upon nineteenth-century experiences by revolutionaries crystallized and refined the idea that the art of insurrection required carefully designed organizations dominated by a professional intelligentsia. While revolution was made *for* the People, it could not be made *by* them. The ambivalence implied by this attitude was especially significant in the writings of those Russians in the late nineteenth and early twentieth centuries who tried to make terror the weapon *par excellence* for the Russian context. Terror was seen as a method to *keep* the masses from engaging in revolutionary activity, for mass revolutionary action was bound to produce titanic blood baths! This view seems quite ironic, even paradoxical, because terror today is justified to the world outside the organization either as the last resort of the powerless or as the only way to provoke mass rebellion.

Terror has been described by those employing it as 'propaganda by the deed' or 'armed propaganda'. But how can we know when a bomb goes off, who exploded it and why? Messages still must be conveyed and bombs must be accompanied by words. Bonnie Cordes examines terrorist literature, especially communiqués, which have rarely been studied seriously, and she provides a framework for doing so which opens a window to underground life. Her materials were issued largely by the 'Euro-terrorists' a union, perhaps the first ever, of national groups (Belgian, French, German, and Italian) whose principal immediate objective is the destruction of NATO. In many ways, the most important audiences for these statements are other terrorist groups, sympathizers or potential recruits, and those elements involved in the attacks. Morale, group cohesion and perhaps the recruiting potential depend upon viewing terrorist action in particular ways. Indeed, the impulse to define a new vision derived from the flagging fortunes of several groups and from a sense that terror was becoming aimless or too blatantly served what Crenshaw would call internal organizational needs. Here, as in the cases discussed earlier by Rapoport, the decision to become international is an indication of serious weakness. The tendency of European officials to see the 'Euro-terrorists' as a cohesive body may be just as mistaken as the earlier Canadian view of the FLQ, described by Crelinsten, because the communiqués, Cordes examines, indicate that component elements are still preoccupied with individual concerns.

In recent years theological concepts have been used to justify terrorist activity; and Mark Juergensmeyer, Khachig Tololyan and Ehud Sprinzak focus on this, our final theme in the volume. It should be emphasized, that although this connection between religion and terror seems odd and unusual to us, virtually all instances of terrorist activity, prior to the French Revolution, which were justified had to be justified in religious terms. And it is also true that many terrorist campaigns which have been treated as secular had important religious elements, for example, the Irgun (Israel), EOKA (Cyprus) and the FLN (Algeria).

There is a widespread tendency, Mark Juergensmeyer notes, to explain examples of sacred terror by more familiar political or economic categories. These explanations certainly have value, but they are normally offered by distant observers of the conflict while those engaged in it use a theological picture of the world which we must understand in its own terms. To illustrate his point, Juergensmeyer uses the Sikhs as his principal example, drawing on the speeches of Jamail Singh Bhindranwale, the most prominent of the terrorist leaders, who was killed in 1984 when the Indian army stormed the Golden Temple.

Terrorists need religion because religion can provide a most compelling legitimacy for killing and dying especially in situations when political appeals are ineffective. Religion, moreover, seems to need terror too, for religion deals with the ultimate issues of order and disorder and of good and evil. The symbols, arts, sacred texts, and myths of all religions, therefore, are full of violence; they retain and domesticate memories of desperate past struggles. But the passions represented in those symbols and rituals are not always contained. When are they released?

It seems to occur when the past represented in those sacred forms provides a paradigm which believers find appropriate for contemporary problems. That is what Ehud Sprinzak suggests, and he goes on to intimate that the character of particular religions shapes their terror patterns. The spectacular victories of the Six Day War, which unexpectedly put all the major Biblical sites in Israeli hands for the first time in 2,000 years, seemed to be a fulfilment of Biblical prophecies and this helped crystallize a messianic movement. The sudden frustration of that movement by the Camp David settlement produced an element which believed that the messianic process could be resumed only if they destroyed the Muslim shrine, the Dome of the Rock, built on the ruins of the Second Temple – Judaism's holiest site. This would occasion the great catastrophe which ancient prophecies foretold would purge and redeem Israel, transforming the nation into a sacred people and kingdom of priests spreading from the Nile to the Euphrates. The plot, which took three years to perfect, was postponed because no rabbi would sanction it. Sprinzak concludes by discussing why the response of messianic movements to setbacks is more likely to be extra-legal and terrorist than those by non-messianic movements to similar circumstances, and how critical the notion of catastrophe is to Jewish messianism.

To understand sacred terror, Juergensmeyer and Sprinzak suggest, one must see how traditional elements of the religous culture are used to explain and to provide models for dealing with present circumstances. Tololyan develops this argument further, illucidating Armenian terror which most people, including the terrorists themselves, mistakenly understand as entirely secular or political – 'a response to the Genocide' of 1915. Tololyan argues that the roots of Armenian activity are, on the contrary, embedded in a very ancient Armenian religious culture which provides paradigms of suffering, daring, rare partial success and heroic death. The willingness to act against very high odds and to accept violent death are pictured as essential elements in the behaviour of those who would live in the most respected or socially approved ways.

Armenian culture is deeply influenced by sets of stories embodying these behavioural models, stories which began in the fifth century and were subsequently re-enacted and added to in other critical periods. Throughout Armenian history, these stories were sustained in learned and popular discourses, in ecclesiastical ritual and, above all, in living songs learned and sung in churches, schools, athletic unions, and youth clubs. Invariably, the terrorist pamplets allude to those original narratives, which are connected to other stories, those concerning Armenian uprisings in the nineteenth century, those about the Genocide, and those relating to the subsequent assassinations of Turkish officials involved in the Genocide. The terrorists thus see themselves as embodying this tradition, and are, of course, often attacked by other Armenians who are outraged by this claim.

It is a mistake to think that Turkey and NATO are *primary* audiences for Armenian terror. The true audience is Armenian diaspora culture which is in danger of assimilation, and whose identity is strengthened by the spectacle. Hence, the dominant cultural narratives create 'conditions that help to produce terrorism and are in turn reanimated by it. Such terrorism produces new heroes for old stories.'

The interest in the relevance of religion displayed in our last three essays and the concern for discovering the history and comparative anatomy of terrorism which most of the others reflect manifests a belief that the phenomena is much more deeply embedded in our cultural traditions, and, therefore, far less tractable than conventional wisdom acknowledges. A sobering lesson but surely a beneficial one.

The concluding sequel by Grant Wardlaw constitutes a separate section. Its subject is the state's use of terrorist groups as an instrument of foreign policy. It incorporates a number of major theses in the preceding articles and is concerned with both the conditional nature of the co-operation in this use of terror and the misperceptions characterizing Western, especially American, counter-policies.

Although there are times when one can speak of an identity of interest between a state and the terrorist body it aids, most often the identify is tentative and precarious especially when the state utilizes national bodies from other states. To understand the problematic nature of this relationship, one must identify the different ranges of interest which characterize each partner. As each party tries to maximize its independence and minimize its vulnerabilities, tension is produced – tension which limits the kinds of feasible cooperative action and thus the threats for other states. Wardlaw offers general guidelines for understanding the problems (guidelines which were implicit in Schiller, and Rapoport's accounts of the terrorist as an international actor). Confusion about the precise character of a particular relationship can lead to catastrophe; thus, in 1914 it was *not* the assassination of the Archduke, but Austria's *misperception* of Serbia's relationship to the terrorist which occasioned the First World War.

American policy has been imprisoned by a public opinion which the government helped create for domestic political reasons. The public has been encouraged to believe that the terror is more threatening than analysis and experience show it is or can be. At the same time the public is told that governments can eradicate terrorism completely, a notion which anyone familiar with the history of the phenomena (or with the contents of this volume) would deem fatuous. The inevitable consequence of an attempt to base policy on unrealistic assumptions is that government cannot act either consistently or responsibly, and this in turn undermines its own credibility.

Governments are either unwilling to define terrorism or to use definitions consistently to direct policy. Political reasons in the narrowest sense of the term have too much weight in determining whether or not a state appears or continues to appear on the list of sponsors and in determining appropriate counter-measures. A peculiar 'ahistorical view' (fostered partly by academics who should know better) has created the conviction that state sponsored terror is a 'unique feature of the contemporary international landscape' – a conviction which encourages arbitrariness since we are in effect assuming that there is no useful experience to gauge the phenomena with. But the plain fact is that historical periods without such problems are much rarer than those with them!

Contemporary attempts to deal with state sponsored terror, Wardlaw says, are intensely ideological; Crenshaw might say that they are subject more to organizational than instrumental interests, and we should not forget Crelinsten's observation that Canadian policy *vis-à-vis* the FLQ could be characterized this way too. Though they will never admit it, governments, like the terrorists they face, respond more to the force of domestic opinion than to that of their adversaries. This should not surprise us for we began the volume by seeking patterns common to all groups.

NOTES

1. David C. Rapoport, *Assassination and Terrorism* (Toronto: CBC, 1971).
2. Amos Lakos, *International Terrorism: A Bibliography* (Boulder, CO: Westview Press, 1986). The items include unpublished papers and dissertations.
3. The counter-terrorist topic has 1,393 items, terrorist strategy and tactics 852, and terrorist psychology 254. Organizational analysis is not grouped under a separate topic in the text itself, but the index lists nine items, four of which are republications. If the title of the piece contains the word organization or some reasonable facsimile the index will pick it up. If not, it will be under some other topic. Much information on the organizational details of specific movements appears of course in the case studies of particular groups.

   One book which seems to be on the subject exists, Kent Layne Oots, *A Political Organization Approach to Transnational Terrorism* (New York: Greenwood Press, 1986). Despite its title, it is largely concerned with analyzing statistics pertaining to particular terrorist incidents. Consequently, the propositions generated have very little to do with organization.
4. The *Memoirs of General Grivas, General Grivas on Guerrilla Warfare*, and Menachem Begin's *The Revolt*, are especially rich. They are discussed in my 'The International World' below, but only with regard to the issue of that essay.
5. Alex P. Schmid, *Political Terrorism: A Research Guide to Concepts, Theories, Data Bases and Literature* (New Brunswick: Transaction Books, 1983), p.422.
6. Martha Crenshaw, 'An Organizational Approach to the Analysis of Political Terrorism', *Orbis*, Vol. 29, No. 3 (1985), p.474.
7. The Thugs were the most proficient terrorists of all time. The British estimated that they murdered 30,000 every year for centuries. Avoiding publicity completely, they killed with the most primitive weapon – a scarf. Likewise the Shining Path, according to McCormick, not only shuns the limelight, but also uses a technology primitive by modern terrorist standards. Despite the conventional wisdom, I suspect that the history of terror would show inverse ratios between the impulse for publicity and the statistics for killing! See my 'Fear and Trembling: Terror in Three Religious Traditions', *American Political Science Review*. 78 (Sept. 1984), 658–77.

I. INTERNAL STRUCTURE AND CONFLICT

Theories of Terrorism: Instrumental and Organizational Approaches

Martha Crenshaw

It is possible to think in terms of two basic explanations for how the conspiratorial organizations that practice terrorism behave.[1] In turn, each analysis yields different policy recommendations. These two approaches, which are derived from established bodies of theory, will be presented sequentially in order to set out the logical premises and the policy implications of each. However, both views may be necessary to understanding terrorism and its consequences.

The first explanation is based on the assumption that the act of terrorism is a deliberate choice by a political actor. The organization, as a unit, acts to achieve collective values, which involve radical changes in political and social conditions. Terrorism is interpreted as a response to external stimuli, particularly government actions. An increase in the cost or a decrease in the reward for violence will make it less likely. However, the second explanation focuses on internal organizational processes within the group using terrorism or among organizations sharing similar objectives. Terrorism is explained as the result of an organization's struggle for survival, usually in a competitive environment. Leaders ensure organizational maintenance by offering varied incentives to followers, not all of which involve the pursuit of the group's stated political purposes. Leaders seek to prevent both defection and dissent by developing intense loyalites among group members. The organization responds to pressure from outside by changing the incentives offered members or through innovation. Terrorist actions do not necessarily or directly reflect ideological values.

The Instrumental Approach

In this perspective violence is seen as intentional. Terrorism is a means to a political end. Government and adversary are analyzed as if engaged in a typical conflict, in which each party's actions are aimed at influencing the behavior of the other. The classic works on the stragegy of conflict, such as those by Thomas C. Schelling, suggest that terrorism is one form of violent coercion, a bargaining process based on the power to hurt and intimidate as a substitute for the use of overt military force.[2] As such, it is similar to other strategies based on 'the power to hurt' rather than conventional military strength. Terrorism is meant to produce a change in the government's political position, not the destruction of military potential.

The non-state organization using terrorism is assumed to act on the basis of calculation of the benefit or value to be gained from an action, the costs of the attempt and of its failure, the consequences of inaction, or the probability of success. Terrorist actions may occur for several reasons: the value sought is overwhelmingly important; the costs of trying are low; the status quo is intolerable; or the probability of succeeding (even at high cost) is high. Extremist groups may act out of anticipation of reward or out of desperation, in response to opportunity or to threat.

This strategic perspective is a conceptual foundation for the analysis of surprise attack.[3] Terrorism is par excellence a strategy of surprise, necessary for small groups who must thereby compensate for weakness in numbers and destructive capability.

Explanations of why surprise occurs frequently emphasize the defender's lack of preparation as much as the adversary's intentions and capabilities. The enemy's intent to surprise is taken for granted. Intelligence failures may preclude warning of impending attack, or, paradoxically, an overload of warnings, especially if they are imprecise, may induce complacency or the 'cry-wolf syndrome'. Specific tactical warnings of impending terrorist attack are rarely received. More seriously, government leaders are likely to be insensitive to warnings they do receive.[4] For example, the political costs of acting in anticipation of an attack may outweigh the advantages to be gained by striking first. Nor may governments wish to expose intelligence sources by revealing the receipt of warnings.

The actions of the attacker are determined by perceptions of incentive and opportunity.[5] The existence of opportunities for surprise attack may generate a political incentive for terrorism where none existed before. An organization may not consider translating its ideological goals into action until the possibility presents itself. Such an opportunity could stem from the vulnerability and availability of symbolic targets (such as the presence of American Marines in Beirut, Israeli forces in southern Lebanon, or British troops in Northern Ireland) or from the offer of resources from foreign governments. In turn, a prior incentive or ideological direction may lead to a search for opportunities, which determined and risk-prone groups may be adept at creating.

What strategic conditions promote surprise? Surprise may simply be aggressive, aimed at winning quickly and cheaply. The short-term victory may involve a propaganda gain that demonstrates the government's weakness. Terrorism may appear to have compelled a government to withdraw from a position to which it was publically committed as, for example, the American withdrawal from Beirut. In such cases, the attack may stem from the opposing organization's perception of its position as dominant. Yet surprise may also be a result of strategic weakness. Terrorism may occur in anticipation of government pressure. Extremist groups may be most dangerous when they feel beleaguered and on the defensive, with little to lose from a suicidal attack. As is characteristic of a balance of power international system, a party may attack because the ratio of forces is likely to become even more unfavorable in the future rather than because an advantage exists in the present.

Bringing about surprise, from an operational viewpoint, is often a matter simply of timing.[6] Governments often know that a terrorist attack is probable and what the likely targets are, but cannot predict the day or the hour of the attack. In addition, surprise may be achieved through technical or doctrinal innovation. Terrorism, frequently referred to as 'a new mode of warfare', is in itself such an innovation. Since the beginning of the modern wave of terrorism around 1968, terrorists have developed new and elaborate methods of hostage-taking, including aircraft hijackings, seizure of embassies or consulates, and kidnapping of diplomats and business executives. As these tactics became familiar to governments and corporations, they ceased to surprise. Furthermore, defending states devised effective protective measures. Terrorism then shifted to bombings that were shocking in their massive and indiscriminate destructiveness and in the apparent willingness of their perpetrators to die with their bombs. The purpose of innovation in terrorism is to maintain the possibility of surprise because it is critical to success.

An organization's success or failure is measured in terms of its ability to attain its stated political ends. Few organizations actually attain the long-term ideological objectives they claim to seek, and therefore one must conclude that terrorism is objectively a failure. The reason it continues in the immediate is that extremist organizations frequently achieve their tactical objectives, particularly publicity and recognition.

Should there be obvious disunity or factionalism within an organization, the instrumětal model would interpret it in terms of disagreement over political goals or strategy. The Palestine Liberation Organization, for example, is divided over the questions of how best to defeat Israel and the character of the future state. The Irish Republican Army split in the aftermath of the civil rights movement in Northern Ireland, as rival leaders disagreed on how to respond to the demands of the Catholic population.

Since the specific intentions of any adversary, particularly a clandestine organization, are intrinsically difficult to determine, it is tempting to focus on the adversary's capabilities and to assume intention from actions. If terrorists are instrumental and calculating, the means they use are logically related to their ends. The targets of terrorism, for example, are symbolically related to the organization's ideological beliefs. Predictability and interpretability of the act of terrorism – whether or not it is understood by the watching audience as its perpetrators mean it to be understood – depend on the existence of this link between victim and purpose. Terrorist ideology, no matter how unrealistic, must be taken seriously as a guide to intentions. Coupled with analysis of capabilities, it provides a basis for expectations. Organizations such as the Italian Red Brigades, for example, which seek to involve the masses in the political struggle, are unlikely to commit acts of violence which might alienate potential supporters. Ideology can thus be a factor in self-restraint. On the other hand, organizations which have no desire for an earthly constituency and possess the necessary resources, such as the followers of the Ayatollah Khomeini, are unlikely to practice moderation.

The escalation of terrorism is a problem that requires explanation. In terms of the strategic approach, escalation is similar to innovation in being primarily a response to government actions. Opponents are sensitive to the strengths as well as the weaknesses of governments; terrorists engage in a process of constant adaptation to the strategic environment. Moving to greater destructiveness may be a reaction to a need to retain the initiative as governments find means of countering exisiting capabilities.

Moreover, if terrorism is a means to an end, then substitutes are possible. The absence of alternatives to terrorism will be important; organizations that do not rely solely on terrorism may be more likely to abandon the strategy in the face of failure. A constant failure to achieve stated goals would presumably lead to internal strife and ultimate collapse. Terrorism will end through consistent failure, when costs are high and opportunities for violence closed.

In meeting a threat that is interpreted in such terms, the government has two basic alternatives: *defense* and *deterrence*. As Glenn Snyder proposed in a classic formulation of the problem,[7] defense means forcefully preventing an enemy from attaining his physical objectives. Defending territory and values may involve not only passive defensive measures – guarding potential objects of attack or erecting barriers – but a tactically offensive response. An effective defense prevents attack by making it impossible. Offensive tactics in the interest of halting an attack would engage an enemy before he reached the target rather than at the point of attack. Anticipatory actions to remove enemy capabilities are of two sorts. *Preemption* occurs when an enemy attack is believed to be imminent. It aims at halting an adversary who is poised to strike. The use of force in the interest of *prevention*, on the other hand, is intended to incapacitate an enemy who plans a future attack but has not yet mobilized. The exercise of prevention is based as much on estimation of enemy intention as of capabilities.

Both preemption and prevention require exceptional intelligence. Decision-makers are unlikely to get the kind of precise warning of impending attack they need in order to preempt effectively. In fact, an indication of an intent to preempt in order to avoid being surprised may provoke premature attack or postponement. Preventive attack to disarm the terrorist at an earlier stage of preparation may be even more demanding of intelligence. It involves detecting preparations for mobilization rather than mobilization itself. Because of inherent uncertainties of information and because public disclosure would compromise intelligence sources, it may be difficult for governments to justify preemption or preventive use of force to their citizens.

Intelligence is also the major problem of response to warning. Governments may be prevented from responding to warning by a variety of constraints that make rational strategy impossible. Domestic public opinion, for example, may restrain governments in the preemptive use of military force against terrorists. Intelligence warnings alone are rarely decisive and concrete enough to use as public evidence. The government may also be insensitive to warning because of doctrines or assumptions that discount the threat. In Beirut, for example, because the American military command was committed to the conception that American forces were on a peace-keeping mission they did not believe that their presence could be construed as hostile. The Long Commission Report noted that perceptual difficulties regarding the nature of the American mission led decision-makers to neglect changing political conditions in Lebanon.[8] Once the United States appeared to have sided with the Christian faction, the tacit immunity once granted American forces was withdrawn. Warnings were then incorrectly interpreted.

In contrast to defensive measures, the purpose of which is to limit the objective opportunities available for terrorism, there is the strategy of deterrence. Its purpose is to influence the adversary's perceptions of opportunity and incentives for attack. Deterrence purports to prevent conflict by convincing the adversary that the costs of the action he contemplates far outweigh any potential benefits he may gain. The defending government influences the opposing organization's decisions by threatening unacceptable damage to collective values should an act of terrorism occur. The value-maximizing adversary will presumably react to an effectively communicated and credible threat by desisting. For the defender, the problem lies in communicating the threat, making it credible, and devising it as a serious threat to the opponent's values. The most feasible and hence most credible threat may not always be the most painful to the adversary. Nor is certainty of implementation always a virtue to the defender. The threat that leaves something to chance may be more potent.

Two forms of deterrence are open to the defender, according to Snyder. The first is *denial*, a strategy resembling and indeed in implementation basically identical to defense. The purpose, however, in deterrence through denying gain to the adversary is to raise the immediate cost of contemplated actions. The prospect of paying a high price for any gain may act as a deterrent.

Yet denial is conventionally thought to be the weakest form of deterrence. It is difficult to make this sort of battlefield cost unacceptable, especially if organizations can recruit members willing to take high personal risks. The demonstration of willingness to die in the attempt may compensate for failure. (And it is of course the followers and not the leaders of the organization who pay this price.) Schelling quotes a memorable passage from Joseph Conrad's *The Secret Agent* to illustrate this obstacle to deterrence. A paradox of deterrence is that it does not always pay to appear rational. The character of 'The Professor', whose only aim in life is to find the perfect detonator for his bombs, carries with him at all times an explosive device wired to go off with the squeeze of a trigger he holds in his pocket. When questioned as to whether he would actually go through with self-destruction, he explains his true intention is not the point: 'What is effective is the belief those people have in my will to use the means.'[9]

The second type of deterrence is its more widely recognized form. Punishment or *retaliation* involves the threat of the use of military force in response to an attack after it has been committed. The prospect of retaliation is presumed to deter the enemy from attacking regardless of the state of the government's physical defenses. This feature makes it attractive for combatting terrorism. Given the terrorist proclivity for civilian targets, for the outrageous, and for the unexpected, defense may require the protection of too many weak links.

Retaliatory threats may be either symmetrical or asymmetrical. That is, the defender can threaten to respond in a manner tailored to the offense, for example, by attacking the base from which a terrorist attack was launched. Given the uncertainties and the unverifiability of intelligence, it is more likely that the defender will issue (and carry out, if deterrence fails) the more credible asymmetrical threats to retaliate against any object of value to the terrorists and to reserve the right to escalate. The government in effect states that punishment may not be in kind or on the same level of damage. Something may be left to chance. Such threats may be effective because they are credible; however, the punishment inflicted on the terrorists may be less severe than symmetrical retaliation against a nerve-center or against leaders. Asymmetrical retaliation may also be less justifiable in the eyes of the public.

If deterrence is a recommended policy against non-states, it should be doubly applicable to the states that sponsor the terrorism of others or engage in it directly. States have a wider range of identifiable values. For states, supporting foreign terrorists is not likely to be an interest of sufficient value to justify limitless sacrifices, whereas for a non-state resistance movement there may be no cost too great to justify abandoning the struggle. Theoretically it should be easier to alter a state's cost-benefit calculations. The US raid against Libya in April 1985 was explicitly described in terms of deterrence of future terrorism, as well as an effort to encourage the overthrow of the Quaddafi regime.

Policy responses consistent with the instrumental explanation of terrorism depend on both denying opportunities for terrorism (mainly a matter of defense) and on affecting incentives to use it. The problem for intelligence is as much to discover the values of a shadowy adversary as to learn locations and plans. Reducing opportunities may also minimize incentives for terrorism. Calculating extremists are presumed to be repsonsive both to raising the cost of attacking and to threatening subsequent punishment.

This approach to combatting terrorism is not without drawbacks. The difficulties of a timely response to prevent surprise attack have been established. Warnings are insufficiently precise and susceptible to misinterpretation. The use of force in anticipation of or in response to terrorism is potentially a contentious domestic issue. Prior conceptions, public opinion, the personalities of leaders, and the emotional frustration terrorism provokes all interfere with control of the defender's response. Deterrence is never simple, and deterring adversaries whose values and risk-taking propensities are imperfectly understood is problematic. Furthermore, the lessons of experience in using coercive diplomacy show that it is ineffective against adversaries with superior motivation.[10] In addition, the use of force may provoke escalation and broadening of conflict. Actions that are intended as defensive may be perceived by others as aggressive.

Organizational Process Theory

This explanation focuses on the internal politics of the organization. In suggesting that terrorism can become self-sustaining regardless of its political consequences, it assumes that the fundamental purpose of any political organization is to maintain itself.[11] Terrorist behavior represents the outcome of the internal dynamics of the organization rather than strategic action. The minimal goal of any organization is survival, but the goals of the people occupying roles in an organization transcend mere survival. Leaders, in particular, wish to enhance and promote the organization. Their personal ambitions are tied to the organization's viability and political position.

The incentives the organization provides for its members are critical to its survival. However, the relationship between actual rewards for membership and the organization's stated objectives is not straight-forward, since recruits often join an organization for reasons other than ideological commitment. Leaders maintain their position by supplying various tangible and intangible incentives to members, rewards that may enhance or diminish the pursuit of the organization's public ends.

The incentives for joining a terrorist organization, especially one that is already established and of known character, include a variety of individual needs: to belong to a group, to acquire social status and reputation, to find comradeship or excitement, or to gain material benefits. The popular image of the terrorist as an individual motivated exclusively by deep and intransigent political commitment obscures a more complex reality. Under certain conditions, membership in an underground organization is a valued social relationship, winning the militant the respect and admiration of peers and family. Joining an organization in order to enhance one's appearance in the eyes of others is characteristic of nationalist and separatist groups, where a popular constituency exists that may deplore the method but applaud the goals of the organization. The practitioners of terrorism in liberal democracies may be acting in terms of a non-indigenous reference group with whom they identify. The radical may genuinely see his or her actions as the continuation of a historic struggle led by distant heroes in the Third World, winning the respect of other revolutionaries. Many West European groups compared themselves sentimentally to the Tupamaros of Uruguay. Since many terrorists are adolescents, joining may be a sign of personal daring or social rebellion more than political belief. Other incentives are those intangible benefits of association in a group: a feeling of belonging, acceptance, and solidarity.

Most organizations offer a mixture of incentives. The issues or causes which the group supports may shift with the organization's need to offer new incentives to members. The Rand Corporation, for instance, notes that in France the group Action Directe, 'in chameleon fashion, rapidly refocuses on the most attractive antigovernment issues'.[12] Since 1979 the organization has opposed nuclear energy, imperialism, Israel, the Catholic Church, and French intervention in Chad. Organizational goals are not necessarily consistent. The operational interpretation of ideology will vary according to the need to ensure organizational survival. The chance for action, no matter what it accomplishes, may be a dominant incentive. Circumstances may alter incentive structures. If an organization is forced into inactivity, substitute incentives must be found. Some groups might shift to dealing in drugs, for example.

However, purposive incentives remain strong for a number of reasons. Collective goals appeal to the individual's sense of satisfaction at contributing to a wrthy political cause. Many members sincerely identify with the organization's purpose; others will be afraid to admit that they do not. In organizations devoted to violence, a premium is placed on group solidarity and cohesion. Relationships within the organization are highly authoritarian.

James Q. Wilson also suggests that there are different categories of political purpose, which affect the stability of the organization.[13] The first purposive incentive offers the pursuit of a single specific objective. The Rand Corporation describes such narrowly-focused groups as 'issue-oriented' and notes that they are common but short-lived.[14] On the other hand, what Wilson terms ideological incentives are based on beliefs that constitute a systematic, comprehensive rejection of the present political world and the promise of a future replacement. These incentives might be distinguished as protest versus revolution. The third incentive is redemption, the appeal of organizations whose efforts concentrate primarily on changing the lives of their members. As violent examples of these moralistic groups, Wilson cites the nineteenth-century anarchists and the Weathermen of the 1960s. These groups are likely to focus on self-sacrifice, on living by stringent moral codes, or on conversion. Wilson suggests that since such groups can never succeed, their despair often results in extreme destructiveness and willingness to take risks.

Such redemptive groups may resemble religious cults as much as ideological organizations. Religious or sacred terrorism falls in this category. Violence has a personal meaning for the individual. It is a path to individual salvation, regardless of the political outcome for the collectivity in the real world. The motivation for terrorism may be to transcend reality as much as to transform it.

Wilson concludes that conspiratorial organizations tend over time to substitute group solidarity for political purpose (whether protest, revolution, or redemption) as the dominant incentive.[15] This development seems likely to be characteristic of tightly compartmentalized underground organizations. Progressive isolation from the environment reduces the amount and quality of the information members receive about external events. They become less concerned with the achievement of political goals and more concerned with maintaining the group. Single-issue groups, whose members are usually part-time rather than professional members of the underground, may find it easier to adapt by creating new incentives through switching issues. Changing position on a single issue is simpler than changing comprehensive belief systems. Given this apparent flexibility, it seems paradoxical that single-issue groups tend to be shorter-lived. Perhaps they are more likely to achieve their goals. On the other hand, when they do not succeed, they cannot recover by offering substitute incentives such as status or solidarity.

Organizational analysis explains not only why terrorism continues regardless of political results but why it starts. It implies that structural explanations of civil violence are of limited use. The objective conditions likely to inspire grievances and hence incite violence are permanent, whereas violence is not continuous or universal.[16] The formation of organizations, not environmental conditions, is the critical variable. Entrepreneurship is an essential ingredient; the leaders who establish an organization must skillfully create and manipulate incentives to attract members. The founders must have an exceptional commitment to the group's purposes and an exaggerated sense of the group's likely efficacy. In a potentially violent organization, this sense of efficacy might come from assessing the government's weakness, observing the apparent success of other, similar groups, or acquiring the support of foreign governments. The existence of a demand for the organization from some actual or potential constituency is also helpful. The extent of mobilizable resources, in turn possibly dependent on foreign assistance or on public support, is another determinant of the establishment of organizations. A third essential condition is that the presence of skilled and determined leaders and some broader demand for action coincide with 'the salience of purposive incentives'.[17] The prominence of ideas that legitimize violence as well as examples set by predecessors contribute to making the organization's purpose salient. If potential terrorists believe that matters of concern to them are being affected by a government whose behavior can be altered – a belief that is likely to emerge when a highly visible enemy appears to pose a serious threat to their values or those of the group with which they identify – they are likely to organize and to act. Organizations are much more responsive to the environment during their inception than in the course of subsequent operations. The older the organization, the more its behavior is explained by organizational imperatives.

Emphasizing organizational maintenance explains why terrorism may persist in the face of evident failure to achieve political purposes. If purposive incentives are overshadowed by others such as social relationships or financial reward, terrorism becomes self-sustaining. In fact, the organization's leaders may be reluctant to see purpose accomplished and the organization's utility ended. They are likely to seek incremental gains sufficient to sustain group morale but not to end members' dependence on the organization.

A second general theory of organizationl behavior focuses on the prevention of decline in firms.[18] Although the comparison between business firms and radical undergrounds may at first seem bizarre, the resemblance has also been noted by the Rand Corporation: 'Organizations are dedicated to survival. They do not voluntarily go out of business. Right now, the immediate objective of many of the world's hard-pressed terrorist groups is the same as the immediate objective of many of the world's hard-pressed corporations – that is, to continue operations.'[19] Albert O. Hirschman's economic theory of organizational imperatives supports Wilson's idea that organizations are more sensitive to their members than to government policy. Yet the implication of his theory is that organizations are fragile; they struggle and often fail to prevent decline. A fundamental precept is that organizations behave differently in competitive than in non-competitive environments. In general, most terrorist organizations appear to confront rivals who have similar political purposes: the Irish Republican Army competes with the Irish National Liberation Army; the Italian Red Brigades compete with Prima Linea; Fatah competes with the Popular Front for the Liberation of Palestine and a host of other factions.

Hirschman proposes that dissatisfied members of an organization have two options: 'exit' or 'voice'. Each is exercised under different circumstances. 'Exit', as it applies to the special circumstances of clandestine extremist organizations, refers to the possibilities of (1) joining another, rival organization that appears more satisfactory, or (2) splintering off and creating a new group. Exit often occurs after a failed attempt to exercise 'voice', or the articulation of complaints in order to persuade the group to follow another direction. Although extremist organizations consistently attempt to define exit as betrayal, factionalism is not uncommon. The possibility of exiting to a rival group of course depends on the existence of an attractive alternative. Where there are no competitors, the dissatisfied must create a new group. The exercise of this option apparently occurs when the most extremist members chafe under the restrictions imposed by the relatively moderate and demand an escalation of violence. The Provisional IRA, for example, developed from the refusal of the parent or 'Official' IRA to adopt a strategy of terrorism against Protestants and the British in the wake of the civil rights movement. To prevent the departure of a sub-group, especially if it endangers the survival of the organization, former moderates may consent to collective radicalization. The Official IRA subsequently followed the Provos into terrorism – both against the British and against each other. Only if there is no possibility of exit can the organization's leaders resist the demands of members for change.

Exit can thus hasten organizational decline. Yet the exercise of 'voice' can also be destructive. Most underground organizations strongly (even forcibly) discourage the expression of discontent. Cohesion and solidarity are important values, both to the organization (for which security is a paramount concern) and to the psychological well-being of members for whom belonging is a dominant incentive. Conspiratorial organizations may therefore be more sensitive to internal disagreement than to defection. The most centralized, secretive, and compartmentalized organizations are likely to be the least tolerant of dissent. For ideological or redemptive organizations, dissent may equal heresy.

The leaders of an organization can avoid the disastrous extremes of exit and voice by soliciting the loyalty of members. In doing so, leaders stress commitment to collective goals and solidarity. If the possibility of exit exists but members choose nevertheless to stay, then group loyalty can be assumed to be strong. Extremist organizations often deliberately build loyalty through ideological indoctrination. However, outlawing both exit and voice heightens the gravity of either offense when it occurs. The consequences of either departure or dissent are then potentially more damaging for the organization. The existence of strong loyalty in itself may create problems if it makes it more difficult for leaders to alter purposive incentives when conditions change. The effort to maintain the organization makes it inflexible.

Another method by which organizations inhibit defection is to establish what Hirschman terms 'severe initiation costs'. If members have invested a lot in joining an organization, they will be reluctant to leave. Terrorist organizations often require the commission of an illegal act for precisely this purpose, to eliminate the individual's option of abandoning the underground. The imposition of this cost, however, does not mean that the member will not be attracted to a close competitor should one exist. Yet the terrorist has developed a certain stake in self-deception. Even if members perceive the organization's failure to achieve collective ends they will 'fight hard to prove they were right after all in paying that high entrance fee' rather than admit error.[20]

Considering the constraints on exit imposed by high initiation costs, discontent serious enough to surface in a clandestine organization is likely to be explosive. However, extreme discontent may provoke not dissolution of the organization but increased activity directed toward the achievement of group goals. The decline of the organization may produce a psychological dynamic in which complacency is succeeded by frenetic activism which goes beyond criticism of the leadership to desperate attempts to salvage the organization. Initiates into a group that uses terrorism have paid a high price to enter the organization and often face an even harsher penalty of exit. They may react not by denying reality but by trying harder to change it. The response to decline, then, may be the escalation of violence.

Experimental psychological studies have in fact indicated that the person who has experienced a severe initiation will find even a low cost exit (for example, to a similarly motivated group also pursuing an active strategy) unsatisfactory. If no alternative to exit exists when voice is prohibited or ineffective, then the disenchanted terrorist will try to reduce the strain of exit by persuading others to join the rebellion against the organization's leadership. Once on the outside, these critics will be extremely hostile to the parent organization. The bitterness of the rivalry among Palestinian factions is explicable in these terms.

These findings also tentatively support the 'fight harder' hypothesis. The dissatisfied terrorist may prefer changing the organization's political direction to departing in frustration. This effort may lead to 'creative innovation' under pressure. The combination of high barriers to exit and dissatisfaction may thus encourage more violence. When members of a terrorist group lack the possibility of exit and are intensely loyal, failure to achieve the organization's stated purpose may only make them strive harder.[21]

This analysis suggests that in competitive conditions, where exit is possible, there may be less internal dissent. Yet organizations may have to devote their efforts to distinguishing themselves from other groups, in order to prevent defection to successful rivals. Competition may inspire escalation, as each group tries to outdo the other in violence in order not only to retain existing members but to attract recruits. Where exit is possible but no competitors exist, a proliferation of organizations may be the result of decline and dissatisfaction. The end result, therefore, may be competition by escalating extremism.

Differences between groups with high and low entrance fees may affect the organization's viability. Groups such as the West German Red Army Faction, for example, which requires the total commitment of members who become professional terrorists with no other life, may find it harder to recover from decline than less structured groups like the Revolutionary Cells. Hirschman feels that all terrorist organizations are in this doomed category. No organization can make itself completely immune to the possibilities of exit and voice. Where both outlets for dissatisfaction are blocked the organization will not survive over the long run.[22] Innovative responses are the exception.

In sum, the organizational process approach to interpreting terrorist behavior assumes a complexity of motivation that goes beyond communicating a political message. Leaders of terrorist organizations struggle to maintain the viability of the organization as much as to challenge governments. The incentives they offer members may require violent actions against the government regardless of cost, if that cost is short of complete destruction of the organization. Ideological purpose, however, is only one incentive among many. Organizational activity will vary according to internal pressures and external competitiveness.

The task of the government is to encourage disintegration without provoking the escalation of violence. Denying reward is difficult. What the outside world perceives as 'failure' may not appear so to such an adversary. The organization's structure of incentives must be altered in order to reduce the possibilities of violence. Offering new, non-violent incentives, increasing opportunities for exit to non-violent political methods, or promoting the expression of internal dissent are policy options that fit this theoretical interpretation. The use of military force is not recommended in the terms of this approach, since retaliation may only strengthen loyalty within the group. At the least, the results of the use of force will be highly unpredictable. Counter-intelligence initiatives combined with judicial and political measures are more suitable.

The Italian experience has been instructive in this regard. The apparent 'repentance' of significant numbers of terrorists in response to offers of leniency from the Italian state has enabled the police to act effectively against the Red Brigades. The offer of reduced prison sentences in exchange for information leading to the apprehension of other Red Brigades members seems to have coincided, perhaps fortuitously, with a period of disarray within the terrorist organization, when numerous members were questioning the group's purposes, especially after the murder of Aldo Moro.[23] The attractiveness of the option of 'repentance' was also increased by a growing perception of the failure of a terrorist strategy. The successful timing of such an inducement suggests that offering the possibility of exit, not to a rival organization but to the aboveground world, at a time of intense discontent can draw terrorists from the underground.

Similarly, with regard to creating opportunities for exit, governments would be advised to consider the wisdom of severe legal penalties for membership in certain underground organizations. Increasing the costs of joining a terrorist organization may restrain some prospective entrants, but establishing high entrance fees also inhibits exit. Offers of amnesty can further motivate exit as well as create suspicion and distrust within the organization.

Where incentives for many terrorists are non-purposive, the government may be able to offer substitutes. Financial rewards may be influential, for example, where incentives are material. Monetary rewards for information leading to the apprehension of terrorists are appropriate. Policy models developed for dealing with criminal organizations or youth gangs may be applicable in some circumstances. However, where incentives are purposive (ideological or redemptive), the government may find it difficult to find satisfactory substitutes unless non-violent organizations with identical purpose exist. Furthermore, if a primary incentive is direct action for its own sake, then the slower, less exciting methods of normal politics may not suffice.

Organizational analysis also suggests that there may be counter-intelligence opportunities for creating dissatisfaction and dissent within terrorist organizations. Schlomo Gazit and Michael Handel, for example, recommend attempts to disrupt terrorist organizations by making it hard for them to recruit new members or to keep the loyalty of existing members.[24] Exactly how this is to be done, however, is left unexplained. It requires the identification of the pool or constituency from which new members are drawn, specification of the incentives offered members, and reduction of the attractiveness of these rewards.

It would probably be easier to affect recruitment (remembering that not all organizations are equally dependent on steady supplies of new members) and support functions by influencing the attitudes of sympathizers than by directly undermining the loyalty of indoctrinated activists. The incentive structures for sympathizers are probably weaker than those for active members. Barriers to both entry and exit are lower, yet there is also little occasion to exercise voice. Sympathizers have little direct control over the organization's decisions. If their frustration should increase, the organization's support basis might erode. The problem is to identify the incentives for sympathizers. Since their participation in the group and its actions is limited, their satisfaction must be vicarious.

Gazit and Handel further recommend that governments try to create conflicts within terrorist organizations or between groups and their rivals. However, accomplishing this objective without infiltrating the activist core of the organization is difficult. Penetrating a hard-core terrorist organization requires the commission of acts of violence that are illegal. Such a policy also runs the risk of creating *agents provocateur* who are dangerous to the government in the long run. On the other hand, groups of sympathizers pose less of a problem.

Gazit and Handel also suggest measures such as misinformation, for example, announcing that a captured terrorist has actually gone over to a rival group. Such propaganda campaigns, however, can backfire in terms of domestic politics if they also mislead the public.

Conclusions

Three questions can be posed about these two theoretical approaches and their policy implications:

> (1) What has more theoretical value, in terms of logical coherence and scope?
> (2) Which better explains the problems of the reality of terrorism?
> (3) Which is used most by policy-makers?

Definitive answers must await further research, but some tentative suggestions are presented here.

The assumptions behind each approach are compared in Table 1. The instrumental theory is simpler and more comprehensible. Because the intentions of actors are inferred from their behavior according to logical rules, it is both intellectually satisfying and relatively undemanding in terms of information requirements. Since data on the small groups that employ clandestine violence are hard to obtain, this relaxation of standards of evidence is a practical advantage. This theory is also familiar to students of conflict. Its premises are deduced from a well-developed body of thought. Its range is thus extremely broad, as it applies to all manner of conflict regardless of the identity of the actors.

TABLE 1

THE PROCESS OF TERRORISM

The Instrumental Perspective

1. The act of terrorism represents a strategic choice.

2. The organization using terrorism acts as a unit, on the basis of collective values.

3. The means of terrorism are logically related to ends and resources; surprise compensates for weakness.

4. The purpose of terrorism is to bring about change in an actor's environment.

5. The pattern of terrorism follows an action–reaction process; terrorism responds to what the government does.

6. Increasing the cost of terrorism makes it less likely; decreasing cost or increasing reward makes it more likely.

7. Terrorism fails when its practioners do not obtain their stated political objectives.

The Organizational Perspective

1. The act of terrorism is the outcome of internal group dynamics.

2. Individual members of an organization disagree over ends and means.

3. The resort to terrorism reflects the incentives leaders provide for followers and competition with rivals.

4. The motivations for participation in terrorism include personal needs as much as ideological goals.

5. Terrorist actions often appear inconsistent, erratic, and unpredictable.

6. External pressure may strengthen group cohesion; rewards may create incentives to leave the group.

7. Terrorism fails when the organization disintegrates; achieving long-term goals may not be desirable.

However, a theory of strategic choice cannot explain how the preferences of actors are determined. Nor does it permit us to distinguish among groups except in terms of their stated ideological objectives. All adversaries are alike in their most important respects. Organizational theory permits us to disaggregate the complexity of the opponent's values and to differentiate among different types of organizations according not only to purpose but to incentive structures and competitiveness. This theory is, however, less coherent and more complex. It may be less satisfying intellectually because the act of terrorism appears to be the random result of unpredictable interactions. This interpretation makes violence less politically meaningful to the observer because its intentions are obscured.

The question of applicability to reality is hard to answer without also considering the views of students of the problem. The two theories should be tested against each other. James DeNardo examined the decision-making of the German Marxists before the Bolshevik Revolution in order to show that their debates over the use of terrorism were founded on explicitly instrumental calculations.[25] He argues that faithfulness to the political reasoning that underlies radical thought requires a strategic theory. Alex Schmid and Janny de Graaf also argue that terrorism is a logical choice for dissidents who lack means of communication other than violence and that such radical oppositions fully calculate the opportunities afforded by a free press.[26]

Leaders of resistance organizations frequently explain themselves in strategic terms. Menachem Begin entitles a chapter of his memoirs 'The Logic of Revolt'. He argues that although emotion gave the Irgun heroism, logic and commonsense provided the strategy that ensured victory.[27]

Organizational theory also has an empirical foundation. Much Palestinian violence appears to be directed against Arafat's authority over the movement as much as against the United States or Israel. The Achille Lauro affair, for example, is considered to be an action by the Palestinian Liberation Front to discourage Arafat's peace initiatives and discredit his leadership. The wealth accrued by organization such as the PLO, the IRA, and Colombian organizations such as M-19 leads one to suspect a financial motive. Analysts of terrorism, however, rarely use organizational theory explicitly. Nevertheless, most case studies present full details of the internal politics of underground organizations, showing that factionalism and struggles for leadership are common.[28]

The public statements of policy-makers in the Reagan Administration have leaned toward the strategic interpretation. The popularity of the 'state sponsorship' theory may represent a desire to make terrorism seem rational. Terrorism is conveniently fitted into a familiar spectrum of international conflict and national security threats. Official pronouncements tend to focus on the response rather than the problem.[29] When the threat is examined, it is seen in terms of destructive capabilities rather than the motivations which might guide such a potential. The intent of terrorism is perceived uniquely as a challenge to the United States. The perpetrators of terrorism are thought to design it exclusively to undermine American values, shatter American self-confidence, and blunt the response. The complexities of the issue and diversities in motivation are neglected.

Many policy-makers seem to believe strongly that hardline policies will prevent terrorism because terrorists want to avoid high costs. The prescriptions of the strategic approach are attractive because they are conventional, compatible with existing political doctrine, easy to implement, and produce immediate, visible, and direct results. The policy recommendations of the organizational approach are difficult, slow to mature, and have few results that can be displayed to the public. Its prescriptions place a premium on secrecy and deception, modes of dealing with the world that the American public may find unacceptable.

Can these two approaches be reconciled in the abstract? Perhaps the organizational theory is one way of completing strategic theory by determining what the values of opponents are, how preferences are determined, and how intensely they are held. Another possibility is that these two approaches describe types of organizations, categories into which real groups can be fitted. Some closely approximate the strategic choice model, while the decisions of others are decisively influenced by organizational politics.

Can they be linked in practice? Policy-makers should be sensitive to the idea that different analyses of the reasons behind terrorist actions can yield incompatible recommendations on how to cope with the problem. Both types of policies are followed in practice, but failure to understand the logical relationship between explanations of terrorism and subsequent prescriptions may impose political costs. Confusion results when rhetorical policy is cast in the terms of strategic theory, sometimes elevated to the status of a moral imperative, but actions are conceived with a view to exploiting the internal politics of underground groups or the states who possess influence over them. The policy debate within the Reagan Administration over how best to deal with terrorism, specifically over the use of military force and over securing the release of hostages held in Lebanon, may be attributable to different interpretations of the political processes that lead to terrorism as well as to bureaucratic and personal rivalries within the government. The result is an inconsistent policy that alternates between contradictory extremes. The political liabilities of confused decisions include charges of hypocrisy and betrayal from Congress and from allies subject to criticism of their weakness in confronting terrorism.

NOTES

An earlier version of this article was presented to the Defense Nuclear Agency's 10th Annual Symposium on the Role of the Behavioral Sciences in Physical Security, April 1985.

1. This approach to analyzing the problem of terrorism is similar to the method employed

by Edward F. Mickolus in 'Negotiating for Hostages: A Policy Dilemma', *Orbis*, Vol. 19, No. 4 (Winter, 1976), 1309–25. He investigates the propositions underlying two policy viewpoints, 'no ransom' and 'flexible-response', each of which is based on 'implicit theories regarding the driving mechanisms of terrorist behavior' (p.1315).

2. Thomas C. Schelling, *Arms and Influence* (New Haven, CT: Yale University Press, 1966), especially 'The Diplomacy of Violence', pp.1–34.

3. See, for example, Richard K. Betts, *Surprise Attack: Lessons for Defense Planning* (Washington, DC: Brookings, 1982), and Klaus Knorr and Patrick Morgan (eds.), *Strategic Military Surprise: Incentives and Opportunities* (New Brunswick, NJ: Transaction Books, 1983).

4. Betts reaches this conclusion; see Chs. 4 and 5, 'Why Surprise Succeeds', pp.87–149.

5. See especially Klaus Knorr, 'Strategic Surprise: The Incentive Structure', pp.173–94, in Knorr and Morgan (eds.).

6. Michael I. Handel, *The Diplomacy of Surprise* (Cambridge, MA: Harvard Center for International Affairs, 1981).

7. Glenn H. Snyder, *Deterrence and Defense: Toward a Theory of National Security* (Princeton, NJ: Princeton University Press, 1961).

8. 'Report of the DOD Commission on Beirut International Airport Terrorist Act, October 23, 1983', Washington, DC, 20 Dec. 1983.

9. Schelling, *Arms and Influence*, p.37. The relevant section in Conrad can be found on p.63 of the 1963 Penguin edition.

10. Alexander L. George, David K. Hall, and William R. Simons, *The Limits of Coercive Diplomacy* (Boston, MA: Little, Brown, 1971). The authors note that the relative motivation of the two sides in a conflict exerts critical leverage on outcomes, since the central task of a coercive strategy is 'to create in the opponent the expectation of unacceptable costs of sufficient magnitude to erode his motivation to continue what he is doing' (pp.26–7). In planning strategy against terrorism, it is imperative to consider the nature and strength of the adversary's motivation.

11. This argument is adapted from James Q. Wilson, *Political Organizations* (New York: Basic Books, 1973). A fuller elaboration of the application of organizational theory to terrorism is found in my article, 'An Organizational Approach to the Analysis of Political Terrorism', *Orbis*, Vol. 29, No. 3 (Fall, 1985), 465–89.

12. Bonnie Cordes *et al.*, *Trends in International Terrorism, 1982 and 1983* (Santa Monica, CA: Rand, 1984), p.29.

13. Wilson, pp.49–50.

14. Cordes *et al.*, pp.3–4.

15. Wilson, p.50 and Ch. 3 in general, 'Organizational Maintenance and Incentives', pp.30–55.

16. Ibid., pp.296–301.

17. Ibid., p.201.

18. Albert O. Hirschman, *Exit, Voice, and Loyalty: Responses to Decline in Firms, Organizations, and States* (Cambridge, MA: Harvard University Press, 1970).

19. Cordes *et al.*, p.50.

20. Hirschman, p.93.

21. Ibid., Appendix, pp.146–55.

22. Ibid., p.121.

23. See Sue Ellen Moran (ed.), *Court Depositions of Three Red Brigadists*, N-2391-RC (Santa Monica, CA: Rand, 1986).

24. Schlomo Gazit and Michael Handel, 'Insurgency, Terrorism, and Intelligence', pp.125–47, in Roy Godson (ed.), *Intelligence Requirements for the 1980s: Counterintelligence* (Washington, DC: National Strategy Information Center, 1980; distributed by Transaction Books).

25. *Power in Numbers: The Political Strategy of Protest and Rebellion* (Princeton, NJ: Princeton University Press, 1985).

26. Alex Schmid and Janny de Graaf, *Violence as Communication: Insurgent Terrorism and the Western News Media* (Beverly Hills, CA: Sage, 1982), Ch. 1, 'Terrorist Uses of the News Media', pp.9–56.

27. Menachem Begin, *The Revolt* (Los Angeles, CA: Nash, 1977), pp.47–58.
28. As an example of a case study that exhibits a sensitivity to organizational politics, see J. Bowyer Bell, *The Secret Army: A History of the IRA 1916–1979* (Cambridge, MA: MIT Press, 1980). A quantititive study that explicitly uses interest group theory to explain the relationship between group size, coalition formation, and terrorist activity is Kent Layne Oots, *A Political Organization Approach to Transnational Terrorism* (Westport, CT: Greenwood Press, 1986).
29. Among many statements about international terrorism made by officials of the Reagan Administration, see as a representative example Robert C. McFarlane, 'Terrorism and the Future of Free Society', *Terrorism: An International Journal*, Vol. 8, No. 4 (1986), 315–26.

The International World As Some Terrorists Have Seen It: A Look at a Century of Memoirs

David C. Rapoport

Scholars rarely study the literature written by terrorists.[1] Even the memoir, a form which terrorists are fond of and one which ought to be very useful and revealing, is ignored. A few memoirs have been examined as part of the analysis of particular groups; no one, to my knowledge, has compared different ones over time, which is the subject of this study.[2]

I will be discussing ten books written by nine persons who were involved in eight different movements.[3] Those people are Vera Figner, a member of the Executive Committee of Narodnaya Volya (The Will of the People), 1879–82 (the first modern terrorist group) and its last leader after 1881, *Memoirs of a Revolutionist*;[4] Boris Savinkov, leader and last commander of the 'Terrorist Brigade' or 'Combat Organization' of the Russian Social-Revolutionists, 1902–14, Narodnaya Volya's major successor, *Memoirs of a Terrorist*;[5] Menachem Begin, commander of the Irgun Zwai Leumi, Israel, 1943–48, *The Revolt*;[6] George Grivas, commander of EOKA, Cyprus, 1955–59, *Memoirs of General Grivas*, and *General Grivas on Guerrilla Warfare*;[7] Sean MacStoifain, Provisional IRA, Chief of Staff, 1969–74, *Memoirs of a Revolutionary*.[8] Two memoirs discuss American activities: Jane Alpert, leader of a tiny New York-based terrorist group in 1969, *Growing Up Underground*,[9] and Susan Stern, a fringe member of the Weather Underground 1969–70, *With the Weathermen*.[10] German activity is described by Michael Baumann, a leader of the 2nd June group, 1971–72, in *Terror or Love*,[11] and Hans Joachim Klein, Revolutionary Cells, 1974?–77? in *German Guerrilla: Terror, Rebel, Reaction and Resistance*.[12] Finally, there is Abu Iyad, founding member, major leader and intelligence chief of the PLO, who wrote *My Home, My Land*.[13]

Let me begin by making a few points regarding the materials, method, and purpose. I chose the memoirs because they were available, seemed interesting, important, and represented groups which encompass much of the history of modern terror. The major kind of rebel terror not represented is sacred or holy terror, and that is omitted largely because I know of no relevant memoir published in a language I can read. My primary concern is with the views expressed, and I did not evaluate the accounts, except in the one instance where they directly contradicted each other. I believe that the memoirs represent sentiments characteristic of particular groups. But since it is not necessary for the argument of the study to demonstrate that contention, I have not tried to establish the point.

Because the definition of terrorism is not settled, virtually every terrorist study is vulnerable to the question of whether the persons discussed really are terrorists. I have my own doubts as to whether Menachem Begin deserves this name or not; and I am sure that many will find reason to question my inclusion of others. My defense is that no matter which of the two major acceptable definitions [14] we use, there will be some reasons for including all of my selections. In any case, certain common themes and interesting problems do emerge in all the works selected, and they do not obscure real differences between the writers.

The essay is part of a larger study still in process whose purpose is to analyze how terrorists describe tensions within their groups and to trace the different expressions of those tensions over the century of modern experience. One such tension pertains to the relations of the group to its international environment. Why should a group function in the international world in the first place and how should it do so? What kinds of support could it mobilize, what targets should it choose, what prices would it have to pay, *etc.*? What sorts of internal disputes are generated by decisions to emphasize international activities?

The conventional wisdom, of course, is that terrorist groups first developed an international dimension in the 1960s, a characteristic resulting from the cumulative impacts of specific developments in modern technology. Individuals and tiny groups had capacities that they lacked previously. Weapons were cheaper, more destructive, easier to obtain and conceal. The 'technological quantum jumps from arrow to the revolver and from the gun to the Molotov Cocktail'. Modern communications and transport allowed hitherto insignificant persons to coordinate activity quickly over vast spaces. Finally, by giving unusual events extensive coverage, the mass media completed the picture; 'you can't be a revolutionary without a color TV: it's as necessary as a gun'. [15]

A second feature of this conventional wisdom is that the international dimensions of contemporary terrorism are elements of strength. Groups are more terrifying because their sanctuaries are more difficult to reach, their range of targets is greater, their supply sources are more secure, and they are supported by a public opinion which transcends national borders. It would seem to follow, though this is nowhere explicitly stated, that a group never would have good reason to avoid international activities.

The major truth this conventional wisdom reflects is that since the 1960s terrorists have become increasingly international. Certain characteristics, in particular, have become more common and visible – cooperation between different national groups, assaults across state borders, attacks against nationals of uninvolved states, state sponsorship for foreign activities, and sympathetic foreign publics.

But it is true also that the memoirs reveal that there always has been an international component in terrorist activity and that characteristics of that component change in time. The political variables in that component are: (1) the terrorist commitment to an international revolution; (2) the willingness of foreign states to support terrorist groups; (3) the degree to which the population terrorists claim to represent is found in areas beyond the primary territory being contested; and, finally, (4) changes which have occurred in the international state system.

The memoirs obviously cannot provide all the material for a comprehensive discussion of the relationship between international activities and the internal life of terrorist groups. But they are one indispensable source. They are quite suggestive too; the comments are invariably cast in political not technological terms, and they make clear that entering the international arena even where it seems necessary may involve great risks and make the organization depend upon the undependable.

The cases will be discussed in chronological order and grouped as manifestations of the three major waves of modern terror which I distinguished initially in *Assassination and Terrorism* (1971). The first wave began in 1879 and lasted until the First World War. The terrorists operating largely within states of European origin, engaged mostly in assassination plots against major officials in the hope of reconstructing the social order. The Russian experience was the most significant because it was the first, most persistent over time, and exercised great influence over other movements and peoples. *Narodnaya Volya* (Figner) and its principal successor the Social-Revolutionists (Savinkov) are our two examples.

A second wave began in Ireland after the First World War and reached its crest in the two decades after the Second World War engulfing the colonial territories of Western states. It normally entailed both guerrilla *and* terrorist activity, military and police units were involved. Begin, Grivas and MacStoifan provide materials here.[16]

In the wake of the new political environment resulting from the Vietnam War, a third wave began in the 1960s. While the aims of the second wave were largely national liberation, more of their successors described themselves as Marxists, and/or Anarchists. The tactics changed too; the guerrilla attacks on military forces of the second wave were abandoned in a continuous search for softer or more defenseless targets.

I. Russian Beginnings (Narodnaya Volya 1879–83, Social-Revolutionists 1900–14)

Revolutions in the West have never been a domestic affair solely. Both the American and French Revolutions attracted enormous attention abroad. Some were attracted for ideological purposes; but others, particularly governments, found it in their interest to provide moral and material support. The same pattern was repeated in various national revolutions of the nineteenth century, a century which also witnessed the development of international revolutionary socialist movements. As revolutionaries the Russian terrorists became interesting immediately to the world outside, Figner emphasized.

We had attracted general attention; the journalistic world seized eagerly upon news concerning Russia, and the events listed in the Russian revolutionary chronicle formed the most absorbing news. In order to check the streams of false rumours and canards of every kind furnished to the European public through the daily press it was necessary to supply systematically the foreign agents with correspondence from Russia covering all the events in the Russian revolutionary world. The Central Committee chose me in the fall of 1880 as the foreign correspondence secretary. I sent Hartman (the international propaganda head) copies of letters, biographies of those who had been executed ... revolutionary publications, ... pictures of arrested and condemned revolutionists ... Russian magazines and newspapers. After the assassination of Alexander II (1881), I sent him a report of the event – the last one – including therein the letter of the Executive Committee to the new Czar Alexander III, a plan of the interior of the Kobozev cheese shop (the operational center for the plot) drawn by Kobozev himself.[17]

'The Will of the People' (Narodnaya Volya), Figner notes,

decided to organize abroad the propaganda of its actual aims ... and to enlist the sympathies of European society by acquainting it with the domestic policy of our government. Thus, while shaking the throne by the explosions of our bombs within the Empire, we might discredit it from without and possibly to the diplomatic interference of a few countries which had been enlightened as to the international affairs of our dark tsardom. For this purpose we had at our disposal those revolutionary forces which had been lost to the movement in Russia, that is the emigrants.[18]

To organize emigrants who would circulate printed materials and provide lectures, Narodnaya Volya sent agents abroad as far away as the US and Canada. Particular interest was paid to revolutionary socialist movements.

All the eminent figures in the socialistic world of Western Europe promised ... their cooperation ... . With some of them, as for instance Karl Marx and Rochefort, the Committee communicated by letter asking them to help their agent Hartman in the work of organizing propaganda against Russian despotism. In answer to this request, the author of *Capital* sent the Committee his autographed portrait together with his expressed agreement to serve. Hartman declared that Marx showed the letter of the Committee with pride to his friends and acquaintances.[19]

How would Narodnaya Volya resolve conflicts between two such different constituencies – on the one hand, a powerful broadly-based Western public interested in encouraging a liberal Russian parliamentary government with a capitalist economy, and, on the other, politically less significant groups of Western revolutionaries who believed in a total reconstruction of society, beliefs which most members of Narodnaya Volya as socialists also shared? It is clear where Figner's own sympathies were. Being a revolutionary meant identifying herself totally with an international revolutionary tradition. Indeed, so essential was that identification for her understanding of herself that she evoked it much later while waiting for a court to pronounce what she imagined would be her death sentence, intimating that the continued existence of that international revolutionary tradition guaranteed her own immortality. 'My thought for some reason turned to the fate of revolutionary movements in general in the West and at home; to the continuity of our ideas and their dissemination from one country to another. Pictures of time long past of people who had died long ago awoke in my memory, and my imagination worked as never before.'[20]

Although Figner does not discuss the problem of conflicting constituencies, the famous letter to Alexander III, which took a week to write, justifying the assassination of his father, the terrorists' most celebrated act, seemed calculated to woo liberal sentiments. Karl Marx understood and approved, declaring the letter, one of 'cunning moderation', and Figner used similar language saying that its great 'moderation and tact ... won the sympathetic approval of all Russian society'.[21] 'Upon its publication in the West it produced a sensation throughout all the European press. The most moderate and conservative periodicals expressed their approval of the demands of the Russian Nihilists finding them reasonable, just, and such as had in large measures been *long ago realized in the daily life of Western Europe.*'[22] It is striking that the letter contained no mention of the terrorists' revolutionary aspirations! And several months later, when President Garfield died of assassination wounds, Narodnaya Volya, in another eloquent letter to the American people, condemned the assassin, taking the opportunity to reiterate that is own aims were identical with those of most Westerners, that Narodnaya Volya believed terror to be abhorrent in free societies always.[23]

Savinkov, on the other hand, who faced a similar situation 25 years later, was either more honest than Figner or the tension between the need to cultivate public opinion in the West and the requirement that the revolutionaries keep faith with foreign revolutionaries, had grown more visibile. After Count Von Plehve (Minister of the Interior) was assassinated (1904), a proclamation issued in Paris by the Central Committee 'addressed in French to all citizens of the civilized world'.

> The compulsory severity of our methods of struggle must not becloud the truth. *More than any others* we condemn publicly, as did our heroic predecessors of the 'Narodnaya Volya', the use of terror as a measure of systematic warfare in free countries. But in Russia where despotism precludes any open political struggle and knows only lawlessness where there is no protection against irresponsible authority, absolutist in all aspects of its bureaucratic structure, we

are compelled to interpose the law of revolution against the law of tyranny (my emphasis).[24]

Many Russian terrorists were bitterly opposed to this proclamation. Kaliayev (who Camus later made the hero of his play 'The Just Assassins') declared,

> I do not know what I would do had I been born a Frenchman, Englishman or German. In all probability, I would not manufacture bombs, and, most probably I would not be interested in politics at all. But why should the Party of Socialist-Revolutionists, i.e. the party of terror, throw stones at Italian and French terrorists ... . Why this hurry? Why this fear of European public opinion? It is not for us to fear – we must be feared and respected. Terror is power. It is not for us to proclaim our lack of respect for it ... . I believe more in terror than in all the parliaments of the world. I will not throw a bomb into a cafe but it is not for me to judge Ravacholle. He is more of a comrade to me than those to whom this proclamation is addressed.[25]

Because Narodnaya Volya and the Combat Organization contained individuals with different political outlooks, it is possible that the three letters represented a minimum acceptable view. Yet, the striking thing is that both Figner and Savinkov point to the crucial importance of meeting the expectations of an international liberal opinion.

Figner, as one initially responsible for coordinating the effort to woo foreign opinion, discusses how it is done highlighting the crucial role of Russian émigrés. (Savinkov, pre-eminently an organizer of assassination teams, reveals no details of propaganda operations abroad.)

Narodnaya Volya uses the international world, additionally, as a place of refuge, creating in the process conflicts over extradition between Russia and other states. In the last phase of Narodnaya Volya, Figner was the only member of the Executive Committee left in Russia not in prison; the others, roughly half of the body, lived abroad. Savinkov describes different details; as members of the Combat Organization constantly moved back and forth over international borders to seek temporary refuge and secure new passports,[26] but there was another important reason – their principal bases are abroad or at least they go there to meet in relative safety to plan new assassinations. Geneva, the home of Michael Gotz, moral leader of the Combat Organization, appeared to be the terrorists' real headquarters; and Geneva seemed close to Russia. Three days after the St. Petersburg assassination of Count Von Plehve, all surviving participants reconvened in Geneva to plan their next move.[27] Meetings of the Central Committee took place in Brussels, Paris and other foreign capitals. The extended trial of Azev, the notorious *agent provocateur*, occurred in Paris. The support of European radicals, moreover, produced new benefits. A successful and prolonged campaign by the Second International prevented the Italian government from extraditing Michael Gotz to Russia.

The Combat Organization was disbanded in 1906 and reconstituted shortly afterwards in Finland – a nation under the Czar's jurisdiction but one with considerable legal autonomy and a revolutionary party sympathetic to the terrorists.

> We chose Finland as the base of operations (headquarters) .... (T)here could be no question at that time of our being extradited to the Russian government from Finland, and should the question have been raised, we would have been immediately warned and given an opportunity to disappear. Members of the Finnish Party of Active Resistance or sympathizers were present in all Finnish government institutions and even among the police.
> The Finns performed many useful services for us. They gave us refuge, supplied us with arms and dynamite, transported supplies to Russia, provided us with Finnish passports, *etc.* ... . It may be said without exaggeration that it was due only to the conditions prevailing in Finland ... that the re-establishment of the Terrorist Brigade (i.e. Combat Organization, DCR) was made possible with a minimum of sacrifices.[28]

As the Finnish case indicates, the terrorists received material, moral, and political support from foreign governments and revolutionaries alike. There are additional examples cited too. The Armenian terrorist organization, Dashnaktzutun, gave a supply of arms. A gift of a million francs was donated, supposedly by American millionaires, but Savinkov later learned that the money was acutally 'laundered' through the Finns by Japan then at war with Russia. The Japanese aim, of course, was domestic turmoil.[29]

II. Colonial Phase (Israel 1943–48, Cyprus 1955–59, Northern Ireland or Ulster 1969–74)

In our next three cases – Begin (Irgun), Grivas (EOKA), and MacStoifain (IRA) – the relationship betweeen the various dimensions of the international context alters significantly. The belief that the revolutionaries are part of an existing international revolutionary tradition abates or is no longer the same serious force. All three speak of common bonds with other revolutionaries (MacStoifain even dedicates his book to 'revolutionaries everywhere ...', and Begin says that all revolutionaries are 'brothers in arms. All the world's fighters for freedom are one family.'[30] But the heroes each invokes are those within their respective national traditions, the Jewish, Greek, and Irish, and no serious effort is made to cultivate the support of revolutionary movements elsewhere. MacStoifain identifies more with other contemporary revolutionaries perhaps because the IRA is less successful in drawing on other sources of international support. Also he lives in a period when this is expected and he needs to compete with the Marxist 'IRA Officials' group.

The international element in these cases comes from at least two principal political facts. The revolts all involve problems which could be perceived as colonial issues; and after the Second World War no matter normally aroused international sympathies more. (Indeed, so successful is the anti-colonial appeal that most terrorist groups today normally claim they are engaging in such a struggle.) Second, a community is involved, Jewish, Greek, and Irish, whose members reside in boundaries beyond the territory being contested drawing other states into the conflict perhaps against their will, or at least exciting hopes among the terrorists that they might be successful in doing that.

How important is the international factor? Grivas, the most systematic of the writers, stresses that EOKA success depended ultimately on it. The first paragraph of his Preparatory General Plan drawn up in Athens two years before the start of the struggle in Cyprus states that 'the objective' is

> To arouse international public opinion, *especially among the allies of Greece*, by deeds of heroism and self-sacrifice which will focus attention on Cyprus until our aims are achieved. The British must be continously harried and beset until *they are obliged by international diplomacy exercised through the United Nations* to examine the Cyprus problem and settle it in accordance with the desires of the Cypriot people and the whole Greek nation (my emphasis).[31]

EOKA did generate pressure through NATO and the UN on Britain which contributed to her decision to relinquish sovereignty. But contrary to Grivas' expectations, violence between Greek and Turkish Cypriots materialized, which aroused Turkey so much against Greece, that the Greeks, fearful of war, abandoned the Cypriots. Grivas was forced to yield or accept a solution (Cypriot independence rather than *Enosis* or union with Greece) which he felt was a clear defeat.[32] Ironically, this defeat occurred in spite of the fact that '[t]he Organization was at the height of its power; [its] men were better armed, better trained and hardened by years of fighting'.[33]

In the Cyprus campaign, unlike the earlier ones in Russia, the diplomatic activity of foreign states, which sometimes moved and other times was moved by an aroused public opinion, proved decisive.[34] (The presence of an international institution, the UN, gave international opinion a forum and focus it lacked before.) For all his sensitivity to the international context, the inability of Grivas to anticipate that it might be possible to arouse the international world in a way which defeated his purpose is puzzling. The documents detailing initial plans show that he simply never appreciated the possibility that Turkey would get involved and made no plans to deal with that contingency.[35] Was he misled by the extraordinary success which Begin achieved in a similar situation only a few years before?

For Begin the international context is seen as critical too.

> Eretz Israel was a centre of world interest. The revolt had made it so ... . [N]o partisan struggle had been so publicized throughout the

world .... While our revolt was in progress, a number of battles of considerable magnitude were fought in the Greek mountains. They were accorded ... a few lines in the world's press. The report on our operations, under screaming headlines covered the front page of newspapers everywhere, particularly in the United States ... . [S]ome people ... argued that it was merely to pander to sensationalism that the American newspapers gave so much space to our operations, and even to our secret broadcasts and public statements. Even if there is a grain of truth in this commercial evaluation, what does it matter? The interest of the newspaper is the measure of the interest of the public.

It is characteristic that even the subsequent operations of the Israeli army were given much less publicity throughout the world than the earlier operations of the rebels. The reason is obvious. The operations of a regular army, even if it achieves great victories, are less spectacular than the daring attacks of a handful of rebels against a mighty government and army.

In this publicity ... sometimes exaggerated but always spontaneous, we recognized the second factor which would preclude a deliberate 'destruction of the Yishuv'. The interest, which our struggle created, built a kind of invisible life belt round the Jewish population .... We never believed that our struggle would cause the total destruction of our people. We knew that Eretz Israel, in consequence of the revolt, resembled a glass house. The world was looking into it with ever-increasing interest and could see most of what was happening inside.[36]

In the Cypriot situation so much depended upon the action of one state, Greece. And the Greek commitment was limited, because the Greeks were also in NATO which contained a Turkey firmly resolved to prevent *Enosis*. Support for Jewish independence was much broader based and, unlike the Greek case, the major contributors had no conflict of interest with immediately apparent consequences. The US was unfriendly to British policy in Palestine;[37] she had a large active Jewish population, the NATO alliance had not yet come into existence, and the American suspicion of Britain was at its post-war height. When it became clear that the British could not suppress the revolt, Soviet support for Jewish independence developed. 'On the heels of the revolt came also the United States' demand for a immediate solution to the Eretz Israel question. It is noteworthy that the American Warren Austin, in supporting the demand for the replacement of British rule in Eretz Israel by a new regime, used language almost identical with that of the Russian, Gromyko.'[38] By contrast Grivas was reluctant to seek Soviet support: apparently he feared the local Communist party which opposed *Enosis*, and he had several communist members executed as 'traitors'.

A decisive difference in the Grivas and Begin cases was the responses of the other resident populations, the Turks and Arabs. Unexpectedly, the Arabs remained passive during the Irgun's struggle *against the British*, and, hence, the Arab states unlike Turkey were not 'forced' to intervene at the most critical moment. Ostensibly, the Arabs believed that the Irgun struggle would make both the Jews and British weaker, but Begin anticipated the possibility that Arabs might have to intervene even against their will and took steps to avert the situation – steps which were absent in Cyprus. No operations, for instance, were permitted in Arab areas even to hit British targets. And his men only received weapons when assigned a particular target. Hence,

> in the early stages of the revolt we achieved an important strategic objective ... . The Arabs not only refrained from hindering us ... some of them actively helped us. Their aid ... was vital. Of the few arms we had, some were bought from the Arabs. Until we found our own means of manufacturing substantial quantities of explosives – the main weapon in the struggle for liberation – and apart from what we 'borrowed' from the British themselves, the major part of our T.N.T. was acquired from Arab suppliers.[39]

The UN was a particularly crucial element because Palestine, as a League of Nations Mandate, was 'ultimately' under UN jurisdiction if Britian could be seen as failing in its trust. The UN, moreover, was perhaps at the height of its powers then; and much strong feeling, so soon after the Holocaust, penetrated world consciousness that Jews were entitled to a state.

The UN involvement gave rise to what Begin labels tongue-in-cheek 'two international scandals', that is, meetings between the Irgun and members of UN Select Committees. And he obviously glows in the warm feelings expressed by particular UN representatives, individuals who were members of ethnic minorities or had come from small Third World countries.[40] It is worth special note that Grivas lacked Begin's opportunities to communicate with foreigners, meeting no officials and no journalists or 'opinion makers'. Begin refers to six interviews with 'opinion makers' (there were probably more); to these we must add those with officials from several foreign governments and the secret meetings with UN personnel. Why is Begin receptive to interviews and Grivas not? One reason may be the very different personal estimates of their own dispensability. Grivas believed that EOKA would collapse if he were captured; he makes the point seven or eight times in the two volumes. On the other hand, Begin repeats several times that the Irgun would go on fighting without him. To the extent that these two beliefs actually did govern them, one could take risks which the other felt he had to avoid.[41]

Grivas certainly complains that his inability to deal directly with the international world was crucial. 'There were many foreigners and even UN representatives who were completely ignorant of why we were demanding our freedom but I had to confine my activities to the home front. It was for those who were handling the political and diplomatic side of the question, namely the Greek Government and Archbishop Makarios, to take care of things abroad.'[42] But the Greek government and the Archbishop finally negotiated a solution with the British which Grivas knew nothing about ahead of time, one which he furiously opposed and one which contained a provision for his own exile![43]

The Russian terrorists sent representatives abroad to solicit material and moral support. In our 'colonial' examples, the 'world' seems to seek EOKA, the Irgun and the IRA or at least media representatives go to the spot where news is being made. While this pattern supplements earlier methods, it is not a substitute for them because the Cypriot Greeks, Israelis and the Irish clearly had developed extensive organizations to mobilize support in the appropriate foreign states.

MacStoifain's account describes events which took place 25 and 15 years later than those recorded by Begin and Grivas, in an age of jet transport, TV, even color TV. Yet fewer foreign states are deeply interested in IRA activities; and this is true despite the fact that the IRA has fought a bitter campaign, one which lasted much longer than either of its more successful predecessors. Certainly, MacStoifain seems quite oblivious to the world outside the British Isles, and he does not even provide an analysis of the international situation let alone make claims about its significance. And it would seem that the absence of deep involvement by parties outside the British Isles has been a serious obstacle for the IRA.

It is difficult to assess the extent of international publicity accorded the IRA from MacStoifain's account. His fragmentary remarks pertain to specific incidents. He describes, a 'press conference' (not simply an interview) held in Belfast 'under British noses' which all the others so far discussed would have envied.[44] 'Contacts abroad' in 1971 persuaded him that IRA activities were 'fully' and 'fairly' reported most of the time;[45] and one suspects that this year may well have been *a*, or indeed *the*, high point of interest in the IRA. To be sure, he complains of the British media's propensity to distort events, but the same complaint against the media appears in every memoir consulted. He does indicate that in paving the way for the IRA, the Civil Rights movement, which carried 'no sectarian symbols or political banners', created a strategy that the Protestants 'did not quite know how to cope with' and was extraordinarily effective in generating world interest. 'The only reason the Unionist system had been able to exist was that the British turned a blind eye to its injustices. Once the reality was dragged out into the light of day *attracting international attention*, it was the beginning of the end (my emphasis).'[46] IRA exploits in MacStoifain's account seem to have comparatively negligible effects. The terrorists do make efforts to carry their message abroad especially to the US, where a large Irish element provides various sorts of support. Still, compared to the 1920s when the IRA successfully struggled to create an Irish state, the Irish-American interest seems tepid although the hope that that interest can be rekindled must always encourage the IRA to persist.

In one sense, the IRA does have a favorable international context.

Events in Northern Ireland always influence the politics of the Republic of Ireland, preventing the Republic from denying its territory and assets completely to the IRA. Perhaps, the current struggle would have been terminated long ago if an effective denial were possible. On the other hand, the Irish government, unlike the Greek one in EOKA's case, patently does not endorse the terrorists.

The comparatively narrow international base of the IRA is indicated by the fact that MacStoifain meets only British and Irish officials while a variety of foreign officials contacted the Irgun and EOKA (via Makarios). MacStoifain refers only once to a UN interest in the Irish question, one that appears early in the campaign and was still-born.[47] He also acknowledges that a concerted, not always successful, effort by governments, especially in NATO countries, to deny the IRA arms exists.[48]

MacStoifain does not discuss, let alone admit, the fact that the IRA failed to generate a wide international concern; and it would be fruitless speculation to imagine why he does not do so. But the plain fact is that the IRA case is not as interesting to the international world as the other two were; and there are political not 'technological' reasons for this indifference.

III. Contemporary (US 1969–71, West Germany 1971–77, Palestine 1957–78)

Our third group includes two Americans (Alpert and Stern), two Germans (Klein and Baumann), and the Palestinian Abu Iyad. For the lack of a better term I will call them contemporary terrorists, part of a phenomenon which began in the late 1960s.[49] Although the careers of the Americans were over before the international activities associated with contemporary terrorism became manifest, they are in many ways 'kindred spirits' of the Germans who together with the Palestinians illustrate what international terrorism has come to mean.

In this last period two basic political reasons for international terrorism are more highly developed than ever. The ties between different national terrorist organizations are more manifest and the involvement of foreign states is greater. By the same token, the contradictions or difficulties these international connections create for the terrrorist, difficulties which were present earlier in the Russian and Cypriot instances, are also more striking now. In these texts the international connection seems to exacerbate weakness without creating strength. One suspects that if the writers could choose freely, they would prefer national to international assets.

The Vietnam War was the initial declared political justification for terror in both the American and German cases, and opposition to the war by those who became terrorists meant identifying with the Vietcong. Stern frequently refers to herself as a member of the 'AmeriCong', persistently asking whether or not the Vietcong would approve of this or that behavior.[50] This acceptance of a Marxist or 'Marxist-like' view of the world, entailed associations with an international revolutionary brotherhood, and an emotional involvement with Communist states as well, especially Cuba and China.

America was pictured as a power which held most of the world under its foot, especially the Third World; and, therefore, all struggles against her were struggles for the same purpose. 'I came', Alpert says, 'to see all anti-establishment uprisings as aspects of world revolution, which in a slightly different form had been predicted by Marx a century ago. I [identified] my own discontent with that of rebels around the globe.'[51] With this view it is not surprising that the first two bombings Alpert's group undertook had nothing directly to do with the war, and were publicly justified as solidarity efforts with Castro and Latin American revolutionaries.[52] This commitment to world revolution did not lead to much direct contact with other revolutionaries, however. There was some interaction; a few persons went to international revolutionary centers, and Alpert learned how to use explosives intitially from two FLQ people from Quebec whom she sheltered.

The German movement was profoundly international in every phase of its life. To begin with Vietnam was not a German war, and the first martyr for the movement was killed in a demonstration against the Shah of Iran's visit to Germany. (The June 2nd organization takes its name from the date of that death). The first bombs used (supplied, incidentally, by a police *provocateur*) were set off in a demonstration against a Nixon visit. The first German terrorist group and a later one as well named themselves the Tupamaros, after a Uruguayan group mistakenly believed to be the first urban terrorists.

The intellectual roots of the German movement were all foreign (Allen Ginsberg, Jack Kerouc, Jack London, Robert Williams, Regis Debray, Mao, Fanon, and Guevara). The American counter-culture, especially its music, had an extraordinary impact, 'We never played the International, but always Jimmy Hendrix'.[53] And the model which inspired the Germans most was the American Black Panthers.

The Germans, like the Americans, understood themselves to be following the lead of Third World revolutionaries.

> The analysis of imperialism tells us that the struggle no longer starts in the metropolis that it's no longer a matter of the working class, but ... what's needed is a vanguard in the metropolis that declares its solidarity with the liberation movements of the Third World. Since it lives in the head of the monster, it can do the greatest damage there. Even if the masses in the European metropolis don't put themselves on the side of the revolution – the working class among us is privileged and takes part in the exploitation of the Third World – the only possiblity for those who build the Vanguard here, who take part in the struggle here, is to destroy the infra-structure of imperialism, destroy the apparatus.[54]

When the Vietnam War was over, the Germans looked for a new

symbol to focus their struggle around and convinced themselves that the PLO was more attractive than any cause in West Germany itself!

> So there was a bomb planted in a Jewish synagogue on the anniversary of Crystal Night. It didn't go off. But everyone flipped out about it, despite the leaflet which explained the problem of Palestine from the viewpoint of the left, that is, that the new strategy of imperialism centers on Palestine. Since Vietnam is finished, the war more or less over, it can't go on forever; people should get involved with Palestine. It is actually much closer to us, which is apparent today with the oil business and has much more to do with us here in the European cities then does Vietnam. This was to become the new framework to carry on the struggle here. But for the press, of course, it was a prize because stupidly enough, it was on Crystal Night, so that the Germans once again set off a bomb in a Jewish synagogue.[55]

The commitment to the PLO was secured by a series of extraordinary actions. Germans trained in Palestinian camps in Jordan (1970) and returned to form the Red Army Faction (RAF), the most effective, certainly the most notorious German group. This was, perhaps, the first time in history one terrorist organization wholly trained another. Soon afterwards German and Palestinian terrorists began cooperating in operations, sometimes across international borders in neutral states and these operations often included persons who lacked a common language, for example, Munich Olympics (1972), Vienna OPEC Ministers' kidnapping (1975), Entebbe (1976) and Moghadishu (1977).

The Revolutionary Cells, the German group most involved in joint operations, and also significantly perhaps, the weakest German group, divided its organization into two sections – the German and the International. Hans Joachim Klein, a participant in the kidnapping of OPEC Ministers, describes how the primary purpose of the International Section, securing help for the release of German prisoners, was compromised or prostituted.

> I want to explain what has become of the guerrilla's political project. The problem is that they claim their actions are independent but they aren't any longer. Each time they were dependent on Wadi Haddad and his group. For every action in support of the liberation of prisoners, the guerillas are dependent on others because they need countries where they can seek refuge. They depend on others for their money and weapons. All that has a price: the participation of German guerrilla members in other actions. Since Haddad needs people who aren't Arabs for his operations, that's exactly what happened at Entebbe.[56]

In view of the importance of Palestinians in the accounts of Baumann and Klein both as a symbol and as members of organizations which give and receive aid, it is disconcerting, though not altogether surprising, to find that Abu Iyad simply does not discuss the PLO's relationships with non-Palestinian terrorist groups.[57] Most instances of cooperation the Germans mention were undertaken by dissident Palestinian groups particularly by the Marxist-Leninist Popular Front for the Liberation of Palestine (PFLP) headed by George Habash, and Abu Iyad denounces them. If incidents where the main body of the PLO itself was involved are acknowledged, he ignores German element.[58]

One cannot pursue the question of what the PLO and other contemporary terrorist organizations mean to each other from Abu Iyad's text, although he makes it abundantly clear that no revolutionary terrorist group has ever been so deeply involved in international activities as the PLO has been.[59] Whereas all our other texts focus on terror operations, this one is preoccupied with international politics, the author being in perpetual motion moving from country to country for discussions.

In the Russian case one could distinguish two international constituencies, one consisting of world revolutionaries and the other of liberal mass publics and/or constituted governments. Choosing to appeal to one or the other created strains within organizations without necessarily splitting them. A similar dilemma exists for contemporaries but the organizational impact may be different, at least it is in a loose confederation such as the PLO, which contains a number of separate and sometimes mutually hostile groups who have used terror against each other, while pursuing different kinds of international activity. The PFLP is one such group. Intermittently in and out of the PLO, and once more powerful than it is today, it developed close relations with German, Italian, and Japanese terror groups and with various Eastern European states, China and North Korea. Fatah, the chief PLO group, has publicly followed a different path, especially since 1974, attempting to create ties with all governments regardless of their political form. To pursue that policy it has renounced certain kinds of terror, largely against those who are not Israelis, and attempted to conceal involvements when it has violated its own declarations.

Only partly visible from Abu Iyad's account, the international character of the PLO is its central feature, one thrust upon it by political necessity, not choice. Abu Iyad suggests many reasons for this feature, though he never enumerates them in a statement. The first is the change in the regional or Arab international system precipitated by the creation of Israel, regarded as an illegitimate body by Arab states and making the Palestinian issue a critical virtually unremovable, issue in their domestic and international politics.

The second is the recognition by Arab states (Rabat, 1974) of the PLO as the legitimate representative of the Palestinians. The UN, which still has jurisdiction over some Palestinian questions, followed suit, granting the PLO a quasi-state or 'observer status' in UN deliberations. To date over 80 states have extended the PLO diplomatic privileges. Most of Abu Iyad's trips are taken to see government officials, and indeed it appears that the PLO has even mediated disputes between Algeria and Morocco, Egypt and Libya.

A third reason derives from what we are told is the PLO's understanding of the meaning of Palestinian history, namely, that the failure of previous rebellions shows that no success is possible without the direct involvement of Arab armies; and, in this respect, the view differs radically from that offered by Begin, Grivas, and MacStoifain who called for moral or political support and sometimes for arms, but never thought the armies of other states necessary or desirable. While the PLO has formally adopted a policy of no involvement in the domestic politics of Arab states, and has made efforts to implement it, the belief that Arab military intervention is required, implies that the PLO must be involved when Arab states are making 'fundamental and crucial' decisions concerning the PLO. He suggests, too, that the PLO will use whatever means it deems appropriate. His discussion of a plot to assassinate different national Arab leaders who were believed opposed to recognizing the PLO as the Palestinian people's legitimate representative at Rabat illustrates the point. The plot, which he claims was the unauthorized actions of individuals, was frustrated. But the fear inspired was effective in producing the result desired, and, therefore, Iyad felt obliged to use his influence to get the fedayeen released and he publicly defended their actions.

> The fourteen fedayeen ... have done their duty. Contrary to the allegations of a malicious propaganda, they never had any intention of attacking all the Arab chiefs of state, but only one of them, King Hussein, the butcher of our people, 'And if it's true, that they sought to execute him', I exclaimed, 'I assume full responsibility for it and the honor of supporting their action'.[60]

A fourth reason for PLO involvement in the international sphere derives from the special competition between rival groups within the PLO. Abu Iyad complains repeatedly that commitment must be constantly demonstrated to sustain credibility and that commitment is best demonstrated through more violent and less compromising politics. (Baumann describes conflict between individuals in his groups similarly.) In such cases, weaker groups seek softer, more defenseless, and innocent targets. Abu Iyad suggests, but he does not state, that this explains why the PFLP brought hijacked European and American aircraft to Jordan in 1970, which was the first time people were deliberately chosen as victims who were neither Israelis nor Arabs. The action contributed significantly to Jordan's decision to expel the PLO but, despite the disaster being wreaked and the denounciation by the PLO, the mainstream body itself soon followed suit by organizing the Black September attacks at the Munich Olympics and the American Embassy in Khartoum both in 1972. Ironically, although the PLO renounced assaults against non-Israeli targets in 1974, as previously indicated, Abu Iyad wondered whether the cost of forbearance has been too high for the organization's revolutionary reputation.[61]

The fifth condition of PLO internationalism, according to Abu Iyad, is perhaps the most important, namely, the diaspora character of the Palestinian community. (Some 60 per cent of the Palestinian population live outside Israeli-controlled territories, 50 per cent live in ten Arab states, and ten per cent elsewhere.) The PLO has never found sufficient indigenous support on the West Bank to mount sustained operations there. From the beginning, its organization work was done in neighboring Arab states, and the political circumstances which permitted this activity kept changing. Fatah – the PLO's chief component – was, for example, initially organized in Egypt, but within a year it had to move to Kuwait. '[W]e could operate more freely in the Gulf state where the security services were less developed and the rulers better disposed towards us than in the countries bordering on Israel.'[62] The Palestinian diaspora, on the other hand, as I have pointed out in our other cases, can provide indispensable logistic advantages for strikes throughout much of the world, and useful political resources to explain the purposes of those attacks. The dispersion of the Palestinian population and administrative offices also means that strikes against the PLO by its various anatagonists will be world-wide in scope too.

Arab states have always been ambivalent towards Palestinian populations in their midst. Sympathy, guilt at not having done enough, and anger at the humiliation those states have suffered at Israeli hands promote Arab support. Still, there is fear of the Palestinians as a potential subversive force, especially since the PLO radical dissidents like the PFLP are pledged to a wholesale reconstruction of the Arab world. Of crucial importance is the recognition that the Palestinians could pull Arab states into unwanted wars. In the years immediately after Israel was established, all bordering Arab states restricted Palestinian raids into Israeli territories. Egypt lifted restrictions briefly in 1955 but the Israelis struck back hard, and those events were a contributing element in the Suez War (1956) after which the restrictions were resumed. The PLO presence later occasioned a civil war in Jordan and then in Lebanon. Abu Iyad admits that the extraordinary restraint such a situation requires broke down in Jordan and Lebanon, partly because the PLO could not control some of its component organizations and even individual fedayeen.[63]

The principal problem, however, is that PLO interests often conflict with those of Arab states. 'All revolutions conceived in Palestine abort in the Arab capitals.'[64]

> We concluded what we thought were strategic alliances with Arab regimes only to discover after, at our own expense, that they were extremely provisional. Such mistakes brought us profound disappointment and unexpected reversals. We thought, for example, that Egypt would be with us forever, that Syria would never, not even briefly, side with the Christian right against us in

Lebanon. We never imagined that Iraq, whatever our political differences, would stoop to having our most eminent militants abroad assassinated.[65]

Whatever its will or public declarations, the PLO, as I have indicated, must upon important occasions involve inself in Arab domestic politics. In turn Arab states, most notably Syria and Iraq, have either captured or established groups within the confederation to influence or weaken the body. The internationalization of the PLO, hence, has made it even more divided; and, Abu Iyad says that the involvement of Arab states in the PLO's internal life has made it impossible to settle for a more limited goal such as the Irgun and EOKA did earlier.

Within and outside the PLO, Palestinian groups controlled by Arab states carry out the foreign policy of those states under the cover provided by arrogating the PLO name. International actions are pursued which would be too repugnant for a state to acknowledge and for which the PLO willy-nilly suffers enormous damage. The most important example, perhaps, is the reckless creation of tensions which led directly to the breakdown of the Lebanese state in 1977.

> [M]ost analyses of the causes of the civil war attribute the major responsiblity to the fedayeen who by their excesses supposedly pushed the Christian rightist parties to take action against the Palestinians. Advocates of this thesis overlook the fact that most of the provocations to which they refer, were committed by fedayeen organizations manipulated by various Arab regimes which traditionally settle their scores on Lebanese territories. For instance, when an article offensive to Iraq is published in the Lebanese [press], it is the Arab Liberation Front, a mere puppet of the Baghdad regime, which takes the matter in hand by dynamiting the publication's building and killing about a dozen people ... . But the press doesn't accuse Iraq or even the ALF. It denounces the 'terrorism of the Palestinians'. And when Saiqah, which dances to the tune of Damascus, kidnaps Lebanese belonging to the pro-Iraq Baath party, the PLO is accused of interfering in Lebanon's internal affairs. Or when Libya decides to seize an opponent, as was the case with its former prime minister Mustafa Ben Halim, it digs up some obscure Palestinian splinter group to do its dirty work. I could go on and on.[66]

These actions are impossible to stop. 'We don't always know who is responsible .... If we do know it would be suicidal to incur the wrath of the various Arab regimes on the pretext of restoring order.'[67]

> Bitter experience has mandated prudence. To illustrate this, I would like to cite an example that haunts our memories after a conflict between Nasser and King Saud in 1957. Nasser demanded that the Palestinian Legislative Council in Gaza, a mere tool of the Egyptian government, adopt a motion criticizing the Saudi monarch.

Whereupon Saud in reprisal promptly expelled all the Palestinian teachers employed in his kingdom. Seventy thousand persons including teachers' wives and children, thus once again lost their homes and their livelihood. And yet Saud knew full well that the Gaza Legislative Council had no choice but to apply the directive from Cairo. His vengence would have been a thousand times crueler had he been criticized by an autonomous organization like Fatah. This gives some idea of why we must go to such lengths to avoid a confrontation with this or that regime, at least when a crucial or fundamental issue is not at stake.[68]

In one other respect the PLO has paid a price for its internationalism. It is in a never-ending struggle against a number of intelligence services from different states simultaneously which know that you can discredit the PLO and pursue another objective at the same time. Lebanon, in particular, was

a favorite stamping ground for intelligence services of foreign powers, large and small, Eastern and Western, Arab and Israeli. Numerous bombings, kidnappings, assassinations, and other 'uncontrolled' incidents throughout the civil war were attributed all too quickly to the Resistance or the left but in fact were nothing more than manifestations of the secret wars being waged among the various intelligence services. For those whose interests were served by the war's prolongation, the incidents were yet another way to revive it when it seemed to lag. Such was and remains our dilemma and dream.[69]

Conclusion

My concern has been to use the memoirs of terrorists, first, to describe their international activities, and, second, to see what conflicts and costs or risks this activity creates for them. I shall focus initially on the first issue, and then take up the second.

Some international context has been part of every experience examined; this suggests, but does not prove, that if one looked at the history of terrorist campaigns since the 1880s, only unusual cases would lack an international component, and, indeed, I have shown elsewhere that international contexts were crucial in religious terror campaigns waged much earlier with primitive technologies.[70] The explanation provided by the texts is that terrorists go to the international scene because they believe in the possibility of international revolution and/or that foreign states have assets terrorists can use in their domestic struggles. The details of the international context varies in individual cases, but the major changes are associated with the three waves of terror. The nature of those changes depend on the specific features of several political variables: namely, the commitment to international revolution, the willingness of foreign publics and governments to help, the availability of an appropriate ethnic population abroad, and changes which have occurred in the international system. Let us illustrate these points by describing the three contexts.

The Russians felt a moral bond with other revolutionaries and that the international arena provided three principal benefits: (1) physical refuge – foreign states were freer and not inclined to extradite; (2) access to potentially sympathetic publics and states; and (3) foreign territories were used by Savinkov to organize terrorist strikes, though not with the complicity of governments. The role of émigrés, Figner notes, was crucial in using this second benefit; and although Savinkov does not discuss the question of arousing foreign opinion, the important role of émigrés earlier and in our later cases makes one feel that they must be significant here too.

What international changes made it possible for the Russian terrorists to operate abroad? The memoirs do not address the question; still, the transformation of Europe in the wake of the French Revolution seems decisive in two respects. The first was the spread of liberal governments willing to grant refuge to revolutionaries, and the second was the development of an international revolutionary tradition.

In our second set of examples, the change is obvious. Western colonial empires suddenly became illegitimate, providing a reservoir of international sympathies for those able to make their anti-colonial claims credible. The commitment to an international revolutionary brotherhood waned at the same time, which probably made it easier to gather foreign sympathies. The UN, especially in its earlier days with its prestige was high, provided an important forum for that sympathy. The Russians had pockets of émigrés, but the colonial terrorists had large numbers of their national or ethnic community living abroad in important interested states. Only one state, Japan, which was at war with Russia, directly supplied material aid in the first wave, but in the colonial cases foreign governments often give diplomatic, moral, and, occasionally, material support.

For the third wave two major changes in the international system are evident. The first is the pre-eminence of the US as a symbol and leader of the West. The ubiquitous evidence of American influence makes belief in its overwhelming dominance plausible and provides specific targets everywhere; and the defeat in Vietnam makes the destruction of the Goliath through audacity and will credible. American and German terrorists succumb first to a notion of world revolution. Most of the targets described by Stern and Alpert, who stay in America, relate to American foreign activity, especially in the Third World. In Germany the world outside seems more important than German issues. Liberal or moderate publics and governments are no longer international constituencies; in their place is a vision of the revolutionary potential of masses in the Third World, and by other terrorist groups, the principal one in time being the PLO or, more precisely, radical groups within that confederation. The German memoirs give little information about the population base of the necessary ground support for operations across national borders.

The second major change initially shaped the international system of the Middle East only. It was the creation of Israel a state whose legitimacy its neighbors would not recognize, making the Palestinian issue both a domestic and international problem for Arab states virtually independent of their will and interests. The sentiment may be comparable to the delegitimization of Western colonialism earlier, except that the mandate for Arab states to involve themselves actively and directly seems so much greater.

The diaspora, furthermore, intensified Palestinian internationalism. The PLO has to move back and forth across borders to get to the population it wants to govern and represent. The dispersion throughout Arab states and even portions of Europe provides potential ground support for operations. Finally, the Palestinian understanding of how their ulitmate objective might be achieved manifests a belief that a revolution or enormous transformation in the Arab world must take place. While Abu Iyad visualizes this change as a natural by-product of a collective effort against Israel (the predominant PLO position), some Palestinian elements think in terms of reconstructing the Arab world first, others think of a world construction as the intitial prerequisite.

The second question I have been addressing is the costs or risks for engaging in the international scene. The memoirs do *not* indicate all the costs paid, nor do they provide an adequate understanding of those they do mention. Still they contain useful material. They show that the necessity to choose between international constituencies may divide organizations. A second risk is that one may increase dependency on the undependable, and a third cost is that a more important local base may be ignored in the effort to get the widest possible international platform. Again, I will illustrate the points by describing their import in the three contexts.

Savinkov indicates that there was considerable organizational opposition to the decision of the Russians to portray themselves as being wholly committed to liberal government, but he neither reveals the significance of that tension nor indicates whether it resulted in splinter groups. One suspects, though the issue is not discussed, that as the members of the Combat Organization constantly moved back and forth across borders, they necessarily forfeited opportunities to develop their shallow local base.

In the second wave the dissipation of the notion of international revolution not only made the sympathies of Western publics and governments easier to attract, it also reduced an important potential divisive force among terrorists. The difficulty of relying on external forces which have interests of their own is suggested by the different outcomes in Cyprus and Israel. Although neither Grivas nor Begin got what he wanted, Grivas ends his book with a bitter description of his exile and Begin concludes on a note of triumph. Grivas depended too much on Greece and Begin was fortunate to have a broader base of international sympathy. Even if one of the major parties had withdrawn support for an Israeli state, the result would probably have been similar.

In the German case the most explicit acknowledgement of a problem resulting from international activity is Klein's observation that the Revolutionary Cells became wholly dependent on the PFLP, whose purpose they began to serve rather than their own. The parallel with the EOKA case is striking. Perhaps more fundamental is the likelihood that the obsession with the world revolution made German terrorists incomprehensible to Germans, a point suggested but not developed by Baumann in his discussion of the attack on Crystal Night.

The PLO case, more clearly than any other, illustrates the costs problem. The base of PLO support from other states is very broad, which should provide maximum independence. None the less, without its own home or place to operate from, it becomes excessively dependent on a particular state at particular times. Sooner or later, the host state feels anxiety about autonomous armed bodies in its midst and/or experiences Israeli counteraction; and then the PLO suffers enormous set-backs.

The internal divisions within the confederation, which frequently lead groups to conduct terror campaigns against one another, are exacerbated because each may be pursuing a different international constituency. The need to compete, to show greater militancy, forces foolish and counter-productive actions. States wanting to influence or use the PLO for their own domestic or international objectives keep fanning smouldering embers, too. And the PLO can never absolve itself completely from outrageous actions committed by others in its name because its past, Abu Iyad admits, is littered with examples of its own use of cover organizations to test the international waters.[71]

The Palestinian diaspora ensures that there will be serious costs for international operations. Palestinian populations can become hostages and the quasi-state status of the PLO means that PLO facilities must be public throughout the international world and are thus vulnerable to attack by Israelis and by rival Palestinian elements. Both circumstances continually result in new tensions with the host countries.

Clearly, the PLO could not avoid becoming an international actor in the Middle East. But Abu Iyad wonders whether the desire to cultivate governments and to make an appeal to Western publics weakened its capacity to inspire local Arab populations.

> What we feared most of all ... has happened. Our movement has become bureaucratized. What it gained in respectability is lost in militancy. We have acquired a taste for dealing with governments and men of power. We take their opinions and wishes into account. We have let ourselves be dragged into the Byzantine intrigues of inter-Arab relations and whether we like it or not we 'went into politics' in the least flattering sense of the term. Recoiling from accusations of terrorism, extremism or adventurism by more or well-intentioned professional diplomats, we knocked ourselves out to demonstrate at all costs our moderation, flexibility and conciliatory spirit, forgetting that such was not our primary vocation.

So we came to be seen less as revolutionaries than as politicians. It goes without saying that this change in our image was very damaging for us among the Arab masses, who had expected more from us. Yet this loss was not compensated for by a corresponding rise in sympathy on the part of Americans and Europeans .... [T]he main reason for our future lay in our ignorance of Western society and the complexity of the democratic mechanisms that govern it.[72]

By the standards of terrorist history, certainly by those of the cases here, PLO resources are enormous.[73] Still, Abu Iyad thinks its achievements disappointing, and in his 1980 epilogue writes that the Palestinians were much closer to success in 1958 when Fatah was founded. Today, in 1987, he must be even more pessimistic.

Has the international scene ever been decisive for success in any of the cases examined? By their own standards, terrorists rarely succeed. The two examples which come closest are colonial cases (Cyprus and Israel) and the relevant memoirs describe their international contexts as decisive. Grivas got the British out, but never achieved *Enosis* or got the Greeks in. International support helped achieve the first objective and international divisions made the second impossible. Turkey might have become involved in any case, but Grivas' failure to avoid attacking Turkish Cypriots brought the Turks in while the British were still there, an outcome Begin avoided in Palestine. It is significant, too, that Grivas had to capitulate when his forces were at their peak. Had Begin refused partition, international support would proably have dissipated, especially since most Jews in Israel were willing to accept it. Both Grivas and Begin understood their refusal would produce civil war. Grivas said the island is too small for a civil war, and Begin remembered that a civil war was the basic reason the land was lost to the Romans 2,000 years ago. (Perhaps both knew, but neither admitted, that they could not win a civil war.)

In the IRA case the failure to get results, or, if you prefer, to get them as quickly as the other groups did, seems related to the fact that there is little international interest outside the British Isles. Perhaps the IRA struggle cannot be so easily defined as a colonial one in the popular mind or perhaps the IRA has less international leverage because it cannot settle for more limited goals as the Irgun and EOKA did, and the IRA in the 1920s had.

The significant character of the international context in these three cases suggests that it probably is just as critical for other colonial instances too. Ulitmately, perhaps, the international context is so important because the imperial power feels uneasy about its own legitimacy. In the case of separatist movements like the Basques or Corsicans who claim to be resisting a colonial rule, neither the nation nor the international world finds those claims credible. Similarly, although the PLO has been recognized by many states, it is unlikely to get further (even though it makes an anti-colonial claim) without changing its ultimate purpose, primarily because Israelis believe their own right to have a state is legitimate.

We shall conclude with several brief points. The memoirs provide a political, not a technological, account for the importance of the international sphere, and the relationships between the two conditions have not yet been discussed in the academic literature. Second, a study of the memoirs reveals a striking irony. We are more conscious of international terror today, but terrorists in the colonial or second contexts were better able to exploit international forces to their advantage than 'our' terrorists are. Third, the population dispersion which is so striking in the Palestinian case has always been a feature of the international terrorist landscape, which is bound to grow in importance. A true diaspora problem may only characterize a few other cases, like the Armenian, but dispersion occurs in many forms and students of terrorism have not yet examined its characteristics and implications.

Finally, important political changes have produced recently a fourth international context. In giving religion new significance, the Iranian Revolution has, in effect, redrawn several international boundaries; state-sponsored terror has become a serious issue, and one state, Lebanon, lacks an effective government, and thus cannot be held responsible for terrorists using its territories. Memoirs pertaining to this context, if they are written, should be interesting.

NOTES

1. The only studies I know based wholly on written materials by terrorists are Nathan Leites, 'Understanding the Next Act', *Terrorism* 3 (1979), 1–46, and Bonnie Cordes, 'Euro-Terrorists Talk About Themselves': A Look at the Literature' in this volume.
2. Ted Gurr's survey ignores memoirs as a source of insight: 'Empirical Research on Political Terrorism: The State of the Art and How It Might Be Improved' in Robert O. Slater and Michael Stohl (eds.), *Current Perspectives on International Terrorism* (to be published). Martha Crenshaw's illuminating review of the literature, 'The Psychology of Political Terrorism', in Margaret G. Hermann (ed.), *Political Psychology: Contemporary Problems and Issues* (San Francisco: Jossey-Bass, 1985), pp.379–413, contains more memoir materials than any study I am familiar with, but they are not an important part of her discussion. The memoir materials used by others are restricted to the 'contemporary period' dating from the 1960s. See, for example, Franco Ferracuti, 'A Sociopsychiatric Interpretation of Terrorism', *Annals of the American Academy* 463 (Sept. 1982), 129–40; Konrad Kellen, *Terrorists: What Are They Like? How Some Terrorists Describe Their World and Actions* (Santa Monica, CA: Rand Corporation, N – 1300 – SL) and *On Terrorists and Terrorism* (Santa Monica, CA: Rand Corporation, N – 1942 – RC); Jerrold M. Post, 'Notes on a Psychodynamic Theory of Terrorist Behavior', *Terrorism* 7 (1984), 241–56.
3. The American and German environments in the 1970s produced a variety of separate tiny groups and I, therefore, have felt justified in treating each environment as producing one movement.
4. Authorized Translation (New York: International Publishers, 1927). Figner's book is abridged, and I have not been able to compare it with the original Russian. One of the reviewers I consulted did note that two versions of the *Memoirs* existed, but he did not illuminate differences between them.

5. Joseph Shaplen (trans.) (New York: Boni, 1931). Shaplen translates 'Boevaya Organizatsiya' as 'Terrorist Brigade'. The more accurate translation is 'Combat' or 'Fighting Organization', and I have decided to use 'Combat Organization'.
6. Ivan Greenberg (ed.) (London: W.H. Allen, 1948).
7. Charles Foley (ed.) (London: Longmans, 1964) and (New York: Praeger, 1964). Grivas' *Memoirs* is not a translation of the original Greek text. Charles Foley introduced fresh material, papers and oral responses while Grivas 'connected and supplemented the work in progress and approved the final text'. *The Economist* reviewer complains that the editor is responsible for the fact that 'several central episodes and controversies are strangely omitted or lightly skipped over'; but the reviewer does not indicate what the controversies are or whether they were in the original text. *The Economist*, Vol. V, No. 212 (26 Sept. 1964), 1247. *Guerrilla Warfare*, a translation from the Greek, is a general treatise as its title suggests, which contains much personal information concerning Grivas' activities in Cyprus.
8. (Edinburgh: Cremonsi, 1975).
9. (New York: William Morrow, 1981).
10. (Garden City, NY: Doubleday, 1975).
11. (New York: Grove, 1977).
12. Jean Marcel, Bouguereau (ed.), (Sanday, Orkney, UK: Cienfuegos Press, 1981). Klein's *German Guerrilla*, an interview extended over several days by Jean Marcel Bouguereau, is not a true memoir even though the original French title describes it as such.
13. With Eric Rouleau (New York: Times Book, 1978).
14. The two standard definitions differ largely on whether the violence can be characterized as normal or extra-normal. I define terrorist activity as being extra-normal violence or the deliberate use of atrocities to achieve particular public ends. It is the method of the perpetrator, not his purpose nor his status which is the distinguishing characteristic. The definitional problem is discussed more in my 'Politics of Atrocity' in Y. Alexander and S. Finger, *Terrorism: Interdisciplinary Perspectives* (New York: John Jay, 1977), pp.45–61; 'Fear and Trembling: Terrorism in Three Religious Traditions', *American Political Science Review* 78 (3 Sept. 1984), 658–77, and my introduction to *The Morality of Terrorism*, edited by David C. Rapoport and Yonah Alexander (New York: Pergamon, 1982).
15. The issue is discussed in more detail in my 'Fear and Trembling ...', op. cit.
16. These examples clearly do not exhaust the colonial experience as I shall indicate, but the label is convenient for the three texts do represent colonial situations.
17. Figner, pp.95–6.
18. Ibid., pp.94–5.
19. Ibid., p.95.
20. Ibid., p.174. James Billington, *Fire in the Minds of Men: Origins of the Revolutionary Faith* (New York: Basic Books, 1980) provides the best most recent study of the international revolutionary tradition; and he discusses terrorism largely in Chs. 14 and 15, pp.386–442.
21. Ibid., p.104.
22. Ibid. (my emphasis).
23. The letter on Garfield is not mentioned in my edition of Figner.
24. Savinkov, p.78.
25. Ibid. François-Claudius Ravachol, executed in 1892, committed several brutal murders for petty theft and some pointless large-scale bomb outrages. At his trial he proclaimed himself an anarchist, and after his execution some anarchists accepted him. But his early career led many to think that he was initially a common criminal and police informer.
    Savinkov names five other members of the 'Combat Organization' who endorsed this view, and indicates that his group was less committed to parliamentary government than was the party it served, ibid., p.76–81.
26. Apparently, movement in Russia was *easier* for those carrying foreign passports than it was for native Russians!

27. Savinkov, p.72.
28. Ibid., p.196.
29. Ibid. The Socialist-Revolutionists tried to establish alliances with the Polish, Armenian, and Macedonian terrorist organizations and had links with many other undergrounds all over the world. Gershuni, the Combat Organization's first leader, met Sun Yat-sen and the Combat Organization's influence reached India. I am grateful to Zeev Ivianski for making me aware of these facts in personal correspondance.
30. Begin, p.307.
31. *Memoirs*, p.204 and *Guerrilla War*, p.91. The translation of the document in *Guerrilla War* emphasizes the international context even more if that is possible, for it states that EOKA will make the Cyprus question 'a source of trouble to them (the allies of Greece) unless a settlement were found that satisfied our claims'.
32. Grivas, *Memoirs*, p.189.
33. Ibid., p.165.
34. One could argue that the failure of foreign states to become more deeply involved is decisive in the Russian case. But the weakness of the Russian terrorist and the strength of the Cypriots puts the action or inaction of foreign states in a different light. *Mutatis mutandis*, all things being equal, the more prolonged the disorder the more likely it is that other states will be drawn into the conflict.
35. *Memoirs*, Appendices.
36. Begin, pp.55–6.
37. Ibid., p.56.
38. Ibid., p.58.
39. Ibid., p.50.
40. Dr Bunche, USA, Dr Granados, Guatemala, and Professor Fabregat, Uruguay are the three identified.
41. I have no doubt that the two believed their claims. But I think Begin was more important to the Irgun than he admits. Grivas did build EOKA by himself, an extraordinary feat.
42. *Guerrilla War*, p.19.
43. *Memoirs*, p.189 ff.
44. MacStoifain, p.190.
45. International media coverage for 1970 is assessed in the following way. Sweden – 'admirably open and well informed', Canada – 'fairly handled', 'the same was true of Denmark and several other countries', the US, 'mixed experiences', 'but at least American viewers saw something of the movement engaged in the struggle', ibid., p.205.
46. Ibid., pp.109 and 111.
47. 'As for hopes of a United Nations peacekeeping force, the Dublin government's call for such a move was merely ... political cynicism. [It was] exploiting the [situation] to build up political capital', p.146.
48. Ibid., pp.308–9.
49. MacStoifain's IRA obviously is a product of the 1960s and shares some features with other movements in this period; still it is different from those we have called contemporary terrorists because the IRA tradtions are so pervasive. With regard to the PLO, it emerged in the 1950s, before the dates given for contemporary terrorism but it became a significant independent body only after 1968–69 when Fatah took it over. The dominant features of contemporary international terrorism which are linked to the PLO began to be expressed shortly after.
50. Stern, p.96.
51. Alpert, p.122.
52. In fact, Alpert explains, the bombings occurred at companies which happened to be 'available', and the reason for the attacks was invented afterwards. These remarkable events are discussed in Ch. X, 'To the Quicksand', pp.194–227.
53. Baumann, p.66.
54. Ibid., p.46.
55. Ibid., p.61.

56. Klein, p.31.
57. Baumann and Klein are no longer members and have less interest in protecting these groups. Abu Iyad is still an important PLO member.
58. The training of the RAF in PLO camps is not mentioned because relations with foreign terrorists is not a subject. The attack at the Munich Olympics by the Black September, which was recruited from Fatah and which Abu Iyad allegedly organized, is discussed in great detail without mentioning German aid.
59. The significance of international relations to the PLO is indicated by the fact that Helene Cobban's study, *The Palestinian Liberation Organization* (Cambridge: Cambridge University Press, 1984) is divided into three parts – history, internal and external relations. No study of any other group has or can give external relations so much attention.
60. Abu Iyad, p.148.
61. Ibid., p.76. The Black September was purported to be an ad hoc group but Eric Rouleau, Abu Iyad's editor, says in the prologue that Fatah organized it and that Abu Iyad probably was responsible (p.xi). The incidents are discussed by the latter on pp.102 and 106. David Schiller's essay 'A Battlegroup Divided: The Palestinian Fedayeen' in this volume quotes Leila Khaled, a PFLP hijacker, as saying that Fatah gave the PFLP no room to operate in Jordan against Israel.
62. Ibid., p.28.
63. Ibid., pp.76 ff. and 168 ff.
64. Ibid., pp.175–6.
65. Ibid., p.220.
66. Ibid., p.176.
67. Ibid.
68. Ibid., pp.223–4.
69. Ibid., p.176.
70. 'Fear and Trembling ...', op. cit.
71. The first operation Fatah undertook used a cover or fictitious name (ibid., p.44) and the practice continued. This is the only memoir which talks about the practice.
72. Ibid., p.221.
73. The size of each group varies in various periods of its history. Narodnaya Volya's Executive Committee never had more than 22 individuals at one time and had some 500 persons in the provinces who intermittently gave vital support. Astrid von Borcke, 'Violence and Terror in Russian Revolutionary Populism: The Narodnaya Volya, 1879–83' in Wolfgang J. Mommsen and Gerhard Hirschfeld (eds.), *Social Protest, Violence and Terror in Nineteenth- and Twentieth-Century Europe* (New York: St. Martin's Press, 1982), p.48. The Irgun, Begin says (p.61), never had more than 30 to 40 full-time members, and he speaks of 'hundreds' and later 'thousands' who carried on with normal occupations and helped when called upon. EOKA seems to have had less than a hundred full-time. The IRA usually numbers several hundred full-time. The PLO after its evacuation from Lebanon recently numbered approximately 17,000. Shaul Mishal, *The PLO Under Arafat* (New Haven: Yale University Press 1986) p.165. The financial resources of the PLO are, by the standards of other groups, enormous. See James Adams, *The Financing of Terror* (New York: Simon & Schuster, 1987).

The Internal Dynamics of the FLQ During the October Crisis of 1970

Ronald D. Crelinsten

Introduction

In his encyclopedic survey of terrorism 'from Robespierre to Arafat', Albert Parry has this to say about the terrorist group, *le Front de libération du Québec* (FLQ), that was active in Canada between 1963 and 1973:

> The Front operated in groups or cells of five to seven members each .... In the Nechayevist way of organizing and running such terror cells, the majority of them only knew members of their own units, but not those of other units. At one time the Canadian authorities even doubted the existence of any central guidance of all the cells. But the government was wrong: the Front was tightly interconnected and thoroughly managed from one principal underground directorate.[1]

Here we have a neat image of a classic cellular structure, with a centralized leadership. Parry accentuates this unified image by saying 'the Front' did this and 'the Front' did that. The problem with this image is that it is wrong.

Martha Crenshaw refers to two models of 'terrorist organizational design': a pyramidal one, with a top echelon which passes decisions down to subordinate but compartmentalized units, and a centrifugal one, with a central leadership radiating its command outward to encircling but compartmentalized units.[2] If we take these two models and apply them to the FLQ, one could say that it was more like a centrifugal model minus the hub of the wheel. Successive groups of friends would decide to form a 'cell' and call themselves the FLQ. But there was no central leadership, only a common ideal of a separate Quebec. What is more, many of these so-called cells had contact through friendship or mutual acquaintances and some individuals were even active in successive cells. Strict compartmentalization was more the result of independent initiatives taken by individuals separated by geography or every-day life than a conscious policy emanating from a central command structure.

In his penetrating study of political violence in Quebec during the decade in which the FLQ was active, Marc Laurendeau identifies nine distinct phases in FLQ activity, beginning in 1963 with attacks on targets symbolizing English domination and culminating in the penultimate phase with the kidnappings of 1970.[3] He identifies the final phase of 1971 as 'attempts at reorganization'. By that time, all active cells had been infiltrated by police informers and, by 1972, the FLQ was, in the words of one researcher, 'a security service colony'.[4] All terrorist activities were either allowed to proceed under the scrutiny of the police or were encouraged through covert facilitation. In some cases, what appeared to the public and even the authorities to be new terrorist communiqués or attacks, were in fact the work of security agents.

Even ideologically, the FLQ was not a uniform, coherent entity. Parry depicts them as 'a curious amalgam of Trotskyites and Maoists'.[5] Yet socialist and Marxist thought only began to permeate FLQ rhetoric in 1966, with the writings of Pierre Vallières and Charles Gagnon. This was already the seventh phase of FLQ activity, which Laurendeau identifies as 'the period of defense of the workers'.[6] Before that, it was primarily nationalist and anti-colonial. If one compares the FLQ manifesto issued in 1963, when the group first made its appearance, with that which was promulgated in 1970, during the October Crisis, the difference is striking. In 1963, the manifesto was addressed to 'patriots', the enemy was 'Anglo-Saxon colonialism' and the solution was 'national independence'. In 1970, the manifesto was addressed to the 'workers of Quebec', the enemies were the 'big bosses', finance companies, banks, and the solution was a made-in-Quebec revolution.[7] Even Vallières and Gagnon, the two who most inspired the Marxist orientation of the later FLQ, eventually split on ideological and tactical grounds. Vallières renounced the FLQ and supported the Parti Québécois at the end of 1971.[8] A few months earlier, Gagnon had decided to devote his energy to the creation of a new workers' party to the left of the Parti Québécois.

Vallières and Gagnon, and especially the former, are often singled out as the leaders of the FLQ, because they inspired a reorientation of the FLQ in the direction of the left-wing revolutionary and urban guerrilla movements that were predominant in the late 1960s. Because it has long been fashionable in the terrorism literature to depict all terrorist groups as left-wing insurgents imbued with some modern variant of Marxist ideology, many groups whose prime goal is some form of national, cultural or ethnic sovereignty are often lumped in with Marxist revolutionaries, even if there is a history of internal factionalism or a strong strain of nationalism within the movement. This seems to be what Albert Parry has done for the FLQ.

As for the relationship between the FLQ and other groups espousing the same goals, Parry again simplifies reality to the point of distortion. Claiming that two terrorist groups emerged in the 1960s, he collapses *le Front de libération populaire* (FLP) into the same category as the FLQ, calling both 'terrorist groups'.[9] In fact, the FLP was an above-ground, left-wing radical group, specializing in organizing mass demonstrations and similar 'agit-prop' campaigns of political protest. Formed in the Spring of 1968 by a splinter group of the socialist independence party, *le Rassemblement pour l'indépendance nationale* (RIN),[10] such groups were common in the late 1960s and often included members who had previously participated in and/or supported FLQ activities. To be sure, for certain activists, such organizations as the FLP constituted legal branches of the same movement for which the FLQ served as a covert, illegal branch, much as the Sinn Fein is the political wing and the IRA is the military wing of the Irish national movement. To the police, certainly, the FLP and other radical protest groups were fronts for the FLQ. But to call the FLP a terrorist organization is to obscure an important distinction, albeit a grey one.

What is becoming more and more clear is that terrorist groups are not monolithic entities that remain constant over time, divorced from the political life in which they exist, impervious to the actions of those who combat them. They evolve and transform in response to internal and external pressures. Like any social organization, they adapt to their changing environment in a variety of ways, often splintering into different entities or merging with other groups. Members move in and out, from clandestine to overt activity and back, sometimes engaging in a mix of legal and illegal action. To simplify this complex reality by forcing everything under the same 'terrorist' rubric is to distort reality. At the same time, such reductionist labelling hinders understanding of how such groups form, evolve and dissolve. Happily, in the ten years since Parry's book was written, researchers are paying more attention to the details of terrorist organization.[11] It is becoming more evident that internal tensions within and among competing groups lie at the root of much terrorist activity. In this article, I shall attempt to demonstrate this by means of a case study. I shall describe the activities of the FLQ in 1970, what groups were involved, how they related to one another, and what problems arose during the double kidnapping in October because of this relationship.

The October Crisis of 1970

Over and above its inherent interest as one of the most important political crises in Canadian history, the October Crisis is uniquely situated at the beginning of what has come to be known as the 'decade of terrorism', as Palestinian and European terrorists began to capture world headlines. Skyjacking and the kidnapping of diplomats, or what has been called 'diplonapping', were relatively new tactics. In fact, the October Crisis represents the first modern case of political kidnapping in North America. What is more, it was a double kidnapping, involving two separate cells and implicating two levels of government. The first victim was James Richard Cross, the British Trade Commissioner in Montreal, and hence an internationally protected person. This immediately implicated the Federal Department of External Affairs in Ottawa, in addition to the Quebec Department of Justice which, in the federal system, is responsible for the administration of justice. The second victim was Pierre Laporte, Deputy Premier and Minister of Employment and Immigration in the Quebec Liberal government. This implicated the provincial government in a much more immediate and dramatic way than had been the case with the first hostage.

The first kidnapping occurred on Monday, 5 October 1970, and was the responsibility of a group of seven individuals calling themselves the Liberation Cell of the FLQ. The leader of this group was Jacques Lanctôt, a 24-year-old taxi driver who edited a newsletter for a group called *le Mouvement de libération du taxi* (MLT).[12] Active in several radical-left protest groups, including the RIN, he had also been involved in the first wave of FLQ activity in 1963, when he was just 17. In the words of Louis Fournier, Lanctôt was both an intellectual, a theoretician who particularly admired Cuba and the Tupamaros of Uruguay, and a man of action, impatient to act.[13] The other members of the Liberation Cell were: Marc Carbonneau, 37, another taxi-driver and colleague of Lanctôt's in the MLT; Yves Langlois, 22, a former court stenographer; Nigel Hamer, 23, an engineering student at the English-language McGill University and the only English-speaking member of the group;[14] Louise Lanctôt, 23, Jacques' sister, and her husband, Jacques Cossette-Trudel, 23, both of whom had been expelled from school the year before for organizing student protests at their junior college; and another woman whose name has never been made public and who has never been formally charged for any crime.

The second kidnapping took place on Saturday, 10 October 1970, and was the responsibility of four individuals calling themselves the Chenier Financing Cell of the FLQ.[15] This name was adopted on the spur of the moment and none of their friends or associates knew that they were planning a second kidnapping. The leader of the Chenier Cell was Paul Rose, 27, a special instructor for maladjusted children. Rose had been active in the student movement and was a member of the RIN and the PQ. The other members of the Chenier Cell were Paul Rose's brother, Jacques, 22, a mechanic for the Canadian National Railway, Francis Simard, 22, an apprentice electrician for Canadian National who had helped Rose found a youth hostel in the east-coast fishing village of Percé in the summer of 1969,[16] and Bernard Lortie, 18, a student from the Gaspé peninsula, who had met the others at the Percé hostel and had just arrived in Montreal days before the Laporte kidnapping.

The acute period of the October Crisis lasted some 15 days. The first kidnapping did not, in fact, precipitate a sense of extreme crisis in government circles. Quebec Premier Robert Bourassa still went to New York City on Wednesday, 7 October, to encourage US investment in the province, the opening of a new session of Parliament proceeded as usual in Ottawa, with all its attendant receptions and ceremonies, and Prime Minister Pierre Trudeau left the day-to-day handling of the kidnapping affair to his Minister for External Affairs, Mitchell Sharp. The two levels of government quickly adopted a joint mode of crisis management and, after stalling the kidnappers for several days with requests for a mediator, finally authorized the broadcast of the FLQ manifesto, on Thursday evening, 8 October. This had by then become the Liberation Cell's minimum demand for continued dialogue.

With the broadcast of the manifesto on Radio-Canada, the French-language national television station, public reaction in Quebec took on a new dimension, with a swell of public sympathy for the terrorist cause. This unexpected wave of sympathy created some strain between the two levels of government and led Quebec Justice Minister, Jérôme Choquette, to take a conciliatory approach in delivering the governments' final offer of safe passage out of the country for the kidnappers in return for the release of James Cross. While the Liberation Cell was apparently willing to accept this final offer, even though it fell far short of the original set of demands, the Rose brothers and their associates were not. In deciding to kidnap Pierre Laporte, the Chenier Cell precipitated that sense of crisis which was not apparent after Cross was abducted. Thus began the second phase of the October Crisis, which lasted some four days. During this time, public support for the FLQ proliferated rapidly, while the Quebec government tried to negotiate with the kidnappers via direct intermediaries. Meanwhile, the Federal government dissociated itself from the negotiations and called troops into Ottawa to guard public buildings and to protect diplomats and leading politicians. Yet covert preparations for a large-scale search-and-arrest operation were carried on throughout the period of negotiations, in full anticipation of increased powers for the police. In addition, preparations were made for the calling of troops into Quebec in aid of civil power, as soon as Premier Bourassa deemed it necessary.

This second phase came to a head with the rallying of all the diverse elements of Quebec political life into a concerted effort to support the Quebec government's search for a negotiated solution, even if it meant releasing imprisoned FLQ activists, who were tried and convicted for previous waves of terrorist violence (mostly bombings). Nationalist, labour and intellectual leaders, including René Lévesque, leader of the PQ, and Claude Ryan, editor of the influential paper, Le Devoir, issued a 'declaration of the sixteen', supporting a negotiated solution and virulently attacking Ottawa's hard line. Meanwhile, the university and college students went out on strike to support the FLQ and their demands. Premier Bourassa finally decided that the time had come for decisive action and phase three began. On Thursday, 15 October, troops were called into Montreal and Quebec City, the provincial capital, and a final offer was made to the kidnappers, excluding release of any prisoners, but reiterating the offer of safe conduct to another country that was made before Laporte was kidnapped. This marked the turning point of the crisis, while the following day, 16 October, marked its climax.

At three o'clock in the morning, having heard nothing from the two terrorist cells, Bourassa requested emergency powers from Ottawa, a state of apprehended insurrection was declared and the War Measures Act was invoked. This piece of legislation allowed the adoption of special regulations which provided the police with extraordinary powers of arrest, search and seizure without warrant, and the preventive detention of suspects for up to 21 days without laying charges and up to 90 days without setting a trial date. By the end of the morning, the police announced that 238 arrests had been made across the province in the early hours of the morning.[17] In an attempt to isolate the active cells from all possible support and to cut off all possible sources of public demonstrations and/or declarations of support for the FLQ, the police rounded up anyone who had ever shown the slightest propensity to participate actively in anything nationalist, leftist, radical, labour-oriented or vaguely progressive. As such, they often reached back to those who had not been active in radical politics for some four or five years. Public support for the FLQ was effectively silenced, the student strike collapsed, and public support for the government action began to build across Canada. While all this was going on, a debate proceeded in the House of Commons in Ottawa on a motion of approval for the action taken by the government.

The tragic dénouement of the Crisis occurred over the weekend. Late Friday afternoon, while his captors were listening to the radio, Pierre Laporte attempted to escape by hurling himself through a window. Cutting himself badly and losing a lot of blood, he pleaded to go to the hospital, but Bernard Lortie merely bandaged his wounds and left the hiding-place to seek the advice of Paul Rose, who was staying with friends in Montreal ever since he escaped a police tail several days before. Laporte was killed the next day and the circumstances surrounding his death remain unclear to this day. While Paul Rose was eventually convicted for his murder and given a life sentence and his brother, Jacques, was acquitted after one hung jury and a second trial, it appears that the elder Rose was not present when Laporte died. The mystery persists because both Roses and Simard claimed responsibility for his death, for reasons of solidarity. Lortie was never charged with the murder, but was convicted for kidnapping.

When news of Laporte's death became public late Saturday night, the parliamentary debate ended and public sentiment rallied even more strongly on the side of the government and against the FLQ. On Monday, 19 October, Parliament approved the adoption of the War Measures Act by an overwhelming majority. Bernard Lortie was captured on 6 November, when police raided the apartment in which the four men were hiding. The other three managed to escape by hiding in an ingenious secret compartment which they had built in a closet. They were finally captured in late December. As for the Liberation Cell and their hostage, James Cross, the police finally found their hide-out in late November, by careful, traditional police work involving surveillance and having nothing whatsoever to do with the emergency powers they possessed by virtue of the War Measures Act. On 3 December, the Cossette-Trudels were arrested upon leaving their apartment hide-out and, after negotiating via a Canadian lawyer who served as the Cuban consul in Montreal, the police secured an exchange of Cross for the release of the Liberation Cell into exile in Cuba. Since Nigel Hamer and the young woman whose name has never been revealed both left the apartment long before the police discovered the hide-out, their involvement in the affair never became public. We have seen that Hamer was never arrested despite police knowledge of his involvement.

With the arrest of the Roses and Simard on 27 December, the October Crisis was officially over. The army left Quebec on 4 January, but the emergency regulations, slightly modified, remained in effect until 30 April 1971. Paul Rose received two life terms for murder and kidnapping and finally received full parole in December 1982 after being turned down several times. Francis Simard received a life term for murder and was finally released in 1981. Bernard Lortie received 20 years and was released in July 1978. Jacques Rose, after a series of acquittals for murder, kidnapping and forcible detention, which lasted several years, received eight years for complicity after the fact in the murder of Pierre Laporte. He was released in February 1979. As for the Liberation Cell, those exiled to Cuba left that country for France in the summer of 1974. With the election of the PQ in November 1976, the exiles began to think of returning to Quebec. The first to actually return were Louise Lanctôt and Jacques Cossette-Trudel, who returned in December 1978. They appeared in court the day after their arrival and were released on bail. On 31 May 1979, they pleaded guilty to charges of kidnapping and forcible detention and received sentences of two years less a day, which allowed them to serve their sentences in a provincial prison rather than a federal penitentiary.[18] They were paroled in April 1980.

The next to arrive was Jacques Lanctôt, who returned to Quebec on 9 January 1979. Unlike the Cossette-Trudels, who renounced their previous activities, Lanctôt never did. Pleading guilty, he received a three-year sentence plus three years probation. Marc Carbonneau returned on 25 May 1981 and was sentenced in March 1982 to 20 months in prison plus 150 hours of community service. Yves Langlois was the last to return, on 9 June 1982. In September of that year, he was sentenced to two years less a day. When he was paroled on 27 May 1983, he was the last of the
principal actors in the October Crisis of 1970 to be released from prison. As for Nigel Hamer, who remained in Montreal throughout the period in which his colleagues were in exile, becoming in the interim an electronics teacher in a junior college, he was arrested on 8 July 1980 and sentenced in 1981 to a one-year prison term plus one year of community service.

Links Between the Two Cells Before October 1970

Despite their use of the word 'cell' to identify themselves during the Crisis itself, those who took part in the two kidnappings knew one another very well. The word 'cell' implies the classic underground structure alluded to earlier of totally independent units isolated from one another, communicating only with a common central leadership. We have already seen that no such central leadership existed. Instead, the individuals clustered around two dominant personalities, Jacques Lanctôt and Paul Rose. Lanctôt and Rose first met two years previously, on 24 June 1968, when both of them were thrown into the same police wagon upon being arrested during a violent demonstration on Quebec's national holiday, St. John the Baptist Day. When they first decided to get involved in FLQ activity, in the Fall of 1969, they operated independently, each surrounded by a different set of people. Lanctôt's group included his younger brother, François, 21, and his best friend, a fellow taxi-driver, André Roy, 23, as well as various people involved in radical labour politics. Rose's group, known as the South Shore gang or the group from Longueuil, a suburb situated across the St. Lawrence river from Montreal Island, included Jacques Rose, Francis Simard, Yves Langlois, who was Simard's close friend, and Claude Morency, a 20-year-old day-labourer.

The activities of the two groups reflected in large measure the different personalities of the two leaders. Paul Rose was an organizer with a keen sense of leadership. His strategy was a long-term one of preparation for a prolonged underground existence. To this end, his group cut off all links with all known separatist hang-outs and went underground. To finance their existence, they engaged in an elaborate system of credit card fraud, using American Express, coupled with bank robberies. Cars were bought, houses rented – four or five in Montreal alone and one on the South Shore. By January 1970, Rose was able to buy an isolated farm in the Quebec countryside, which was intended to serve as a base of operations, a training camp, and a 'people's prison' for eventual hostages in the style of the Tupamaros. Francis Simard describes how the group worked throughout the winter and into the spring to adapt the place to their needs. On the surface, it was to be a sheep farm, and, underneath, a veritable subterranean village, where they could meet and live in security. Meanwhile, the system of safe houses in and around Montreal would serve as a communication and distribution network for FLQ activists and sympathizers.[19]

By contrast, Jacques Lanctôt was an idealist who was oriented to dramatic acts which would make a statement. Kidnapping seemed the ideal tactic to achieve maximum impact. In February of 1970, Lanctôt and Pierre Marcil, 25, were arrested after police stopped their rented van because of a defective tail-light and found a sawed-off shotgun inside. Charged with illegal possession of a firearm and released on bail, Lanctôt immediately jumped bail and went underground. In pursuing their investigation, the police found a large wicker basket in the van, as well as a piece of paper with journalists' phone numbers and the word 'Golan' written on it. A month later, after the police had passed this information on to the Montreal anti-terrorist squad, an arrest warrant was issued in the name of Lanctôt and Marcil for conspiracy to kidnap the Israeli consul in Montreal, Moshe Golan. While Marcil was arrested, Lanctôt was nowhere to be found. In fact, he was living with his wife and child at the farm bought by Paul Rose earlier that year. Having been forced underground by his brush with the police, he had turned to the group that was best prepared for a clandestine existence.[20]

In June 1970, the anti-terrorist squad dismantled a second kidnapping plot, aimed this time at the American consul in Montreal, Harrison Burgess. One of the people arrested in connection with the Burgess plot was Lanctôt's brother, François. Another was André Roy, Lanctôt's closest friend, and Claude Morency, a member of the Rose group. Material seized by police during the break-up of the Burgess plot included a photocopy machine, paper with a specially designed FLQ letterhead and copies of a manifesto which, according to Louis Fournier, had been drafted by André Roy and Jacques Lanctôt.[21] During the October Crisis, the Liberation Cell's communiqués were written on almost identical 'FLQ paper' and the manifesto eventually broadcast by Radio-Canada was identical to that seized by police in June. In addition, the police found a communiqué announcing the abduction of US consul Harrison Burgess in Montreal and listing four demands which were among the seven demanded by the Liberation Cell in October.

Louis Fournier points out that the break-up of the Burgess plot led police to the farm which Paul Rose had bought in January to serve as an FLQ base. A piece of paper with directions on how to get there scribbled on it was their clue. When the provincial police raided the farm on 22 June 1970, several key members of the future Liberation and Chenier cells were present, including Jacques Lanctôt who was wanted by the police. Some of them, including Lanctôt, hid in the attic and were not found during the search, and the remaining members gave false names to the police, who never bothered to verify them. No arrests were made. However, the result of this raid was to render the farm useless as a base of operations and, coupled with the June arrest of three other members, the FLQ suffered a major set-back.[22] From that point on, the Lanctôt group and the Rose group were essentially one.

The impact of these two events – the June arrests and the farm raid – on the immediate plans of the FLQ network that was active in the Spring of 1970 was significant. Jean-François Duchaîne puts it succinctly: 'The organization that existed in the month of June 1970 was in effect much more solid than that which took action in the Fall of 1970'.[23] The Lanctôt–Rose group had to completely reorganize over the ensuing summer. Duchaîne describes some of the problems faced by the group: 'All organizing activity stopped, since all the money that was collected went to clothing the group's members. It was therefore impossible to accumulate the necessary funds for large-scale actions.'[24] The group's options narrowed down to two: wait and organize, or act now. Here we have one of the most basic tensions which plague clandestine groups and which seems to be a leitmotif in the history of such organizations. Martha Crenshaw rightfully points out that it is this dichotomy which separates purely terrorist groups from revolutionary ones: 'Historical forces, not individual actions, create revolutionary conditions. Terrorism can play little part in this scenario, and it has historically been at this juncture in decision-making that terrorist groups have split from larger revolutionary movements.'[25] She then cites Provisional IRA leader, Sean MacStoifain, as a proponent of immediate action:

Guerrillas who want to bring social and political change do not wait
for conditions to become 'ripe' for revolutionary action, because
they could be waiting forever. Instead, they take the field and
gradually build up popular support through their successes.[26]

Jacques Lanctôt could have spoken these exact words. In hiding from
the police, his brother in jail, Lanctôt favored immediate action. Paul
Rose favored the long wait, coupled with careful preparation. Francis
Simard describes the Rose strategy: 'Priority had been given to clandestine action, to setting in place a clandestine network that was effective and
secure. The legal network of houses and distribution that we wanted to
construct rested on our capacity to organize secretly.'[27] Clearly, any
immediate action, such as kidnapping, would compromise the careful
build-up of a secure underground organization. And, in fact, this is exactly
what had happened. With the June arrests and the farm raid, which were
precipitated by the kidnapping plots of the Lanctôt group, all the Rose
group's careful work of early 1970 was undone, and pressure mounted for
immediate action.

Francis Simard describes how the need to organize was supplanted by
the need to free friends and colleagues from prison: 'We were joined by
other people. The necessity of organizing became a minority position.
Priority was given to a plan to kidnap an American diplomat to secure the
release of political prisoners. Everyone worked on it. The project had a
name: Operation Liberation.'[28] Jean-François Duchaîne speaks of the
same source of tension:

> Jacques Lanctôt was impatient with the slowness of preparations,
> the financing that went nowhere and the organization that dragged
> on forever, and announced that he was ready for action. Paul Rose
> calculated that the group's resources (house, weapons, money, etc.)
> were insufficient to sustain a large-scale operation.[29]

This fundamental disagreement over strategy resurfaced during the
October Crisis and was reflected in the actions of the two kidnapping cells.

After the discovery of the farm by the provincial police, the headquarters of the Lanctôt–Rose group were transferred to a house rented by
Paul Rose: 5630 Armstrong Street in Saint-Hubert, a Montreal suburb on
the South Shore. It was here, at a strategy session early in September, that
the group decided, by a vote of five to four, to proceed with Operation
Liberation. One member of the Rose group who voted in favour was Yves
Langlois. In the wake of that decision, the Rose brothers and Simard
decided to follow an independent course and to continue their strategy of
financing and organization. When they heard that Operation Liberation
was planned for late September or early October, Paul and Jacques Rose
and Francis Simard decided to leave the country.[30] On 24 September 1970,
they embarked on a trip to the United States with the Rose brothers'
mother, Rosa, and a younger sister, Claire. The group which decided to
undertake Operation Liberation took the name 'Liberation Cell' (la

cellule Libération).[31] The day before the actual kidnapping, they were still unsure whether to kidnap an American or a British diplomat. Hesitating between the new US Consul, John Topping, and the British Trade Commissioner, James Cross, they finally chose the latter.

Jean-François Duchaîne states that when the Rose brothers and Francis Simard, *en voyage* in the United States, learned of Cross's kidnapping, they were surprised. Not because a kidnapping had occurred, but because it was the only one and the target was British, not American.[32] According to Francis Simard, the original plan had never been to kidnap Cross alone, for fear that this would relegate the conflict to one of language and race, between the English and the French, whereas the conflict went much deeper than that.[33] The idea had been to kidnap a British diplomat, as a protest against cultural colonialism, and an American diplomat, as an attack against economic imperialism.[34] Note once again the combination of anti-colonial and anti-capitalist ideologies. By choosing to kidnap only James Cross, the Liberation Cell appears to have opted for the symbolic blow for cultural sovereignty over an attack on American economic domination.[35] Since the kidnapping of the British diplomat had originally been conceived as a symbolic expression of the fight for national independence, it had even been decided beforehand that he would not be killed. In fact, after Justice Minister Jérôme Choquette made his first public statement at a press conference on the day James Cross was abducted, the diplomat's captors actually told him that he would not be killed and that he would eventually be released and a businessman would be the next victim.[36] Rather than a double kidnapping, the Liberation Cell seems to have decided on two consecutive ones.

However, the Rose brothers and Simard did not know this and, upon hearing the news, they were surprised and disappointed. For them, the Liberation Cell had acted precipitously and, in kidnapping Cross, placed the fight against economic imperialism on a back burner. In choosing what they perceived as the weaker component of the original plan, the Liberation Cell was undermining at the outset their chances of imposing the conditions for their hostage's release. Their decision not to execute their hostage would only force them to continually delay their deadline in the face of a government refusal. Several members of the Liberation Cell would later admit that they had expected their demands to be granted within four or five days and that they were surprised when the government stuck to its minimum concession of publishing the manifesto and granting safe conduct to Cuba.[37] Fearing such an eventuality, the Rose brothers and Simard decided to cut short their trip and to return to Quebec. The objective: another kidnapping. The rationale: to strengthen the bargaining power of the Liberation Cell.

Here again, we see how the different strategic goals of the two cells led to different tactical decisions. In the remainder of this article, I shall examine in greater detail the strategies and tactics of the two cells in an attempt to demonstrate how their differing objectives led them to aim for different things, despite their use of the same tactic of kidnapping. What is more, we shall see how the appearance of the Chenier Cell on the scene created considerable problems for the Liberation Cell, let alone the authorities.

The Cross Affair: Successful Negotiation

This is how one member of the Liberation Cell assessed the outcome of Operation Liberation during the weeks following Laporte's murder and preceding the eventual discovery of their hide-out.

> Nevertheless we can speak of victory at this point since one of our principal demands has been accepted: the broadcast of the manifesto which evoked all that sympathy. For the first time, the patriots of the Front succeeded in expressing themselves practically by stepping into each household, by means of Radio-Canada which read our manifesto. They were in touch for the first time, a contact with us that was quite direct and blunt.

The statement was part of a recorded conversation made by the Liberation Cell in mid-November and released to the media after the Cross affair was terminated.[38] In this political testament of sorts, members of the Cell discussed their motives for Operation Liberation and their assessment of how it went. In the course of their discussion, they provided insights into their overall strategy.

> In any case, whatever happens, we're certain of victory, because everything we had to say has, for now, been said. We used the same means as the bourgeoisie, which the bosses use to disseminate their ideas. We used the big capitalist press, we used the radio stations to make our ideas known, to show that we agree with the claims of the Quebec people.

This emphasis on speaking to the Quebec people highlights one of the main purposes of Operation Liberation: 'to restore the Front's image'. One of the speakers on the tape spoke of the necessity of showing the general public that the FLQ was an organization that was here to stay, even though it only manifested itself occasionally. In other words, part of the strategy underlying Operation Liberation was to demonstrate that the FLQ was a force to be reckoned with in Quebec politics. Here we have an excellent example of a terrorist strategy being adopted as a means of claiming recognition, as a means of justifying the group's own existence. The FLQ was operating against a cacophonous backdrop of advocacy and debate in which well-known political and labour leaders, professional organizations, leading intellectuals, radical lawyers, influential artists and newspaper editors were promoting and attacking all shades of political opinion and all sorts of causes, many of which were consistent with those of the FLQ. One's voice could easily be drowned out in such a commotion, unless one could attract a wide audience by means of some dramatic terrorist act.

To do this the Liberation Cell had to reach the widest possible audience, and the electronic media provided the ideal vehicle. However, it was one thing to simply make news via a single dramatic act and totally another thing to control the media coverage over a protracted period of time via an act necessitating negotiations. For this latter approach, the terrorists needed something more than a hit-and-run tactic such as bombing. One of the cell members pointed out during the taped conversation that past bomb attacks had allowed the press to interpret the FLQ actions in their own ways. According to the speaker, the media tried to terrorize everyone, not just the English-speaking population. What was needed was a tactic that would allow them to control the media and to use it to publicize their cause. Kidnapping was that tactic. By using the media, and, in particular, the competition for news, the Liberation Cell was able to force the government to negotiate in public and thereby, to maximize publicity for its political goals.

Here is the key to the central strategy of the Liberation Cell: to change the image of the FLQ from a marginal group of criminal fanatics to an organized political force with a concrete political programme. The Liberation Cell's widely touted tactic of playing one radio station against another by sending copies of communiqués to competitors in order to maximize media coverage now takes on a new significance. Before Pierre Laporte was ever kidnapped, the Liberation Cell had already used the tactic to establish consistent and rapid reporting of its communiqués by one Montreal station, CKLM. Once this was achieved, the Liberation Cell consistently refused to name a direct mediator for negotiations with the government officials – at least until Laporte was kidnapped. Instead, they preferred to negotiate via communiqués broadcast publicly by the radio stations. The reason for this is obvious. By forcing a government to negotiate with them in public, terrorists thereby gain the status of equal partners in a political dialogue. As such, the terrorists are transformed from marginal criminals into political actors.

The Terrorists' Demands

If we now turn to the specific demands of the Liberation Cell, the overall strategy is also reflected here. They were originally seven in number: (1) the cessation of all police activity designed to find the kidnappers or their hostage; (2) the publication of a political manifesto on the front pages of all major Quebec newspapers and its broadcast on Radio-Canada during a special prime-time broadcast in which released FLQ prisoners would be permitted to read and comment on the text; (3) the release of 20 'political prisoners' (including François Lanctôt, André Roy and Claude Morency) in prison or in custody awaiting trial, as well as three others currently on bail, with permission to leave the country; (4) the provision of a plane to fly them to Algeria or to Cuba, accompanied by their lawyers and at least two reporters; (5) the rehiring of a unionized group of postal drivers, known as the Lapalme boys, who had been replaced with another company by the Federal Minister of the Post Office several months before, triggering a bitter and protracted labour dispute which had attracted the support and sympathy of many radical groups; (6) a 'voluntary tax' of 500,000 dollars in gold ingots to be placed on the plane with the political prisoners upon their release; (7) the publication of the name and photo of the presumed informer who had led to the break-up of the Burgess plot.

On the third day, 7 October, the first two demands became the minimum requirement for the government to show its good faith in the negotiations to come. The second demand was reduced to a simple broadcast of the manifesto by Radio-Canada during prime time. Once the government agreed, on 8 October, to broadcast the manifesto, the Liberation Cell reduced their demands to release of the prisoners and cessation of police activity. The money, the informer and the Lapalme boys were never mentioned again. While the name of the operation implies that freeing the prisoners was the main goal, it is clear that the broadcast of the manifesto was an essential part of the plan. When the government continued to refuse to release any prisoners, and simply offered the kidnappers safe conduct out of the country if they released their hostage, the Liberation Cell seemed prepared to accept the offer, without pressing the issue of the prisoners. After watching Justice Minister Jérôme Choquette deliver the governments' final offer on television on Saturday evening, 10 October, James Cross asked his captors what they were going to do. He was told that they would continue to hold him for several days, just to taunt the police, and then they would let him go.[39] Since Jacques Lanctôt's name and photo had been publicized by that time, the offer of safe passage meant he could avoid prosecution. But the Chenier Cell struck before the Liberation Cell had a chance to act. At 6.18 p.m., minutes after Choquette finished his television address, Pierre Laporte was scooped off the street by four masked, armed men in a car, while the Minister was tossing a football with his nephew in front of his home.

Does the accent placed on police activity mean that this, too, was a central demand of the Liberation Cell, especially since they persisted in this demand throughout the negotiations? It is very probable that the Liberation Cell fully realized that police activity would never cease. Yet, by making this a central element in their hierarchy of demands, they focused public attention on the ongoing police work. Rumours concerning police activity were rife throughout the week of negotiations preceding Laporte's kidnapping. Conflicting reports over the extent of such activity were common. By the time Laporte was abducted, several illegal arrests had already been made and certain groups, such as the Quebec Journalists' Union, were beginning to criticize the police and the public prosecutor. This public criticism contributed to the newly acquired legitimacy of the FLQ in the wake of the manifesto's broadcast. Those who criticized police actions could be seen as validating in some way the FLQ demand that police activity cease. Therefore, the propaganda value of the demand outweighed the inevitability of its being ignored. Yet, for this reason, it cannot be considered a central demand. Rather, it served a tactical purpose in contributing to the legitimizing process of public negotiations.

The question remains as to how the two central demands – publication of the manifesto and release of the prisoners – were related. The key lies in the political dimension raised previously. The Liberation Cell's insistence upon publication of the manifesto as their minimum demand suggests that the primary aim of the operation was, as previously suggested, to paint a political image of the FLQ, oriented in particular toward the working class (hence the demand for reinstatement of the Lapalme union) and toward revolutionary aspirations linking independence and socialism. The Liberation Cell may have initially set out to free their colleagues, hence the title 'Operation Liberation'. Faced with unexpected government intransigence, however, they ended up using this demand to draw the government into a public debate where it was forced to address the FLQ's political programme. By insisting that the manifesto be published first, the terrorists ensured that the public knew what this programme entailed.

It is clear that the Federal government perceived the main goal of the demand to release the prisoners as a propaganda one rather than a real hope that it would be met. Toronto reporter, Anthony Westell, whose reporting tended to reflect official thinking in Ottawa, made this assessment once the Crisis was over:

> As Trudeau emphasized, the key demand for release of FLQ members in jail, was not a Robin Hood attempt to rescue comrades, but a calculated effort to weaken authority by creating a parallel power able to enforce its will on the government, if only for a few hours.[40]

To the extent that the Liberation Cell really did intend merely to rescue their comrades-in-arms, they totally underestimated the political impact of their demand and that is why they were surprised that the government never gave in.

The Liberation Cell also stated in their recorded conversation that the rehiring of the Lapalme boys was their third major demand. There is good reason to suspect, however, that this was also propaganda, again related to image-building. The Liberation Cell abandoned this demand along with all the others except for the two main ones and the cessation of police activity. The Chenier Cell, on the other hand, placed consistent emphasis on the Lapalme workers and it is likely that the Liberation Cell mentioned this as an afterthought while making the tape, as an expression of solidarity with the Chenier Cell. While useful as an opening gambit, as one element in the general picture of a legitimate political group concerned about the plight of workers, the demand to rehire the Lapalme drivers soon became secondary, once the legitimacy of the kidnappers had been reinforced by ongoing negotiations.

As for the remaining demands, two – the provision of a plane and the transport of the political prisoners and their families to Cuba or Algeria –

were merely ancillary to the release of the prisoners. The remaining two –
the gold and the naming of the alleged informer – served as foils to the
main demands. When they were abandoned in the early stages of the
negotiations, the terrorists acquired an image as reasonable, conciliatory
people. In addition, the remaining demands seemed less unreasonable by
contrast to the original set of demands. Pressure was placed on the
government to respond in kind, and this, above all other factors, probably
led to the broadcast of the manifesto. Here we have an excellent example
of a rarely recognized terrorist tactic: de-escalation of demands down to a
point where a government finds it difficult not to accede.

A Successful Compromise: A Dialogue in which Both Sides Won

The period between the abductions of James Cross and Pierre Laporte can
be conveniently divided into four phases. First, there was the battle over
the means of communication, in which the authorities blocked publication of FLQ communiqués and the terrorists sent duplicates to the media.
This lasted for two and a half days and was finally won by the Liberation
Cell.[41] The second phase was the day and a half leading up to the broadcast
of the manifesto. In this phase, the governments tried to stall and, instead
of suppressing communiqués as they had done before, officials tried to
draw the kidnappers away from their use of the media and towards direct
and secret negotiations. At the same time, federal officials tried to delay
broadcast or publication of the manifesto as long as possible, even to the
point of phoning newspaper publishers directly to request that they
refrain from publishing the text. However, the redundancy created by the
Liberation Cell's provision of multiple copies to the media ultimately
undermined these attempts. The third phase was the 24-hour period
following the broadcast of the manifesto. Here, the conditions were ripe
for effective negotiation, but any good faith that existed was destroyed
when the Liberation Cell's sixth communiqué, in which they responded to
the manifesto broadcast in a conciliatory fashion, was never found due to a
mix-up in its delivery. Believing that the police had once again intercepted
a communiqué, the Liberation Cell set a final ultimatum for the release of
the prisoners. The fourth phase involved the drafting of the final offer in
such a way as to appease public sentiment which sympathized with the
manifesto, while offering safe passage to the kidnappers.

If one examines the communiqués and official statements made by both
kidnappers and government officials during this period preceding
Laporte's kidnapping, it becomes clear that both government and
terrorist strategies worked. However, each side paid a price for their
success. While the FLQ gained widespread publicity and public sympathy
for their cause, they failed to free their friends in jail and paid the price of
exile. They paid this price because they underestimated the firmness of
the two governments, in particular the Federal government. While the
governments would have achieved the release of Mr Cross, they paid the
price of widespread sympathy for the FLQ cause and opened the way to

their legitimation as political actors. They paid this price because they underestimated the extent of public support for aspirations such as those espoused by the FLQ and the degree to which they resonated with those of a wide variety of activists and symphathizers who would, themselves, never resort to violence.

If the incident had ended there, it is quite likely that the public debate on the political grievances raised by the FLQ would have continued long after the specific demands of the terrorists had faded into memory. The newly gained credibility of the FLQ may have forced the government to address the broader political issues sooner, but this may have happened eventually anyway. After all, the Parti Québécois did gain power six years later. Instead, the Chenier Cell, listening to what Jérôme Choquette considered a conciliatory speech, heard only condescension and paternalism. They felt that the Liberation Cell had lost, not won. In order to strengthen the FLQ's bargaining position, or so they thought, the Chenier Cell set out to kidnap Pierre Laporte. In doing so, they altered completely and irrevocably the delicate negotiation process which had evolved over the preceding week.

The Laporte Affair: A Test of Strength

The Terrorist Strategy

The Rose group had voted against Operation Liberation for both strategic and tactical reasons. On the tactical level, they felt that they did not have enough resources to launch an adequate operation that was likely to succeed. On the strategic level, they felt that kidnapping could not achieve the kind of large-scale organization they were aiming for and could even work against such a goal by provoking an overly repressive atmosphere which would impede organizing on a large scale. Clearly, from a strategic point of view, the Lanctôt group and the Rose group differed fundamentally. This difference was reflected in the way each group operated during the October Crisis. The former was anxious to take action immediately and, in doing so, prepared carefully. They set limited objectives commensurate with the tactic chosen: kidnapping. A major aim was propaganda and publicity, in conformance with standard urban guerrilla dogma on the proper use of kidnapping.[42] If they also succeeded in freeing their colleagues, so much the better.

By contrast, the Rose group had concentrated their efforts upon financing an underground organization capable of mounting some large-scale offensive at a later date.[43] Yet their participation in Operation Liberation was spontaneous, impulsive and ill-prepared. Using their headquarters at 5630 Armstrong Street in Saint-Hubert, they decided to kidnap Laporte because he lived close by. They never believed he would be so easy to abduct. They had no money and little food and, during the first day of Laporte's captivity, Sunday, 11 October, he gave them the $60 in his pocket so they could buy food. Paul Rose used most of it for taxi-cabs to downtown Montreal, where he deposited a series of three different communiqués within the space of a single day.

In their first communiqué, the Chenier Cell returned to the full set of demands set by the Liberation Cell at the outset of the Crisis and demanded compliance by ten o'clock that same evening or Laporte would be 'executed'. They also stated that the Liberation Cell would shortly issue a communiqué concerning the technical details of the operation. This was an obvious attempt to elicit some response from Cross's captors and to marshall their cooperation in this new escalation. Having acted impetuously and without any prior planning or warning, it was now imperative to coordinate their action with the other group. Each successive communiqué reiterated the demands and the death threat and made some reference to the Liberation Cell. The second one stated that the Liberation Cell would shortly be issuing their own communiqué, summarizing the entire situation. In the third, the Chenier Cell explicitly mentioned that no word had yet been received from the other cell and then proceeded to summarize the situation themselves. If Cross were still alive, the Liberation Cell would shortly issue an eighth communiqué summarizing the situation. If he were dead, the Chenier Cell would proceed alone. If Cross were still alive but technical difficulties impeded the release of a communiqué, then both hostages would be released when the demands were met.

As for the Liberation Cell, their immediate reaction to the Laporte abduction had been total surprise. While it certainly complicated their plan to release Mr Cross within a few days, they were initially delighted at this unexpected turn of events, since they hoped that it would help them achieve their goal of freeing the political prisoners. However, with the broadcast of the first communiqué from the Chenier Cell, they soon began to feel as if they were being pre-empted. When they realized who the perpetrators actually were,[44] it struck them that the most cautious group of all had launched into pure improvization.[45] This contradiction between the strategic philosophy of the Rose group and the improvised, slapdash nature of their action is important for understanding the behavior of the Chenier Cell during the week following Laporte's kidnapping.

The primary motive behind the decision of the Chenier Cell to kidnap a second person was supposedly to strengthen the hand of the Liberation Cell in their ongoing negotiations with the authorities. By choosing a high-ranking member of the Quebec government, they felt that they would give the FLQ the edge which, to them, had been lost in the first week. By returning to the full set of demands, they attempted to sabotage the negotiations which had been completed, since, in their eyes, the governments had clearly acted in bad faith. In addition, they placed a different emphasis on the various demands set originally by the Liberation Cell. At several points in his account of the Crisis, Francis Simard implies that had the Federal government reinstated the Lapalme workers and freed the prisoners, Laporte would never have been kidnapped.[46] When they abducted Laporte, the Chenier Cell told him that these were their central demands and, in a letter to Premier Bourassa which accompanied the third communiqué, Laporte emphasized the importance of the Lapalme workers. However, in their own communiqués, the Chenier Cell never differentiated between these central demands and the other ones, except to suggest that, if the prisoners were freed, the death threat to Laporte would be suspended.

By focusing upon the reinstatement of the Lapalme union as their central demand, and using the release of imprisoned felquistes as a minimum demand, the Chenier Cell escalated the demands beyond the limited propaganda scope embarked upon by the Liberation Cell. This suggests that the Chenier Cell had not grasped the propaganda strategy underlying the Liberation Cell's specific hierarchy of demands. The overall handling of negotiations by the Chenier Cell suggests that they were not interested in or appreciative of the kinds of propaganda gains inherent in a flexible approach to negotiations. For example, after Premier Bourassa implied, in a radio address Sunday night, that direct negotiations were possible, the Chenier Cell issued a fourth communiqué, naming radical lawyer Robert Lemieux as their *'interlocuteur'*, but insisted that Lemieux's mandate was simply to negotiate the implementation of their demands and not their substance. It is clear that the Chenier Cell, having decided to take action despite their belief that such lightning strikes as bombing and kidnapping were inappropriate means to achieve their long-term goals, then proceeded as if it were indeed possible to adapt a limited tactic, kidnapping, to their broader strategic goals.

Besides returning to the original set of demands, Paul Rose, in drafting his communiqués, consistently set out to depict the FLQ as stronger and more organized than it really was. For example, the first communiqué begins with the following preamble: 'Faced with the pig-headedness of the authorities in power who refuse to accede to the FLQ's demands and in conformance to plan 3 previously established in case of such a refusal, the Chenier Financing Cell has just kidnapped ... Pierre Laporte'. Of course, no such 'plan 3' existed. Even the one conciliatory gesture made publicly by the Chenier Cell in their fourth communiqué of Monday morning, 11 October – a promise to suspend their activities – was coupled with a call to other, fictitious cells to do the same. This was just another attempt to depict the FLQ as a strong, well-structured organization with a concrete, well-prepared plan of action.[47] The language of Rose's communiqués, the insistence that each new communiqué was the last, the admonition that any hesitation on the part of the authorities would be taken as a refusal, the pessimistic way in which they predicted the Liberation Cell's continuing silence throughout the 24 hours following Laporte's abduction – suggesting that Cross might have been executed – all reflected an attempt to counter the flexible image of the Liberation Cell with a new firmness and intransigence designed to force the governments to capitulate to their demands.

When the Liberation Cell finally did respond to the Laporte kidnapping, they stuck to their original two demands, the release of the prisoners and cessation of police activity, and promised that both Cross and Laporte would be freed if these demands were met. They also named Robert Lemieux as their mediator. This communiqué was only published on Monday morning, 11 October, several hours before the Chenier Cell's 'conciliatory' fourth communiqué was published, in which they suspended their deadline but refused to negotiate the substance of the six remaining demands. The contradiction between the two morning communiqués created considerable confusion in the media and amongst the crisis managers, and Robert Bourassa delayed his announcement of the appointment of a government mediator, lawyer Robert Demers, until late evening.

In the meantime, the Chenier Cell responded to the Liberation Cell's communiqué with its fifth communiqué, disassociating themselves from the Liberation Cell's stand. Retaining the full set of demands as a pre-requisite for Laporte's release, the Chenier Cell backed the Liberation Cell's reduced demands for the release of Cross. However, in flagrant contrast to the Liberation Cell, they suggested that Cross would be executed if the prisoners were not released. The Liberation Cell had explicitly set no deadline for the release of prisoners and had previously suspended the death threat to Cross. The only truly conciliatory gesture made by the Chenier Cell in this communiqué was their promise to suspend Laporte's death threat if the prisoners were released. But they claimed that they would hold their hostage until the remaining demands were met. In view of their lack of preparation for a long captivity, one can only assume that the Chenier Cell expected the government to capitulate quickly or that they merely had not thought through the consequences of a government refusal.[48]

A Two-Headed Monster is Born

In *post-hoc* justifications of his actions in drafting communiqués depicting the FLQ as much stronger than it really was, Paul Rose has claimed that this image-building was designed to accelerate negotiations.[49] Yet the Chenier Cell's stubborn and persistent refusal to negotiate the substance of their demands suggests otherwise. The Chenier Cell was not seeking a negotiated settlement at all, but a total capitulation by the governments. While the Liberation Cell was willing to abandon its central demand for the release of their comrades-in-arms, in the face of unexpected resistance on the part of the governments, and to content themselves with the propaganda gains made through negotiating their release, the Chenier Cell appeared really to want their demands met. To them, this was the only true measure of success and negotiations only meant that they would have to compromise or be compromised in some way. Faced with government intransigence, they became intransigent themselves.

The Chenier Cell's lack of interest in the propaganda gains of negotiation became clear when Paul Rose and Jacques Cossette-Trudel finally managed to meet on the evening of 13 October. This was the very first time that members of the two cells had made direct contact since the beginning of the Crisis.[50] While Cossette-Trudel was willing to settle for less than the complete set of demands, Rose was not. The two worked out a compromise arrangement which suggests that they had reached an impasse and had simply agreed to disagree: in the event of a government refusal, Cross's life would be spared but Laporte's death threat would not be suspended. In the meantime, the two decided that all communication with the authorities would be left to the Liberation Cell, who would issue a joint communiqué the next day, and that, henceforth, the Chenier Cell would retreat into silence. The stated rationale for this tactic was again to force the government to negotiate seriously.[51]

A possible key to the Chenier Cell's attitude is the following statement by Francis Simard: 'For us, if October made a statement, it was not solely by means of a manifesto, but by the action itself. By revealing a force, that of those who never get a chance to speak.'[52] Here is the classic propaganda of the deed. Compare Simard's words with the following statement made at the London Congress of the Anarchist International in 1881: 'any action against existing institutions is far more likely to grip and find the support of the masses than thousands of leaflets and a stream of words'.[53] According to Ulrich Linse, in his analysis of anarchism in the late nineteenth century, '"propaganda by deed" was held to be a far more effective tool of advertisement for anarchism than the written or spoken word'.[54] From this perspective, the Chenier strategy becomes much clearer. By standing firm, by refusing to negotiate, by naming a spokesman merely to discuss implementation of the demands, and by retreating into silence on all other matters, the action was left to speak louder than any words could possibly have done. As such, kidnapping Laporte represented a spectacular show of force, a blinding display of sudden power designed 'to grip and find the support of the masses'.

Having aimed their sights on a large-scale action in the long term, in which a mass organization could yield real power, the Chenier Cell lost sight of the inappropriateness of the kidnapping tactic for such a plan and tried to adapt Laporte's abduction to their old strategy.[55] Their insistence on the centrality of the Lapalme demand reflected their long-term goal of establishing a mass base of support amongst the working class and organized labour. Little matter that, on the day following the Cross kidnapping, the Lapalme union had expressed no interest in FLQ support.[56] Because a mass base of support was indeed lacking, the action was destined to be short-lived. But the authorities could not know the true paucity of the FLQ infrastructure and so the sudden display of power did trigger real panic and shock for a short, intense period. For a while, the FLQ did seem powerful, invincible, a force to be reckoned with, and the second kidnapping did evoke a wave of admiration and excitement in pro-independence circles. However, the inevitable response, which the Chenier Cell did not foresee, was a real show of force in return.

For the Liberation Cell, it is clear that the kidnapping of Laporte did not change their overall strategy and that they stood firm against the Chenier

Cell's pressure to escalate their demands. The only difference was that they decided to try again for the release of the prisoners. They also seemed content once again to extract maximum propaganda value out of the ongoing negotiations. In a joint communiqué issued on 14 October, after the meeting between Rose and Cossette-Trudel, the Liberation Cell suggested that both hostages would be released after the prisoners were freed, despite Paul Rose's insistence that Laporte's release was contingent upon all demands being met. At the same time, however, they attacked the good faith of the authorities and filled their communiqué with political rhetoric. Yet they gave their mediator, Robert Lemieux, carte blanche in negotiations, which was correctly viewed by the press as backing off from the Chenier Cell's intransigent position. While there was mention of the $500,000 in gold once again, the general impression during the negotiations between Lemieux and the government mediator, Robert Demers, was that the release of the prisoners remained the central demand, despite the fact that the Chenier Cell had never backed off from the total set of demands.

What is clear is that, after Laporte's kidnapping, the FLQ became a two-headed entity, with conflicting strategies which permeated the two cells' communiqués and the public and private stances they took *vis-à-vis* each other, their hostages and their demands. The limited propaganda goal of the Liberation Cell led them to be flexible in their interaction with the governments and this flexibility continued into the second week despite the efforts of the Chenier Cell to stiffen their resolve. For the Chenier Cell, the FLQ was engaged in a test of strength, a battle of wills with the authorities. Unlike the Liberation Cell, they did not wish to be reasonable. They simply wanted to humiliate the Federal and Provincial governments. In one sense, however, the Chenier tactic of reinstating the full set of demands worked in favour of the Liberation Cell. There is an upper threshold over which terrorist demands can safely be ignored by governments. If the demands are too unreasonable or extreme, refusal to meet them will usually be supported by the general public. Conversely, the more reasonable and less extreme the demand, the greater the pressure on government to negotiate. This is what seems to have happened after Laporte's kidnapping. The widespread sympathy created by the broadcast of the manifesto was channelled into public support for the release of the FLQ prisoners. The instransigence of the Chenier Cell's position made the Liberation Cell's demand appear more reasonable. Thus, the issue of the release of the prisoners became the central focus for the continuing and proliferating public debate in the second week.

By the time that the army was called into Quebec and the War Measures Act was invoked, the kidnappers and their hostages had become secondary to the larger political debate over the right of the Quebec government to pursue an independent course from Ottawa. On Saturday, 17 October, the day Laporte was killed, the Liberation Cell did issue a tenth communiqué, but it was suppressed by the authorities and never publicized. Among other things, they announced the indefinite suspension of the death threat hanging over their hostage and announced that the Chenier Cell was deciding the fate of their hostage and that word would arrive soon. Clearly, they were simply following the agreement that was made between Paul Rose and Jacques Cossette-Trudel several days before, to go their separate ways.

Conclusion

Alex Schmid, in his now classic work on political terrorism, speaks of the importance of detailed case studies. He writes that 'the most general deficiency of most of the literature on terrorism is that the terrorist organization or movement is studied in isolation rather than in its socio-political context'.[57] In this article, I have tried to examine the FLQ in such a way as to avoid this error. In concluding, I wish to identify three different levels of analysis which I feel came to the fore during my case study and which should be addressed when we study the infrastructure and internal dynamics of terrorist groups. I shall demonstrate how each level was reflected in the preceding case study and how each might be applied to the study of other groups.

First, there is the level of the organization itself, its infrastructure, its internal dynamics. Here, issues such as membership profiles, division of labour, strategic and tactical decision-making, rules and procedures, methods of operation come to the fore. We have seen how the adoption of a name by a group of actors does not necessarily mean that a coherent group with a well-developed infrastructure exists. Nor does it mean that internal divisions and frictions are absent, even if public statements present a unified image. Although the FLQ-1970 was perceived as a centralized, efficient organization, both at the time and in subsequent descriptions in the literature, we have seen the disparity between that image, as reinforced in Paul Rose's communiqués, and the real state of affairs. Furthermore, the persistence of a name over a number of years does not necessarily indicate the endurance of a single terrorist organization over that same period. Our case study makes clear that different groups may adopt the same name at different times, without any central command structure or any coherence in objectives, strategies or tactics. As recently as December 1986, the name 'FLQ' was used by perpetrators of several Molotov cocktail attacks on a chain of Montreal department stores using bilingual signs instead of unilingual French ones. Does this signal the revival of the FLQ, which has simply lain dormant for the past 15 years, organizing in secret? More likely, a few people decided to adopt the name precisely to give the impression that the Phoenix has risen once again out of the ashes of the 1970s. Montreal police officials consider the bomb attacks to be the work of a few crackpots. Only time and research will tell if any organization really exists behind the façade of these isolated incidents.

We tend to have a monolithic view of 'the terrorist', attributing to particular groups a coherence they do not always deserve. This is particularly true in the case of ideology, where many groups are cast in a single ideological mold whereas, in actual fact, they suffer from internal dissension and factionalism. As we saw with the FLQ, the reality is often more complex than depicted in the literature. This is true for other groups as well. For example, Bruce Hoffman has recently shown how neo-Nazi groups in West Germany are beginning to adopt left-wing rhetoric and to select targets that are the traditional choice of left-wing groups. Until police caught on to this shift, it was generally assumed that certain bombings were the work of left-wing groups.[58] Much terrorism in the Middle East is the result of internecine rivalry, as groups vie for the loyalty of young militants and extremists who are impatient with negotiations and diplomacy. Much of the Middle East-inspired international terrorism of recent years can be attributed at least as much to such factionalism as to any united front against Israel or the United States. For example, the bombings at the Rome and Vienna airports in December 1985 may have had as much to do with scuttling the *rapprochement* between Yasser Arafat and King Hussein as it was meant to terrorize American and European tourists. The PLO is no more monolithic than the FLQ, particularly considered over a period of 15 years. Internal dissension could also be the reason that Direct Action in Europe now has an international wing, which targets NATO installations and personnel, and a wing which is more oriented toward domestic, labour-oriented issues. Fernando Reinares[59] points out that differences between factions of the Basque organization, ETA, are often minimized or ignored. The same could be said for many groups. The tension which Reinares describes between political and military factions of the ETA, which culminated in a split in 1974, is reminiscent of the tension between the Rose and Lanctôt groups that was described in this article.

The second level of analysis which emerges from the preceding case study is the socio-political environment in which the terrorist organization operates. Here, issues such as recruitment, individual careers of terrorists, and relationships between overt and covert groups or between different terrorist groups are important. No terrorist group exists in total isolation from the political, economic, social and cultural life within which it is embedded, no matter how divorced from reality it has become due to the exigencies of clandestinity. Terrorist groups, like many secret societies or cults, emerge, evolve and dissolve along with, in reaction to, in competition with or in cooperation with other groups which advocate or contest similar or opposing goals. The classic split between an overt, political wing and a covert military wing of the same organization, such as Sinn Fein and the IRA, is one kind of relationship. One could perhaps characterize the relationship between the FLP and the FLQ in such a way, although the FLP was not a political party as such and never fielded candidates in an election.

Another kind of relationship is the rivalry between radical political parties and their extremist fringes who differ on strategy, such as the use of violence, though they share the same goals. In Chile, at least before 1980, the Communist Party of Chile (PCCh) and the Movement of the Revolutionary Left (MIR) exemplified such a relationship, the former adamantly opposing the use of violence and vociferously attacking the latter for its terrorist tactics.[60] Clearly, the extremist fringes of the RIN and the PQ provided a pool of potential recruits or supporters for FLQ activities. In the case of the PQ, René Lévesque consistently viewed the FLQ as a threat to the legitimacy of his party, denouncing each successive act of terrorism or violence while warning that continued refusal to address his party's agenda would push more and more of his followers into the terrorist camp. Because such relationships between overt and covert groups exist, it is important to understand the relationship between a terrorist group and the other groups which are active before, during and after its lifetime. Terrorists do not spring, full-blown, out of the woodwork, nor do they remain terrorists forever. Individuals move between overt and covert, legitimate and illegitimate activities. They adopt, then renounce, violence or particular ideologies of violence, and vice versa. Careers of individual members often reveal patterns which help to understand the rise and fall of the terrorist strategy in the life of a particular political conflict. The careers of Jacques Lanctôt, Paul Rose and Pierre Vallières are cases in point. Bruce Hoffman's recent work on the hitherto unrecognized links between right-wing terrorist groups in West Germany and Palestinian groups is based in part on analysis of individual careers.[61]

The third and final level of analysis to be considered is the social reaction to the terrorist organization, in particular, that of the agents of the state. Here, issues such as the selection of targets, the relationship with captured terrorists, and the role of informers and covert facilitation are important. The relationship between the terrorist group and those state organizations responsible for combatting them is often an important element in understanding the internal dynamics of the terrorist group itself. We have seen how the successful break-up of two kidnapping plots by police in early 1970 set the stage for the October kidnappings. The crucial vote taken in September tipped the balance in favor of freeing prisoners instead of long-term preparations. Martha Crenshaw[62] describes how the IRA's targetting of off-duty police and soldiers in 1971 was justified as a response to the government's policy of internment. Internal divisions often revolve around how to react to official measures to counter terrorism. This was clearly shown by the preceding case study. Factions can differ over whether to target state officials or the general public. According to Crenshaw, Maria McGuire left the Provisional IRA in part because she disapproved of bombing civilians.[63]

The repressive response of the state can serve as a reason for escalating tactics (for example, to kidnapping, from bombing) or for lying low and reorganizing. Such opposing options can polarize a group and create splits, as we saw with the FLQ-1970. Often a group can find itself devoting all its efforts to trying to free imprisoned members that have been captured, tried and convicted, losing sight entirely of its original political goals. According to Wolfgang Mommsen, this was exactly what happened to the Red Army Faction in West Germany: 'from 1971 onwards it has been engaged in a sort of private war with the authorities, with the primary objective of pressing for the release of RAF-members, while politically it has manoeuvred itself into a totally defensive position'.[64]

Internal tension amongst the counter-terrorists can trigger or even mirror internal tension amongst the terrorists. In the October Crisis, the divergence between the Federal and Provincial governments in the wake of Laporte's kidnapping mirrored to a certain extent the divergence between the two cells. The Liberation Cell reacted to and profited from dialogue and negotiation with the Quebec government, while the Chenier Cell reacted to firmness from the Federal government with escalation and intransigence. Just as terrorist organizations are treated as monolithic entities, so we tend to paper over the divisions and heterogeneity of views amongst those who combat the terrorists. Critics of Israeli counter-terror policy ignore the internal debate, dissension and factionalism within Israel and the Knesset. Just as we speak of 'Arab terrrorism' without differentiating amongst the dizzying array of groups vying for power in the Middle East, so we speak of 'how the West can win', without recognizing the competing interests which exist amongst Western allies.[65] Much can be learned about the infrastructure and dynamics of terrorist groups by studying their relationship with those who combat them. It is not necessary to label the state 'terrorist', to equate counter-terror with terror or to claim that 'international terrorism' is the logical outcome of the geopolitical terrorism of superpowers to see that many of the parameters of group cohesion and decision-making are the same for terrorist and counter-terrorist organizations. Each reacts to the other and, over time, a distinct kind of dialogue can be discerned.[66] To study the terrorist in isolation from the social reaction to him is to miss this level of analysis.

In sum, then, there are three levels of analysis which emerge from the case study presented here: the terrorist organization itself, the social and political environment within which it operates, and the official reaction that it evokes. At each level of analysis, a different set of parameters is involved in understanding the internal dynamics of the terrorist organization. By combining all three 'dynamics', it is possible to gain a better understanding of how terrorist groups evolve and function in specific times and places.

NOTES

1. Albert Parry, *Terrorism: From Robespierre to Arafat* (New York: Vanguard Press, 1976), p.368.
2. Martha Crenshaw, 'An Organizational Approach to the Analysis of Political Terrorism', *Orbis* 29 (Fall 1985), p.469.
3. Marc Laurendeau, *Les québécois violents*, 2e édition, revue et augmentée (Montréal: Boréal Express, 1974). See especially his Appendix II (pp.222–4), which lists the

personnel of the various FLQ groups active in each phase and identifies those individuals who are related by birth or marriage to other FLQ members. See also his Appendix I (pp.213–21), which provides a chronology of events from 1962 to 1972. Having been written before many of the revelations which occurred during subsequent government inquiries and before the publication of Louis Fournier's definitive history of the FLQ, Laurendeau's information is not entirely consistent with more up-to-date accounts published in the 1980s. However, on the whole, it accurately reflects the diverse and loosely organized nature of the FLQ which later accounts only confirm. See Louis Fournier, *F.L.Q.: Histoire d'un mouvement clandestin* (Montréal: Québec/ Amérique, 1982). In translation: Louis Fournier, *FLQ: The Anatomy of an Underground Movement*. Trans. by Edward Baxter (Toronto: NC Press, 1984).

 4. See Jean-Paul Brodeur, 'Legitimizing Police Deviance', in Clifford Shearing (ed.), *Organizational Police Deviance* (Toronto: Butterworth, 1981), pp.127–60, especially pp.149–51. Brodeur was principal researcher for the provincial inquiries looking into the October Crisis (The Duchaîne Inquiry) and the activities of the police during and after this Crisis (the Keable Commission), both of whose final reports were published in 1981. He cites a police officer's testimony before the Keable Commission as follows: 'in 1972, we [the police] were the FLQ', ibid., p.159, note 57. For the Duchaîne report, see Jean-François Duchaîne, *Rapport sur les événements d'octobre 1970*, 2nd ed. (Québec: Gouvernement du Québec, Ministère de la Justice, 1981). For the Keable Report, see Québec, *Rapport de la Commission d'enquête sur des opérations policières en territoire québécois* (Québec: Ministère de la Justice, 1981).

 5. Parry, op. cit., pp.365–6.

 6. Marc Laurendeau, op. cit., p.223.

 7. For the two texts, see Documents 95 and 110 in Daniel Latouche and Diane Poliquin-Bourassa (eds.), *Le manuel de la parole: Manifestes québécois. Tome 3: 1960–1976* (Montréal: Boréal Express, 1979), pp.33, 127.

 8. The Parti Québécois (PQ) was formed in the fall of 1968 as a legally constituted provincial political party, seeking Quebec independence via traditional electoral politics. Headed by René Lévesque, a former journalist and Cabinet Minister in the Provincial Liberal Government, the PQ combined both nationalist and socialist elements in an effort to create a broad coalition – a 'national front' – of independence-minded people united behind the charismatic popularity of its leader. At its inception, the PQ was oriented toward the Scandinavian model of social democracy and managed to attract a fair number of left-wing militants. Several groups, including the FLP, occupied the far left of the political spectrum, and viewed the PQ with some suspicion. In 1976, the PQ finally gained power and instituted many social reforms consistent with its social democratic image. Four years later, in 1980, the PQ government presented a referendum on independence to the Quebec people. The Yes side lost, but the PQ was returned to power a year later. During this final term of office, the party lost its most fervent advocates of Quebec independence, as Lévesque struggled to strike a balance between those who felt that independence was primordial and those who felt that staying in power was primordial. Lévesque resigned the leadership in 1985 and, shortly afterward, the PQ government was defeated in an election by the same party, the Liberal Party, that had been defeated in 1976. The Liberal leader was the same person, Robert Bourassa, who was Premier of Quebec during the October Crisis. In French, there is a saying: *Plus ça change, plus c'est la même chose*. The more things change, the more they stay the same.

 9. Albert Parry, op. cit., p.366.

10. The group that formed the FLP bolted the RIN in protest against negotiations which the RIN had begun with the PQ with a view to merging the two parties. The two parties did finally merge, under the PQ banner, in the fall of 1968. See note 8.

11. See, for example, Martha Crenshaw, 1985, op. cit.; J.K. Zawodny, 'Infrastructures of Terrorist Organizations', in Lawrence Zelic Freedman and Yonah Alexander (eds.), *Perspectives on Terrorism* (Wilmington, DE: Scholarly Resources, 1983), pp.61–70.

12. The MLT, or Taxi Liberation Movement, was involved in fighting the Murray Hill Limousine Service, which had a monopoly on the shuttle service between Montreal and

its airport. Comprised of around 150 taxi drivers, the MLT engaged in radical agit-prop ostensibly aimed at fighting for the rights of Montreal's cab drivers, who numbered in the thousands. During the Montreal Police strike in October 1969, the MLT and other radical protest groups, such as the FLP, organized a protest march – actually a drive, since protesters drove in a caravan of some 75 cabs – to the Murray Hill garage, where violence broke out. Buses were set on fire and guards on surrounding rooftops began firing into the crowd with shotguns. In the mêlée, several persons were hit with shotgun pellets, including another MLT member, Marc Carbonneau, who would also participate in the Cross kidnapping a year later. Ironically, the one death in this incident was Corporal Robert Dumas, a member of the provincial police force's security service, who had infiltrated the demonstration.

13. Louis Fournier, op. cit., p.240.
14. Although the Montreal anti-terrorist squad knew of the participation of Hamer as of December 1970, due to an informer, Hamer was never arrested or charged until his role was made public a decade later, in the course of the Duchaîne Inquiry. He was eventually tried and convicted and, in May of 1981, he received a one-year sentence. To this day, it remains a mystery why the police failed to act on their information about Hamer, although one researcher who had access to the confidential records of the Commission rejects the hypothesis that he was a police informer. See Jean-Paul Brodeur, 'La Crise d'octobre et les commissions d'enquête', *Criminologie 13* (No.2, 1980), 78–98, at p.94.
15. Dr Jean Olivier Chénier was one of the leaders of the unsuccessful 1837 rebellion in Lower Canada (Quebec before Confederation in 1867). Chénier was killed during the revolt. The word 'financing' (*financement*) was probably a reference, recognizable to insiders, to the group's previous activities involving credit card fraud and bank robberies which were carried out to finance FLQ operations and organization.
16. The hostel also served as a drop-in centre for local youth throughout the summer and quickly became very popular. Harrassed by the local authorities, who disliked the presence of so many young people in their quiet, tourist-conscious town, the hostel became somewhat of a *cause célèbre* when the authorities maladroitly tried to expel the occupants with water hoses.
17. By the end of the Crisis, 453 people had been arrested. Of these, 403 were eventually released without charges ever having been laid and, of the remaining 50 people, only 35 were ever charged under the War Measures Act. The other 15 were charged under the Criminal Code for participating in or supporting the actual kidnappings. In June 1971, two of the 35 charged under the War Measures Act were acquitted and the Crown dropped all remaining charges against the rest.
18. Sentences of two years or more must be served in a Federal Penitentiary.
19. Francis Simard, *Pour en finir avec octobre* (Montréal: Stanké, 1982), pp.170–71. This account of his role in the events preceding and during the October Crisis was written in collaboration with the other members of the Chenier Cell.
20. While each group operated independently, the individual members not currently involved in an operation would keep in touch. Francis Simard (op. cit., p.173) states, for example, that his group knew about the kidnapping plans, but went about their own business. But this autonomy was soon to end.
21. Louis Fournier, op. cit., p.268.
22. See Louis Fournier, op. cit., pp.249–50 for details concerning the plot to kidnap the Israeli consul, pp.267–70 for details concerning the Burgess plot and p.271 for an account of the police raid on the farm. In his final report on his inquiry into the October Crisis, Judge Jean-François Duchaîne describes these incidents as well. His report was based on police records and testimony and on interviews with the terrorists. See Jean-François Duchaîne, op. cit., pp.11–14. See also Francis Simard, op. cit., pp.171–3.
23. Jean-François Duchaîne, op. cit., p.14.
24. Ibid., p.15.
25. Martha Crenshaw, 'The Persistence of IRA Terrorism', in Yonah Alexander and Alan O'Day (eds.), *Terrorism in Ireland* (New York: St. Martin's Press, 1984), pp.246–71, at p.254.

26. Ibid., p.255.
27. Francis Simard, op. cit., p.170.
28. Ibid., p.173.
29. Jean-François Duchaîne, op. cit., p.15.
30. Bernard Lortie only joined the group after their return.
31. For the early September vote, see Louis Fournier, op. cit., pp.289–90; Jean-François Duchaîne, op. cit., p.15, note 20; Francis Simard, op. cit., pp.175–6. For the departure of the Roses and Simard, see Louis Fournier, op. cit., p.291; Jean-François Duchaîne, op. cit., p.17; Francis Simard, op. cit., p.176. For the concrete steps taken by the Liberation Cell in preparation for the 5 October kidnapping, see Jean-François Duchaîne, op. cit., pp.16–19; Louis Fournier, op. cit., pp.289–92.
32. Jean-François Duchaîne, op. cit., p.34.
33. Francis Simard, op. cit., pp.19, 174.
34. This is what Paul Rose told the police in his statement taken after his capture. See John Saywell, *Quebec 1970: A Documentary Narrative* (Toronto: Toronto University Press, 1971), pp.55–6.
35. This was consistent with Jacques Lanctôt's more intellectual approach. It is probably no coincidence that he is now owner of a small Montreal publishing house, VLB Press, which specializes in publishing young Quebec authors. The initials stand for Victor-Lévy Beaulieu, the original owner and a noted Quebec writer. Lanctôt bought the publishing house shortly after coming out of prison. In a 1984 interview, he stated that, since his return in 1979, he had learned that the political fight could be continued on the cultural front as well. See Nathalie Petrowski, 'Que sont nos militants devenus? 1. Le dur retour à la "réalité"', *Le Devoir*, 5 May 1984, pp.1, 12.
36. This is what Mr Cross told police in a statement made on the day he was freed. See Jean-François Duchaîne, op. cit., p.35.
37. During the October Crisis, while still holding James Cross, the Liberation Cell, notably Jacques Lanctôt and Jacques Cossette-Trudel, arranged to have a discussion of theirs recorded and distributed to the pro-independence alternative press. It was published after the members left for Cuba.
38. After the Liberation Cell's departure into exile, the conversation was published in the December issue of the monthly review, *Choc*, and, in part, in the weekly, *Québec-Presse*. Both *Choc* and *Québec-Presse* were pro-independence publications.
39. Ron Haggart and Aubrey E. Golden, *Rumours of War* (Toronto: James Lorimer, 1971), p.232.
40. Anthony Westell, 'War Measures Act: Ottawa used it to restore confidence', *Toronto Daily Star*, 16 Jan. 1971, p.14.
41. For a more detailed analysis of the role of the media in the October Crisis, see Ronald D. Crelinsten, 'Power and Meaning: Terrorism as a Struggle for Access to the Communication Structure', in Paul Wilkinson (ed.), *Contemporary Research on Terrorism* (Aberdeen: University of Aberdeen Press, forthcoming).
42. Carlos Marighela, in his Minimanual for the Urban Guerrilla, writes: 'The kidnapping of personalities ... can be a useful form of propaganda ... provided it occurs under special circumstances, and the kidnapping is handled so that the public sympathizes with it and accepts it'. Cited in Denis Smith, *Bleeding Hearts ... Bleeding Country: Canada and the Quebec Crisis* (Edmonton: M.G. Hurtig, 1971), pp.54–5.
43. For an account of the Rose group's activities by one of its members, see Francis Simard, op. cit., pp.141–53.
44. When the police announced the licence number of the car used to kidnap Laporte, the Liberation Cell recognized it as the Roses' car. Realizing that it had been the object of a police check already and had been at the Rose farm when it was raided, they were amazed that the Rose group would use it in a kidnapping.
45. Jean-François Duchaîne, op. cit., p.62.
46. Francis Simard, op. cit., pp.24, 37, 50.
47. When Rose drafted a communiqué six days later, announcing the death of Pierre Laporte, he signed it the 'Dieppe Cell (Royal 22nd)', again to depict the FLQ as larger than it really was. Here, he also engaged in some sarcastic propaganda, since it was the

famous French-Canadian Royal 22nd Regiment which had fought at Dieppe in the Second World War that was standing guard duty in Montreal. On 27 October, in hiding from the massive police manhunt, Rose also issued an ostensibly joint communiqué from the Liberation, Chenier and Dieppe Cells which he alone actually wrote. Since much of these details only emerged during the Duchaîne Inquiry a decade later, it is perhaps not surprising that researchers publishing before 1980 would attribute a well-defined infrastructure to so loosely defined an organization as the FLQ-1970.

48. In an interview with political commentator and columnist Marc Laurendeau, conducted ten years later in prison, Paul Rose admitted that he had never heard of the War Measures Act before the Crisis and had never expected the government to invoke emergency powers. See Marc Laurendeau, 'Entrevue avec Paul Rose en prison', Le Devoir, 1 Oct. 1980, p.A8.

49. See Jean-François Duchaîne op. cit., p.89.

50. While members of the Chenier Cell did not know the whereabouts of the Liberation Cell, they had previously arranged that a friend of Paul Rose's would be able to contact them. Since Laporte's kidnapping, they had been phoning this person (from pay phones) regularly. Finally, while Rose was in her apartment, having just escaped a police tail, Cossette-Trudel phoned. Learning that Rose was there, he came right over.

51. Jean-François Duchaîne, op. cit., p.89. Paul Rose had been tailed by police that morning and only managed to lose them in the evening, just before his meeting with Cossette-Trudel. From that day on, he never returned to the house where Laporte was being detained, but stayed with various friends in Montreal.

52. Francis Simard, op. cit., p.28. This is a loose translation of the original vernacular French.

53. Cited in Ulrich Linse, '"Propaganda by Deed", and "Direct Action": Two Concepts of Anarchist Violence', in Wolfgang J. Mommsen and Gerhard Hirschfeld (eds.), Social Protest, Violence and Terror in Nineteenth- and Twentieth-century Europe (New York: St. Martin's Press, 1982), Ch.13, p.202. See also David C. Rapoport, Assassination and Terrorism (Toronto: CBC, 1971), pp.49 ff.

54. Ibid.

55. In the same vein, Linse suggests that the original concept of propaganda by deed, which was linked with the ideal of armed insurrection, was later deformed into the notion of individual acts, such as political assassination and 'dynamite terrorism'. Ulrich Linse, op. cit., pp.201–3.

56. See 'No interest in FLQ help: Former Lapalme drivers', The Gazette (Montreal), 7 Oct. 1970, p.5.

57. Alex P. Schmid, Political Terrorism: A Research Guide to Concepts, Theories, Data Bases and Literature (New Brunswick: Transaction Books, 1983), p.422.

58. Bruce Hoffman, 'Right-Wing Terrorism in West Germany', Rand Paper P-7270. Santa Monica: The Rand Corporation, 1986, pp.8–15.

59. Fernando Reinares, 'Statements about the Dynamics of Terrorism during the Transition from Authoritarianism to Democracy in Spain', paper presented at the International Academic Conference, 'Research on Terrorism', University of Aberdeen, April 1986.

60. It was only in the wake of the 1980 Constitution and Pinochet's expressed intention to stay in power until 1995 that the PCCh began to advocate the use of violence.

61. Bruce Hoffman, op. cit., pp.17–22.

62. Martha Crenshaw, op. cit., 1984.

63. Ibid., p.269, note 27.

64. Wolfgang J. Mommsen, 'Non-Legal Violence and Terrorism in Western Industrial Societies: An Historical Analysis', in Wolfgang J. Mommsen and Gerhard Hirschfeld (eds.), op. cit., Ch.22, p.401.

65. The same principle was at work, in a backhanded sort of way, in the foreign policy débâcle in the US concerning the Reagan administration's apparent policy of shipping arms to Iran in exchange for the release of hostages in Lebanon. Having depicted Iran for years as a monolithic monster, sponsoring terrorism against US targets and interests throughout the Middle East, the administration's claim that it was attempting to

develop a more flexible policy which recognized and tried to play on internal divisions within the Khomeini regime simply came across as blatant hypocrisy and opportunism. It is clear that dogmatic adherence to a monolithic view of one's perceived enemy narrows the options that are available for dealing with that enemy. In particular, an over-reliance on pejorative rhetoric precludes the possibility of negotiation and reduces the chances of conflict resolution. Strident rhetoric is most useful in justifying a policy of no negotiation and overt hostility, including the resort to violence. This is as true for state actors as it is for non-state actors, and as pertinent for counter-terrorists as it is for terrorists.

66. See Ronald D. Crelinsten, 'Terrorism as Political Communication: the Relationship between the Controller and the Controlled', in Paul Wilkinson (ed.), op. cit., forthcoming.

A Battlegroup Divided:
The Palestinian Fedayeen

David Th. Schiller

On 27 December 1985, two hit-teams of the Abu Nidal group attacked simultaneoulsy El-Al ticket counters at the Rome and Vienna air terminals. The handgrenade and machinegun attacks killed 18 passengers and wounded 114. The locations of these terrorist attacks were well chosen from the standpoint of the attackers. The governments of both countries targeted had been sympathetic to the Palestinian cause and supported a negotiated solution to the conflict which would include the mainstream PLO. The choice of the Israeli airline counters as initial targets and the presence of Americans among the victims were of secondary importance to the masterminds behind the attack. In the queer logic of inter-Palestinian rivalries these acts were aimed at Arafat, meant to embarrass him in the eyes of Austria and Italy, the two European countries most sympathetic to the leader of the mainstream PLO. Furthermore, they were designed to disturb the ongoing joint PLO–Jordanian initiative.

To long-time observers of the Palestinian struggle, the Rome and Vienna attacks came as no surprise. They fell into a set pattern which had governed the actions and politics of Palestinian terrorist organizations for decades – a series of splits, inner tensions and internecine feuds, for which nearby Europe has become a convenient battleground, presenting an abundance of soft, convenient targets with better media coverage than is available in the Middle East. In one way or another, these internal dynamics have dominated the fate of Palestinian nationalists since the 1920s, resulting in the repeated defeats of Palestinian attempts to gain a foothold in the battle for national self-determination. Viewing the current dilemma of the PLO from a historical perspective the observer is struck with a sense of 'deja vue': it has all happened before, and one is tempted to compare yesterday's warlords – the Mufti, Abdel Kader, Abdel Rahim or Hassan Salameh – with today's Arafat, Habbash, Hawatmeh, Abu Moussa and Abu Nidal.

The development of Palestinian nationalism can be analyzed into four stages which correspond to the widening of the conflict and its changing appearances:

I: 'Palestinism' or Palestinian nationalism (as opposed to pan-Arabism or the pan-Syrian movement) was first generated as a separate political element after the First World War in reaction to the British Mandate and Zionist immigration to Palestine. This coincided with the ascendance of a new generation of local politicians in the wake of the Ottoman Empire's disintegration, replacing the older Damascus-oriented notables. Lasting from 1920 to 1939, this first phase saw the emergence of Amin el Husseini, Mufti of Jerusalem, as the national leader of the Arab population in the British Mandate. These years were accentuated by a series of riots and armed clashes, finally climaxing in the 'Arab Rebellion' of 1936–39, which changed the conflict over Palestine from a local affair to an all-Arab concern of international dimensions. The second half of this period was dominated by anti-British and anti-Jewish guerrilla and terrorist gangs, operating within the framework of the traditional structures of the Middle Eastern peasant society.

II: The ten years from 1939 to the end of the first Israeli–Arab war in 1949 presented the stage for the Mufti's machinations. Attempts to change the courses of Mandate politics by rallying pan-Arab support were followed by the alliances with non-regional powers (first Mussolini's Italy, and later Hitler's Reich), which supported the Palestinian struggle with arms, money, sanctuaries and training.[1] The obsession with the armed aspects of the Palestinian struggle and the inability to settle with a negotiated compromise solution of the problem led directly to the outbreak of open hostilities in 1947 and to what is known in the Palestinian literature as '*al-naklak*', the catastrophe, namely, the foundation of Israel, the exodus of large parts of the Arab population, and the annexation of the West Bank by the Transjordan Emirate.[2]

III: During the two decades following the foundation of Israel, Palestinian nationalism fell prey to the polarization of Arab politics: Palestinian exiles were engaged in various political movements, ranging from fundamentalist Islam to Nasserism. Those paramilitary groups and representations which existed among the Palestinians were closely linked to one of either two major Arab powers, Syria or Egypt, and were meant by those nations to be useful pawns in the inter-Arab power struggle.

IV: The power vacuum resulting from the crushing defeat of the Arab armies during the Six Day War of June 1967 permitted the rise of a new set of paramilitary groups, the 'fedayeen' – 'those willing to sacrifice themselves'. Under the leadership of Yassir Arafat's Al Fatah, the fedayeen groups took over the PLO which became the new vehicle of Palestinian nationalism. When the propagated 'popular war of liberation' in the Israeli-occupied territories failed, Palestinian guerrilla activity degenerated quickly into terrorism. While Israeli counterstrikes forced the movement more and more into the defensive, the precarious PLO attempt to steer an independent course in inter-Arab politics led the Palestinians directly into two devastating civil wars in Jordan and Lebanon.

Throughout these decades the Palestinian movement was never a unified element in the Middle East, where the Israeli–Arab dilemma is only one among many highly complicated conflicts. Looking back over some 70 years of strife it appears that the Palestinians have been their own worst enemies; Jewish nationalism, British imperial policies, the superpowers and Arab governments were not as efficient at preventing the realization of national self-determination as the Palestinian leaders themselves.

The following factors shaped internal dynamics within the movement – whether at the time of the Mufti or in the current PLO:

(a) the traditional social structure of Palestinian Arabs rooted in clannism, tribalism and ethnic-confessional parochialism.

(b) rivalling, conflicting support states and political powers, on which the movement's groups are dependent for financial and logistical support, as well as political and ideolgical differences among these factions, which are generated as much by the support states as by the individual leader's need to acquire status and image.

(c) unrest and impatience among the ranks, resulting from stagnation and lack of successes, leading to the repeated emergence of rebels from among the lieutenant level of the fedayeens.

In wondering about the internal strife which has plagued this national movement since its beginning, it is often forgotten that the Palestinians have never overcome the drawbacks of the traditional Middle Eastern social structure as a 'mosaic system'[3] of various clannish, tribal and ethnic in-groups with strong vertical loyalties and local 'zu'ama' leadership.[4] Political leaders are not elected, but gain their position because of their economic situation as landowners or through business wealth, through appointment by another higher authority or as charismatic figureheads who achieve and maintain their status as leaders through the extension of privileges to their followers, supported by a clique of old friends and family members. Parties are thus less a program-oriented alliance of members than a power-clique closely linked with regional or ethnic-confessional influence spheres.

Urbanization, the uprooting of rural family structures and other elements of modernization can only insufficiently camouflage these traditional structures. As in the Iranian revolution or in the Lebanese Civil War, the traditional identifications, loyalties and leadership patterns dominated the conflict. None of the religious, national or ideological trends which have come to the fore in the Arab world could really achieve a horizontal breakthrough, uniting its segmented societies.

The same holds true for the idea of a Palestinian identity. Although it can fire the imagination of the afflicted it does not provide enough momentum to fuse the different elements of the Palestinians into an encompassing political movement. Militant activism takes the place of policital action; and in this context a maverick like Abu Nidal is not an exceptional case but a symptom of the problem, which afflicts the whole movement. Palestinism remains linked to other motors, be they Marxism, Islamic fundamentalism or the loyalty to foster states such as Syria and

Iraq – whose own purposes are served under the disguise of the struggle for Palestine. Thus Nasser used the Palestinian question as a political vehicle and rallying point to enhance his own image in the Arab world, and the Libyan leader, Gadhafi, views the Palestinians as an avant-garde of the overall Third World revolutionary movement he dreams of promoting. For Syria Palestinian nationalism is just a stepping-stone on the way to a Greater Syria. From Damascus Palestine is viewed as South Syria, and the need for an independent Palestinian nationalism is ultimately denied in favor of a Syrian-centered Arabism. For conservative Arab regimes the Palestinian cause has functioned as a useful safety valve, focusing the revolutionary zeal of their own radicals towards a distant battlefield. By contributing large sums of money to the different Palestinian groups, countries like Saudi Arabia and the Gulf Emirates kept the revolutionaries at bay purchasing immunity. By urging its own unruly elements to harness their energies to the liberation of Palestine, they siphoned off what could have otherwise led to rebellion and unrest in their own states.

Early Rivalries

Despite declarations to the contrary, the Palestinian national movement with its rivalling factions presents a picture of the traditional Middle Eastern social structure more than of a modern political goal-oriented organization. The movement was born out of the quest for power by young scions of landowning families who feuded among themselves for leadership of the Palestinian Arabs. The clashes among the Husseinis, Khalidis and Nashashibis provided much of the background of the first two phases of the Palestinian conflict. The political organizations formed, like the 'Arab Club' and the 'Literary Club' of the 1920s or the 'Palestinian Arab Party' and 'National Defence Party' of the 1930s were 'fronts' for the Husseini and Nashashibi clans respectively.[5] Although independence and the struggle against Jewish settlements were definitely issues of concer, they were employed as useful means to rally support by rivals for leadership. Neighboring countries, on the other hand, used the problems in Palestine to lay the groundwork for the planned annexations after the British retreat.

While the Jews were busy creating a modern political infrastructure aimed at nationhood, with political parties and unions, a welfare and defense system and elected representatives to negotiate with the Mandate authorities, the Arabs failed even to produce an equivalent to the 'Jewish Agency', despite much prodding by the British. The main problem of Palestinism was – and remains to this day – that this nationalism only defined itself in reaction to Zionism and found its expression only in militant activity. From the early start of the movement it labored under the illusion that the only way in which the course of events could be changed was through the use of arms. Long before the 'National Covenant' of the Palestinian movement was written, the phrases of Articles 9 and 10 referring to *al-jamal al-fidai*, fedayeen action, as the only way to the liberation of Palestine would have amply described the overruling mindset of Palestinian nationalists. While the Jewish armed underground groups of the Mandate were an outgrowth of existing political organizations and parties, and were subject to them, the Arab paramilitary groups *were* the national movement.

In the beginning the Palestinian resistance against Jewish settlements had all the signs of rural village feuds and tribal raiding so prevalent in the Middle East with its long history of 'faza'a' – the mobilization of all the youngsters and men of a village or region to ward off an attack by foreign intruders. In the years of the 'Arab Revolt' the activation of armed gangs and terrorist cells masterminded by Amin al Husseini for his revolt soon lost its political overtones and turned to brigandage, terrorizing of the Arab population. Extorting money from villages, the 'gangs' (arabic: *ursabi*) as the rebels were known in contemporary parlance, were soon feuding among themselves, killing alleged traitors by the dozens, and recruiting common criminals from the Mandate and neighboring countries. Once commited to armed resistance, any negotiated compromise or political cooperation with the Mandate government, which could have curtailed Jewish immigration and settlement was regarded as treason by the Palesinian militants. Moderate voices were subdued by terror. Bloodfeuds resulted from the excesses of the gangs and all chances for a settlement were lost. The Arab revolt was also a climax of the Palestinian inter-clan rivalries, which finally led to the assassination of Fakhri Bey Nashashibi in 1941 by a Mufti follower.[7] By 1937 the rebels had killed more Arabs than Jewish or British enemies, the police records of the Mandate indicate.

The necessities of a guerrilla war waged against the authorities forced the Mufti and other Palestinian leaders of the period into exile. Thus the Palestinian movement became dependent on neighboring countries, accepting logistical and financial help from outside powers, and thereby losing independence. The Mufti turned to Italy and Germany for help, an alliance which greatly discredited the Palestinian movement. The years leading up to partition and the first Israeli–Arab wars appeared as a repetition of the Arab Revolt, featuring the same antagonists and the same uncompromising militancy. When the Mufti was outlawed as a war criminal, the Palestinians' future increasingly passed into the hands of neighboring potentates, who financed rival mercenary leaders such as the Syrian generalissimo Kauqji to pave the way for their own armies invading Palestine. The local leadership remained either muffled or hopelessly divided due to the bloodshed of the 1930s and in the end had no say in the negotiations leading to the division of Palestine. By 1947 the Palestine problem had become an Arab affair, a cornerstone of Middle East power politics.

A Pawn of Inter-Arab Squabbles

The exodus of Palestinian Arabs, the foundation of the Jewish state, the annexation of the West Bank by the Emirate of Jordan, and the occupation of the Gaza-Rafiah area by Egypt spelled an end to the old generation of Palestinian leaders. The neighboring Arab states now became the caretakers of the Palestinian cause, with exiled Palestinian politicians relegated to a position of unimportance. The Palestinian refugee camps quickly became recruiting sources to whatever power or political movement promised a return to the lost homeland. In the 1950s and 1960s Egypt and Syria both created Palestinian paramilitary organizations in their conflicting quests for the leading role in the Arab world. Maintaining the *casus belli* with Israel was one way to achieve that goal, and the Palestinians became willing cannon-fodder for the low-intensity border clashes which marked the Israeli–Arab conflict after the rise of Nasser to power.[8]

The new phase of guerrilla activity against Israel was prompted by the example of anti-colonial resistance provided by the Vietminh and the Algerian FLN. The success of these popular wars of liberation against the war-weary European nations triggered expectations among young Palestinians who founded clandestine revolutionary cells.[9] Later, with the support of Arab nations or other political movements, groups like Arafat's Fatah or Habbash's Popular Front for the Liberation of Palestine, linked to the Arab National Movement (ANM), grew.[10] The short-lived union of Syria and Egypt, the United Arab Republic (UAR), brought increasing instability to the region between 1958 to 1961, but raised the hopes of the refugees. In early 1959 Nasser introduced for the first time the term of a 'Palestinian entity' into the debate; Iraq's General Kassim demanded the foundation of a 'Palestinian Republic' in Gaza and the West Bank. While earlier attempts at destabilization by the United Arab Republic in Lebanon were foiled by American reaction, the Hashemite Kingdom now became the main target. The intelligence services of the Syrian and Egyptian armies began to support various Palestinian groups, among these the element around Arafat and various ANM cells.[11]

Nasser tried to canalize the reawakened Palestinian national sentiments by establishing the 'Palestinian National Union'. This led finally in 1964 to the establishment of the 'Palestine Liberation Organization' (PLO), in a growing militant atmosphere caused by Israeli–Syrian clashes over the Jordan waters. It should be noted that the PLO's first Congress in Jerusalem was viewed with strong suspicion by King Hussein, and that the Beirut-based 'Arab Higher Committee', a group of old-time Palestinian leaders headed by the ageing ex-Mufti Amin el Husseini denounced the PLO as an Egyptian tool.[12]

Syrian and Egyptain activities were aimed at drawing Lebanon and Jordan into confrontation with Israel. The Palestinians were meant to fufil a role within another game of inter-Arab power politics, a game in which they had very little influence. Few illusions were harbored in Damascus or Cairo in regard to the military effectiveness of a few saboteurs. Damage to Israel was of secondary importance, the political impact on Israel, and her reactions against Jordan was primary. Thus, the infiltrations by the paramilitary groups organized either by the PLO or the

Syrian army were launched from Lebanese or Jordanian territory as part of a low-intensity warfare scheme.

Attempts by the Lebanese and Jordanian authorities to prevent such attacks led to clashes. Fatah's first infiltration into Israel was curtailed by the quick action of the Lebanese Secret Service. Fatah's first 'martyr' was shot by a Jordanian patrol returning from the notorious first raid in January 1965. In the strategic planning by Syrian and Egyptian leaders, the fedayeen activities were just one element in heightening tensions along the borders with Israel, thereby forcing the Arab nations into a union against the common enemy. Nasser's long-time dream seemed to become reality in May 1967 with the signing of a military pact between Egypt, Jordan and Syria.

The Illusion of Independence

Great hopes were entertained by Arafat and his comrades for a united Palestinian national movement, independent from the influence of the Arab states, and this dream seemed to be within reach after the Six Day War. Hundreds flocked to the training camps in the Jordan valley, and the clever propagandistic exploitation of the fedayeen's stand at Karameh made the Palestinian guerrillas the new heroes of the Arab world.

By the end of 1968 Arafat had taken over the PLO and replaced the old functionaries with representatives of the fedayeen groups, carefully ensuring that the important positions were filled by Fatah leaders or by members of his own family. Indeed, over the years recurring charges of corruption and nepotism were thus levelled at Arafat by dissident groups, pointing out that the PLO's financial administration is largely controlled by Fatah functionaries and that Arafat has given his relatives key positions. One brother, Fathi, is head of the Palestinian Red Crescent. Another brother, Jemal, is the PLO representative in South Yemen. Arafat's cousin Haj Matlek leads the PLO's military office. One nephew Musa commands the security detail guarding the PLO leadership, while another nephew, Nasser, acts as the general secretary of the influential Student Union.[13] In a similar vein, the PFLP and its various splinter factions are dominated by a similar old-fellow network often dating back to the pre-1967 days of the Arab National Movement and by family connections. Thus Marwan Haddad stepped into the command vacuum left when his brother died in March 1978, collecting the remnants of Wadi Haddad's PFLP-Special Operations group.

While Arafat's take-over of the PLO had broken Nasser's control over the organizations, the fedayeen groups were far from being united and independent from outside influence. Although Fatah's leading role within the Palestinian movement was acknowledged for the time, it did not remain unchallenged for long. Whereas Fatah attracted mainly recruits from the Sunni majority of the Palestinian peasant society, members of the Greek-Orthodox Christian minority among the

Palestinians flocked to groups like Habbash's PFLP whose secular approach fitted intellectuals and students coming from an urban background. Traditional social structures still played their role in the mobilization of the fedayeen organizations, whose new leadership generation fell very much into the zu'ama pattern.

By financing upstart leaders interested in founding new fedayeen groups or supporting dissenting existing ones, nations like Iraq, Syria, Egypt and later Libya kept a handle on PLO politics. After the 1968 takeover the PLO was raised to a new role as a dominating element in the Israeli–Arab conflict, but now the PLO itself became the new stage for inter-Arab power competition.

The emergence of terrorist attacks abroad, which started in the summer of 1968 with hijackings and airport attacks, has to be viewed in the light of internal PLO rivalries. The main 'front' with Israel in the Jordan valley was monopolized by Fatah and presented few, if any, chances to distinguish oneself. Already the conflicting, exaggerated claims by different fedayeen groups had become a source of irritation and derision in the Arab world. The 'international battlefield' gave even the smallest groups an opportunity to gain reputation beyond their actual size and capabilities. It should be noted in this context that the spree of Palestinian international terrorism was started by Habbash's PFLP, the most serious challenger of Arafat's and Fatah's leadership role.[14] Other groups took up the example, recognizing the apparent lack of risk and the publicity effort of operations in Europe. Soon hijackings and other terrorist acts followed each other in rapid succession as fedayeen groups tried to outdo one another, capitalizing on the group's media exposure. At times, even the Fatah felt the need to compete in this field, to ascertain its role, and to rally its rank and file who demanded action and successes. Examples are the activities of the 'Black September Group' in the 1970s, masterminded by Salah Khalaf and other high-ranking Fatah functionaries, and later the operations of 'Group 17' which carried out the Barcelona murders and the killing of three tourists in Cyprus in September and October 1985.

The activities abroad soon went out of control. They provoked Israeli reactions and brought the PLO onto a colliding course with the host countries, which suffered from Israeli retaliation raids. At the same time the host countries became increasingly worried about the presence of the armed autonomous entities in the refugee camps. Openly defying the power of the host governments, groups like the PFLP drove the PLO into two devastating civil wars. The multiple hijacking ending at Dawson's Field near Amman perpetrated by the PFLP in September 1970 was 'the straw which broke the camel's back' for King Hussein's government. George Habbash wanted to force the mainstream PLO into a showdown with the Hasemite Kingdom, following the PFLP's (and the ANM's) dictum that the road towards liberation of Haifa and Jaffa led through Amman. A similar set of events in the years prior to 1975 preceded the outbreak of the Lebanese civil war. Again clashes with the authorities were the result of independent actions by PLO splinter groups which negated all agreements between the Lebanese government and the PLO leadership. The splinter groups also armed and supported local radical elements, destabilizing the precarious balance of the multi-confessional community in Lebanon, thereby provoking the state-supporting Maronite organizations into action.

The activities of radical splinter groups which repeatedly forced the mainstream PLO into confrontations it tried to avoid, underline the major weakness of the Palestinian national movement. At best the PLO is a roof-top organization of paramilitary groups which drift apart at the slightest instance of disagreement. The only common denominator of the fedayeen is their will to fight Israel, but even here the question of how to achieve this always creates dissent and divisions.

As in the days of the Mandate, the Palestinian movement has been lacking a binding political concept more explict than the National Covenant. As the PLO leadership for the sake of outward appearance and its own role has gone and will go to any length to avoid dissension in the ranks of the movement, it has been easy for splinter groups to manipulate the mainstream. Arafat has only turned against those dissidents who openly challenged his leadership, while he has failed again and again to control maverick radicals.[15] In the long run, these factors have increased the rifts in the Palestinian movement to a point where the dissent has now achieved dramatic dimensions.

The Growth of Dissent

If there ever was a chance for unity, it was after the expulsion from Jordan. The delegates of the Eighth Palestinian National Congress clearly recognized what led to the disaster: a lack of overall discipline within the movement, its sectarianism and the uncontrollable radicalism of splinter groups and camp militias. However, except for resolutions and declarations, nothing was done, and the existence of the many factions was blamed on the interfering politics of various Arab nations.[16] What this analysis lacked was an understanding of why it was so easy for the regimes in Damascus, Baghdad and Tripoli to maintain partisan groups within the ranks of the PLO. The underlying causes were never remedied, and after establishing themselves in Lebanon, the PLO groups continued their course as before.

The variety of fedayeen factions grew each year, ranging ideologically from Marxist revolutionaries to nationalist Syrian to Iraqi Baathist, to Islamic fundamentalists. In Lebanon, Palestinians became involved with the local quagmire of radical militant organizations which further complicated the internal situation of the PLO. One is at a loss to explain the ideological differences between the various splinters. Note, for example, the history of the PFLP of George Habbash:

The Popular Front for the Liberation of Palestine (PFLP) was built in December 1967 from the 'Heroes of the Return', sponsored by the

Lebanese branch of the ANM, and led by Shafik al-Hut and Ahmed el-Yamani, and 'The Youth of Vengeance' led by Habbash, Naif Hawatmeh and Wadi Haddad, all long-time functionaries of the Palestinian ANM in Lebanon. In November 1968 the 'Palestine Liberation Front', a Syrian-sponsored fedayeen group headed by two former Syrian army officers, Ahmed Jibril and Ali Bushnak joined this new PLO sub-group.

Within a few months the disintegration began with Jibril leaving the organization and establishing his own 'PFLP-General Command', relying on sponsorship from Syria and later Libya.

The following year Achmed Zahrur left the PFLP-GC, creating the 'Organization of Arab Palestine' with help from Egypt.

1976 another one of Jibril's lieutenants, Abbas Zaida, split to organize the 'Palestine Liberation Front' with support from Libya.

In January 1969 Hawatmeh split off from the PFLP and founded the 'Democratic Popular Front for Liberation of Palestine' (DPFLP), supporting Arafat within the PLO.

In 1970 the 'People's Organization for Liberation of Palestine' emerged from Hawatmeh's group only to enter the Syrian-sponsored 'Saiqa' (Thunderbolt) by 1972.

In 1972 Abu Shihab, formerly of the Lebanese ANM, and his group of followers declared their independence from the PFLP, founding the 'Revolutionary People's Front'.

By 1976 Wadi Haddad, Habbash's closest confidant in the PFLP, had opened his 'PFLP-Special Operations' with help from Iraq, Libya and the People's Republic of Yemen.

Sifting through the mass of theoretical tractates and mutual accusations generated by these rival factions, it becomes obvious that the revolutionary verbiage is only a facade. All employ the same Marxist terms, declaring their solidarity with the other progressive movements in the Arab and Third World, and emphasizing their revolutionary zeal in fighting against Zionism and Imperialism. There is no ideological difference since they all refer to reactionary Arab regimes and the needs for revolution in those regimes to reach the liberation of Palestine. Ideological distinctions between these groups are hard to substantiate and cannot be seen as reason for divisions. The key to the emergence of splinter groups lies in shifting alliances, dependencies on sponsor states, and rivalries among the leading personalities.

More and more, groups made their appearance without ideological pretensions, simply challenging the existing PLO leadership. Perhaps the establishment of a government-in-exile outside the framework of the PLO could have altered this development. This was the view of a number of moderate Arab politicians (foremost among these Anwar Al-Sadat) searching for a way to include the Palestinians in the negotiations with

Israel after the 1973 war. But such a political body would have minimized the importance of the fedayeens, and these proposals were rebuffed. Further, when it appeared for a short time after the UN recognition of the Palestinian movement that the PLO could be a partner in a future all-out Middle East conference to settle the conflict, the glowing embers of internal dissent were fanned into a violent firestorm.

The PLO's undeclared policy under Arafat's leadership consists of creating and maintaining an independent role for the Palestinians in Arab politics by manouevering between the poles of power, using Saudi Arabia as a political and financial safety net. Arafat's arrangements, first with the Syrians, later with Egypt and most recently with the Jordanians have to be understood as an attempt to prevent the exemption of the PLO from whatever political opportunities materialize. If the Palestinian people (read: PLO) are the most important element in the Middle East equation, as Arafat has repeatedly claimed, then the organization cannot stay apart from any political development taking place.[17] The PLO's freedom of movement, its ability to make independent decisions, and its veto power were to be assured by a precarious tightrope walk, changing sets of alliances with the rival Arab powers, more often than not pitting Egypt against Syria, trying to harness Iraq, Libya, even Iran to the PLO carriage, and looking for support in Moscow and Riyadh.

In the Middle Eastern multiple-conflict arena, such a criss-cross balancing act is doomed to failure: in 1970, when the PLO hoped for support from Iraq and Syria in their confrontation with Russia, they were left with empty promises. In Lebanon, when the Maronite Falange stormed Tal al-Zaatar, neither Libya nor Egypt nor Syria sent help. On the contrary, when the PLO tried to hamper the establishment of a Pax Syriana, Hafez al-Assad's armoured brigades made short work of the PLO resistance. While the government in Damascus has always been ready to use the fedayeen as elements in its own strategy, it had increasingly become suspicious of the Fatah leadership clique, having once or twice attempted to replace Arafat by one of their own. When that failed, Syria decided to assemble all those fedayeen factions which opposed Arafat or mistrusted his diplomatic game.

Rejection or 'salvation' fronts began to emerge, uniting the radical Syrian-dominated fedayeen groups against the mainstream PLO. Open fighting broke out among the followers in Lebanon. This was complicated by a Syrian–Iraqi border war whose sideshow in the streets of Beirut and Tripoli took place among PLO-sections linked to these antagonists. All of this led to the outbreak of the Lebanese civil war, and brought the direct involvement of Syria.

The years between the October War and Camp David could have opened new political avenues for the Palestinian movement, bringing at least a chance for a West Bank homeland as envisioned in the Camp David accord. But for the fedayeen it was back to square one in Lebanon. The continuation of military confrontation with Israel resulted only in harder retaliation raids, finally entangling the PLO in a confrontation with the

Lebanese state authorities and state-supporting militias. On the other side of the fence, the Israelis – angered by border clashes and terrorist acts – became more and more entrenched politically. Terrorist acts abroad by Black September or the hostage killings of Quiriat Schmoneh, Maalot, Nahariyah, etc. supplied the arguments for hardliners refusing any compromise with the Palestinians.[18]

Spiral of Violence: The Case of Abu Nidal

The more there appeared a chance for peace in the Middle East, the more terrorist acts occurred. Not only were certain acts aimed at sabotaging the development of *rapprochement* in the wake of Sadat's trip to Jerusalem, but the internal Palestinian dissent accounted for even more victims. Fatah officials or PLO representatives reputed to be 'moderates', were killed in cold blood by rejectionist hit teams. Countries which supported PLO politics such as Austria or Italy became battle zones in the inter-Palestinian feud. Germany, which maintained clandestine contacts with the PLO's security apparatus to prevent Palestinian terrorist acts, learned the hard way that this very policy provoked radical factions into perpetrating acts in order to compromise PLO leadership.[19]

The career of one notorius radical, Sabri al-Banna, a.k.a. Abu Nidal, provides an interesting insight into the internal dynamics of Palestinian terrorism.

One of the founding members of Fatah, Sabri al-Banna, was the PLO representative in Baghdad and apparently also had a hand in organizing Black September. Al-Banna, who already in 1971 had voiced criticism of the Fatah and PLO leadership's strategy regarding Jordan, finally broke with Arafat in 1974. His rebellion was sponsored by Iraq's president Al-Baqr, who confiscated the PLO holdings in Baghdad and turned them over to Abu Nidal. Fatah retaliated by announcing death sentences on Al-Banna and his followers. One of these, the former PLO representative to Libya, Ahmed Abdel Ghaffur was consequently killed on his return to Lebanon. According to Al-Banna, Fatah executed some 150 of his friends.[20]

As a first 'act de presence', of the Abu Nidal Group, the 'Commando Abdul Ghaffur' hijacked a British airliner from Dubai to Tunis. Abu Nidal then tried to achieve a union of radical Palestinian groups to unseat Arafat by inviting the fedayeen groups to a Palestinian National Congress in Baghdad – an endeavour which failed miserably. At the height of the Syrian–Iraq feud, Abu Nidal operated on behalf of the Iraqi secret service against Syria, attempting twice to kill the Syrian Foreign Minister Khaddam among other acts. His 'Black June' is named after the month in 1976, when the Syrian 'peace-keeping force' intervened against the PLO in Lebanon. In an interview with *The Middle East* magazine, Abu Nidal called the struggle against 'the reactionary regime in Syria, Jordan and Lebanon ... our second priority' after combatting Zionists.[21]

The Camp David Accord provided the political background for a new Iraqi-inspired campaign against 'traitors'. In London PLO representative Said Hammami was shot in January 1978. Six months later the Kuwait-based PLO diplomat Ali Jassin was killed. Meanwhile, Fatah loyalists struck back attacking Iraqi embassies in Paris and Karachi and gunning down an Iraqi diplomat in Tripoli. In August two PLO men fell victim in Paris, while an attack on the PLO office in Islamabad the following day killed three PLO members and a Pakistani policeman. The internecine war soon spread to other factions in Lebanon, where rival groups shot it out in the streets of Beirut and Tripoli. A bloody climax occurred, when a large bomb levelled a PLO headquarters building in Beirut, killing some 155 people, mostly affiliated with the pro-Iraqi Palestine Liberation Front. Arafat, himself, had left the building half an hour prior to its destruction and at least ten Fatah men died in the rubble. While the origins could never be ascertained, suspicions focused on a pro-Syrian splinter group, Ahmed Jibril's PFLP-Gener al Command.

During these years, Baghdad became a rallying place for various terrorist groups operating transnationally. The German Federal Investigation Bureau was able to track various Baader-Meinhof members to an army camp in Habbanijah near the Iraqi capital, where they and members of the Wadi Haddad PFLP section underwent training.[22] Only after Saddam Hussein's rise to power were these activities curtailed and an attempt made to mend Baghdad's fences with the PLO. Sabri al-Banna moved his operational base to Syria, turning his wrath now against Austria which he viewed as engineering contacts between Israel and the PLO. In May 1981 Heinz Knittel, a pro-Israel politician of the socialist democratic party was killed, and this was followed by threats against Chancellor Kreisky. The next month, Naim Chader, the PLO man in Brussels, was murdered. The most spectacular of these activities – Abu Nidal claimed to have organized close to one hundred – was the assassination of PLO delegate Issam Sartawi during the Lisbon conference of the Socialist Internationale in April 1983.

More terrorist acts followed against a wide variety of targets by elements employing different names: 'Fatah Revolutionary Council' for attacks against Palestinian and Israeli targets, 'Revolutionary Arab Brigades' against Kuwait, 'Revolutionary Organization of Socialist Muslims' against objectives in Great Britain and 'Egyptian Revolution' for acts in or against Egypt, such as the November hijacking of an Egypt Air plane to Malta. There is also strong suspicion that Abu Nidal had a hand in the re-emergence of 'Black September' in December 1984, attacking the Jordan–PLO *rapprochement* at a time when Syria was opposed to Jordan.[23]

Abu Nidal's switch in 1979/1980 from Iraq to Syria was a remarkable and astonishing feat. Apparently, his earlier bombings and assassination attempts against Syria were forgiven and forgotten, which gave rise to rumors that Abu Nidal had acted all the time as a double agent paid by Damascus to furnish the Syrian government with the pretexts for their crack-down against the PLO resistance in Lebanon in 1976. There is another interesting feature in Nidal's sketchy career. The rebellion of al-Banna and Ghaffur occurred at a time when Libyan leader Mu'ammar Gadhafi tried his best to prod the PLO into a more active stand against Israel, finally stopping his donations to Arafat. By autumn 1973 Ghaffur had well established himself in Libya, opening a branch of Abu Nidal's rebel group, the 'Revolutionary Organization of Al-Assifa'. On 17 December an attempt to attack US Secretary of State Henry Kissinger during a flight-stop at the airport in Rome was discovered, resulting in a shoot-out and the hijacking of a Lufthansa airliner to Kuwait. There the five terrorists, claiming to belong to the 'Arab National Youth for the Liberation of Palestine' (ANYLP), gave themselves up and divulged information on their connection to Ghaffur and Abu Nidal. After Ghaffur's death, remnants of this Libyan-based fedayeen section apparently were taken over by Marwan Haddad, a relative of Wadi Haddad who operated at that time from Baghdad.[24]

Libya's criticism of the PLO leadership was underlined during the siege of Beirut, when Gadhafi demanded that the PLO leadership commit suicide rather than leave Beirut. The rebellion aginst Arafat within Fatah, coming in the wake of the 1982 defeat, found the support not only of Syria but also of Gadhafi who, according to press interviews given by the rebels, financed at least some of the field-grade Fatah commanders who opposed Arafat.

It is strongly suspected that the Abu Nidal group at that time also turned to Colonel Gadhafi for support and moved its operational base to Libya. As in earlier years when Abu Nidal switched sides from Iraq to Syria, this new change from Syria to Libya might be explained as an attempt to maintain a certain amount of independence from any one single sponsor-state. The use of Shi'ite activists and the possibility of joint operations by radical Shi'ites and Palestinians, which is suspected in recent events in Spain, Greece and Turkey, could present another avenue of opportunity used by state-sponsored fedayeen factions in an attempt to cover their tracks more efficiently.[25] That Abu Nidal is not an isolated case, but a symbol of the ever-present dissension in the PLO, was underlined in the events following the PLO exodus from Beirut.

The Current Dilemma

No defiant gestures from the departing fedayeen and no declarations to the contrary can hide the fact that the Israeli invasion of Lebanon and the ensuing retreat from Beirut was a political and military catastrophe for the PLO. Lebanon was the last base bordering on Israel where the fedayeen group could operate without control: Syria, Jordan and Egypt always keep tight reins on any fedayeen activity along their ceasefire lines with Israel. Thousands of tons of military hardware, installations, bureaus and other holdings were lost too. Within a few weeks the PLO had lost its role as a central element in the Lebanese power game and turned from a well-entrenched, affluent paramilitary organization into a pauper at the mercy of their new Arab hosts. The armed contingents were split up and sent piecemeal to different countries, such as Yemen, Iraq and Tunisia.

Although the defeat led to some soul-searching by members of the PLO leadership[26] it triggered another round of internal strife, this time originating within Fatah. Criticizing Arafat's *rapprochement* with Jordan as abandonment of the National Charter's principle proclaiming fedayeen action as the only way to the liberation of Palestine, a group of Fatah field commanders under the direction of Abu Moussa, Abu Khaled al-Amla, and Nimr Saleh rebelled openly. The crisis, which started in May 1983 over the promotion of two unpopular Arafat followers, led to armed clashes between loyalists and rebels. The Fatah rebels found themselves supported by Libya, whose news media provided them with a platform to voice their views. They also received logistical and financial aid from Syria which saw another chance to unseat Arafat. Rejectionist groups like the PFLP-General Command, the Palestine Liberation Front, and Saiqa threw their weight behind the rebels. By October the fighting escalated to open war directed against the last strongholds of the mainstream PLO in Tripoli. With the help of Syrian artillery and tanks, the rebels forced Arafat and his loyalists to leave Lebanon in a dramatic evacuation by sea.

However, an attempt by Syria to gather the Palestinian opposition groups into a new PLO-type organization designed to isolate Arafat failed. The Syrian government succeeded in mentoring a union of rejectionist groups called the 'National Revolutionary Alliance' consisting of Abu Moussa's Fatah rebels, the Baathist Saiqa, Jibril's PFLP-GC and the small 'Palestinian Popular Struggle Front'. This fell short of Damascus' expectations to form an all-encompassing 'National Front'.

George Habbash (PFLP) and Naif Hawatmeh (DPFLP) – though representing the staunchest opposition to the alleged PLO 'policy of surrender' – shied away from the final consequence which would cement the rift already existing within the Palestinian people. Calling themselves the 'Democratic Alliance' they continue to negotiate with the PLO leadership, meanwhile openly advocating 'armed operations' to stop Arafat's diplomatic moves with Jordan. Not until March 1985 did Habbash announce his joining of the National Revolutionary Alliance.

The PLF became divided over which side to take. One faction headed by politbureau member Abdel Fattha sided with the rebels, while the PLF general secretary Talaat Tacoub pleaded for neutrality and finally sided with PFLP and DPFLP. A third PLF-section under Abbas Zaida, a.k.a. Abul Abbas, switched to Arafat. Its rewards were an unproportionally large PLF representation in the Palestinian National Council and a seat for Zaida in the PLO executive committee.

Arafat's power base has consisted of his own loyalist Fatah, the Iraqi-supported Arab Liberation Front and the Abul Abbas PLF faction,[27] while negotiations were underway to establish a *modus vivendi* with the Democratic Alliance. In terms of international terrorism, these divisions over the Jordan–PLO *rapprochement* accounted for much of the terrorist attacks witnessed after December 1983, including the killing of Fahd Kawasmeh, PLO executive committee member, in December 1984, the shooting of a Jordanian diplomat in Ankara in July 1985 and the bombing of an Iraqi Airline office in Cyprus in November 1985. The PLO fedayeen groups countered these attacks by assassinations and bombings directed against the opposition groups and Syrian installations abroad (for example, the attempted bombing of the Syrian embassy in London in June 1985).

In a new attempt to gather support, Arafat improved his relations with Baghdad and Algiers by early 1986. Both countries increased their support of the mainstream PLO, training Fatah and PLF cadres and supplying military bases, weapons and instructors. PLO members have been engaged on the Iraqi frontline for commando operations against Iranian positions. In the spring of 1986 another spree of terror bombings in Syria, initiated by Iraq as a retaliation for Syrian's persistent support of Iran occurred. While Syria regularly blames 'Israeli agents' for such acts, it is apparent that at least some of the earlier bombings in 1985 were the result of the cooperation between the oppositional Muslim Brotherhood and Fatah, which was renewed in 1984. (In his younger days Arafat had been an activist of the Brotherhood in Palestine and Egypt.) Obviously, PLO contacts with the opposition in Syria proved to be helpful for the new wave of attacks which, according to the Syrian newsagency SANA, killed 140 and wounded 144.

Another twist to this ongoing drama occurred in the summer of 1986. The Jordanian government in the course of a sudden and unexpected *rapprochement* with Syria, closed the PLO offices in Amman, ousted a number of mainstream PLO representatives, and supported Atallah Atallah, another critic of Arafat's leadership. After a PLO delegation headed by Arafat met with Syrian Foreign Minister Khaddam and Libya's Gadhafi (for the first time since 1982) during the Harare summit of the non-aligned nations, the PLO revoked the Jordanian–Palestinian agreement of 11 February 1985. Such a move had been demanded by the Popular Front for the Liberation of Palestine as a precondition for its participation in an upcoming session of the Palestinian National Council, which hopes to bring about a unification of the Palestinian ranks. It would also herald one more reorientation of Arafat, this time mending his fences with Syria in order to save his position in the face of growing dissension within the Palestinian movement.

No Hope for the Future

Whatever the motives for these latest developments, they will not spell an end to the tensions dividing the Palestinian camp, nor will they provide a new political direction for the PLO. The fedayeen groups have experienced now more than two decades of set-backs and defeats, with no tangible results for years of troubles and bloodshed. Unrest is fomenting among the rank and file as recent rebellions indicate. As no new alternatives are in sight, it is quite foreseeable that new friction within the Palestinian movement will present the world with another round of internal strife. As in earlier cases, this will spill over into the international arena with more senseless terrorist acts adding to the seemingly endless list of previous outrages.

Under the current set of circumstances the Palestinian national movement as represented by the PLO and its fedayeen groups will not be able to join any negotiated settlement of the Israeli–Arab conflict, nor will it be satisfied by any compromise solution as envisioned in the various proposals for a future West Bank homeland. This is as much a result of the influence of radical sponsor states, such as Syria or Libya as of the structure of the movement itself and of its domination by paramilitary groups. The fixation on the armed struggle will always permit outside powers to influence the Palestinians, exploit their rivalries and ambitions, and use them as pawns; and radical Arab nations like Libya or Syria will continue to manipulate the Palestinian organizations.

Historically, factionalism and internal strife has been an integral part in all four phases of the Palestinian national movement since the early days of the British Mandate. If šme progress can be seen, it is wholly in the organizational establishment of the PLO, which changed some of the conditions under which the movement existed. Although leadership generations changed over the years, this did not diminish internal dynamics leading to dissent. Nor did political recognition affect the basics of Palestinism, especially the dominating role of the fedayeen myth, from which most of the rivalries derived. The current phase differs from the earlier decades of Palestinian history only in the way in which the utilization of the international stage for the internal battles has been perfected. Radical factions like Abu Nidal's have appeared before in the long-drawn out Palestinian tragedy (for example, Wadi Haddad's PFLP-Special Operations), but none orchestrated international terrorist acts against third parties quite as cleverly as this group, while balancing its dependency on various sponsor states.

As compared to other terrorism-dominated conflicts, the Palestinian is distinguished by the astonishing multiplicity of groups, sponsor states and alliances, each with conflicting strategies and ideological pretensions. In their desperately forlorn hope for return to the homeland, the Palestinians appear constantly in search of new remedies for their débâcle, willing to embrace any messiah – be it Nasser, Mao or Khomeini – for the crusade against Israel. No other terrorists, not the IRA or ETA, the Corse separatists nor any of the Latin-American and West-European groups, have ever been as diversified as the Palestinians. The Palestinians have failed to establish a political infrastructure which could arbitrate quarrels and controversies through a democratic process, thereby allowing a united front against outside intervention. Militancy and revolutionary rhetorics are not enough. As a political movement, the Palestinian nationalists have not progressed much and every crisis or defeat has thrown them back to square one, where their only expression is terrorism and internal strife.

In the Middle East the Palestinian cause is only one of many factors contributing to the different conflicts. It is highly questionable whether any Arab state of the region is really willing to permit the realization of an independent Palestinian state. Perhaps the best chances for Palestinian self-determination have already been lost in the past: time appears to be running out. The PLO and the fedayeen groups will exist as long as they serve a purpose for the Arab states confronting Israel. If that confrontation ceases to maintain its importance in the face of other and probably more pressing problems of the Arab world, the Palestinians are likely to suffer the same fate as the Armenians or Kurds.

NOTES

1. Yehoshua Porath, *The Emergence of the Palestinian-Arab National Movement 1918–1929* (London: Frank Cass, 1974) and *Palestinian-Arab National Movement: From Riots to Rebellion* (London: Frank Cass, 1977) are still the best analyses of these years. For Amin el-Husseini's role in inter-Arab rivalries see also the *CID-Reports to Sir Charles Tegart*. Private Paper Collection, St. Anthony's College, Documentation Centre, Oxford, and Bayan Nuweihid Al-Hout, 'The Palestine Political Elite during the Mandate Period', *Journal of Palestine Studies* (JPS), No.33, Vol.IX/1 (Autumn 1979), S.85-111. On the Husseini-Nazi contacts, see Lukasz Hirszowicz, *The Third Reich and the Arab East* (London: Routledge & Kegan Paul, 1966).
2. Aref el-Arev, *El Naklah* (Beirut: NPI, 1958).
3. Carleton Coon, *Caravan, The Story of the Middle East* (New York: Henry Holt, 1951) is still one of the best descriptions of traditional structures in the Middle East. See also C. van Nieuwenhuijze, *Sociology of the Middle East: A Stocktaking and Interpretation* (Leiden: E.J. Brill, 1971).
4. See Arnold Hottinger, 'Zu'ama in Historical Perspective', in L. Binder, *Politics in Lebanon* (New York: John Wiley, 1966).
5. Porath, p.75f and V.F. Abboushi, 'The Road to Rebellion: Arab Palestine in the 1930's,' *Journal of Palestine Studies*, Vol.VI, No.3 (Spring 1977), pp.24–46.
6. A good example of this glorification is Leila Khaled's autobiography *My People Shall Live* (London: Hodder & Stoughton, 1973). See also H. el-Yacoubi, 'The Evolution of Palestinian Consciousness' (Boulder, CO. Ph.D. dissertation, 1973) and his description of 'fida'i', p.239f. See also 'Status from Fire', *Fateh* 302 (1971).
7. Porath, p.190f.
8. For a report of the UNO commander at that time, see E.L.M. Burns, *Between Arab and Israeli* (Toronto: I. Obolensky, 1962), p.61. Also Ehud Yaari's book in Hebrew on the Egyptian use of infiltration, *Mizraim wa HaFedayee 1953–1956* (Givat Haviva: 1975).
9. The early years of Arafat's Fatah are amply described by Abu Ijad (Salah Khalaf) with Eric Rouleau, *Un Palestinian sans Patrie* (Paris: Fayolle, 1978). On the connections between the Arafat group and the Syrian intelligence see E. Yaari, *Strike Terror: The Story of Fatah* (New York: Sabra Books, 1970).
10. Yaari, p.32f. Issa Al-Shuaibi, 'The Development of Palestinian Entity Consciousness', in *JPS* 9 (1979).
11. Leila Khaled – in an attempt to diminish Fatah's role as the first independent fedayeen group – lays claim to sabotage raids by the ANM as early as 1953.
12. For a summary of the pre-1967 PLO development, see R. Hamid's 'What is the PLO', *JPS* 4 (1975). Paul Jureidini and W.E. Hazen, *The Palestinian Movement in Politics* (Lexington, MA: Lexington Books, 1976) detail the role of the PLO in inter-Arab

squabbles.

13. Such accusations of corruption were again levelled against the PLO leadership in August 1986 by rebel leader Abu Musa, see a series of articles in the Lebanese newspaper, *Al Watan Al-Arabi* of that month.

14. Khaled's description – pp.99ff. 140ff – of her role in the PFLP hijackings and of the ideological legitimization of these acts are revealing and clearly indicate that the hijackings were meant to force Fatah into an all-out confrontation with King Hussein.

15. Jureidini, p.95.

16. This is even acknowledged by Salah Khalaf in Abu Ijad, p.112ff. Also see Khaled el-Hindi, 'An End' in Russell Stetler (ed.), *Palestine: the Arab-Israeli Conflict* (San Francisco, CA: Ramparts Press, 1972), pp.289–97.

17. For a view of inter-PLO rivalries as seen by the Fatah leadership, see Helena Cobban, *The PLO – People, Power and Politics* (Cambridge: Cambridge University Press, 1984); she also gives a good account of the PLO's inter-Arab manuevers.

18. The role of Palestinian infighting and terrorist attacks as a critical factor in the development toward the Lebanese Civil War only has been randomly analyzed by those writing about the tragedy. The 1986 Shi'ite onslaught against Palestinian armed groups can only be understood in the light of earlier Shi'ite experience with the PLO presence in South Lebanon.

19. Some of these PLO contacts were reported in *Der Spiegel* 51 (1979), 8 (1980) and 17 (1980) when Palestinian terrorists were caught smuggling large amounts of explosives into West Berlin and Bavaria.

20. In October 1985 Abu Nidal, countering rumors of his death, gave an interesting interview to *Der Spiegel* from which some of the following information is drawn.

21. Interview with Abu Nidal in the London-based monthly, *The Middle East*, July 1978. See also *Arab World Weekly*, 2 Dec. 1974 on the PLO rebels and 'Why PLO and Iraq are at Loggerheads', *The Middle East*, Aug. 1978.

22. *Der Spiegel*, 21 (1978) and 23 (1978). Also *Stern* 48 (1977) and 8 (1986) on Baader-Meinhof members in Iraq and Yemen.

23. Ariel Merari (ed.), *Inter 85* (Tel Aviv: The Yaffee Institute for Strategic Studies, 1986), p.42ff.

24. *Conflict Studies* 41 (1973), p.7, *BBC Foreign Broadcasting Information Service*, 17 April 1973 and *Arab World Weekly*, 7 Dec. 1974.

25. Merari, p.45.

26. An indication of this was given in an interview of Abu Ijad, *Der Spiegel* 10 (1985).

27. Ariel Merari, 'The Future of Palestinian Terrorism', *TVI Journal* 5 (1985) estimates the manpower within these camps at mainstream PLO 8,000 men, National Alliance 4,500, Democratic Alliance 4,500.

The Shining Path and Peruvian Terrorism

Gordon H. McCormick

Sendero Luminoso (Shining Path) was born in the department of Ayachucho, high in the Peruvian Andes. The region, long ignored by the government in Lima, is among the most impoverished departments in the country. Politically, culturally, and economically, Ayachucho has existed as a world apart. Though isolated on the Andean altiplano, more than 300 miles from Lima, Ayachucho has played an important role in Peruvian history. It was the site of the Huari Confederation, the first of the pan-Andean empires. It was in Ayachucho also where Tupac Yupanqui defeated the Huancas to found the Inca empire. In 1824, it was the site of the last great battle for Latin American liberation. Since its original conquest by Spain, it has also been the focal point of numerous Indian uprisings.

Peru is a country long plagued by political violence. Today alone, there are at least five known terrorist groups operating on Peruvian soil: the Movement of the Revolutionary Left (MIR), Puka Llacta-Red Flag, People's Revolutionary Commandos, the Tupac Amaru Revolutionary Movement (MRTA), and the Communist Party of Peru–Sendero Luminoso. Of these groups, Sendero Luminoso requires particular attention. First, the Shining Path is by far the largest and most successful of Peru's terrorist organizations. Sendero initiated its first operations against the Lima regime in 1980. In the intervening seven years it has grown to become the most serious security problem facing the Peruvian government. Second, Sendero reveals a number of organizational and ideological features that are quite unique. The movement is rooted in a combination of Andean mysticism, Maoism, and the world view of its leader and organizer, Abimael Guzman. Few political movements, inside or outside Peru, can match its fanaticism and extreme parochialism. Finally, Sendero must be singled out for its simple ruthlessness. Murder, dynamite bombings and arson are the instruments of political violence. Few terrorist groups in modern times, however, have employed high-order violence with the same determination, lack of discrimination, and widespread effect as the Shining Path. In the space of the first six years of operations, Sendero may have carried out as many as 12,000 terrorist actions, resulting in a possible death toll as high as 10,000.

It should be noted at the outset that very little is known of the Shining Path. Sendero, for one thing, is a relatively recent creation. Observers have not had the same opportunity to study the behavior and organizational development of the Shining Path as most other prominent terrorist organizations. Clandestine organizations are, by their very nature, secret. Patching together a clear and reliable portrait of the inner workings of such a group on the basis of available intelligence is generally a slow process. This problem has been compounded by Sendero's own relative silence. In contrast to most terrorist groups which thrive on the exposure provided by an international press, Sendero has largely avoided the media, preferring instead to publicize its cause by means of 'armed propaganda', relying on actions rather than words. The purpose of the present article, within the limits of the available data, is to provide a brief overview of Sendero's leadership, organizing concepts, and style of operations. The article concludes by assessing the apparent strengths and possible vulnerabilities of the group based on this analysis.

The Thought of Comrade Gonzalo

Sendero Luminoso was founded in 1970 by Abimael Guzman, then a professor of philosophy at the University of Huamanga in Ayachucho. Guzman was born in 1934 into a middle-class family. He grew up in the home of his father and stepmother until he entered San Agustin National University in Arequipa. Guzman received two degrees from San Agustin, a Ph.D for his dissertation on Immanuel Kant's theory of space and a second degree in law for his thesis on 'The Bourgois Democratic State'. Acquaintances remember him as a quiet and serious student, with a close knowledge of classical music and a taste for pre-Socratic philosophy and the literary works of Joyce and Hemingway.[1]

Guzman's initial involvement in radical politics is believed to have begun in the late 1950s with his membership in the Communist Party of Peru (PCP). In 1964, Guzman and other pro-Chinese party members split from the PCP to follow the Maoist splinter group, Bandera Roja, a move prompted by the Sino-Soviet rift and Moscow's newly established doctrine on 'the peaceful road to socialism'. Guzman's final break with the conventional left occurred in 1970 when he and a small group of followers were expelled from the movement for doctrinal heresy and 'occultism'. For his part, Guzman accused the Red Flag of betraying its Maoist origins by promoting the 'privilege' of the cities and having 'scorn for the countryside'.[2] Guzman vowed to continue his efforts to lead a rural-based revolt against the Lima regime under a Maoist banner.

With his expulsion from Bandera Roja, Guzman moved to take control of the radical left at Huamanga and establish the true Communist Party of Peru – Shining Path. Membership in the new organization grew rapidly during the early 1970s. Guzman, who became personnel director of the university in 1971, was well placed to make sure that only ideologically compatible faculty were hired at Huamanga – and through the establishment of a radical faculty – to indoctrinate and recruit a generation of student followers. Sendero soon moved beyond Huamanga to begin recruiting among the Indian populations of Ayachucho. By the mid-1970s, Sendero had begun to establish local cells in the surrounding departments of Cusco, Apurimac, Huancavelica and Junin. Its largest pool of recruits was drawn from the non-Spanish speaking peoples of the highlands, and Indian slum-dwellers in the area of Lima and several other major cities. At this time, few people other than his followers and his enemies within the traditional left had yet heard of Guzman and the Shining Path. The movment spent years recruiting and preparing for its ultimate debut before it turned to violence. In 1978, however, Sendero went underground to lay the groundwork for the final struggle for power.

Sendero Luminoso finally burst onto the scene in May 1980 during the presidential election in a series of attacks against polling places in Ayachucho. Since this time, the organization has been both a source of growing concern for the government in Lima as well as a mystery. Sendero has issued very few public statements concerning its goals, political and economic agenda, or strategy of armed struggle. Most of what we know of the movement's ideology and world view has come from two short texts. The first was issued in July 1981 and the second in March 1982.[3] These have been supplemented by the trial testimony of captured Senderistas, the occasional communiqué, and slogans scrawled on the walls of public buildings. For years, the Senderista leadership refused to even be interviewed by the press, which it condemned out of hand as paid agents of the Lima regime. This rule was not broken until September 1986, when Guzman, in an unusual move, accepted an interview with *El Nuevo Diario*, a Lima-based newspaper.[4] As a rule, Sendero continues to pursue a policy of 'propaganda by the deed', rather than one of proselytizing through the mechanism of the press.

Little is known of Sendero's organizational make-up and decision-making structure. What is known suggests that Guzman, despite rumors of his death, retains tight authority over the movement, even as its range of operations has spread into most of Peru's 24 departments. Guzman's influence is exercised through a National Directorate and a Central Committee, which together oversee the movement's operations. The organization also appears to be broken into several regional commands that are responsible for recruitment and play a role in selecting local targets. Rank-and-file members are organized along cellular lines and draw upon the assistance of local sympathizers and part-time activists. Decision-making authority within the movement appears to be highly centralized. The organization itself, however, is highly atomized. Guzman operates through others. Very few Senderistas are reported to have actually had contact with or even seen Guzman.

Second-order leadership within Sendero appears to be shared among a number of individuals. Prominent among these are Julio Cesar Mezich, a mestizo, believed to be the number two man in the movement after Guzman; Osman Morote Barrionuevo, one of the few original leaders of Sendero still alive; and Augusta La Torre, the wife of Guzman and an important ideologue of the organization who is believed to have recently returned to Peru after residing for some years in Paris. Over the past few years Sendero has suffered the loss of much of its original leadership group. One of the first to die was Edith Lagos, who was killed by the army shortly after her escape from Huamanga prison in 1982. Antonio Diaz Martinez, reputed to be the number three man in the organization, was captured in December 1983 and killed during the uprising at Lurigancho penitentiary in June 1986. Diaz's replacement, Claudio Bellido Huaytalla, 'Comrade Caszely', who was thought to be the chief of operations for Sendero's central command (incorporating the regions of Ayachucho, Apurimac, and Huancavelica) was killed in October 1986 in a battle with security forces. Thirty-nine terrorists, including 13 ranking members of the organization, were reported to have been killed in the action when the army attacked a series of Sendero base camps in the area of Pomatambo, in a remote region of Ayachucho department.

What role the surviving leadership group plays in Sendero decision-making remains unclear. Though Guzman retains undisputed authority over the organization, the dispersed nature of Sendero's operations and the natural and imposed difficulties of maintaining timely communications in the back areas of highland Peru, suggest that Sendero's regional commands probably operate with some degree of tactical independence. This must also be the case at the level of individual cells, which for reasons of security as well as distance, appear to have limited day-to-day contact with Sendero's leadership, at any level. This autonomy, however, does not extend to the level of strategy, which resides in Guzman's hands alone. Sendero's command apparatus, while playing some role in coordinating organizational strategy, plays little identifiable role in the formulation of that strategy in the first place. It appears to serve principally as a means of transmitting orders and direction from Guzman and his immediate entourage down to the level of the local cell, Sendero's 'working level'.

Guzman, in short, remains the force behind the scenes. Under the *nom de guerre* of Comrade Gonzalo, he has carefully cultivated an image of genius and omnipresence among his followers. Photographs of Guzman reveal a plain, overweight, and uninspired-looking individual. Within Sendero, however, he is known as the 'Fourth Sword of Marxism', after Marx, Lenin and Mao. By force of personality, he has shaped Sendero in his own image, determining its agenda, direction and ideological orientation. Isolated and aloof, Guzman nevertheless exercises a strong hold over the movement's leadership and rank and file alike. To the highland peasantry, he is presented in an almost religious manner, an image designed to appeal to local superstition and custom as well, one suspects, to Guzman himself. Despite its national presence and size – 1,000 to 3,000 cadres – Sendero remains a highly individualized organization, established and based on a cult of personality of Comrade Gonzalo.

Authority and control within Sendero, in this respect, appears to hinge on some variant of what has been termed the charismatic leader–follower relationship. Such a relationship, according to one recent analysis, is based on four properties: (1) the group leader, in this case Abimael Guzman, is believed to possess a unique vision and superhuman qualities; (2) group followers unquestioningly accept the leader's views, statements and judgements; (3) they comply with his orders and directives without condition; and (4) they give the leader unqualified support and devotion.[5] While this relationship can be subject to breakdown over time, when it is operative it results in a unique bond of command between the leader of an organization and its rank-and-file membership. The leader under these conditions is much more than the simple head of the group. For a period of time, at least, he commands an absolute authority. He is viewed as a heroic figure by his followers, who assume the role of his disciples. A relationship of this nature will result in a high degree of group unity. It also delimits the role of the organization's secondary or mid-level leadership, whose principal role is to serve as a link between the charismatic leader and those who are sent out to do his bidding.

Sendero is a self-proclaimed Maoist organization. Its political agenda is based on Mao's writings and deeds, appropriately reinterpreted as the thought of Comrade Gonzalo. Sendero has called for the abolition of a national market economy, industry, the banking system, all foreign trade, the use of currency, and the establishment of a communal village-oriented economy based on a system of barter exchange. From what we know of this program it might resemble the rural economic schemes of the Khmer Rouge or the economic experiments of the Chinese leadership during the Great Leap Forward or the Cultural Revolution. These measures have sometimes been carried out in a small way in areas 'liberated' by Sendero forces. Upon moving into a village, Senderistas have been known to round-up and slaughter local landowners and turn their holdings over to the peasantry in two-hectare parcels. Anyone owning land of over two hectares is subject to be shot, as are those engaged in the cultivation of cash crops or the use of currency. Similarly, trade with the cities or other villages through the mechanism of local markets is halted, and the peasantry is forced to plant only for its own needs and those of the immediate community. The object of these measures is to hasten the end of the money-based economy and isolate the cities from the countryside.[6]

Sendero's stated goal is the creation of a 'new state of workers and peasants'. While expressly Maoist in orientation, Guzman's view of what this new state would look like owes much to the work of Jose Carlos Mariategui, the spiritual prophet of the Shining Path.[7] According to Mariategui, the original basis for Peruvian socialism lies in the pre-Columbian peasant community. This system, which was destroyed by the Spanish conquest and kept down by the inherited order in Lima, is to serve as the blueprint for a rejuvenated Andean socialism. The roots of this revolution lie logically in the traditional Indian populations of the altiplano, which are the descendants of this earlier order. While Sendero's operations have been largely confined to Peru, the movement has international goals.[8] According to Guzman, the scope of the revolution must ultimately be broadened to include the Quechua-speaking peoples of Bolivia, Columbia, Ecuador, Argentina, and Chile. Sendero's goal, in this respect, is not simply the overthrow of the government in Lima, but a larger Latin American revolution uniting the Quechua nation in a new socialist state.

Strategy and Operations

Armed struggle, in Guzman's view, is the only means of achieving victory. In the absence of an ability to confront the Peruvian state directly, this has meant a concerted campaign of terror against the symbols of Lima's authority, the economy, and foreign imperialism in all its various forms. Terror is also used as an instrument to enforce a revolutionary order in areas that have fallen under guerrilla control. According to the testimony of captured Senderistas, Guzman has planned for a protracted struggle to evolve roughly in three stages, not unlike the theory of guerrilla war developed by Mao Zedong in the 1930s.[9]

> Stage one is a period of 'agitation and propaganda'. The purpose of this stage is to mobilize a base of support in the countryside, establish a dedicated cadre and the first rudiments of a guerrilla army, and lay the groundwork for an expanded armed struggle.

> Stage two involves the creation of selected 'liberated zones'. These will serve as both strongholds and symbols of achievement. According to a document released by Sendero in March 1982, *Let's Advance the Guerrilla War!*, the movement has entered this period. Sendero's actions in this stage are expected to develop slowly, as the movement works to polarize society, continues to widen its area of rural control, and makes its first move to bring the war into the cities by establishing a network of urban supporters.

> Stage three involves a general uprising in the countryside, the collapse of urban society, and the destruction of the Lima regime. This is to be accomplished by gradually surrounding and besieging the cities and finally striking from within with an urban network.

As noted, Sendero first struck on the day of the presidential election in May 1980. Ironically, this date marked Peru's return to a civilian government after some 12 years of military rule. Sendero's initial actions, which were dismissed as an aberration, proved to be an ominous portent of things to come. Since this time, Sendero's campaign of terror has escalated rapidly, both in scope and character. From its initial base in Ayachucho, the movement's range of operations has since expanded to include most of Peru's administrative departments. During the first two years of the new Belaunde administration, attacks were primarily directed against rural targets. Over the past four years, the frequency of these attacks has increased while the list of targets has broadened to encompass many of the country's important urban centers. Government authorities now fear that Sendero may have also recently moved its headquarters out of the mountains into the Lima metropolitan area. At the very least, Sendero is known to maintain a network of supporters within Lima and several departmental capitals.[10]

Sendero's early operations (1980–81) were largely confined to minor acts of sabotage. Most of these were implemented in and around

Ayachucho. Attacks during this period were launched against local government offices, electric power stations and transmission lines, telecommunication facilities, and a wide variety of economic targets. Other actions included staged 'people's trials' to punish landowners, corrupt officials, or village merchants; and the establishment of the first 'zones of liberation' within the interior. While Sendero issued few communiqués during this period, proclamations were frequently attached to dead dogs hung from lamp posts, an act meant to symbolize the movement's condemnation of the 'running dogs' of international imperialism.

Sendero, then as now, rarely claimed credit for its actions. Many of the movement's early operations were consequently discounted as the work of other groups or unaffiliated terrorists. On the basis of this premise, and fearing that a counter-terrorist campaign could end only in the use of counter-terror by the army, the Belaunde administration resisted early calls by the military to enter Ayachucho to deal with the threat. By early 1981, however, the administration was forced to act. In March it passed a broad anti-terrorist law, imposing a range of stiff penalties on any person or group aiding or cooperating with terrorists. This was followed in October with the first declared state of emergency in Ayachucho. This move proved to be a desperate act of an increasingly besieged administration. It imposed a strict curfew in the departmental capital, suspended constitutional protection against arbitrary arrest, and opened the way for the first concerted use of force against the guerrillas. Following the imposed state of emergency the government sent 1,400 'Sinchis', the Peruvian Civil Guard, into Ayachucho to impose order.[11]

These measures were ultimately ineffective. As Belaunde had feared, the imposition of martial law and the use of the Civil Guard resulted in numerous excesses, probably doing more harm that good to the government's efforts to contain the Shining Path. Sendero, for its part, responded by widening the war. On 2 March 1982, the guerrillas launched a daring raid against a prison in Ayachucho city housing a large number of Senderistas. The battle for control of the prison lasted five hours and was carried out by between 50 and 60 guerrillas. It resulted in the escape of 54 convicted or suspected terrorists and 193 additional prisoners, most of whom were being held for drug-related crimes.[12] This operation was followed by a series of strikes against local police barracks, various public works, and a dynamic attack against the presidential palace in Lima. Responding to these actions, the government immediately renewed the state of emergency in Ayachucho.

In August, Sendero bombed five high-tension towers supplying electricity to the Lima-Callao Area. Though attacks against the country's electric power assets had been carried out as early as 1980, this was the largest and most effective operation to date. The bombings were expertly conducted, leading some officials to speculate that the guerrillas had received inside assistance. The attack effected a 525-mile corridor from the coastal cities of Trujillo to Ica. Nine million people – half the nation's population – were without electricty for 48 hours. Under cover of darkness, terrorist teams in Lima drove through the streets throwing sticks of dynamite into private shops, banks, and government facilities. Some 50 public buildings were bombed in the first night of the blackout, including the Palace of Justice, the Ministry of Economics, the government's Housing Bank, and the Ministry of Foreign Affairs.[13]

Sendero launched a second major attack on Lima's electrical grid in December. Four high-tension towers were destroyed in the attack, causing a complete failure in the capital and six other cities. Minutes after the blackout, Sendero lit a huge hammer and sickle that glowed from a hill overlooking Lima in celebration of Abimael Guzman's 48th birthday. Some 15,000 police and Civil Guards were rapidly mobilized and sent into the streets in anticipation of a general attack by Sendero's urban-based network. Two people were killed and 100 were arrested during the emergency. Documents found on one captured Senderista indicated that the blackout was to be the first in a series of planned actions against the capital city. The offensive, which was to involve both sabotage attacks and the killing of a number of government officials, was slated to be carried out over the Christmas holiday and given the designation of 'Operation Santa Claus'.

This action seems to have marked the opening salvo in a concerted campaign to bring the war to the capital. As one commentator has noted, terrorist strikes in Lima occurred on almost a daily basis during this period. Businesses were sacked, movie theaters, restaurants, and other public gathering places were bombed, and numerous police and bystanders were gunned down in the streets. In several cases, Sendero was reported to have seized schools, holding school officials at gunpoint while the students were treated to lectures on the goals of the revolution.[14]

Sendero's financial support appears to come from several sources. Its most important source of support are the Indian communities of the altiplano. While early contributions to the movement were often made willingly, today it appears that the majority of local aid is gathered as 'taxes', or forced donations. Additional support is garnered through bank robberies and 'expropriations' from local landowners, petty capitalists, and elements of the peasantry who are judged to be hostile to the objectives of the revolution. A final source of support seems to have been provided by elements in the drug trade, who have reportedly contributed to Sendero's cause in an effort to distract the authorities from their own illegal operations. Peru is thought to grow almost 50 per cent of the world's coca. Most of this comes from the upper Huallaga valley, the area of Cuzco, and parts of Cajamarca department, all of which are guerrilla strongholds.[15] By supporting Sendero, local *traficantes* have managed to buy some protection for their operations, both by avoiding becoming a target and by making it difficult for Peruvian authorities to enter their growing areas to control local production.

Sendero's most important source of weapons, mainly dynamite, has been the thousands of small mining camps dotting the Peruvian highlands.

These camps have proved to be impossible to protect. In one attack launched last year, a guerrilla team made off with over 92,000 sticks of TNT, providing it with the means to carry out local operations for months. The guerrillas have also become adept at producing molotov cocktails, pipe bombs, and home-made grenades. The latter are made from soft drink cans packed with gunpowder and nails. These have been known to be hurled from *huranos*, a traditional slingshot used by the highland Indians. Dynamite is supplemented by weapons stolen from the police. In contrast to the army and Civil Guard, the Senderistas are poorly armed and equipped. They manage to compensate for this deficiency, however, with surprise, their ability to select the time and place of attack, and a penchant for daring operations. While there is reason to believe that the balance of advantages may have recently shifted to the military, these factors, coupled with a fanatic ruthlessness, have kept Sendero in business.

Sendero's range of targets has continued to expand over the past three years. The first attack against a Peruvian military installation took place in June 1983, when guerrillas struck an army barracks outside of Lima. Until this time, Sendero had sought to avoid confronting the army directly, generally confining its attacks to isolated police posts against which it might organize a temporary superiority in numbers. Other attacks have been conducted against resort hotels, the American, Soviet, Chinese, East German, and Nicaraguan embassies, the Coca Cola bottling plant in Lima, Sears and Roebuck, offices of the Ford Motor Company, the Bank of America, and the Fiat Corporation, the US cultural center, the residences of the US and British ambassadors, a beauty contest, telecommunications facilities, the home of the Cuban military attaché, the headquarters of the ruling American Popular Revolutionary Alliance (APRA), the offices of Aeroflot, several Kentucky Fried Chicken concessions, scores of factories, bridges, dams, and other public works, and the Peruvian hydroelectric facility at Viconga.

Such attacks, far from being isolated incidents, are numerous and frequently conducted in a coordinated, if pre-planned, manner. In one operation, Sendero planted bombs at eight embassies and the same number of public and private buildings in a single night.[16] In another case, synchronized bombs were planted at targets as diverse as the US embassy, the Peruvian Sports Institute, and at two ARPA facilities in Lima, all of which are widely dispersed through the city. According to the Ministry of Interior (see Table 1), the number of attacks by Sendero has risen every year between 1980 and 1985. Guzman himself has claimed that the movement has conducted over 30,000 operations. As noted above, while estimates vary, Sendero may actually be responsible for carrying out as many as 12,000 terrorist actions over the past seven years resulting in a possible combined death toll of as high as 10,000.[17]

One of its most effective tactics has been the coordinated use of assassination and posted death threats to disrupt and paralyze local institutions. Targets have included local political institutions, labor

TABLE 1
SHINING PATH OPERATIONS

Year	Attacks
1980	219
1981	715
1982	891
1983	1,123
1984	1,760
1985	2,050
TOTAL	6,758

Source: Peruvian Ministry of Interior, cited in *El Nuevo Diario*, 5 Sept. 1986; *Terrorism*, Joint Publications Research Service, 1 Dec. 1986.

organizations, peasant associations, and even the police. Moving into an area, Sendero will declare the region to be a 'zone of liberation'. Large numbers of local administrators, community leaders, and 'traitors' will then be rounded-up and, after a brief 'trial', will invariably be shot, hung, mutilated, or beaten for their various crimes against the revolution. In certain cases, entire villages are reported to have been massacred either for refusing to cooperate with the guerrillas or cooperating with the authorities. After setting an example, Sendero will next publish a 'death list' of all those in the region who are to be brought to justice. Terrified, those whose names appear on the list, teachers, minor officials, priests, and other local leaders flee for their lives, leaving the peasantry to their fate and large areas in the hands of the Shining Path. In certain high risk areas – notably Ayachucho – orderly administration has required a permanent military presence.

The use of the army, which was finally authorized in Ayachucho in December 1982, has not been without its costs. While the military did succeed in stabilizing the situation within the department – though it by no means succeeded in stamping out all guerrilla activities – it did so at a significant toll. Six months after its intervention, the death toll in Ayachucho numbered almost 1,000. Even elements within the army leadership admitted that many of those arrested or killed were probably not connected with Sendero. As one ranking commander was quoted as saying, however, if the army kills 60, at least six can be expected to be Senderistas.[18] Recent efforts to combat Sendero through the creation of village militias have also led to abuses, encouraging vigilantism and providing villagers with the opportunity to settle personal scores under the guise of the law. In one incident in early 1983, eight journalists investigating the war in Ayachucho were attacked and killed by 100 machete-wielding peasants who allegedly mistook them for guerrillas. Most Peruvians, according to a poll taken shortly after this incident, did not accept the official account, believing instead that the army was behind the murders to discourage reporters from entering the area.[19]

Reports of abuses by the military, the Sinchis, and the police continue to be rife,[20] despite efforts by the new Garcia government to keep them in check. The security forces, which are frequently unable to distinguish Sendero supporters from its victims, have often operated on the premise that entire village populations were Sendero sympathizers, conducting mass arrests, indiscriminate interrogations, and village-wide searches. In other cases, the security forces are reported to have bribed village communities to attack others believed to be supporting guerrilla operations. The most serious single incident to date occurred in June 1986, in a counter-attack against a coordinated uprising by Sendero inmates in three Peruvian prisons.[21] Some 260 Senderistas were reported to have been killed in the assault. According to the military, the inmates, who were armed with crossbows, dynamite, and a handful of weapons seized from the guards, were all killed in the process of recapturing the prisons. It was later learned, however, that as many as 130 prisoners were captured alive, only to be executed by the Civil Guard. The incident created a crisis in the Garcia administration and resulted in the arrest of more than 100 individuals believed to be involved in the murders.[22]

Operational Pressures and Organizational Limits

Sendero has not been subject to the same internal divisions and factionalization that have characterized such groups as the PLO and the IRA. The organization has manifest a high degree of group cohesion and internal discipline. Though it has suffered very high casualties over the past six years, the morale, motivation, and solidarity of Sendero's membership still appear to be strong. To date, there have been no known challenges to Guzman's leadership, few defections, and no apparent success in penetrating the organization. The movement has also been able to show results. While measures to contain the spread of the insurgency have proven to be partially successful, Sendero is still able to operate in large areas of the country with little interference from government forces. This has tended to sustain group cohesion.

Sendero's early vitality seems to have been due to several factors. First, in form and expression, Sendero exhibits many of the qualities of a religious cult.[23] It is founded, in a sense, on the revelations of Comrade Gonzalo, has divided the world sharply between good and evil, maintains a highly rigid belief system, and demands absolute commitment on the part of its membership. Second, Sendero is completely isolated from society. In contrast to such groups as the Farabundo Marti National Liberation Front (FMLN), Freedom for the Basque Homeland (ETA), or Irish Republican Army (IRA), it maintains no legal or open front that might serve as a source of intra-organizational conflict, or as an alternative avenue of expression for individuals who have tired of the underground. Finally, Sendero, until the recent resurgence of Tupac Amaru and MIR, has virtually monopolized the resort to revolutionary violence. Group unity, as a number of commentators have noted, is always more difficult to preserve if there are competitors and, hence, alternatives in pursuing the armed struggle.[24]

One, however, must guard against exaggerating Sendero's potential based on the drama of its past actions. Despite its successes, Sendero is still a young organization. Until recently it has been a group in ascendency, expanding its size, reputation and range of operations with little apparent effort. There is reason to believe, however, that Sendero's future may not be as promising as its past. An examination of Sendero's structure, *modus operandi*, ideology, and world view suggest a number of important weaknesses that could lead to increasing organizational pressures within the group over the coming years. These could have important implications for Sendero's internal stability and will almost certainly have an important bearing on its future effectiveness.

First, Sendero's isolation and extremism, though an early source of strength, will ultimately prove to be a serious detriment to its ability to adapt to changing circumstances, expand, and possibly even maintain its membership. As suggested earlier, Sendero has rejected any and all associations with the legal left, or any other underground organization. Guzman has denounced Peru's legal left as 'parliamentary cretins', while such competitors as Tupac Amaru and Puka Llacta-Red Flag are dismissed as 'objective allies of reaction'. During its early years of operation, Sendero's sectarian quality helped to give the organization a distinct identity and probably played some role in boosting its early membership. Today there is reason to believe that its parochialism may have already become a serious liability.[25]

This rigid belief system has prohibited Sendero from creating a united opposition front against the regime and severely restricted its base of potential supporters. The united front concept has played an important role in most successful revolutionary struggles. One of its most ardent exponents ironically was Mao, who made it the centerpiece of his political strategy during the period of the Chinese civil war and later instituted it as a key principle in Chinese foreign policy. The purpose of the united front, as demonstrated most recently by the Sandinista National Liberation Front (FSLN), is to mobilize the largest possible level of opposition against the target regime by appealing to a broad range of potential supporters. The magnitude of the resulting opposition provides the revolutionary movement with an aura of legitimacy and a sizeable base of militant support. Sendero, however, has moved in quite the opposite direction. Its parochial view of Peruvian society and uncompromising ideology have made any association with even the underground left impossible, with a resulting dimunition in both its support and effectiveness.

Second, and related to this, Sendero has avoided affiliating its struggle with any potential outside sponsor or even establishing ties with other underground organizations operating in the region. During the early 1980s, the Belaunde administration made periodic claims that the movement was receiving assistance from foreign sources, including Cuba, foreign priests, West European 'hippies', the Spanish left, and other regional guerrilla groups. Far from seeking its assistance, however, the international left has been roundly condemned by Sendero as 'Fascists', 'traitors', and 'revisionists'. Guzman once dismissed Che Guevera as a 'choir girl', while the Soviet Union is condemned for its corruption and treasonist ideology. The current Chinese leadership has been singled out for particular abuse for its 'betrayal' of Mao Zedong. Similar views are expressed toward other regional guerrilla groups such as the April 19 Movement (M-19), MIR, Armed Revolutionary Forces of Columbia (FARC), or Alfaro Lives Damnit, all of which are considered to be the 'puppets' of 'foreign masters'. Sendero's only known foreign contact was established with Albania during the mid-1970s. Since this time, however, even the late Enver Hoxa has been condemned for his revisionist tendencies.

In short, at a time when most Latin guerrilla groups appear to be broadening or at least strengthening their foreign or intra-regional ties, Sendero remains isolated and aloof as a matter of policy.[26] Such ties have played an important role over the years in the comparative success and certainly the durability of groups like M-19, FARC, or the FSLN. In Sendero's case, the movement unilaterally has distanced itself from the material aid and stature that can be gained through foreign sponsorship or assistance. This has worked to restrict its influence, level of support, and area of operations. This has become a particular problem because of the movement's international objectives. Guzman appears to have made a number of attempts to expand Sendero's range of operations into Columbia, Bolivia, and possibly Ecuador. Individuals operating under Sendero's banner have also surfaced in Venezuela.[27] In each of these cases, however, his efforts have never taken root because of a lack of any local network of support.

Third, Sendero's use of terror has already probably become self-defeating. Terrorism alone has rarely led to a successful revolutionary outcome. Where it has been used effectively, it has been employed as a selective component in a larger program of armed struggle. As Chalmers Johnson has noted, successful guerrilla movements, as a simple matter of survival, characteristically behave well toward the civilian population. If they are to persevere, much less win, they will require the active assistance of the local peasantry, for material support, intelligence, as an aid to mobility, and as a base for recruitment. Although they may be able to acquire much of this assistance at gunpoint in the short run, their longevity will ultimately depend upon the active cooperation of a supportive populous.[28]

Sendero's early base of support has not survived its liberal use of terror to enforce obedience and unpopular 'revolutionary reforms'.[29] Sendero has made a regular practice of assassinating local community leaders, disfiguring peasant voters, indiscriminately destroying crops and live-stock, and killing or maiming anyone suspected of cooperating with the government or resisting Sendero's authority. In the end, its crimes against its own chosen constituency are probably more severe and certainly more frequent than those committed against the Peruvian government or the rest of the population. As a result, Sendero has been having increasing difficulty over the past two years replacing its losses and maintaining its level of rural support. The recruitment problem has been complicated by the organization's geographic isolation. Sendero appears to have lost its once strong university connection when it went underground. What ties remained have gradually dwindled over the years, further severing its association with mainstream Peruvian society.

Fourth, Sendero faces a number of technical constraints. These are, once again, the result of its parochialism, which has kept it in Peru, constrained its target set, and limited the weapons, tactics, and technologies that it has at its disposal. As noted earlier, Sendero's only weapons are guns – the largest of which are automatic rifles – and dynamite. All of these must be gathered from local sources such as the police. For the first time in recent years it has also reportedly begun to use two-way radios. While it has certainly managed to kill a lot of people over the past seven years, it has never posed a direct threat to the regime which, in the final analysis, has more guns and is better organized.[30] Nor has it ever been able to bring its operations into the world arena, despite its list of international enemies and its interest in hitting such international targets as embassies, foreign dignitaries, multinational corporations, and other symbols of foreign imperialis, whether on the right or left. Sendero is very much a 'home-grown' organization, with international pretensions but no international contacts, experience, or presence.

Finally, Sendero may well face certain important organizational limits. As noted earlier, the movement appears to be organized along cellular lines. While ultimate decision-making authority on matters of strategy, tactics, and ideology presides with Abimael Guzman, the organization itself is highly compartmentalized.[31] Decisions are made at the top and communicated downward to cells operating throughout the country. A structure of this nature, while difficult to defeat, can also prove to be quite difficult to control. In the case of Sendero, the control problem is complicated by the dispersed nature of its operations and the geographic isolation of many of its cells. On a daily basis, local units or groups of units are self-sustaining and may need little in the way of central guidance or support. Local cells play a large role in selecting their targets and their general operating instructions are clear: carry out as many actions as possible in the shortest period of time. The movement's loose organizational structure, however, has made it difficult to carry out coordinated operations on a national level unless these attacks are carefully planned in advance. This has, in turn, significantly restricted its ability to pose a real threat to the regime, by limiting its initiative, its ability to take advantage of opportunities or react to changing circumstances, and the degree to which it can mobilize against the state.[32]

Sendero may also be unusually vulnerable to the death of Abimael Guzman. The movement, as we have seen, is highly personalistic.[33] It is a reflection of Guzman's world view, personality, and ideological idiosyncrasies. While it possesses a nominal doctrine and chain of command, it remains highly dependent on Guzman's personal authority. Little effort apears to have been made to institutionalize the decision-making process or even hedge against the day when Comrade Gonzalo might pass from the scene. The risk this poses is increased by Sendero's decentralization which, in this case as in others, serves as a constant threat to the movement's cohesion and internal identity. Sendero has been able to overcome this problem in the past because of the bond established between the rank and file and the 'Thought of Comrade Gonzalo'. The loyalty of the movement's membership, however, appears to be to the man and his image rather than to the organization and its loosely articulated objectives. Guzman, in this respect, is much more than Sendero's founder and current head, he serves as its spiritual leader and guiding light. Whether the organization could survive his death in its present form and configuration seems problematic.

These factors have placed inherent limits on Sendero's range of operations, its ability to endure, and its future effectiveness. These constraints are already beginning to be felt. For one thing, the sharp rise in incidents witnessed between 1980 and 1985 does not appear to have been repeated last year. It is even possible that Sendero may have carried out fewer major operations in 1986 than in 1985. Sendero's actions have also assumed a certain repetitive quality. Dynamite attacks by Senderistas have become a routine. While this indicates, on the one hand, that Sendero is still ablëto operate with relative freedom, it also reveals the limits of the group's repertoire. Sendero, to be sure, can still capture the headlines. It is also capable of killing people with disturbing regularity. As its actions have become more commonplace, however, large elements of the population have become desensitized to its presence. There is only so much one can accomplish with dynamite and small arms. It is quite possible that Sendero has reached or is approaching its technical and tactical ceiling. If so, it will be difficult for the group to maintain its current profile in the face of mounting efforts by the government to defeat it.

Sendero's parochialism and rigidity, furthermore, are likely to limit its ability to adapt to these and related challenges. If true, this could lead to increasing pressures within the organization for a change in strategy and, with it, the first challenge to Guzman's authority. As noted earlier, cohesion and group solidarity within Sendero still appear to be strong. Significant dissension or growing dissatisfaction with Guzman's leadership, if present, would be revealed in a reduction in the group's propensity to take risks, a high rate of defection, a decline in prisoner morale, an increase in 'enforcement' killings, and the possible establishment of a breakaway front. We have seen no evidence of this to date. While not an issue today, however, these are likely to become increasing problems over the coming years. Sendero has only recently begun to confront its limitations. Unless it is able to transcend these limits with flexibility and innovation, the movement is likely to be subject to increasing internal conflict.

None of this means that Sendero is facing an immediate crisis. Nor does it mean that we will necessarily see any significant reduction in Sendero's operations in the next few years. For all its limitations, the Shining Path remains an established and resilient organization. Attempts on the part of the Belaunde and Garcia administrations to find common ground with the movement have not succeeded in the past and can be expected to fail in the future. Its decentralized structure, while posing problems of control, has also made it very difficult to contain and defeat. Even the eventual death or capture of Abimael Guzman is not likely to lead to the group's immediate demise; as martyr or legend he would probably remain a force behind the movement and an example for those who would succeed him for some time to come. Given the strength of Peruvian security forces, however, the limitations within which it has chosen or been forced to operate, the movement's organizational profile, and its apparently limited popular base, it is not possible that Sendero will succeed in seizing power in Peru. Indeed, it seems possible that the organization has already passed its prime. Its own excesses and lack of a popular and well-defined political agenda have severely constrained its ability to mobilize new supporters and have and will continue to restrict its range of operations.

The real problem lies not in a Sendero takeover, but in the threat the movement poses to Peru's fragile democratic institutions. The Garcia administration faces the dilemma confronted by all democratic societies attempting to combat widespread domestic subversion: how to defeat the threat successfully without undermining the very institutions and principles one is fighting to preserve. This dilemma is all the more profound in the case of Peru, where the government faces the additional threat of military intervention. The Garcia administration is walking a fine line between the competing objectives of defeating Sendero, guarding against the use of counter-terror by the army and police, and avoiding alienating the military or providing it with any incentive to take matters into their own hands. Sendero, as an organization, will eventually be defeated. The future of Peruvian democracy, however, will ultimately depend on how successful the Garcia government is in managing this challenge.

NOTES

1. Gustavo Gorriti Ellenbogen and Carlos Torres Enriquez, 'The Path of Abimael', *Caretas* (Lima), 7 June 1982. Special Translation, 'Biographic Data on Sendero Luminoso Leader Abimael Guzman Reynoso', Foreign Broadcast Information Service (FBIS), 3 Aug. 1982.
2. David P. Werlich, 'Peru: The Shadow of the Shining Path', *Current History*, Feb. 1984, pp.80–81.
3. These are *Nuevo Gobierno y la Perspectiva Economica Politica y de la Lucha de Clases en General*, 1981 (The New Government and Prospects for Economics, Politics, and

Class Struggle in General), and in 1982, *Desarrollemos la Guerra de Guerrillos!* (Let's Advance the Guerrilla War!).

4. See *El Nuevo Diario* (Lima), 15 Sept. 1986. Translation, 'Peru: Shining Path Leadership, Plans, Policies', *Terrorism*, Joint Publications Research Service (JPRS), 1 Dec. 1986, pp.11–56.

5. Ann Ruth Wilner, *The Spellbinders* (New Haven, CT: Yale University Press, 1984), pp.18–29. See also the analysis by Jerrold M. Post, 'Narcissism and the Charismatic Leader-Follower Relationship', N.D., unpublished manuscript, George Washington University Medical School.

6. Michael Radu, 'Sendero Luminoso', in *Insurgent and Terrorist Groups in Latin America*, DIA-Report (Philadelphia: Foreign Policy Research Institute, 1984), pp.529–30.

7. Jose Carlos Mariategui (1894–1930) was the founding father of the Peruvian Socialist Party in the 1920s. His views on rural socialism are developed in his most prominent work, *Siete Ensayas* (Seven Essays). Peter Gaupp, 'Peru: A "Shining Path" of Darkness', *Swiss Review of World Affairs*, Jan. 1984, pp.27–31.

8. Jesus Reyes Munante, *Oiga* (Lima), translation, 'Shining Path Goals, Philosophy Reviewed', *Latin America* (JPRS), 9 Aug. 1984, pp.66–72.

9. See the discussion by Raul Gonzales, *Debate* (Lima), Sept. 1983, pp.24–46. See also Mao Zedong, 'On Protracted War', in *Selected Military Writings* (Peking: Foreign Language Press, 1968), pp.210–19.

10. Adolfo Huirse, *El Nacional* (Lima), translation, 'Aims, Tactics, Organization of the Shining Path', *Terrorism* (JPRS), 22 May 1986, pp.1–13.

11. David P. Werlich, pp.81–2.

12. Robert F. Lamberg, 'Dynamite and Democracy in Peru', *Swiss Review of World Affairs*, Oct. 1982, pp.14–15.

13. Data on Sendero operations, unless otherwise noted, are drawn from the RAND Chronology on International Terrorism.

14. David P. Werlich, p.82.

15. Mark S. Steinitz, 'Insurgents, Terrorists, and the Drug Trade', *Washington Quarterly* (Fall 1985), pp.142–3; and Richard B. Craig, 'Illicit Drug Traffic and U.S.–Latin American Relations', *Washington Quarterly* (Fall 1985), pp.108–11.

16. Adolfo Huirse, p.2.

17. These figures represent a composite based on the RAND Chronology of International Terrorism.

18. Quoted in Raul Gonzalez, *Debate*, p.46.

19. Cynthia McClintock, 'Sendero Luminoso: Peru's Maoist Guerrillas', *Problems of Communism*, Sept.–Oct. 1983, p.31.

20. See, for example, Tim Johnson, 'Peruvian Military Charged With Fighting Terror With Terror', *The Christian Science Monitor*, 20 Feb. 1985; and Jackson Diehl, 'Legal Process Strained in Peru', *The Washington Post*, 4 March 1985.

21. Reported in the *Los Angeles Times*, 19/20 June 1986.

22. Such incidents have been widely reported. The reaction on the part of the Garcia administration to the excesses of the army and other security forces has been quite vigorous. This has led to widespread speculation that the military, at some point, will be compelled to move against the regime and prosecute the war without civilian constraints.

23. For a general discussion, see William S. Bainbridge and Rodney Stark, 'Cult Formation: Three Compatible Models', *Sociological Analysis* (Winter 1979), pp.283–95.

24. See the discussion by Martha Crenshaw, 'An Organizational Approach to the Analysis of Political Terrorism', *ORBIS* (Fall 1985), pp.465–89. It is interesting that such rigidity is a common trait of religious or quasi-religious terrorist organizations. See David C. Rapoport, 'Fear and Trembling: Terrorism in Three Religious Traditions', *American Political Science Review* (Sept. 1984), pp.658–77.

25. David Scott Palmer, 'The Sendero Luminoso Rebellion in Rural Peru', in Georges Fauriol (ed.) *Latin American Insurgencies* (Washington, DC: NDU Press, GPO,

1985), p.88.

26. Richard A. Finney, 'Growing Unity Among South American Guerrillas', *Journal of Defense and Diplomacy* (July 1986), pp.21–4, 71.
27. Michael Radu, pp.541–4.
28. Chalmers Johnson, *Revolutionary Change*, 2nd ed. (Stanford, CA: Stanford University Press, 1982), pp.149–50.
29. The evidence suggests that Sendero was able to elicit widespread support in Ayachucho among the peasantry during the early 1980s. See the discussion by Cynthia McClintock, 'Why Peasants Rebel: The Case of Peru's Sendero Luminoso', *World Politics* (Oct. 1984), pp.50–62.
30. As Johnson notes, revolutionary subversion will not succeed in the face of a capable and cohesive army. Insurgent bands are no match for professional troops. While they can create havoc on a selective basis, they cannot topple a regime that commands an effective army determined to preserve the status quo.
31. Some of the implications of such an organizational structure are discussed by J.K. Zawodny, 'Infrastructure of Terrorist Organizations', *Conflict Quarterly* (Spring 1981), pp.24–31.
32. It is again ironic that Mao's own theories of guerrilla warfare emphasize the critical importance of strategic, operational, and tactical flexibility. 'An entire gamut of means may be utilized to achieve a single end; and frequently negotiations, intrigue and persuasion are perceived as more efficacious than violence.' Howard L. Boorman and Scott A. Boorman, 'Strategy and National Psychology in China', *Annals of the American Academy of Political and Social Science* (March 1967), p.149.
33. Guzman is believed to suffer from irreversible kidney disease characterized by the gradual deterioration of the renal filtering process. The disease has been tentatively diagnosed as nephritis. If accurate, the question of transition may become an issue sooner than is commonly assumed. See the report in *El Nacional* (Lima), 6 Nov. 1986.

II. MOTIVATIONS AND JUSTIFICATIONS

The Terrorist Revolution: Roots of Modern Terrorism

Zeev Ivianski

De Tocqueville was the first to detect the rise of the professional revolutionary. He describes the phenomenon, Melven Richter tells us, as

> a new human type, formed by total revolution and destined to play a prominent role in the politics of the nineteenth and twentieth centuries. The professional revolutionary promises to realize the doctrine of the movement in all its purity. The price he exacts is the absolute obedience of his followers and the exclusive right to speak in their name.

De Tocqueville also foresaw that the rise to power of such revolutionaries would be inextricably bound up with a total disregard for the will of the people, and hence that one of the manifestations of their rule would be expressed in actions taken 'in the name of nations, without consulting them and claiming their gratitude while trampling them underfoot'. 'Until our day', de Tocqueville writes, 'it had been thought that tyranny was odious in all its forms. Now it has been discovered that there are legitimate tyrannies and sacred injustices, provided that they are exercised in the name of the people.' He also correctly assessed the tremendous force of the professional revolutionaries, which derives from the conjunction of the sacred aim of changing the face of society and resurrecting humankind, with the fervency of those instincts that are so directly connected with the self-interest of the revolutionaries.[1]

Filippo Michele Buonarotti* is the man whose personality, thought, and work most typify the modern professional revolutionary. Buonarotti served as the archetype in whom were already obvious those signs that later characterized the revolutionary underground and the dual personality of the modern revolutionary – the two different faces, one for the outside world and the other for the underground. This duality included a complex network of activities carried on simultaneously in different fields, the apparent fitting into legal society and the secret conspiracy with the underground. The complicated structure of the secret society developed a general staff, a central committee, a secret lodge, anonymous in name and identity, and a network of agents and cells on different levels of involvement, responsibility, and information. To these were added the principle of infiltrating various bodies and organizations,

---

* F.M. Buonarotti: 1761–1837 revolutionary, active in the Radical Jacobin wing and later in the Babeuf conspiracy (1793), published in 1824 his *Histoire de la Conspiration de Légalité*, which had a tremendous impact on the socialist movement.

including the army and the civilian government's bureaucracy and, above all, the principle that no means were to be rejected that could lead to achieving sacred ends.[2]

From Blanqui** the revolutionary underground absorbed the concept that the social revolution was dependent upon the seizure of political power. Blanqui's own personality expressed the full ideal of total commitment, the complete surrender of one's private life for the sake of the cause. 'Communism', Blanqui wrote, 'must abstain from straying into utopian by-ways and must never diverge from politics'. By politics he meant the revolutionary struggle for control of the regime: this constituted the essence of conspiracy, of insurrection, of the revolution itself. From this there followed the stress on the present action. 'Let us concern ourselves with the present day', says Blanqui, 'for tomorrow does not belong to us ... our only obligation is to ready good materials for the building of that tomorrow, the rest does not lie within our capabilities'. He rejected parliamentarism and feared the majority decisions that would result from a general election. 'The majority that is won by fear or by the lash is no majority of true citizens, but rather one a herd of slaves', Blanqui claimed.[3] In the course of time, Blanqui's and Buonarotti's secret societies were to prove abortive, and their conspiracies equally ineffectual, yet the principles they championed and on which they based these societies were later – in the hands of the professional, determined and intelligent revolutionaries amid favorable historical circumstances – to become the cornerstones of the modern revolutionary underground. From Blanqui and Buonarotti that terrorist warfare and the underground that conducted it were to derive their organizational patterns and the laws that governed their struggle. Blanquism drew lessons and new patterns of revolutionary activity from the experience of the abortive revolutions in nineteenth-century Europe. The seizure of power by any and all means was essential, whether as the starting point of all revolution or as the essence and purpose of the revolution itself.[4] Importance was placed on the worship of the revolutionary deed and not on high-flown revolutionary rhetoric, patterns of hierarchical organization were cultivated along with the myth of the 'Executive Committee' and the 'Central Committee' which were at time nothing more than mere phantoms of imagination and legend. Also cultivated was the myth of a great force, even if this, too, was at times nothing more than the systematic deception of the members of the revolutionary association themselves.[5] The revolutionary needed to acquire two-facedness and to penetrate into every facet of government and society. A hero of a thousand faces, the revolutionary agent was to be found everywhere, to see and yet not be seen. To engage in underground activity and yet to maneuver openly the movement required a revolutionary elitism and was to develop an echelon that served as its shock force, its vanguard, acting in the name of the mass but turning

** Louis Auguste Blanqui (1805–81) French revolutionary leader. A passionate extremist and master of insurrection, he spent 37 years of his life in prison.

aside from them in scorn. The art of revolutionary warfare or insurrection was raised to a scientific level with the adoption of modern systems of military strategy, technology and propaganda.

The Revolutionary Party as the General Staff in Revolutionary Warfare

The degeneration of revolutionary warfare, and a vicious struggle between terror and counter-terror, generally speaking precedes ideological formulation of terror as a revolutionary strategy, for ideologies usually attempt to explain events which they themselves did not bring about. The insurrections of the mid-nineteenth century were in essence spontaneous, engendered by the invisible machinery of mass ferment and decided by a confrontation between those who manned the barricades and the armed forces of the existing regime. That situation changed with the developments of the second half of the century. The battle of the barricades became a historical anachronism: the soldier no longer saw his opponent as a man of 'the people', but rather as a rebel, a plunderer, a wild thing, an 'outcast of society', and the soldier had more sophisticated ways to fight. This led Engels to conclude, in the *Introduction* to Marx's *The Class Struggles in France, 1848–1850*, that 'the time of surprise attacks, of revolutions carried through by small conscious minorities at the head of unconscious masses, is past'.[6] As Engels sees it, the time of the mass parties has now come. And yet the revolutions of the early twentieth century were not carried out by mass parties but by small conscious minorities. The art of revolutionary warfare did change, but its standard bearers continued to be that conspiratorial nucleus, the general staff of the revolution. From here on, no revolution succeeded unless the minority heading it adopted an organizational pattern, an ability to command resources and manpower, and a capacity for decision which surpassed those of the ruling regime. Thus, Jules Monnerot claims that all the revolutions of the twentieth century that proved to be successful were led by revolutionary general staffs.

The modern army and system of warfare posed a further problem – how should one construct an army to oppose that of the regime? 'This new army', as Monnerot characterized the Party, 'was to wage a new type of war ... not against the enemy, but against its own government; it was not intended for open campaigns or for attacking fortified positions, but for undermining the social order'. The revolutionary organization would have an advantage in that it accepted none of the limitations and reservations of conventional warfare, namely, the distinction between war and peace, between military and civilian. Essentially, it was a general staff that had no need of declarations of war. 'The mere existence of the Party reveals or implies a state of war which can only end with the final destruction of all pre-existing social structure.'[7]

The central problem of revolutionary warfare lay in the successful coordination of the party's organization, planning and initiative – the work of the general staff of professional revolutionaries – with the people's insurrection. The difficulty lay in correlating the spontaneous act of the masses with the conscious actions of the revolutionary nucleus. Trotsky believed that

> Just as the blacksmith cannot seize the red hot iron in his naked hand, so the proletariat cannot directly seize the power; it has to have an organization accommodated to this task. The coordination of the mass insurrection with the conspiracy, the subordination of the conspiracy to the insurrection, the organization of the insurrection through the conspiracy constitutes that complex and responsible department of revolutionary politics which Marx and Engels called 'the art of insurrection'.[8]

Thus, the central committee was responsible for organizing the chaos of public insurrection as a tool of revolutionary change.

The Blanquist Formulation

Marx and Engels adopted the art of revolutionary warfare, essentially the conspiratorial action by a revolutionary minority, only in the course of the 1848–49 revolution, and even then as part of the Jacobin–Blanquist tradition. The question of their allegiance to this tradition is also open to discussion and dispute,[9] but Marx never retracted his *Address of the Central Bureau to the Communist League*. Nor are his various comments of the questions of revolutionary terror uneqivocally negative. The Blanquist elements revealed in Marx's and Engels' works that were seized upon by Lenin and Trotsky and elevated to the status of an all-encompassing doctrine of the art of revolutionary insurrection and justifying revolutionary terrorism were, it is true, stressed by them arbitrarily, but they were genuinely in Marx's texts. Lenin's dictum that 'in revolutionary times the borders of the possible are extended a thousandfold', and that 'during a revolution the objective situation changes rapidly and suddenly' is certainly in the spirit of the attitude adopted by Marx and Engels during the 1848–49 revolutions, the Paris Commune and the terror of the Narodnaya Volya movement. When Trotsky writes that 'an element of conspiracy almost always enters to some degree into any insurrection. Being historically conditioned by a certain stage in the growth of a revolution, a mass insurrection is never purely spontaneous', his critique is Blanquist, and he admits as much.[10] Terrorist warfare of the Narodnaya Volya was also given a distinctly Blanquist flavor. Thus, Oshanina writes that the members of the Executive Committee, who were all (excepting herself) of a populist background, 'ended up by becoming Jacobians, more or less', she explained, 'the members began less and less to believe in the ability of the people to achieve anything by their own efforts and began instead to attach increasing importance to the initiative taken by the revolutionaries'.[11]

The demand for a re-evaluation of the tactics and techniques of revolutionary warfare and the call to learn some lessons from the defeats of the past in barricade warfare and insurrection came in Blanqui's *Instructions pour une prise d'armes*, written apparently in 1869, but not published until 1930.[12] In the course of analysis of the failures of the 1848–49 revolutions and the reasons for the defeat of the war of the barricades, Blanqui listed the advantages enjoyed by a revolutionary elite: 'They fight for an ideal, it is enthusiasm and not fear that motivates them ... they have heart and brains. No army in the world can compare to this elite corps of men.' What was missing however was organization, unity, and integrated action that follows a single plan, for 'organization spells victory'. Thence Blanqui went on to define his new approach to the art of warfare. 'The heroes behind the writing desks', he declared, 'scorn the sword just as the officers scorn their empty works'. Unlike Engels, Blanqui continued to believe in barricade and street warfare. In 1906, Lenin again expressed enthusiasm for a new tactic of barricade warfare that had emerged as a result of the adoption of modern military techniques and the widespread use of dynamite and hand-grenades. The partisan warfare he preached in 1906 also included the use of individual terror and expropriation of the state's monies. Thus, he wrote in 1906,

> The phenomenon in which we are interested is the *armed* struggle. Armed struggle pursues two *different* aims, which must be *strictly* distinguished: in the first place, this struggle aims at assassinating individuals, chiefs and subordinates in the army and police; in the second place, it aims at the confiscating of monetary funds both from the government and from private persons.

Rejecting the 'stereotype' condemnation of this struggle as Blanquist or anarchist, Lenin went on to stress that 'It is not partisan actions which disorganize the movement, but the weakness of a party which is incapable of taking such actions *under its control*'.[13]

V. Burtsev, however, anticipated Lenin in calling for a close study of the art of insurrection. In his pamphlet, *To Arms*, published in London in 1903, he described the art of warfare as having progressed to a high level. 'One must think of the victory even during the struggle', he says, 'we must not let our thoughts be distracted by concern as to how we are to win the support of the bourgeoisie.' Burtsev here also preached the taking of hostages from the ranks of the leading personalities and 'favorites' of the bourgeoisie and the authorities so that they could afterwards be used to regain prisoners and win compensation for the people. 'The taking of hostages', he wrote, 'is the only way in which the enemy can be forced to relate to the people as a party to the struggle'. Further, 'He who devotes himself to the affairs of the revolution cannot do otherwise than place himself at the behest of its awful laws'.[14] Following the 9 January 1905 episode, Lenin gave himself up to researching the 'art of warfare', translating a treatise on street fighting by Cluseret – the 'red general' of the Paris Commune – studying Clausewitz, and trying to fathom the attitudes of Marx and Engels on the art of insurrection.

The Art of Terrorist Warfare

Two modern pamphlets published in Geneva in 1880 discuss the art of revolutionary warfare and sum up the lessons to be drawn from the century's abortive revolutions, the defeat of the Paris Commune, and revolutionary action in Russia. Both were the work of émigrés, members of the Narodnaya Volya, temporarily removed from the fray. These were Nicholas Morozov's *Terrorist Struggle* and V. Tarnovski's (G. Romanenko) *Terrorism and Routine*.[15] Neither of these works served as a practical guide to revolutionary struggle, nor were they a source of its inspiration, but at the same time they clearly laid down the path to terrorist warfare as an art of modern, scientific revolutionary war. To them it was the only system of struggle that provided any answer to the supremacy of the reigning political and military establishment.

Morozov

Nicholas Morozov was an early champion of terror to promote revolution. When, in 1874, the 'Going to the People' movement started, he was an early secret enlistee where he became an apprentice blacksmith and woodchopper.[16] Subsequently, he went through every single one of the movement's developments, starting with the 'Propaganda Association', via the 'Circle of the Troglodytes', the 'Chaikovskyists', the 'Land and Liberty',[17] and finally into the extreme terrorism of Narodnaya Volya. In 1875 he was sent to Geneva to take part in the editing of the *Robotnik*. There he met Tkachev who gave him Schiller's *William Tell* to read, and he perceived 'a new report of armed struggle', that was to replace 'the old, cruel struggle in which so many thousands had fallen in vain'.[18] He later poured out his heart-searchings to Kravchinsky (Stepniak, as was his literary pseudonym): 'I have given much thought to the course of armed struggle, to all those popular insurrections, to the barricades, to those clashes between the masses and the armed soldiers, all of which were so fearfully cruel. Thousands have perished in vain, leaving behind many a broken heart.' 'Would it not be better to adopt a David and Goliath system?' he asks. Kravchinsky, who, though he was one of the first to have carried out terror acts, never adopted terrorism as a system, replied that the danger was that if William Tell was thus made into a hero worthy of emulation, there would subsequently arise dozens of feeble-minded imitators, capable of taking pot-shots at the enemies of mankind as freely as could be until the system eventually sank so deep into the mire that 'you yourself will be ashamed'.[19] Perhaps he did not know how truly his prophecy was to be fulfilled. When, on 24 January 1878 Vera Zasulich's shot rang out, Morozov finally felt that 'now something is about to happen that was bound to occur after three years of this awful persecution. Now our Charlotte Corday has appeared, and the William Tells will follow soon.'[20]

Neo-Partisan Warfare

The years of prison sentences, executions and the life of suffering led by the thousands involved in the Going to the People movement all combined to convince Morozov of the need to embark on face-to-face armed struggle against Czardom, though this was totally opposed to his character and personality. His autobiographical notes show the constant inner struggle by which he was torn, drawn as he was to theory and science and yet at the same time sensing always a moral compulsion to accompany his comrades in the face of every danger. Olga Lyubatovich[21] described the strange figure he cut: a dried-up man, tall, with the face of a scholar, yet bristling with pistols and preaching terror. He took part in terrorist actions and in attempts to free comrades from prison, though they nearly all ended in failure. With the establishment of the 'Land and Liberty' movement and the founding of its journal, Morozov became a member of the editorial board together with A.D. Klements and Kravchinsky, both of whom were later replaced by Plekhanov and Tikhomirov. Disagreements between Mozorov, Plekhanov and Tikhomirov led to the split in the 'Land and Liberty' movement and to the setting up of the Narodnaya Volya. Morozov's articles calling for a neo-partisan struggle, that is, terrorism, and Solovyev's 1 April 1879 attempt on the life of Alexander II were the direct cause of the split. At that time, Morozov urged the adoption of a 'neo-partisan system whose sole aim would be to ensure for all freedom of speech, of print, of assembly and of social parties'.[22] Because of the bitter differences of opinion that emerged among the editorial board (Plekhanov was totally opposed to all political struggle waged by violence, while Tikhomirov was prepared only to endorse agrarian terror), it was suggested that Morozov put out a special bulletin in which he would be free to advance his ideas – this was the *Bulletin of the Land and Liberty* whose first issue appeared on 12 March 1879. But this, he saw, was no solution. 'Life itself has inexorably set us on a new path', he claimed. Thus, from among former members of the Going to the People movement there emerged within the ranks of Land and Liberty a new faction – the 'Freedom or Death' group – among whom were found those who were later to become the members of the Executive Committee, Alexander Kvyatkovsky, Mikhailov, Zundelvich, Shirayev and Morozov.

An article by Morozov in the *Bulletin of the Land and Liberty* of 14 March 1879, under the title of *Political Assassination* made the point that

> political assassination is in the present circumstances, the sole means of self-defense and one of the best methods of agitation. By dealing a blow at the very centre of governmental organization, its awful force will give a mighty shock to the whole regime. This blow will transmit itself, as an electric current, thoughout the entire state and will cause disruption and confusion in all its activities.

Political assassination should be carried out by secret societies, he said, for it was this 'secrecy which gives a small group of daring men the ability to fight against millions of organized, obvious and visible enemies'. When to secrecy there is added

> political assassination, as a systematic means of attack, then these men become truly terrifying to their enemies. From this point onwards, the enemy will have no choice but to go always in fear of his life never knowing whence and when the avenging hand will strike. Political assassination is the carrying out of revolution in the present.

It was, he wrote, a truly terrifying weapon, for 'there is no defense against it, no mighty armies or legions of spies can vanquish it'.[23]

It is not suprising that this article became the center of controversy at the Voronezh gathering where the split in the movement emerged. Morozov avoided the use of the term 'terror' which was already accepted by the public since in his view, it did not fit the course he was advocating. But to his regret the term was already too deeply rooted within public consciousness and eventually he adopted it. Thus, he entitled his pamphlet on neo-partisan struggle as *The Terrorist Struggle*, and even described himself as a 'terrorist' at his trial.[24]

Morozov drew up the statutes and programmatic statements at the Lipetsk conference where the Czar's assassination was in effect decided upon. The conversation that took place between Morozov and Mikhailov typifies the mood current in Lipetsk among those who initiated the swing towards political assassination: Mikhailov expressed his conviction that great changes would eventually sweep over Russia but that these would be brought about 'at the expense of our own lives'. 'What does it matter whether these changes are achieved by us or at our expense?' asked Morozov, 'What is important is that we prepare the way for them to come about!' And, like Savinkov some 30 years later, he added, 'He who wields the sword shall die by the sword!'

Morozov in the Narodnaya Volya

Morozov was a member of the Executive Committee of the Narodnaya Volya, and, together with Tikhomirov, the editor of its journal. In the course of time, disagreements appeared between the two, and subsequently, between Morozov and other members of the Committee. Lyubatovich, Morozov's wife and herself a member of the Committee, claims that these differences of opinion revolved around the question of seizing power after the revolution, pointing out that she and Morozov were opposed to the Jacobian tendencies of Tikhomirov and Oshanian. But Vera Figner contends that it was Morozov, the most extreme terrorist in the ranks of the Executive Committee, who advocated the idea of a revolution without the people's participation. A letter from Morozov to Vera Figner written at that time casts light on the controversy, for in it Morozov explained his temporary withdrawal from the Executive

Committee by saying that he had been checked in his stride and his articles
censored because he adhered to the viewpoint put forward in Lipetsk and
opposed the idea of a constituent assembly (to be called into being after
the seizure of power). In view of these differences, he had asked that he
and Lyubatovich be sent to the south to work among the youth there.
Their request was not granted because Zhelyabov and Mikhailov felt that
the couple would be likely to have a harmful influence on the youth.
Hence, they were compelled to leave the country and try to set up abroad
an organization more in tune with their ideas.[25] Yet despite his testimony,
it seems that the true reason for the quarrel lay more in Morozov's
reservations about the centralization which so characterized the
movement, for he feared that the system would undermine the
membership and lead to a concentration of power around those who held
key offices. As to the significance of the alleged controversy surrounding
the constituent assembly, a letter from Morozov to Tkachev of 25 May
1880 makes it clear that Morozov felt that in the existing circumstances a
constituent assembly would simply give sanction to the present regime by
holding a plebiscite. In other words, Morozov had adopted a clearly
Blanquist stand in supporting a revolutionary struggle that was to be
waged by a revolutionary elite which was then to enforce its revolution on
the people once victory was theirs.[26]

'The Terrorist Struggle' – Morozov's Pamphlet

Morozov's 1880 pamphlet 'The Terrorist Struggle' was reprinted by the
Social-Revolutionary Party in 1907 as a document of historical importance
and one that provided 'a brilliant justification for political terror'. 'In our
opinion', it was stated there, 'this pamphlet by Morozov and the article he
wrote in the *Land and Liberty Bulletin* gives perfect expression to the
outlook of the majority of active terrorists of that time'.[27]
    The pamphlet opened with quotations from St. Just and Robespierre
concerning the right to assassinate a tyrant. 'Every man is entitled to kill a
tyrant and the nation cannot deprive any citizen of this right.' 'The right to
execute a tyrant is similar to the right to overthrow him. As far as liberty is
concerned, there is no man lower than the tyrant; as far as humanity is
concerned, no man is more guilty than he.' In other words, the starting
point for this discussion of terrorist warfare was again the old question of
tyrannicide, for Morozov was indeed profoundly influenced by the
romanticism of the French Revolution particularly with respect to the
Reign of Terror. From here Morozov surveyed the changes that had taken
place in modern times and transformed earlier peasant insurrection into
historic anachronism. Vast material resources and the growth of modern
armies have, he said, shifted the center of revolutionary activity to the
urban concentrations and their people. The alleys of the new towns and
their rows of cramped houses had created ideal conditions for barricade
warfare. The growth of large populations of urban workers, the proximity

of the nerve centers of the enemy's power and the ability of the people to
strike a blow at the enemy had bred in the masses a belief in their own
strength and, at the same time, increased the chances of their success.[28]

But all of this Morozov pointed out, was true only for the West. In
Russia, with its vast plains and its poor villages, its few towns and its
dispersed working population, the situation was quite different. The
tremendous might of the central government made any organization of
peasant insurrection impossible, while the numerically small size of
the proletariat had brought about a situation in which this group was
incapable of constituting a real danger to the regime and the existing
order. This accounted for the different form and unique quality of the
Russian revolution. In Russia there was no choice but to seek out a new
form of struggle which may be termed 'the terrorist revolution' and which
needed to be waged by the revolutionary intelligentsia.

Against the omnipotent government, with its army, its spies, its prisons
and its millions of police, there was to be set up a small fighting group
whose members would know no equal in daring and in ability to organize
insurrection. Against the might of the government this small group would
be armed with an impenetrable secrecy, an unassailable loyalty of one
member towards the others. The group's primary weapon would be the
element of surprise, the fact that the members of the organization cloaked
themselves in invisibility. 'Never before in history were there such
convenient conditions for the existence of a revolutionary party and for
such successful methods of struggle', Morozov proclaimed. Moreover, 'if
a long chain of independent, regional organizations range themselves
alongside the small, fighting terrorist group, then the days of the
monarchy and the tyrany are numbered indeed, and the road towards
socialist activity in Russia is open!' Organization and secrecy also ensured
that attacks, even Czaricide, would not be suicidal to their perpetrators.
The attackers would be able to level their blows and then disappear
without a trace only to return later to attack further. Up till then the
struggle was one of desperation and of self-sacrifice. From that point on it
would be 'a war of force against force of equal against equal, a war of
heroism against despotism, a war of science and education against the
bayonet and the gallows'.[29]

Czars and despots could no longer live quietly and reign in peace. The
ground shook beneath their feet, the unseen avenging hand wrote again
and again the news of their fall on the walls of their palaces. Yet for all that,
there existed the danger of a rebirth of tyranny in the future. A new
tyranny was likely to arise on the ruins of the old, and this time by the will of
the people themselves. An oppressive constitutional regime could be
established along the lines of Bismark's Germany. For this there was no
remedy other than a *continuation* of individual terror, for such regimes
depended for their strength on individuals, and when these are done away
with the regime itself comes to an end. Individual, political, limited terror,
but terror of a permanent nature, alone would set the limit for any
tyrannical regime. Such terror had a good chance of fulfilling its aims if it

grounded itself in ideology, for ideology cannot be destroyed, even though individual fighters can. In other words, Morozov's conception of the role of terror in Russia was not limited to putting an end to the existing tyranny. As he saw it, Russian terrorism was to become a continuing system of permanent struggle, 'popular, historical, and traditional'.[30]

'Terrorism and Routine' – Gerassim Romanenko (1855–1928)[31]

Gerassim Romanenko was to become the second prophet of the 'terrorist revolution', one in thought with Morozov and himself the author of the pamphlet *Terrorism and Routine*. In 1879 Romanenko arrived in Zurich where he came into contact with the *Nabat* group and with Morozov with whom he planned the establishment of a group supporting consistent and systematic terror. The two wrote their separate pamphlets while maintaining close contact, each correcting the work of the other. Romanenko, like Morozov, was also at the time an emissary of the Narodnaya Volya abroad. Both returned to Russia in 1881 in order to take their part in the struggle and act as representatives of a consistent terrorism. Morozov was arrested immediately, while Romanenko was co-opted to the Executive Committee. Before his own arrest in November of that year, he initiated, wrote and published the infamous call to pogroms against the Jews.[32] Vera Figner describes him in her memoirs as an intelligent and educated man, handsomely built, with a refined face bearing the marks of consumption on its features.[33] While in gaol, attempts were made to use him in order to arrange some sort of meeting between the authorities and the Executive Committee. Romanenko, for his part, presented the Czar with a long, detailed memorandum in which he outlined the programme of a Marxist social and economic revolution. Here he pointed out Russia's pyramidal structure, the base of which was formed by the great indifferent mass of the people, while the top was composed of two rival terror nuclei – those responsible for the White Terror perpetrated on behalf of the ruling elite, and the small group of revolutionaries waging their own terror from the underground. Romanenko was treated leniently and got a five-year term of exile to Turkestan, being permitted to return to his native Bessarabia in 1887. Here he turned his coat and became a convinced monarchist, serving as advisor to the notorious pogrom-instigator Krushevan.

The pamphlet *Terrorism and Routine*, composed in his youth, was written in reply to N. Dragomanov's *Terrorism and Freedom*.[34] The latter was the work of one of the representatives of the liberal-revolutionary camp in exile and it drew a distinction between the plague of attacks that had taken place in the past, which Dragomanov described as belonging to the category of murders which happened time and again throughout history, and the new terror of Russia that was, he claimed, 'a serious matter' that was developing into a system. As regards political terror in

Russia, Dragomanov claimed that from the historian's point of view it was impossible to understand its causes, nevertheless one must not 'applaud this murder from an ambush and evaluate it to the status of a system and an example to be emulated'. Dragomanov did not ignore the fact that Russia's reality was one of violence and that violence was thus unavoidable, but he called for an open confrontation. He praised the attempts to free prisoners by armed force and attacks on the secret police, the mainstay of the existing regime; yet at the same time he stressed that the 'sanctity of the gaol obligates an equal sanctity of the methods used to achieve it'.[35]

Romanenko's sharply worded reply was a complete dissociation from the milk-and-water liberalism that Dragomanov represented. It set forth what he saw as the scientific and moral principles of the terror system as a strategy that was designed to *prevent* the honors of a mass revolution and the blood-letting of popular insurrections. Thus Romanenko pointed to the unique nature of Russia's development: the society that resulted from the wedding of capitalism to the Byzantine tyranny of traditional Czarist rule, and to the continuing struggle between the intelligentsia and the regime that had known no cessation since the days of the Decembrists. He went on to describe the excesses of the White Terror. The question to be asked, was what would be the most effective form of insurrection for Russia.[36] Preaching political insurrection to the people would be to give advice as useless as telling a man dying of starvation and cold to get up, get dressed and feed himself properly. 'What is the way out of this blind alley in which the Russian revolutionary movement has become trapped?', Romanenko asked, 'It is history that suggests a way – a terrorist revolution!' 'The revolution must become a system and it must demonstrate – in considered and thought-out action that will really penetrate deeply into the consciousness of the tyrants – that every attack on the rights of the people will bring reprisal and punishment.' Thus, Romanenko advocated, throwing off the concepts of accepted morality: 'From the point of view of supreme justice every revolution designed to liberate the people is unqualifiedly moral' for the simple reason that the revolution endows the people with the possibility of leading a normal life. Further, 'it is unconceivable to think of any morality beyond liberty ... socially speaking, the only morality is that which helps in the establishment of liberty and the development of society and its material advancement'.[37] Romanenko goes even further in finding yet a further moral justification for terrorist revolution: it is moral to carry out the revolution in a manner that will reduce the people's suffering to a minimum. Thus, a people's revolution results in the death of some of its finest sons and in the spilling of much innocent blood; as opposed to this, a terrorist revolution, 'even if it does result in some innocent casualties, as was the case with the soldiers in the Winter Palace explosion, results only in war casualties; terrorism itself aims its blows against those who themselves are directly to blame for the evil'.[38]

'Political Terror in Russia' – L. Shternberg[39]

Another pamphlet advocating terror was the work of Lev Shternberg (1861–1927), a member of the Narodnaya Volya student group and one of the small remnant (mostly Jewish students) who tried, in the years 1884–87, to re-establish the movement after the crippling blow dealt it with the imprisonment of Lopatin. Published in hectograph form in 1884, Shternberg's *Political Terror in Russia* concerned itself with the strategic aspect of political terror as the weapon of the revolutionary intelligentsia and as the only alternative to revolutionary struggle in Russia. It was marked by a conviction that political terror is unavoidable, moral and effective.

Shternberg opened his treatise with a description of the reactionary measures which the White Terror aimed at the vital interests of the intelligentsia in an attempt to choke it to death after the defeat inflicted on the fighting nucleus of the Narodnaya Volya. He claims it was particularly difficult to endure such assault on the liberties of the individual, for those liberties constituted the very breach of the intelligentsia's life. He then proceeded to an examination of the social forces in Russia and their revolutionary potential. The peasantry still had room to breathe within the reforms, yet no matter how cramped its circumstances, it would in any case only very rarely be prepared to gamble on an uncertain future. The dispersion of the peasantry, the individualistic economic ideals that inspired it, combined with the existence of an army of millions at the disposal of the regime, all made it impossible that there should be an insurrection. Moreover, it is the duty of the intelligentsia to prevent such a happening since it had no chance of success and would spell total disaster. Should such an insurrection break out, the intelligentsia would in any case be incapable of leading it or giving it any direction. The most that could be expected of the peasantry was that they will not interfere in the ongoing struggle between the intelligentsia and the regime. Shternberg's view of the bourgeoisie and petty-bourgeoisie was that they lacked any consciousness of solidarity and readiness to sacrifice for a common goal. Some of them, he thought, might be drawn to the barricades when these were thrown up by the working class or might, at the last moment, when it was obvious that there was a clear chance of success, join a conspiracy to seize power. In other words, all one could expect from this class was *post factum* support and cooperation. Meanwhile what characterized them was 'a criminal indifference and faint-heartedness'.

The proletariat, the only group which lived in large concentrations, existed under miserable conditions, and came into contact with other groups, might form a political movement. However, the regime's spy-network and its oppressive policies conspired to prevent any real consolidation of such a movement to the point where insurrection might be viable.[40] The most that could be expected here was that a small group drawn from the proletariat might ally itself to the revolutionary minority when the time for action came. Shternberg's view of the situation led him to the conclusion that there was no hope and no chance of a revolution in Russia other than that which would be carried out by a revolutionary elite, that is, by the intelligentsia, which was possessed both of consciousness and of a sense of mission. From here Shternberg then proceeded to an examination of the goals of the revolutionary party – the minority group among the intelligentsia.

In his view the revolutionary party's aim was to achieve those goals formulated as the 'terrorists' revolution' by Morozov and Romanenko – and this they needed to do with a minimum of casualties and in the shortest possible time. This, for Shternberg, was the revolutionary intelligentsia's historic mission; for this it was worth paying the price of their own lives. They were to 'cushion with their own flesh and blood' the path that would lead to the revolution's fulfillment. Such a party would end, even if its own members were denied the privilege of seeing for themselves the realization of their vision, by carrying out the supreme task of serving as the vanguard for a popular social revolution. The path to such a revolution was the path of terror whose aim was to overthrow the rule of the Czar and to gain the support of the masses by systematically murdering the Czars and the enemies of the people.[41]

Shternberg stressed the universal nature of terror which, he pointed out, had been used in many different historical periods and circumstances by various groups and for many unrelated purposes. Hence, he claimed, one must consider always what its purpose is, weighing this according to the concrete circumstances of the time and of the struggle waged. Terror is in essence 'the violent removal of certain persons' (individual terror) and it further appears always as the last choice of a group that is incapable of engaging in open battle. Those who use terror for unrealistic goals are doomed to disappointment and failure. This was what happened in the French Revolution and in Ireland – for in both bases the terror was aimed not against specific individuals or specific privileges, but against an entire class.[42] As for anarchist terror in the West, it produced an exchange of fire and of blows, but no real progress. According to Shternberg, the achievement of parliamentary institutions had cost the workers of the West so much that they now refused to explode them anew and to turn their backs on them.

The situation in Russia, said Shternberg, was quite different, for here the purpose of the terror should be to overthrow tyranny and establish the institutions of political theory. In Russia all the institutions of oppression and tyranny were concentrated in the hands of but a few people as, simple as it might be to remove these people, it would be difficult to weld the masses together for an open struggle. Hence terror in Russia would not be a matter of revenge, of compensation, of the people's justice, or of desperate protest. It would comprise rather 'a temporary struggle, balanced and properly considered, undertaken by the revolutionaries against the very pillars of the tyranny'. Russian terror was thus directed against an arbitrary regime detached from the masses with no public support. The regime depended on a mighty army which was only all-powerful in confrontations with open mass movements but which would be condemned to helplessness in fighting against a hidden enemy that uses the element of surprise in its attacks. Facing up to the army of gendarmerie and secret agents, the terrorists would enjoy a great advantage, as they were armed with moral strength, endurance and a readiness to sacrifice themselves.[43] The last section in Shternberg's pamphlet dealt with the moral question of terror. Moral reservations about terror, he argued, always come from people who had no objection in principle to revolutions likely to result in massive casualties among the innocent. Victor Hugo, for example, had declared that he would not sacrifice one single child for the sake of the state and yet for all that he had no scruples in calling for a bloody war against tyrants. As for those who claimed that even the enemy had an ideology, Shternberg says that the Pobedonostsevs and the Metternichs merely 'cloak their bestial impulses in principles' but that at any event the war was not being waged against them – the really fierce struggle would be engaged against the crimes of the tyrants and their perverted deeds.[44]

Summary

It was not merely considerations of tactics and morality that led Russia's revolutionary intelligentsia to adopt terror as their weapon; they were also to some extent motivated by a profound fear of the cruelties and horrors that might result from a mass insurrection. It was thus that the myth of the people became transformed into the myth of the elite, the heroes of history. It was in this spirit that, in a leading article in the reborn *Bell*, No.1, 2 April 1870, Nechayev wrote as follows: 'A fearful catastrophe threatens us all from below. Everyone feels its inevitable approach ... everyone prophesies its coming with trepidation, yet meanwhile no one so much as lifts a finger in order to save himself and Russia from this spontaneous elemental revolution, from the horrors of this revolution ...'.[46] Ten years later, this same claim was again and again made in the Narodnaya Volya publications.

Romanenko, pointing to the fact that terrorist warfare was to be preferred, warned against the attempt to overthrow the terror waged by a revolutionary minority, because, he claimed, 'history, when it finds the front door blocked, is bound to end up by breaking down the windows, and then its path is strewn with horrors'.[47] Morozov, for his part, explained that he had come to know the extent of the people's ignorance and its unpreparedness for any socialist regime, thus he anticipated the institution of a 'republic of the intelligentsia rather than a democratic republic'.[48] Zhelyabov, one of the Narodnaya Volya's leading members, and a man who himself came from peasant stock, gives a gloomy description of the likely outcome of a peasant revolution – total chaos and free rein for unbridled animal instincts. Rysakov, Zhelyabov's disciple and one of those involved in Alexander II's assassination, described the organized terror movement as the preferred alternative to a blind, witless insurrection of 'dumb people'.[49] Tikhomirov too echoed these sentiments when he asked in a programmatic essay written after the destruction of the Narodnaya Volya, 'What can we expect of the revolution? – We are heading for a catastrophe!' He warns the authorities that their attempts to check and root out the forces of revolution will merely hasten the awful moment when Russia will rush headlong into revolutionary destruction and sink to the very depths.[50] In 1908, the same warning was uttered by Alexander Blok who described the intelligentsia's fear of a mass revolution, which he likened later to a troika being galloped *'straight at us ... a sentence of execution from which there is no escape. For in throwing ourselves into the midst of the people we are casting ourselves beneath the wheels of a runaway troika, straight into certain death.'*[51]

The revolutionary intelligentsia was continually torn between admiration for the 'people' and the 'masses' and a fear of these same forces; between the myth of the 'people' and the 'bandits' on the one hand, and the myth of the elite, of the revolutionary party, on the other; between a worship of the people and a revulsion from it; between what it imagined to be 'the people's will' and what that will was in reality. This conflict itself reflected the intelligentsia's frustrations, hesitations and perplexities, but it also reflected that group's appetite for power. It was at one and the same time a reflection of its heroism and yet of its perversion and its treachery. This perhaps accounted for the long list of odd and colorful revolutionaries that came up from the intelligentsia, a mixture of rebels, rulers, tyrants, perverts, traitors, saints and martyrs. All populist thought, starting with the Chaikovyists and going through the Land and Liberty groups, the People's Will, the Black Partition, the Social Revolutionaries, right up to Lenin's *What is to be Done* are marked by this conflict between a worship of the masses and of revolutionary spontaneity, on the one hand, and the consciousness of mission and of constituting a revolutionary elite, on the other. Examining the heated disputes over the drafting of programmes, the ideological struggles waged with such deathly seriousness over philosophical and theoretical issues that accompanied virtually every act of the Russian revolutionary movement, one must surely recall Leo Tolstoy's analogy as it was reported by Krupskaya; walking along the road one day he saw a strange figure apparently bending over something and making the oddest movements with his hands and feet; aha, what a madman, he thought to himself. However, when he drew nearer what he beheld before him was a man down on his hands and knees sharpening a knife on the side of the paving stone .... [52] Looking at the Nechayev–Bakunin encounter, one cannot but feel that in its juxtaposition of the intellectual-revolutionary with the conspirator drawn from among the people, there is again reflected all those conflicts of guilt and admiration, faith and suspicion that so characterized the clash between Russia's intellectuals and its people. The episode of the pogroms against the Jews provides yet another illustration of the dilemma of the intellectuals. Thus Pavel Axelrod relates in his memoirs that when he asked the members of the Black Partition 'and what will happen if the people should want to attack the Jews?', Plekhanov answered him, 'We are on the side of the people to the extent that its ambitions are progressive, but we can under no circumstances support those of its ambitions that are reactionary!'[53] On the other hand, Romanenko, the theoretician of terrorism by a small minority, was unable to withstand temptation, and it was he who published the infamous call to pogroms. In the sixth issue of *Narodnaya Volya*, he discusses the pogroms and claims that though 'from the moral point of view one cannot justify such acts', nevertheless it remains a fact that the people's revolution in France also witnessed atrocities that sprang from 'the wrath of the people'; thus, 'if bombs again prove ineffective, if the stupid crooks again continue to torture our land, there will be a swift wave of popular terror and we shall again be witness to the horrors of the French Revolution and the Pugachev uprising ...'. His hint was quite sufficient.

NOTES

1. Melvin Richter, 'Tocqueville's Contribution to the Theory of Revolution', in Carl Friedrich and Roland Pennock (eds.), *Revolution* (New York: Atherton, 1967); op. cit., pp.75–121, especially pp.87, 88, 94; A. De Tocqueville, 'De la Democratie en Amerique', *Oeuvres, Papiers et Correspondence* (Paris: Gallimard, 2e edition, 1951), p.413; Alexis de Tocqueville, *Oeuvres Completes*, T.II (Gallimard, 10e edition), '"Fragments" et Notes inedites sur la Revolution', Livre IV, pp.337, 8; 349, 50.
2. E.L. Eisenstein, *The First Professional Revolutionist, Filippo Michele Buonarotti* (Cambridge, MA: Harvard University Press, 1959), pp.37–49; 24–6. A. Lehning, 'Buanarotti and His International Secret Societies', *International Review of Social History*, Vol.I (1956), pp.115–22. The social programme was not made known to the lower echelons of the secret society. Entry into the upper echelons brought with it a greater acquaintance with the doctrines. In his *General Ideas of a Secret Society*, Buonarotti writes that his secret society is in principle democratic, but that its organizational form must not be democratic, op. cit., pp.117–22.
3. A. Blanqui, *Critique Sociale* (Paris: Fexix Alcan, 1885), pp.196, 201, 206.
4. Pilsudski, a former terrorist himself, wrote in 1910: 'What revolution is it that we must prepare ourselves for? It is a struggle for power, carried out violently and relatively quickly' – and thus he expressed one of the Blanquist principles of twentieth century revolutionaries. Jozef Pilsudski, 'Zadania praktyczne rewolucji w zaborze rosyjskim', *Pisma-Mowy-Rozkazy* (Warszawa: wyd. Polska Zjednoczona, 1930), T.II, p.340.
5. Buonarotti likened himself to a secular Loyola, and regarded his society as 'the private army of the professional revolutionary' (Eisenstein, op. cit., pp.40–49). The secret societies that he headed, and the others that were set up at his inspiration, adopted for themselves the rules of the Freemasons' lodges: a strict organizational hierarchy accompanied by varying levels of involvement of knowledge. Rank and file members were not privy to the secret structure, and the final aim, too, was to be kept secret. The fact that upper echelons existed was also kept from their knowledge. A routine venture was the penetration of as many other bodies as possible, in order that these might be overturned from within. A. Lehning, 'Buanarotti', op. cit., pp.115–20; J.M. Roberts, *The Mythology of Secret Societies* (St. Albans: Paladin, 1974), pp.134–9; 168–81; 233–49; 354–60. Blanqui adopted the principle of 'systematically cheating the members into believing that they are a great army' as one of the systems of the 'democratic

phalanx'. 'The great revolutionary committee' in whose name he addressed the
uprising of 1839 was part of this fraud. M. Nomad, *Apostles of Revolution* (London:
Secker & Warburg, 1939), p.23.

6. F. Engels, Intro. to K. Marx, 'The Class Struggle in France', *Selected Works* (Moscow:
   Foreign Languages Publishing House, 1950), Vol.I, pp.120–27.
7. Jules Monnerot, *Sociology and Psychology of Communism* (Boston: Beacon Press,
   1953), pp.27–37.
8. L. Trotsky, *History of the Russian Revolution* (London: Sphere Books, 1967), Vol.III,
   pp.160, 161.
9. See Bertram D. Wolfe, *Marxism 100 Years in the Life of a Doctrine* (London:
   Chapman & Hall, 1967), pp.150–64. G. Lichtheim, *Marxism, An Historical and
   Critical Study* (London: Routledge & Kegan Paul, 1964), pp.51–62; 122–9. J.L.
   Talmon, *Political Messianism* (London: Secker & Warburg, 1960), pp.512 ff; S.
   Avineri, *The Social and Political Thought of Karl Marx* (London: Cambridge University Press, 1968), pp.196 ff.
10. Trotsky, *History*, op. cit., Vol.III, p.162.
11. 'Pokazanya M.N. Polonskoy K. Istoryi Partyi N.V.', *Byloye* (1907), N6/18; pp.6, 7.
    Polonskaya (alias Oshanina, alias Olovennikova,, alias Barannikova) member of the
    Executive Committee of the N.V. was the only woman who participated in the Lipetsk
    Conference. This statement of hers was given in 1893.
12. A. Blanqui, 'Instructions pour une prise d'armes', *La Critique Sociale*, Revue des Idees
    et des Livres (Paris, Oct. 1931), pp.108–17.
13. Lenin's attitude and his connection with the tradition of Narodnaya Volya have been
    the subject of several recent studies. S.S. Volk, *Narodnaya Volya, 1879–1882*, izd.
    Nauka (Moskva-Leningrad, 1966); V.A. Tvardovskaja, 'Krizis Zemli I Voli V Konce
    70-ch godov', *Istorya S.S.S.R.* 4 (1959), pp.61–74; J. Frenkel, 'Party Genealogy and
    the Soviet Historians, 1920–1938, *Slavic Review*, Vol.XXV, No.4 (Dec. 1966),
    pp.566–7; 590–93. R. Pipes (ed.), 'The Origins of Bolshevism – The Intellectual
    Evolution of Young Lenin', *Revolutionary Russia* (Cambridge, MA: Harvard
    University Press, 1968), pp.28–62; R. Pipes, 'Russian Marxism and Its Populist
    Background', *The Russian Review*, Vol.19, No.1 (Jan. 1960), pp.316–37. In any event,
    Lenin's stance on 'Individual Terror' was far from clear-cut. His 1899 reservations
    about the programme of the Emancipation-of-Labour group, 1885, as it related to
    terror, raised two important points: 'that every programme leaves the questions of
    means open; and that terror is not advisable as a means of struggle *at the present
    moment*' (italics in original). V.I. Lenin, 'A Draft Programme of Our Party', *Collected
    Works* (Moscow, 1960), Vol.4, pp.238 ff. in an article of 1901 he wrote, 'In principle we
    have never rejected and cannot reject terror. Terror is one of the forms of military
    action that may be perfectly suitable and even essential at a definite juncture in the
    battle, given a definite state of the troops and the existence of definite conditions' (V.I.
    Lenin, 'Where to Begin', *Collected Works*, op. cit., Vol.V, p.19). In 1906 Lenin
    endorsed expropriation and even terrorist activities so long as 'the sentiments of the
    masses be taken into account', and that 'the conditions of the working class movement
    be reckoned with' and that 'care be taken that force of the proletariat should not be
    fritted away', V.I. Lenin, 'Guerrilla Warfare', *Collected Works*, Vol. II, pp.222; 213–
    23.
14. V. Burtsev, *K. Oruzhyu* (London, 1903), pp.4–9.
15. N. Morozov, *Terroristicheskaya Bor'ba* (London, 1880), V. Tarnovsky (G.
    Romanenko), *Terrorism i Rutina* (London, 1880). Both pamplets were published at
    the same time, their authors maintaining close contact with the 'Nabat' group, while
    they were abroad in 1880. (Both returned to Russia in 1881.) The British Museum
    catalogue mistakenly dates Romanenko's pamphlet as 1875.
16. *Going to the People* – the movement of students and young revolutionary Russian
    intelligentsia influenced by the teachings of Herzen, Chernishevsky, Lavrov and
    Bakunin to spread the gospel of socialism ('Narodnichestvo' – populism in its Russian
    version) among the peasants and masses. In the year 1874 more than 2,000 persons
    threw aside their careers, positions, studies and went to the villages, dressed up as

peasants to work as teachers, nursed, doctors, blacksmiths and log-cutters among the people. Government persecutions sent 215 to prison in 1877. Mass trials were staged in Moscow and St. Petersburg. The persecutions and the fiasco of the peaceful movement led to the emergence of the more organized, disciplined and radical 'Zemlya i Volya' ('Land and Liberty') organization.

17. *Zemlya i Volya* – Revolutionary organization of the *narodniks* (populists) founded in 1876. Their slogan was *Land* for the peasants and *Freedom* for the people. The road to socialism in Russia, they believed, led through the transformation of the peasant village commune (the 'mir' or 'obshchina') into a socialist system for the whole country, evading capitalism. Government persecutions made them turn to political struggle adopting terrorism as its main weapon. In June 1879 a split occurred at the Voronezh conference. The majority decided to adopt the 'terrorist struggle' and the assassination of the Tsar as their first goal, to achieve political and civil rights. They formed the 'People's Will' Party (Narodnaya Volya). A very tiny minority headed by G. Plekhanov formed the 'Black Partition' group ('Chernyj Peredel'), that is, all land to the peasants, a pure populist group sticking to the old narodnik slogans, refuting terrorism and political struggle.

18. N. Morozov, *Povest Moyey Zhizni* (Moskva-Leningrad: izd. Akademyi Nauk, 1947), T.I, pp.468–72.

19. Ibid., T.II, pp.149, 950.

20. Ibid., T.II, p.252.

21. Olga Lyubatovich, member of the Executive Committee, was married to N. Morozov. Her memoirs are an important source for the history of the turn towards terrorism. See O. Lyubatovich, 'Dalekoye i Nedavnoye', *Byloye* 5 (1906), pp.208–45; 5 (1906), pp.102–157.

22. N. Morozov, *Povest*, op. cit., T.II, pp.500, 501.

23. *DA Zdrastvuyet Narodnaya Volya*, No.9 (Paris, 1907); pp.15, 16. This is the later reprint of Morozov's article published by the S"Rs.

24. N. Morozov, *Povest*, op. cit., T.II, p.508.

25. Ibid., T.II, pp.451, 452.

26. Lyubatovich and Kuzmin (Kolosov) notes that Morozov was the first editor of the party's newspaper after the split. See Lyubatovich, 'Dalekoye', op. cit., p.112; O. Kuzmin, *Narodovolcheskaya Zhurnalistika* (Moskva: izd. Politkatorzhan, 1930), p.58. For the reasons for the estrangement see 'Dalekoye', ibid., pp.121, 2; and Vera Figner's notes on Kuzmin's book in *Nar. Zhurn*, Ibid., pp.231–74; and particularly pp.238–47, which gives the text of Morozov's letter to her of 1880. The letter eluded Venturi who accepts Lyubatovich's version of the causes of the quarrel. The Narodnaya Volya's Executive Committee letter to its members abroad, written at the end of 1881 and causing considerable upset and dispute, rejects Morozov's and Romanenko's pamphlets. F. Venturi, *Roots of Revolution* (New York: Grasse & Dunlap, 1966), p.673, pp.827, 8, N 98; S.N. Valk (ed.), *Revolutsyonnoye Narodnichestvo* (Moskva-Leningrad: izd. Nauka, 1965), T.II, pp.315–22; p.387, N.169.

27. Lyubatovich, 'Dalekoye', op. cit., pp.129–31. Vera Figner, *Zapechatelnyj Trud-Polnoye Sobranye Sochinenyj*, Vol.I (Moskva, 1932), pp.295, 6. Olga and Mark Nathanson also gave up their children in favour of continuing the struggle. The children were left with Olga's father and died subsequently in a diphtheria epidemic. See A. Pribyleva Korba, V. Figner, *Zapechatelnyj Trud-Polnoye Sobranye Sochinenj* (Moskva, 1932), Vol.I, pp.295–6. See A. Pribyleva Korba – V. Figner, *A. Mikhailov* (Moskva-Leningrad, 1925), p.199.

28. *Da Zdrastvuyet N.V.*, op. cit., N p.17.

29. N. Morozov, *Terroristicheskaya Borba*, op. cit., ibid., pp.3, 4.

30. Ibid., pp.5–9.

31. Ibid., pp.11–15.

32. S.N. Valk, 'G.G. Romanenko,' *Katorga i Ssylka* 48 (1928), pp.36–58.

33. Romanenko, who was not alone in his assessment, saw the pogroms against the Jews as 'a purely popular movement'. In his opinion, the reason for the outbursts of violence was to be sought in the socio-economic realities; while local circumstances in the south

gave the movement an 'anti-Jewish' character. He cites the *Russkiye Vedomosti* which claimed that the Jews were the focus of attack not out of any principle, but simply because they presented 'the weakest form of resistance'. Romanenko goes even further, claiming that the landowners in the south were an anachronistic force, and that 'in the external struggle for a crust of bread' the masses no longer saw them as the main enemy. Their whole attention was turned to the 'new exploitative force': the shop-owners, the inn-keepers and the usurers – that is, the Jews. His long article on the subject appearing in *Narodnaya Volya*, No.6 (Oct. 1881). (*Literatura Narodnoy Voli*, Paris, 1905, pp.419–39 still shows a reluctance to take up the cudgels on behalf of the pogromists in any open manner. Discussing the horrors of revolution, he asks whether Robespierre, St. Just and Desmoulins should have surrendered their roles in the history of France because of the extremist acts perpetrated by the masses (ibid., pp.438–9). Shortly thereafter he wrote the infamous pogrom broadsheet in the name of the Executive Committee, despite the objections of more prominent members. (Vera Figner tore her copy to shreds when it reached her in Odessa and Tikhomirov wrote an article condemning the pogroms in *Narodnaya Volya*, No.10, Sept. 1884.) See S. Valk, 'G.G. Romanenko', op. cit., pp.50–54; 'Literatura', op. cit., pp.674–5. Further on the pogroms, it is worth noting that it was in the *Narodnaya Volya* that there first appeared the formulation permitting attacks on 'Jews' while at the same time protesting hatred against 'Hebrews' (a later version made it permissible to attack 'cosmopolitans', 'Zionists', etc., while pronouncing that this in no way expressed hatred for Jews as a whole). 'One must distinguish between Yevreis, as a depressed national group, and Zhids, as the representatives of the exploiting classes, and hence as those who are to be attacked', proclaimed the Listok *Narodnoya Volia*, in issue No.1 (July 1883), *Lit. Nar. Voli*, op. cit., pp.622–8; it was not merely the French Revolution that served in this case as an exuse; Marx, too, was cited: 'the Jews, as a people that has been pursued throughout history, sensitive and nervous, hold up the mirror as it were, to all the perversions of the regime', and thus 'when an anti-semitic movement starts one can be certain that in its wake will come a more profound move against the regime' (ibid.).

34. Vera Figner, *Zap. Trud.* op. cit., pp.293 ff.
35. M.P. Dragomanov (1841–96) of Cossack background (his parents were small landowners), had an academic career, but was forced to give up his Chair at the University of Kiev because of his pro-Ukrainian feelings and his stand in regard to self-rule. From 1876 onward he was in exile, first in Vienna and later in Geneva. He saw terrorism as a pathological expression of Russian reality, and warned against the individual arbitrariness that was likely to overwhelm it, also sounding the alarm against the presence within the ranks of terrorists of men of doubtful repute, traitors and the like, and against the principle of the 'holy deceit'. See M.P. Dragomanov, *Sobranye Politicheskich Sochinenyj*, izd. Redaktsyi 'Osvodozhdenya', T.II (Paris, 1906), pp.VII–LIX; T.N. Soch, 'K biografyi A.I. Zhelyabova' published in *Volonoye Slovo* (1882), N.39, 40, pp.413–36.
36. On his stand on Terrorism see *Terrorizm i Svovoda, Muravyi i Korova*, Otvet Na Otvet, 'Golosa', M. Dragomanova, Zheneva, 1880, Imp. du 'Robotnik' et de la 'Hromada'; pp.1–11; *Sobranie Sochinenyj*, T.II, op. cit., pp.285–310. *Le Tyrannicide en Russie et L'Action de l'Europe Occidentale* (Geneva, 1883).
37. V. Tarnovsky, *Terrorism i Rutina*, op. cit., pp.3–8.
38. Ibid., pp.7–17.
39. Ibid., pp.17–19.
40. Lev Shternberg had a traditional Jewish background. Returning from prison and exile he was active in the Jewish Ethnographic-Historical Association and became its chairman, succeeding Dubnow. After the 1917 revolution, he became Professor of Ethnography in the University of Leningrad. See Tsvi Rudi, *Heavar* 16 (1969), in Hebrew, pp.182–91; M.A. Krol, *Stranicy Moyej Zhizni* (New York, 1944), pp.9–22. A. Schechter-Minor, 'Yuzhno Russkaya Narodovolcheskaya Organizatsya', *Narodovoltsy* (Sbornik Statey) (Moskva: izd. Politkatorzhan, 1928), T.I, pp.131–9.
41. L. Shternberg, *Politicheskiy Terror V. Rossiyi* (1884, Hectograph Edition), pp.2–8. I am grateful to Dr B. Sapir of the 'Institute for Social History' in Amsterdam for giving

me access to the rare copy of this pamphlet, ibid., pp.2–8.
42. Ibid., pp.9–11.
43. Ibid., pp.12–14.
44. Ibid., pp.14–18.
45. Ibid., pp.19–24.
46. B.P. Kozmin, *Iz Istoryi Revolutsyonnoy Mysli v Rosiyi* (Moskva: Akademyi Nauk, 1961), p.566.
47. V. Tarnovsky, *Terrorizm i Rutina* op. cit., p.24. Valk claims that the difference between Romanenko and the other members of the Executive Committee is seen, inter alia, in the fact that they viewed the success of terror as offering a chance for the outbreak of a popular uprising that should follow in its wake, while Romanenko prophesied some bloody apocalypse and presented terrorism as an alternative. S. Valk, 'G. Romanenko', op. cit., p.48.
48. N. Morozov, *Povest*, op. cit., T.II, p.500.
49. P.B. Akselrod, *Perezhitoye i Peredumannoye*, izd. Gzhevina (Berlin, 1923), p.313; 'Pokazanya Rysakova', *Byloye* (1918), pp.245, 258.
50. L. Tikhomirov, 'Chevo nam zhdat' ot revolutsyi', *Vestnik Narodnoy Voli*, No.2 (Zheneva, 1884), p.248.
51. A. Blok, *Rossiya i Inteligentsya*, izd. Skify (Berlin, 1920), pp.43, 45.
52. N. Krupskaya, *Memories of Lenin* (London, 1970), p.84.
53. P. Axelrod, 'Perezhitoye', op. cit., p.335.

When Terrorists Do the Talking: Reflections on Terrorist Literature

Bonnie Cordes

Introduction

Much research has been devoted to examining what terrorists have done in the past and to identifying trends for predicting what they might do in the future. Less attention, however, has been focused on terrorist motivations, mindset or indeed, on *terrorists'* self-perception. By using the primary materials provided by the terrorists themselves, that is, memoirs, statements, interviews, and communiqués, much information about the terrorist mindset and decision-making can be gleaned.

While sending a message of fear and intimidation through their violent actions, the terrorists must also use written and spoken language to legitimize, rationalize, and justify their actions. Although there are ample historic examples of appealing causes and precedents for terrorism,[1] the rationales for terrorism today frequently undergo severe strain. In the 1980s violence is directed against societies with more ample means than ever available to its citizens to express and redress grievances. Such a paradox requires extensive explanation by the terrorist to rationalize and justify his actions not only to an audience of perceived or potential sympathizers, but also to himself. Although terrorism is often described as a form of communication, terrorists are rather poor communicators. Like many poor writers, what they lack in clarity they often make up for in quantity. Yet what terrorists do say about themselves is often more revealing than they intend.

The fundamental contradiction the terrorists must deal with is that while they deliberately employ what we in fact regard as terrorist violence, they characterize their actions as something else.[2] While a criminal may accept that he is indeed a criminal, a terrorist goes to extraordinary lengths to deny that he is a terrorist. This denial may consist not only of semantic denial but of recharacterizing themselves as freedom fighters, revolutionaries, etc., and at the same time depicting the state and its representatives as the criminals and the terrorists.[3] This war of labels becomes terribly important in the contest between authorities and the terrorist challengers to win the sympathies of the public. Rather than be ignored, this terrorist 'name-calling' should be listened to carefully. Terrorist statements give us our best, and sometimes, only inside view of terrorist life and thinking within the group. To comprehend the terrorist mindset it is crucial to uncover the rationale, motivations, and mechanisms for denial. The rebels claim to be using terrorist violence as only a part of a larger, revolutionary strategy. Terrorism, they often claim, is merely one, necessary step in a broader struggle. Yet the revolution they propose is difficult to grasp – it demands that they communicate their own purpose, role, rationale, and legitimacy to the people for whom they claim to wage the battle. They must show that the violence is useful; thus they engage themselves in a necessary verbal, as well as violent strategy. And to convince others, they must themselves be convinced.[4]

In 1979 Nathan Leites recognized that, although much work of varied nature is being conducted on what terrorists do and some on what makes them do it, very little at all considers 'what they thought they were doing', or more precisely 'what good [they thought] it would do'.[5] There are several reasons for this gap. First of all, there is a paucity of relevant data provided by the rebels themselves. When terrorists write or speak about themselves it is often indirectly. Terrorist violence is meant to carry a message that is not always heard or understood as the terrorists would like it to be: rather than communicating 'mayhem and destruction' with a particular bombing, for instance, they would prefer that their audience read 'solidarity with the oppressed peoples of the Third World'. So, not only do they throw bombs, but they also have to write. Often unconsciously, it appears, the purposes of communiqués are not only to explain their actions to others but to persuade the terrorists themselves that what they have done was justified, was appropriate, and carried sufficient weight in the pursuit of their cause. Most material, however, is event-related, that is, written for or just after a particular terrorist action, or in the form of declaratory communiqués. Occasionally the terrorists will issue explanatory political tracts, give patchy interviews with often sympathetic journalists, or – on the *very* rare occasion when a terrorist lives long enough and has the inclination – write memoirs. What does exist of this sort of material is rarely published and even more difficult to obtain in the original. Last but not least, the terrorist literature that is available provides ponderous, and often repetitive, reading. Consequently, a valuable primary source is frequently neglected.

By listening to what some terrorists have to say, this analysis suggests how terrorists see themselves, what they think they are doing, and what they think their actions will accomplish; it also proposes a simple framework for a more systematic examination of the terrorists' view of themselves and their actions. Terrorist communications can be analyzed from two different aspects: how they persuade (or intend to persuade) others (what I call the *propaganda aspect*) and how they persuade them-selves (the *auto-propaganda aspect*). Keeping these two ostensible pur-poses in mind when reading terrorist literature we can perhaps address Leites' question '... how do they make it plausible to themselves that their acts serve the attainment of their goal?'[6] It is the mechanics of such self-explanation that provide us with valuable insights into the workings and mindset of the group.

Focus

The existence of several different types of terrorist groups, many with differing aims and socio-political contexts, further complicates the study of terrorist literature and thwarts most attempts at generalization. Part of the complexity of terrorism is the fact that it is conducted by a variety of idiosyncratic individuals with widely divergent national and socio-cultural backgrounds. Efforts to provide an overall 'terrorist profile' is misleading, for as Jerrold Post cautions, 'there are as nearly as many variants of personality who become involved in terrorist pursuits as there are variants of personality'.[7] To mitigate the errors inherent in making generalizations, a study must necessarily limit itself to an examination of terrorists from a particular geographical area, and with similar ideological bent. Such categorization simplifies and minimizes error through over-generalizations. Eventually it may be possible to make useful cross-national, cross-cultural, and cross-ideological comparisons. In the cases taken for this study the assumption is that, although a number of nationalities are represented, they share the experience of being 'Western' and 'European' and claim similar ideological frameworks of the radical left.

Post makes a useful distinction between 'anarchic-ideologues' such as the Italian Red Brigades or the German Red Army Faction and 'nationalist-secessionist' groups such as the Spanish Basques of ETA or the Irish Republican Army, stating that

> There would seem to be a profound difference between terrorists bent on destroying their own society, the 'world of their fathers,' and those whose terrorist activities carry on the mission of their fathers. To put it in other words, for some, becoming terrorists is an act of retaliation for real and imagined hurts *against the society of their parents*; for others, it is an act of retaliation against society *for the hurt done to their parents* .... This would suggest more conflict, more psychopathology, among those committed to anarchy and destruction of society ... .[8]

To illustrate the proposed framework for examining terrorist literature, this study uses a variety of material written and spoken by European 'anarchic-ideologues' – specifically, the major left-wing groups found in France, West Germany, Italy, and Belgium, frequently categorized in very general terms as anarchist/millenialists or, more recently, 'Euro-terrorists'.[9] This analysis employs material from Belgian groups such as the Communist Combatant Cells (CCC) and the Revolutionary Front for Proletarian Action (FRAP); from French groups such as *Action Directe* (AD); from German groups such as *Rote Armee Fraktion* (RAF), Revolutionary Cells (RZ), and *Rote Zora*; and from Italian groups such as *Brigate Rosse* (RB) and *Prima Linea* (PL).[9]

Although these particular groups have different ages,[10] all trace their roots and initial inspiration to the student revolts in Europe in 1968, originating in the protest movement against the Vietnam War. Focusing most of their energies on changing or overthrowing the governments of their respective countries, they share a common hatred for the United States and claim allegiance to a revolutionary brotherhood dedicated to solidarity with Third World liberation movements. It was in 1981 that the Red Brigades, considered purely an Italian problem, first struck out at NATO with its kidnapping of US General Dozier. Periodically, thereafter, other anti-NATO attacks occurred throughout Europe, culminating in 1984 and 1985 with a declaration of unity announced by the German Red Army Faction and the French *Action Directe*. Joint actions by these groups, with implied Italian inspiration, along with continued and apparently co-ordinated attacks against American, NATO, and Israeli targets by the entire spectrum of radical left groups throughout Europe (from Greece, to Portugal, to Belgium), led to the coining of the phrase 'Euro-terrorism' and the suggestion that an international master cell was in place guided by a single objective of destroying the Western alliance. European terrorist groups enjoyed an increase in stature while European countries scurried to work together as cooperatively as they imagined the terrorist groups were already doing successfully.

Although these groups are particularly interesting because of their longevity and attempt at unification, the choice of these groups as illuminators of the framework is purely arbitrary. The conclusions to be drawn, however, about the usefulness of terrorist literature are by no means limited to these groups.

The Framework

Behavioral assessments have been made of terrorist literature, using psycho-linguistics, psychiatric assessments, psychologic analysis, propaganda analysis and even graphological analysis.[11] More appropriate for this type of literature is the use of traditional content analysis which examines the texts as a whole rather than breaking them down into phrases and words. Although the original work is the most valid object for study, much information of less specific nature can still be derived from translations. And for any such study a familiarity with the group and the political context is essential.

The problem is to organize such a general content analysis so as to reach beyond speculative surmising and make available information about the inner workings of the terrorist group. If one accepts Jerrold Post's argument that a key motivation for membership in a terrorist group is the sense of belonging and the fraternity of like-minded members, it follows that there will be enormous apprehensions that the group may fall apart. With little or nothing to belong to what does a terrorist do? This issue can be monitored through the consistent readings of terrorist literature with a view to specifically pinpointing the group's sensitivities, the internal disagreements, and moral weaknesses to ascertain vulnerabilities. First, the audience of a communiqué or tract must be delineated. Normally, the purpose of the writing is to reach more than one audience. The government is the most prominent one. The communiqué claims credit and offers justification for an action. It threatens further action, and often demands specific changes or moves to prevent their further use of violence. A second prominent audience is the group's 'constituency' – 'the people', 'the workers', or 'the oppressed peoples of the Third World'. Their purpose is to inform this audience of their purpose, their courage, and their selflessness; to proclaim their love and sacrifice for this people they no longer see, to engender support amongst them, to draw sympathy and perhaps, to mobilize them.

A third important and crucial, but less prominent audience is the members of other like-minded groups. Whether in competition or in cooperation with one another, terrorist groups nurture large, sensitive egos. Their pride requires that they transmit their worth to all others – acceptance into the 'terrorist community' is not only essential to their national and/or international standing but also generates a pool of sympathizers and potential recruits. Proclamations of solidarity for other groups enhance their image and buy them matched salutes of solidarity, creating the effect of a larger and more powerful organization.

The most important and least obvious audience is the terrorists themselves. To maintain morale, the members of a group must feel good about themselves. Writing is the expression of the group's immediate feelings and an attempt to adjust them constantly upward. Thus, the *auto-propaganda* effect of the communiqués is to applaud and glorify the terrorists, to justify and even to criticize their actions, as well as to motivate members for further activity, and, as described by Albert Bandura, to promote what he calls the 'moral disengagement' of the group.[12]

Assuming that terrorists are products of the society in which they live (setting aside for the moment psychopaths or otherwise disturbed persons who may be, but rarely are members) we can also expect that they have incorporated to some extent certain moral standards and rules of conduct. This assumption is further strengthened when we realize that terrorists are deliberately overstepping moral bounds and therefore *must* be aware of what they are doing.[13] Violating the rules brings social condemnation, but interestingly enough and more importantly, it also brings *self*-condemnation activated, Bandura asserts, by learned 'internal regulators'.[14] Bandura describes ways in which one can turn off these regulators and be 'disengaged' from inhumane conduct, and those mechanisms are particularly relevant in an examination of terrorist literature.

Although he points out that this act of 'disengagement' is not unusual (people frequently must rationalize actions they carry out that have or could have injurious effects) it appears that it is an overriding concern of the terrorists. It has long been known that an indoctrination process is necessary to prepare members of a terrorist group to carry out violent acts.[15] Bandura calls this the generation of 'self-exonerations needed to neutralize self-sanctions'[16] or what we might call rationalizing guilt.

Because so much of the 'Euro-terrorist' literature serves the auto-propaganda purpose and since the aim of this study is to show how terrorists understand themselves, the remainder of the essay elaborates auto-propaganda themes. One tends to picture terrorist activity as wholly extraordinary but ironically it is striking how often and how emphatically terrorists describe their activities in moral language ordinary society is accustomed to using. Euro-terrorists' pamphlets are written to support a 'war', and that term is used in a literal not a metaphorical sense. For it is in war, Franco Ferracuti says, that society permits violence, and 'The "normal" [not insane] terrorist is therefore like a soldier outside of time and space living in a reality of war that exists only in his or her fantasy'.[17] Comparing real war with the terrorists' war he argues that the terrorists are actually attempting to replicate certain conditions which must exist for a war we can justify to take place. The process involves identifying a crisis (or creating one), building an organized collectivity of opposition, transforming the 'enemy' into something 'alien and hostile', and building a reciprocal 'maniacal feeling of increasing power and invulnerability'. Elements such as these are abundant in terrorist literature with constant references to the 'armed struggle', 'war on imperialist war', and to characterizations of themselves as 'soldiers'.

> BUILD UP THE POLITICAL-MILITARY FRONT IN WESTERN EUROPE AS PART OF THE WORLDWIDE STRUGGLE BETWEEN THE INTERNATIONAL PROLETARIAT AND THE IMPERIALIST BOURGEOISIE.
>
> NEVER BE DETERRED BY THE ENORMOUS DIMENSIONS OF YOUR OWN GOALS.
>
> THE WEST EUROPEAN GUERRILLAS ARE CONVULSING THE EUROPEAN CENTER.[18]

To maintain the 'war footing' it is at the same time necessary to discredit legal or peaceful attempts to fight the battle. In the following excerpt, the italicized words (my emphasis) demonstrate this fascination with the image that the terrorists are 'at war' because of the imminence of war, and the futility of other non-violent means, in a declaration of responsibility for the bombing of a computer office of the French Ministry of Defense:

> *Wars, war economy*, a continuing economy based on *arms*: This is the central characteristic of the economy of imperialism, a question of *the two great wars, the cold war of the 1950s, the some 250 armed conflicts* the world experienced from 1945 to 1984, the intensification of *weapons* spending ... *militarism* clearly appears as the lifesaver to which capitalism systematically clings whenever the

forces inherent in its own system risk sinking it in the abyss of *crisis*. Confronted with the need inherent in the system, *it is ridiculous to look to peaceful pacifism.*[19]

To the terrorists the time is long past for engaging the legal system of the state or using peaceful protest to change the system. The 'capitalists'' cards are stacked against them. The reigning system has built-in mechanisms for 'pacification of the antagonism of the masses'. While 'the bell jar of state security that is in place over society does not disappear, but rather is felt by increasing numbers of the people, the screw of impoverization that they have applied begins to take hold'.[20] The terrorist is not deluded.

It may be that violence, terror, *illegal* actions breed more satisfaction and *possible* results despite the higher risks. Always the terrorist effort is described, as any just war would be, as the strategy of last resort. It is not seen as a more expedient course, nor is there ever a limit outlined in the pamphlets, as contrasted with the memoirs, which indicate that the desire to act frequently determines the decision to take up arms.

> Our original conception of the organization implied a connection between the urban guerrilla and the work at the base. We would like it if each and all of us could work in the neighbourhoods and factories, in socialist groups that already exist, influence discussion, experience and learn. This has proved impossible .... Some say that the possibilities for agitation, propaganda and organisation are far from being eradicated and that only when they are, should we pose the question of arms. We say: it will not really be possible to profit from any political actions as long as armed struggle does not appear clearly as the goal of the politicisation, ...[21]

The auto-propaganda effect of these messages is to persuade the terrorist the enemy is real, the cause just, and the terrorist's existence not only justified, but called for due to the 'urgency' of the moment. It is very difficult but necessary to maintain this sense of urgency. For while they wait, discuss, and delay action the enemy is overtaking them: 'the period of small steps [by the imperialists] and of hitting individual targets is over; the acceleration of the process of reconstruction is now proceeding with the regularity of a steam roller ... [over the bodies of the workers].'[22] Indeed, the terrorists are endowed with particular qualities that allow them to carry on the struggle, 'to work towards a strategy of communist liberation of the proletariat' because they can 'regard the present with the insights of tomorrow ...' and recognize that the 'historic task of the communists – both as a faction and as an organized avant garde of the proletariat – is to understand the movement of capital in its entirety ... to understand ... the development of the revolutionary consciousness of the proletariat ...'.[23] Although the terrorist relies upon 'Marxist analysis in order to understand reality',[24] without violent action such 'Marxist methodology would deteriorate to a static theorizing about reality'. With both methodology *and* action, the terrorists feel they can 'really develop the dynamic of construction/destruction'.[25]

Although at times difficult to comprehend, terrorism is a rational strategy, one in which the benefits exceed the costs for its employers. The driving force and justifications for the group's existence are moral. Thus, the 'just' war is the battle against evil, and always in self-defense. Going against the prevailing system and mores, and using violence in a 'legitimate' fashion can provide individuals with personal satisfaction far beyond the stated 'cause'. Obviously, there are many motives for engaging in such unconventional activities.

When the media 'misrepresents our combat' by introducing 'questioning and suspicion'[26] and by labelling the combatants as 'anarchists', more explanations are needed, and more communiqués are generally issued. Terrorists treasure their commitment to the people, believe the feelings are reciprocal, and fashion themselves as adventurous young people who, with little trouble and much ingenuity, are able to make an impact on the state. Intrigue is the exciting part of the game and 'intelligence [covert action] is not a shameful disease ... but a necessary practice ...'.[27]

Memoirs of defectors and depositions given by repentant terrorists reveal that terrorists themselves have debated the issues of the morality of violence and just what constitutes 'terrorism'.[28] Living underground, such individuals slowly become divorced from reality, descending into a world in which they wage Ferracuti's 'fantasy way'. They can never rest or withdraw from the struggle, however. The German defector Klein describes the misery of his life after leaving the group still hiding underground, but this time without his comrades, living in fear of *them* as well as of the authorities. Klein has swapped one struggle for another.[29]

Because the abstract boundary between political terror and crime is not clear, there is a continuing need to elevate the terrorist motive above that of the criminal, a need that becomes elemental to the terrorist's perception of his success.[30] This need to justify and validate his violent actions becomes a consuming part of his existence, for the terrorist is *aware* of the moral, legal boundaries he oversteps which is why he must fashion himself to be a soldier.[31] But not only is he a soldier, he must also be a victim, one whose pain assures that he will prevail: 'Not those who cause the most suffering will be victorious, but rather those who suffer the most!'[32] Dying for the cause is the ultimate propaganda act and proof of one's dedication to others as well as to oneself. Turning the terrorist violence against the terrorist becomes an exquisite paradox – passively killing oneself so as to believe oneself.[33]

Apparently, the auto-propaganda aspect of words and actions can at times become too powerful and dominating, to the point that the group loses touch with reality. Popular support can hardly be gained by a group that does not become a symbol of justice and liberty. Between 1980 and early 1984, limited to avoiding arrest and running from police, and occasional seemingly meaningless bombings, the European terrorist groups lost what minor public support and interest they had previously enjoyed. There was a tendency to lose sight of their strategic need to mobilize the masses and to open up the 'path' to their goal. Condemning aimless violence (and a violence which must have appeared self-serving) AD, RAF, and new CCC communiqués tried to correct this situation in a stream of written material during the summer and fall of 1984 in the wake of the European peace movement and the addition of nuclear missiles to the continent.

The 'enemy' was now characterized on a grander, more evil scale, and its 'true character' was more evident than before. The time was right, according to the terrorist, to achieve some remarkable results:

> Attacks on the multinational structures of NATO, on its bases and strategies, on its plans and propaganda, are bringing about a transformation of the awareness and practices of the proletariat, going beyond its national characteristics and bringing about an international organizational advance.[34]

While 'this situation is understood by all workers ...' (it is tactfully added so as not to condescend to the prized constituency), the response to the terrorism provides a further augmentation of 'the capital of sympathy and unification which we were in the process of accumulating ...'.[35]

What has been called 'Euro-terrorism' actually developed as a concept years before its manifestations in joint communiqués and action. The shift from clearly indigenous groups to a 'West European guerrilla' was more an expansion of a state of mind than a radical change in type of operations. Terrorists in Italy and Germany have histories stretching back to the late 1960s, when as purely indigenous groups, they held programs to overthrow their respective establishments. Although they had all, to one extent or another, engaged in activities or at least in rhetoric, targeting 'imperialist' and US institutions, the focus had been on domestic targets. Concentrating on such actions now was to be considered 'utopian presumptiveness' since 'detaching one's own territory from the imperialist chain' is not only impracticable but selfish.[36] Within the new concept, it is admitted that each national struggle is equally necessary and must take place simultaneously, but that unity in the struggle should supercede. Yet the newly declared association of the French AD and German RAF (in January 1985) has not kept either group, or the newly formed Belgian CCC, from persisting in their purely national-minded attacks or statements. In practice, despite the talks of unity, the groups remain greatly concerned with anti-establishment actions, with political developments in their own countries, and particularly with the fate of their own comrades and the treatment of 'political prisoners'. Such concerns are reflected in page after page of communiqués explaining the failure of operations, and condemning actions by authorities against incarcerated comrades.

The 1985 announcement of unity had declared that 'It is now necessary and possible to open a new phase in the development of a true revolutionary strategy in the Imperialist Centers ...' with the purpose of creating 'a West

European guerrilla',[37] where each of the European groups was to continue acting on its own national program. Keeping in mind the shared struggle, although recognizing that 'Each one must fight in the sector where he has the most strength', the rebels would at the same time 'always offensively [link] the fight to those of other proletarians involved in other sectors of the same struggle'.[38] The apparent shift in strategy of several European terrorist groups simultaneously brought out a spontaneous reaction from government officials used to flirting with the notion of terrorist conspiracies. The media was full of talk of the need for European cooperation against the united terrorist front. The terrorist campaign of joint actions and communiqués was credited, and rightly so, with having tremendous impact:

> There is a specter going around in Europe: the specter of 'Euro-terrorism'. All forces of old Europe have aligned themselves in a holy crusade in order to hunt down this specter: the Pope and NATO, Paris and Washington, Scelfaro and Barrionuevo, Fabius and Kohl, etc. The entire repressive apparatus of old Europe, the Europe of the alliance, has placed itself in a state of emergency in view of the rise of revolutionary guerrillas.[39]

An educational process was necessary, they state, part of which would be effected through writings, part through joint actions. The union was envisaged by the terrorists as a requisite step in revolutionary strategy where 'Today it is important to regard Western Europe as a homogeneous territory, where the formation of a unified revolutionary pole is possible ...'[40] but not to be accomplished overnight. 'Concretely put: we regard the process of the new-formation of the totality of the European proletariat into one single proletarian faction as a process that has not yet been concluded'.[41]

This union of 'internationalization of the proletariat' is necessary *because* the *enemy* is unified. But the unification of the European terrorist groups into a 'metropolis proletariat' will not be 'a soup in which all experiences are blended ...'[42] but will recognize national differences. Although the very idea of a 'front' is called an 'open concept', it is insisted that there must be resistance to any purely independent structures.

Ironically, the union of revolutionary groups into an 'anti-imperialist front in Western Europe' is required to fend off the unification of Western Europe, which is considered the next step in 'imperialist domination'. The most 'aggressive of the capitalist factions' is the military-industrial complex, considered responsible for the impetus to militarize, homogenize, and 'Americanize' Western Europe into 'one counterrevolutionary bloc'.[43] The crisis is imminent and action, not pacifism, is necessary *now* because of 'the reality' of the coming 'imperialist war' and the risk of being 'damned to be "cannon fodder"' in the coming conflicts and, until that point, to be "profit fodder" in the Near East, Africa, etc.'.[44] Exhorting to action is not to take the offensive, however. Revolutionary acts are in response to what is characterized as an offensive threat. Thus, an action is justified if it is accepted that, 'That which is destroying us must itself be destroyed ...'.[45]

To believe these words and be able to act on them is a whole process in itself. The techniques for the necessary 'moral disengagement' are heavily disguised and not easily recognized. Bandura suggests that part of the process is carried out by what he terms 'euphemistic labelling' and 'dehumanization'.[46] Renaming themselves, their actions, their victims and their enemies accords the terrorist respectability. What they say and what they do are actually two entirely different things. A May Day bombing, for instance, is an 'intervention on behalf of the works', or an 'affirmation of the proletarian value of the world holiday of the oppressed'. Much effort goes into characterizing the enemy. The David and Goliath theme is prevalent – there is nobility and honor in the courage and determination of an oppressed party who dares to strike out at the 'oppressor'.

The use of euphemisms or name-calling is profuse throughout the communiqués of every group (that is, 'pigs', 'imperialist exploiters', 'carrions and their consorts', etc.). Often the name-calling process degenerates to the point where, to further ascribe guilt and worthiness of punishment, the terrorists divest the enemy of human qualities. By imputing 'bestial qualities' to the targets they choose to attack makes them subhuman or even animals. 'Pigs' deserve nothing more than what the terrorists deliver them.

Frequently the state is labelled *terrorist*, particularly with regard to treatment of the rebels themselves (such as 'the terrorist program against the prisoners') and frequently with regard to actions seen as directed against the rest of the people in general: 'the major power of NATO has raised state terrorism against the anti-imperialist guerrilla groups, the liberation movements and the population, which are refusing their loyalty, to an official government policy'.[47] Some analysts would label this technique as projection on the part of the rebels, but they are not the only ones to do so:

> The demonizing of the guerrillas, the witch hunt, the *projection of terrorism* onto the guerrillas are losing their effectiveness, and no longer mobilize on behalf of the state. On the contrary, terror is the concept that clings like tar to a system that only destroys, suppresses and stands in the way of any kind of human development (emphasis mine).[48]

It was previously noted that a terrorist prefers to call himself a 'revolutionary' or a 'freedom fighter'. Often reference is made to historical moments and historical figures for validation, in what Bandura terms 'advantageous comparison'.[49] A technique used to elevate the terrorist sense of what he is and what he is doing, such comparisons frequently use quotes from illustrious revolutionary figures – Marx, as we have seen with the use of the Communist Manifesto, or Lenin, or Che – and are used to explain that 'The present belongs to the struggle; the future belongs to us. (Che)'[50] and that the terrorists are merely carrying on the struggle.

Again, through recitations of the cruelties carried out by the state, the terrorists appear relatively innocent. Often this technique is employed when terrorist members are arrested and held in prison. The RAF used such an occasion to spell out the atrocities (solitary confinement and 'sensory deprivation') committed against their comrades by the German authorities, resulting in their suicide/'murders'.

> As a symbol of the revolutionary potential that exists in every corner of W. German cities, the RAF had to be annihilated before they became heroes and examples for the malcontents to follow. And so on 18 Oct. 1977, Andreas Baader, Jan Carl Raspe and Gundrun Ensslin were murdered in Stuttgart-Stammheim prison.[51]

> The number of political prisoners suffering from the terrorist conditions of prisons are not limited to urban guerrillas, but include lawyers, authors, publishers and bookshop keepers.[52]

Such restructuring of their own behavior in contrast to that of the state provides not only self-exoneration but also, states Bandura, self-glorification and a source of self-pride.[53] Dehumanizing the enemy becomes automatic with practice. Klein, in an interview given from hiding after his defection from the RAF, spoke of his fear of having a weapon with him *now* because he was unsure of his control over it. Possession caused what he called an 'over-estimation of your opponent' and subsequent use became easily justified with little forethought.[54] When no one technique will satisfactorily transform or 'whitewash' a violent act, there is always a way to deny responsibility for it in the first place.[55] Unfortunately for them, the hard-sought exposure given to the terrorists is not to their liking. When actions have unintended consequences, groups have been known to withdraw their claims. In 1981, when *Action Directe* was still very young and as yet inexperienced in the fine arts of assassination, it found itself in a cooperative venture with a Lebanese group in Paris (the so-called Lebanese Armed Revolutionary Faction or LARF) which was involved in the elimination of American and Israeli diplomats and functionaries. A bomb placed under the car of Roderick Grant, then American diplomatic councillor at the embassy in Paris, was discovered, but not before AD claimed responsibility for placing it. LARF also claimed to have taken part in the action. Two members of the Paris bomb squad were killed instantly as they attempted to defuse the device. When news of their deaths hit the press, AD members, presumably dismayed by this turn of events, promptly telephoned authorities to disown their part in the action. Such a disclaimer is instructive of a number of possible tendencies: either the deaths were actually unintended or some or all of the members decided belatedly that they wanted no part of such violence; possibly there was disagreement within the group about the prudence or justification for such action; or, once the news was broadcast, the group feared the negative public reaction.

If a disclaimer is not practical, elaborate explanations may be required. The CCC May Day bombing, which claimed the lives of two firemen at the scene of the burning van containing explosives, prompted the group to displace responsibility for the deaths. To punctuate their accusation, they bombed the 'head financial and logistics office' of the Brussels gendarmerie. According to the CCC, 'The entire world will understand the selection of this target for attack because of the responsibility of the gendarmerie ...',[56] presumably for the firemen's deaths. The firemen were the first fatalities of the extensive bombing activity initiated by the CCC in October 1984. The media and government response was outrage, but communiqués suggest that the CCC experienced a severe reaction to the event as well. Rather than expressing remorse or guilt, however, they express their indignation: 'The deaths of these two men shock us deeply and arouse our rage at those responsible ...'.[57] Several pages are dedicated to explaining how the responsibility for the firemen's deaths could and should be placed at the doorstep of the 'gendarmerie' and not at their own. Their dismay lies more in the fact that 'the deaths of these public servants has destroyed and obviated the power of our initiative, has concealed the correctness of the attack ...' and that 'the police campaign which is being carried out in the media concerning our so-called "contempt for human life" is a despicable falsification of our political texts ...'.[58] Although they regret the deaths, they are convinced of the appropriateness of the target. It is the deaths that 'in a tragic way' made the act 'incomprehensible and inaccessible to the population as a whole'.[59] The explanation is that the 'pigs' sent the firemen to their deaths, probably because of the 'scorn that the bourgeoisie has for the workers ...' and so that the authorities could 'exploit' the accident.

It is difficult not to hear the remorse of the terrorists, particularly in one passage that nearly sounds like a plea for forgiveness: 'We bow down before the victims and respect the pain of their families and comrades. We understand their rage, but we ask them in view of our explanation to consider against whom this rage should be directed ...'.[60]

Much more difficult to detect in terrorist written works is the attempt to justify actions based on what Bandura terms the 'diffusion of responsibility'[61] where all members of the group share the onus of an action but at the same time no one individual is to blame. Presumably this could be revealed in terrorist confessions or when a group has fractured.[62] This technique is enhanced in groups with rigid hierarchical structures. Here, individual members relinquish personal control over their actions, while honoring their obligation to the group and their commitment to the cause. Group decision-making and collective action can also have the same effect, so that no one person need feel *he* made the choice or the move that brings moral condemnation.

What They Think It Will Accomplish

Most terrorist actions are perfectly suited to distancing oneself from the effects of one's actions. The majority of terrorist attacks are hit and run operations where the actual damage, destruction, and/or deaths need not be witnessed first-hand. As long as the terrorists keep themselves insulated from the effects of their violence, that is, leaving the scene, not dwelling on the news of the dead and injured but rather on the reactions of the authorities, they can avoid dealing with their moral anxieties.

Yet whatever the terrorists believe they will accomplish is fairly well hidden. That they believe they are successfully moving toward this unknown is often stated and with confidence. According to one imprisoned terrorist, 'It is fairly certain that the extent of the armed actions and the massive actions in solidarity with the revolutionary militant prisoners *justify the fear* that has been unleashed on the governments of the member states of NATO ... the success of all of this activity is undeniable.'[63] In piecing together allusions to this future a picture emerges of destroying one society so as to replace it with a new one. This new social system is to be based on the free development of the individual, the emancipation of the proletariat and 'can only come about through the destruction of capitalism and the opening of a path to communist liberation'.[64] Not one of the terrorist authors seems to be able or interested in specifying what the new social system will be like, but all are agreed that 'We want to destroy this society in order to build up' another, one that will be 'a just and classless society, in which production meets the needs of all, not only the needs of a privileged few, ... a society in which ''equality for all'' no longer has to be demanded, because it has already been realized'.[65] To justify acts of violence, the situation must be black and white, with little room for hesitation. Often using the claim of conspiracy, the groups build the evil enemy, explaining here why violence is necessary and why it is necessary *now*:

> We arrive at this step from the objective situation: The central importance of Western Europe for the reconstruction of imperialism which has become weakened as the result of the liberation struggle of the peoples of the South ... which in turn has resulted in a collision between the growing forces of productivity and the limitations of the world markets. This has led to a global political, economic, and military crisis in the imperialist chain of states, and has now touched the entire imperialist system.[66]

The tone of alarm communicates the necessity of the organization while the murky, sometimes confused explanation portrays the revolutionaries as dedicated, hard-working intellectuals who have clearly thought all of this out. It is hard to imagine the average man on the street getting this message from the widely distributed flyer. Instead, the tract impressed its writer, making him *feel* that this generation of the Red Army Faction had been created in response to a threat. Characterizing the enemy as a conspirator allows the terrorists to refuse to believe what is so apparent and obvious to everyone else. The terrorist plays the part of self-appointed detective with a superior ability to recognize and decipher the state's *real* intentions.

Although he may pose himself as particularly knowledgeable about the purposes of the 'imperialist conspiracy', it is evident that much internal group friction results over these debates. The discussions themselves can lead to disagreement and cleavage with factions following a new, self-determined rationale. All revolutionary groups – terrorist or guerrilla – have had their internal critics. Sometimes these critics, like Hans Joachim Klein and Michael Baumann of the German millenialist groups, for example, have left the underground and written or talked about how the clandestine life of terrorist violence had gone wrong. Debates over the justification for violence, the types of targets, the issues of indiscriminate versus discriminate killing, are endemic to a terrorist group. Such differences of opinion within terrorist groups have on occasion led authorities to believe that a schism existed. Because of the new 'internationalist' focus of AD communiqués, for instance, and the continuation of AD anti-establishment actions, French authorities are convinced of a group split.

Concluding Reflections

Terrorism entails the use of violence for effect, 'speaking with action' rather than with words. Yet the meaning of an act is not always clear, and therefore an integral part of most terrorist activity is the explanation later provided in written and oral forms. Although this explanation is ostensibly directed at the state authorities, or a constituency, or potential recruits, it has rarely been recognized that the explanations are developed to convince the terrorists themselves that what they are doing is correct and justified. An awareness of the auto-propaganda aspect brings a richer dimension to the information normally available to the analyst in terrorist communiqués.

Some groups write more than others. The Belgian Communist Combatant Cells (CCC) has been quite prolific since its inception, while the French *Action Directe* (AD) was never able to sustain a flow of written materials. Save for some interviews and a few short papers, AD's communiqués have often been rather short and brutally to the point, while the CCC will take five pages or more to explain a particular action. The Italian Red Brigades (RB) are known for their voluminous works and painfully detailed documents, while the German Red Army Faction (RAF) wrote about itself and its actions consistently in the early years, but only sporadically since then. Indeed, the absence of any significant declarations by the RAF since 1982 led authorities to believe this was one more indication that the movement was in disarray and weakened.

A necessary caution in analyzing written materials of terrorists is that, while we tend to attribute the declarations to the entire group, the individual author or authors certainly imbue the text with personal elements. It is usually unknown to what extent the texts are approved or censored by other members, although such practices undoubtedly exist. The frequency and quantity of writing may, as mentioned, indicate the health of the group, yet much written material is issued from prison cells by incarcerated members. More likely, it appears that the frequency, quantity, and style of writing depends as much on the availability of an intellectual member prone to written expression as on the overall condition of the group, although it may be this very lack of intellectual leadership that also indicates a group in decline.

Without the 'proper' justification and explanation of the group's violence, and periodic assessment and/or realignment of strategy, terrorist activity tends to deteriorate into mindless or self-serving violence. 'Communication and discussion are necessary because they are the prerequisites for all to learn ...'[67] but at the same time, 'Communism does not develop via radical positions in texts. It expresses itself in a precise analysis of the situation and in a transfer to actual practice ...'.[68] Similarly, during the early days of the RAF, then leader Ulrike Meinhof dedicated herself to espousing revolutionary doctrine for the group, concluding, however, that 'Writing is shit, now let's make the revolution'.[69] With Meinhof's death, Brigitte Monhaupt took over the pen as well as the intellectual leadership of the RAF rather effectively, but with her demise 'on the whole, at least toward the outside, the RAF has become less verbal, and the men and women now prominent in it make very few statements. For example, we have no statements at all ... from current co-leader Christian Klar. But that does not mean he is not a true fanatic.'[70] Klar has since written some rather unintelligible material from his prison cell in Germany, accompanied by some superficially theoretical tracts from Brigitte Monhaupt – it appears that some individuals simply choose to write more than others.

Certain personalities carry the weight and responsibility of writing for the group. Pierre Carette, presumed leader of the Belgian CCC and probable author of their extensive communiqués, has a history of radical activity and as a professional printer, has an intimate association with the written word. The Red Brigades owes its literary debt to figures such as Curcio and Moretti, and the Germans to Mahler, Monhaupt and Meinhof.

An additional caution is necessary in such an analysis of terrorist literature. Each type of material presumably has a particular purpose: policy papers are for internal as well as external consumption to outline strategy and rally support; communiqués are to explain and persuade a larger public and a perceived constituency; memoirs are personal therapeutic autobiographies to justify and evaluate the past. Yet all this material can be seen as focusing on several audiences. The very need, even compulsion, to explain and justify, works to deny the real appearance of the violent actions. And this denial is directed as much at an outer audience as it is to an inner one. Not only need they convince themselves, but other terrorist groups as well. They have a 'constituency' they must answer to, be it fringe sympathizers or potential recruits or the terrorists of other groups. A certain prestige and intellectual sophistication is required to be considered legitimate. The least important audience of all, perhaps, is the government, although the communiqués are often directed to the authorities. The group and the individual author(s) require the written and spoken exercise to build conviction amongst the members and in its audience. There is no greater fan of the terrorist, however, than the terrorist himself. Analyzing the material from these two different aspects should separate one fiction from another and perhaps even provide some useful facts.

Text analysis can be useful in a number of ways. Changes can be detected in the mood and thinking of the group, and at times disharmony can be illuminated. It can provide obvious clues to tactical procedures and changes. Most importantly, however, it can reveal the methods and level of 'moral disengagement' necessary to head off internal disagreements and disenchantment of individual members. Although the analysis should ideally be carried out using the original work, translations can provide a lot of otherwise unavailable information and insights.

Idiosyncratic differences emerge from group to group because of different writers, different nationalities, and different national programs, but the basic characteristics of the European 'anarchic-ideologues' are the same. The groups share (1) obviously, but importantly, a common use of terrorist violence; (2) denial that they are terrorists; (3) the need to portray themselves in a favorable light in order to attract support; (4) the need to rationalize and justify what they do; and (5) the need to feel good about themselves to maintain group cohesion.

A number of basic conclusions consequently emerge. According to the memoirs of defectors and the depositions of repentant terrorists, a life of violence tends to harden or defeat its adherents. Once in the underground it is nearly impossible to leave it intact. Those who do escape are more demoralized than renewed, as Klein indicates in his written work from hiding.

Another impression, but certainly not conclusion from terrorist literature, is that it may be true that European anarchists, unlike other terrorists, belong more to the 'province of psychologists than political analysts ...'.[71] Reality in their terms, is dramatically unreal to us; their continuing attempts to convince themselves and others of this abstract vision is remarkable in its energy and persistence.

A closer assessment needs to be made, but this brief look suggests that, difficult as it is to gauge systematically the frequency and quantity of writing by terrorists the impression is that not only do the groups appear to write less frequently as they age, but by deduction this suggests they may care less about the consequences of their acts. These observations are less evident in the communiqués than in the memoirs or statements of repentants.

The stress of life underground and the continuous struggle to survive often distorts the already 'strange' perceptions of terrorists, according to members of terrorist groups who have defected or recanted. Another form of 'underground life' – the prison – appears to have similar effects on the terrorists. After several years of incarceration, virtually cut off from the outside world, the images they conjure of the people and of the enemy become more and more bizarre.

What about 'Euro-terrorism?' Declarations of 'unity', 'comradeship', 'brotherhood', etc., do not disguise the fact that cooperation is elusive. The 'Western anti-imperialist front' is more a loose confederation of like-minded groups than an actual organizational structure. Intuitively, this failure to unite can be attributed to idiosyncratic group rationales and strong, uncompromising personalities. Attempts at cooperation with each other appear difficult to execute in practice and, if achieved, are often short-lived.

Despite the claims of union, the real focus of these groups is the problems they see in their own countries and political systems. It is not simply a matter of ageing as a group and expanding horizons. On the contrary, the older and more sophisticated the group, the stronger the realization appears to be that because of the inherent imbalance between the group and its chosen enemy the state, no notable changes can be forced into the international environment. The prospect for change at home can be nearly as futile, but time and again these groups have felt they made an impact, if only by the attention they generated from the security services of the state and media coverage. A recent document put out by remnants of the Red Brigades of Italy makes this sentiment clear when its author thanks all the other European revolutionaries for their actions and declarations of solidarity, but insists that the Red Brigades not be distracted and continue with the business at hand – the problems of politics at home. The union of the European groups remains more in the mind of authorities than in the minds of the terrorists, where there is actually more an absorption with self than with the enemy.

Text analysis can be useful if carried out with caution and consistency. Following the writings of a particular group can provide invaluable insights to the workings and mindset of the group, can detect changes in mood and thinking and illuminate disharmony amongst the members or with the members of other groups. Besides providing obvious clues to tactical procedures and changes, terrorist literature unintentionally reveals the methods and intensity of 'moral disengagement' that may be creating tension and conflict within the group. Only by reading and analyzing this material (or, of course, through the rare and difficult procedure of communicating with a successful plant in the group) can such information be obtained. Not only is the quantity and quality of such literature a measure of the health and cohesion of a group, but it also appears to be a most important window into their otherwise clandestine, underground life.

NOTES

An earlier version of this paper is being published in Paul Wilkinson (ed.), *Current Research on Terrorism* (Aberdeen: University Press, 1987).

1. Frequently cited are the examples of the French and American revolutions and successful colonialist revolts.
2. Issues of definition, of course, have presented a problem to many parties seeking a clear boundary for what should be considered terrorism. The label has become so burdened with value connotations that the actors themselves reject it, a distinct change from the turn of the century when anarchists and revolutionaries proudly adopted it. Terrorism in this essay refers to a definition first used by Thornton in 'Terror as a Weapon of Political Agitation', *Internal War: Problems and Approaches*, edited by Harry Eckstein (1964), p.73; 'Terror is a symbolic act designed to influence political behaviour by extranormal means, entailing the use or the threat of violence'. Additionally, it is determined by the nature of the act and not by the nature of the perpetrator. See also Brian Jenkins, *The Study of Terrorism: Definitional Problems* (The Rand Corporation, Dec. 1980).
3. For the purposes of this article, I will risk the criticisms of the rebels by labeling subnational groups employing violence as 'terrorists' throughout.
4. David Rapoport was, to my knowledge, the first to make such an assertion about the terrorist mentality. In his 1971 primer on *Assassination and Terrorism* he states, 'All terrorists must deny the relevance of guilt and innocence, but in doing so they create an unbearable tension in their own souls, for they are in effect saying that a person is not a person. It is no accident that left-wing terrorists constantly speak of a "pig-society"; by convincing *themselves* that they are confronting animals they hope to stay the remorse which the slaughter of the innocent necessarily generates, *Assassination and Terrorism*, (Toronto: CBC Merchandising, 1971), p.42.
5. Nathan Leites, 'Understanding the Next Act', Terrorism, Vol.3 (1979), p.1.
6. Ibid., p.2.
7. Jerrold Post, 'Notes on a Psychodynamic Theory of Terrorist Behavior', *Terrorism* (1984), p.242.
8. Ibid., p.243.
9. The sources enlisted in this study are representative, and not a comprehensive compilation of all such primary source material.
10. The French AD, for instance, was created in 1979, and the CCC not until 1984, while the Italian Red Brigades and the German RAF were well into their second generation by that time. Several current groups are the result of the decline, splitting, or 'regeneration' of previous groups.
11. See Joyce Peterson's *Using Stylistic Analysis to Assess Threat Messages* (The Rand Corporation, Oct. 1985), for a description of these techniques still being developed. She suggests using accepted literary tools as well. For other work on the psychological mechanisms, personality, and social backgrounds of those drawn to political violence, see works by Konrad Kellen, *On Terrorists and Terrorism* (The Rand Corporation, Dec. 1982), and A. Kaplan, 'The Psychodynamics of Terrorism', *Terrorism* (1978).
12. Albert Bandura, 'Mechanisms of Moral Disengagement', unpublished paper presented at the Interdisciplinary Research Conference on 'The Psychology of Terrorism: Behaviors, World-Views, States of Mind', Washington, DC, March 1987.
13. Again, this point has been suggested earlier by David C. Rapoport: 'To speak of the systematic use of terror for publicity and provocation purposes is to presume, of course, that the antagonists in some critical senses share a moral community.' See 'The Politics of Atrocity' in Yonah Alexander and Seymour Maxwell Finger (ed.), *Terrorism: Interdisciplinary Perspectives* (New York: John Jay Press, 1977), p.51.
14. Bandura, p.1.
15. See, for example, Menachem Begin, in his chapter on going underground 'We Fight, Therefore We Are', *The Revolt*, pp.26–46.
16. Bandura, p.1.

17. Franco Ferracuti, 'A Sociopsychiatric Interpretation of Terrorism', *The Annals of the American Academy of Political and Social Science* (Sept. 1982), p.136.
18. 'Communiqué of Action Directe', June 1985.
19. 'Communiqué from Direct Action', *Ligne Rouge*, 13 July 1984.
20. Brigitte Monhaupt from prison, 26 March 1985.
21. 'RAF Philosophy', *The German Guerrilla: Terror, Reaction, and Resistance* (Orkney, UK: Cienfuegos Press, undated), p.98.
22. 'Communiqué from Direct Action', *Zusammen Kaempfen*, July 1985.
23. *Zusammen Kaempfen*, July 1985, pp.3–6.
24. Ibid.
25. Ibid.
26. 'Concrete Answers to Concrete Question', CCC Communiqué, May 1985.
27. Ibid.
28. See, for instance, Menachem Begin's defence of the actions of the *Irgun* and denial that its members were terrorists in *The Revolt* (New York: Nash Publishing, 1978), pp.45–56 and 59–61.
29. Hans-Joachim Klein, 'Les Memoires d'un Terroriste International', *Liberation*, 8 Oct. 1978.
30. Early anarchist theory in Russia and Western Europe at the end of the nineteenth century and during the 1960s explicitly endorsed all criminal activity as revolutionary.
31. To further illustrate the relationship of military violence to terrorist violence see David C. Rapoport, 'The Politics of Atrocity', in Alexander and Finger (eds.), op. cit., p.59, footnote 14: 'When a war begins, each military act (as long as it stays within the boundaries of military convention) does not have to be justified morally. Precisely because conventions are always being violated, terrorists feel compelled to justify each successive action.'
32. Brigitte Monhaupt quoting Irish hunger striker Patsy O'Hara, 26 March 1985, cited in the Spring 1986 issue of *Open Road*, Vancouver, Canada.
33. This paradox is portrayed in Albert Camus' play *The Just Assassins*, in which Yanek, an imprisoned terrorist, hangs for his crime rather than accept a pardon.
34. 'Communiqué from Action Directe', claiming credit for the assassination of General René Audran, 25 Jan. 1985.
35. 'CCC communiqué', 6 May 1985.
36. Communiqué from FRAP, July 1985.
37. 'For the Unity of Western Europe's Revolutionaries', RAF communiqué early 1985.
38. 'Communiqué from Directe Action', *Ligne Rouge*, 13 July 1984.
39. This remarkable quote taken from *Zusammen Kaempfen*, July 1985, pp.14–16, is undoubtedly a conscious paraphrasing and restatement of Marx's Communist Manifesto which I cite here for comparison: 'A spectre is haunting Europe – the spectre of Communism. All the Powers of old Europe have entered into a holy alliance to exorcise this spectre: Pope and Czar, Metternich and Guizot, French Radicals and German police spies.' (Quoted from 'The Manifesto of the Communist Party', in Robert C. Tucker (ed.), *The Marx–Engels Reader* (New York: W.W. Norton, 1978, p.473.) It is clear that the author using Marx had a sense that his own movement was at a turning point and thus deserved this historic description.
40. Unknown author, 'Internationalization of the Struggle', *Zusammen Kaempfen*, July 1985, pp.3–6.
41. Ibid.
42. Ibid.
43. *Zusammen Kaempfen*, July 1985, pp.8–9.
44. Ibid.
45. 'Communiqué by FRAP', April 1985.
46. Bandura, pp.8–9 and 17–21.
47. 'Christian Klar from prison', 26 March 1985.
48. Ibid.
49. Bandura, pp.9–11.
50. *Zusammen Kaempfen*, July 1985, pp.28–31.

51. 'RAF Philosophy', p.100.
52. Ibid., p.101.
53. Bandura, p.10.
54. 'Interview with Hans Joachim Klein', *Liberation*, 8 Oct. 1978.
55. This Bandura terms simply as 'displacement of responsibility'. See his 'Mechanisms', pp.11–13.
56. 'CCC on 1 May Action', 6 May 1985.
57. Ibid.
58. Ibid.
59. Ibid.
60. Ibid.
61. Bandura, p.13.
62. The European groups in focus here did not provide such an example. Just such a split did take place in an Armenian terrorist group, however, in July 1983. The defectors subsequently wrote pages of accusations of their former leader and in many instances attempted to absolve themselves of the blame for terrorism conducted while they were members. See 'The Reality' presumably authored by Monte Melkonian.
63. *Zusammen Kaempfen*, July 1985, pp.14–16.
64. Ibid.
65. 'Communiqué of FRAP', April 1985.
66. 'For the Unity of Western Europe's Revolutionaries', RAF communiqué approximately early 1985.
67. Unknown author, 'Anti-Imperialist Front', *Zusammen Kaempfen*, July 1985.
68. 'Communique' of Action Directe', June 1985.
69. Quoted in Leites, p.32.
70. Konrad Kellen, Unpublished 'Primer' on the Red Army Faction, 1982.
71. Bowyer Bell, 'Old Trends and Future Realities', *Washington Quarterly*, Spring 1985.

PRIMARY SOURCE MATERIAL

Belgian Groups

Fighting Communist Cells Communiqué', dated 26 Nov. 1984, *Open Road*, Vancouver, Canada, Spring 1986.
'Concrete Answers to Concrete Questions', CCC Communiqué, May 1985.
'Communiqué to CCC', 1 May 1985
'CCC on May 1 Action', 6 May 1985, in *Zusammen Kaempfen*, July 1985.
'CCC Communiqué No. 3 from the Karl Marx Campaign', 4–5 Nov. 1985.
'CCC Communiqué and Addendum', 28 Jan. 1986.
'FRAP Communiqué', May 1985.
'Communiqué by FRAP', in *Zusammen Kaempfen*, July 1985.

French Groups

'Interview with "Action Directe" Leader Rouillan', *Liberation*, Paris, 17 Aug. 1982, p.3.
'Action Directe Leader Rouillan on Attacks, Goals', *Le Matin*, Paris, 5 Oct. 1982, p.19.
'Un Manifeste d'Action Directe', excerpts of lengthy AD communiqué, *Le Monde*, Paris, 21 Oct. 1982.
'Action Directe Communiqué, Anti-Apartheid Bombings', 4 Sept. 1985, *Open Road*, Vancouver, Canada, Spring 1986.

German Groups

RAF Texts, Bo Cavefors Publishers, Malmo, Sweden, 1977.
'RAF Communiqué', 8 Aug. 1985.
Baumann, Michael, *Terror or Love? Bommi Baumann's Own Story of His Life as a West German Urban Guerrilla*, Grove Press, NY, 1978.
Baumann, Michael, 'The Mind of a German Terrorist', *Encounter*, Vol. LI, No. 3 (Sept. 1978), pp.81–8.

Klein, Hans-Joachim, *La Mort Mercenaire: Temoignage d'un Ancien Terroriste Ouest-Allemand*, Editions du Seuil, Paris, 1980.

Klein, Hans-Joachim, 'Les Memoires d'un Terroriste International', *Liberation*, 8 Oct. 1978.

'Revolutionary Cells Communiqué', dated both 24 April 1985 and 2 Sept. 1985, in Spring 1986 issue of *Open Road*, Vancouver, Canada.

'Revolutionary Cells and Rote Zora, Discussion Paper on the Peace Movement', *Open Road*, Vancouver, Canada, Spring 1986.

Italian Groups

Court Depositions of Three Red Brigadists, ed. Sue Ellen Moran, The Rand Corporation, N–2391–RC, Feb. 1986.

'Document 142', excerpts of Red Brigades communiqué in *Le Point*, 2 April 1984.

Prima Linea, 'Des deserteurs du terrorisme temoignent', *Liberation*, No. 2072, Paris, 13 Oct. 1980.

The Logic of Religious Violence

Mark Juergensmeyer

'When the struggle reaches the decisive phase may I die fighting
in its midst.' – Jarnail Singh Bhindranwale

In the mid-1970s, when militant young Sikhs first began to attack the
Nirankaris – members of a small religious community perceived as being
anti-Sikh – few observers could have predicted that that violence would
escalate into the savagery that seized the Punjab in the 1980s. The Sikhs as
a community were too well off economically, too well educated, it
seemed, to be a party to random acts of terror. Yet it is true that militant
encounters have often played a part in Sikh history, and in the mid-1960s a
radical movement very much like that of the 1980s stormed through the
Punjab. The charismatic leader at that time was Sant Fateh Singh, who
went on a well-publicized fast and threatened to immolate himself on the
roof of the Golden Temple's Akali Takht unless the government made
concessions that would lead to the establishment of a Sikh-majority state.
The Indian government, captained by Prime Minister Indira Gandhi,
conceded, and the old Punjab state was carved in two to produce a Hindu-
majority Haryana and a new Punjab. It was smaller than the previous one,
and contained enough Sikh-dominated areas to give it a slim Sikh
majority.

The violence of this decade, however, seems very different from what
one saw in the 1960s.[1] For one thing, the attacks themselves have been
more vicious. Often they have involved Sikhs and Hindus indiscriminately, and many innocent bystanders have been targeted along with politically
active persons. The new Sikh leader, Jamail Singh Bhindranwale, was
stranger – more intense and more strident – than Fateh Singh was, and the
goals of Bhindranwale and his allies were more diffuse. Government
officials who were trying to negotiate a settlement were never quite
certain what their demands were. In fact there was no clear consensus
among the activists themselves as to what they wanted, and the items on
their lists of demands would shift from time to time. In 1984, shortly before
she gave the command for the Indian Army to invade the Golden Temple,
an exasperated Indira Gandhi itemized everything she had done to meet
the Sikh demands and asked, 'What more can any government do?'[2]

It was a question that frustrated many observers outside the government as well, a good many moderate Sikhs among them. But frustration
led to action, and those actions made things worse. The Indian army's
brutal assault on the Golden Temple in June 1984, and the heartless
massacre of Sikhs by Hindus in Delhi and elsewhere after the assassination
of Mrs Gandhi in November of that year caused the violence to escalate.

Still, it is fair to say that quite a bit of bloodshed originated on the Sikh side of the ledger, and within the Sikh community anti-government violence achieved a religious respectability that begs to be explained.

The Rational Explanations

The explanations one hears most frequently place the blame for Sikh violence on political, economic and social factors, and each of these approaches is compelling. The political explanation, for instance, focuses on the weakness of the Sikh political party, the Akali Dal, and its inability to secure a consistent plurality in the Punjab legislature. This is no wonder, since the Sikhs command a bare 51 per cent majority of the post-1966 Punjab. Moreover, the Muslims, who comprised the Punjab's other non-Hindu religious community before 1948, were awarded a nation of their own at the time of India's independence, so it is understandable that many Sikhs would continue to long for greater political power, and even yearn for their own Pakistan.[3]

The economic explanation for Sikh unrest is largely a matter of seeing the achievements of the Sikhs in relation to what they feel their efforts should warrant, rather than to what others in India have received. Compared with almost every other region of India, the Punjab is fairly well-to-do. Yet Sikhs complain, with some justification, that for that very reason they have been deprived of their fair share: resources from the Punjab have been siphoned off to other parts of the nation.[4] Agricultural prices, for example, are held stable in India in part because the government maintains a ceiling on the prices that farmers in rich agricultural areas like the Punjab are permitted to exact. In addition some Sikhs claim that industrial growth has been hampered in the Punjab as the government has encouraged growth in other parts of India, and that the Punjab's agricultural lifeblood – water for irrigation from Punjabi rivers – has been diverted to farming areas in other states.

The social explanation for Sikh discontent is just as straightforward: the Sikhs are a minority community in India, and their separate identity within the Indian family is in danger. Since the religious ideas on which Sikhism is based grew out of the nexus of medieval Hinduism, Sikhs fear they could be reabsorbed into the amorphous cultural mass that is Hinduism and dissappear as a distinct religious community.[5] The possibility is real: Sikhism almost vanished in the latter part of the nineteenth century. But in this century secularism is as much a threat as Hinduism, and like fundamentalist movements in many other parts of the world, Sikh traditionalists have seen the secular government as the perpetrator of a dangerous anti-religious ideology that threatens the existence of such traditional religious communities as their own. In the perception of some Sikhs, these two threats – the religious and the secular – have recently combined forces as the Hindu right has exercised increasing political power and Mrs Gandhi's Congress Party has allegedly pandered to its interests.[6]

There is nothing wrong with these political, economic and social explanations of Sikh unrest. Each is persuasive in its own sphere, and together they help us understand why the Sikhs as a community have been unhappy. But they do not help us understand the piety with which a few Sikhs have justified their bloody acts or the passion with which so many of them have condoned them – even the random acts of destruction associated with terrorism. Nor are they the sort of explanations one hears from Sikhs who are most closely involved in the struggle. The socio-economic and political explanations usually come from observers outside the Sikh community or from those inside it who are least sympathetic to the militant protesters. The point of view of the activists is different. Their frame of reference is more grand: their explanations of the conflict and its causes achieve almost mythical dimensions. To understand this point of view we have to turn to their own words and see what they reveal about the radicals' perception of the world about them.

The Religious Rhetoric of Sikh Violence

To understand the militant Sikh position, I have chosen to focus on the speeches of Jamail Singh Bhindranwale, the man who was without dispute the most visible and charismatic of this generation's militant leaders.[7] He was also the most revered – or despised, depending on one's point of view. During his lifetime he was called a *sant*, a holy man, and a few Sikhs have been bold enough to proclaim him the eleventh *guru*, and thus challenge the traditional Sikh belief that the line of ten gurus ended with Gobind Singh in the early eighteenth century.

Jarnail Singh was born in 1947 at the village Rodey near the town of Moga. He was the youngest son in a poor family of farmers from the Jat caste, and when he was 18 years old his father handed him over for religious training to the head of a Sikh center known as the Damdani Taksal. The leader came from the village Bhindran and was therefore known as Bhindranwale, and after his death, when the mantle of leadership fell on young Jamail Singh, he assumed his mentor's name. The young leader took his duties seriously and gained a certain amount of fame as a preacher. He was a stern one at that: Jarnail became famous for castigating the easy-living, easy-drinking customs of Sikh villagers, especially those who clipped their beards and adopted modern ways. He carried weapons, and on 13 April 1978, in a bloody confrontation in Amritsar with members of the renegade Nirankari religious movement, he showed that he was not afraid to use them. This episode was followed by an attack from Nirankaris that killed a number of Bhindranwale's followers, and further counter-attacks ensued.[8] Thus began the bloody career of a man who was trained to live a calm and spiritual life of religious devotion.

Although he was intitally at the fringes of Sikh leadership, during the late 1970s Bhindranwale began to be taken seriously within Akali circles because of his growing popularity among the masses.[9] He seemed to have been fixated on the Nirankaris: his fiery sermons condemned them as evil. He regarded them as a demonic force that endangered the very basis of the Sikh community, especially its commitment to the authority of the Sikh gurus. And in time he expanded his characterization of their demonic power to include those who protected them, including the secular government of Indira Gandhi.

Much of what Bhindranwale has to say in sermons of this period, however, might be heard in the sermons of Methodist pastors in Iowa or in the homilies of clergies belonging to any religious tradition, anywhere on the globe. He calls for faith – faith in a time of trial – and for the spiritual discipline that accompanies it. In one sermon he rebukes the press and others who call him an extremist, and explains what sort of an extremist he is:

> One who takes the vows of faith and helps others take it; who reads the scriptures and helps others to do the same; who avoids liquor and drugs and helps others do likewise; who urges unity and cooperation; who preaches Hindu-Sikh unity and coexistence ... who says: 'respect your scriptures, unite under the flag, stoutly support the community, and be attached to your Lord's throne and home'.[10]

Like many Protestant ministers, Bhindranwale prescribes piety as the answer to every need. 'You can't have courage without reading [the Sikh scriptures]', he admonishes his followers: 'Only the [scripture]-readers can suffer torture and be capable of feats of strength'.[11] He is especially harsh on backsliders in the faith. Those who cut their beards are targets of his wrath: 'Do you think you resemble the image of Guru Gobind Singh?' he asks them.[12] But then he reassures the bulk of his followers. Because of their persistence in the faith, he tells them, 'the Guru will give you strength', adding that 'righteousness is with you'.[13] They will need all the strength and courage they can get, Bhindranwale explains, because their faith is under attack.[14]

Lying only slightly beneath the surface of this language is the notion of a great struggle that Bhindranwale thinks is taking place. On the personal level it is the tension between faith and the lack of faith; on the cosmic level it is the battle between truth and evil. Often his rhetoric is vague about who the enemy really is. 'In order to destroy religion', Bhindranwale informs his congregation, 'on all sides and in many forms mean tactics have been initiated'.[15] But rather than wasting effort in explaining who these forces are and why they would want to destroy religion, Bhindranwale dwells instead on what should be the response: a willingness to fight and defend the faith – if necessary, to the end.

> Unless you are prepared to die, sacrificing your own life, you cannot be a free people .... If you start thinking in terms of service to your community then you will be on the right path and you will readily sacrifice yourself. If you have faith in the Guru no power on earth can enslave you. The Sikh faith is to pray to God, take one's vows before the Guru Granth Sahib [scriptures] and then act careless of consequences to oneself.[16]

At other times Bhindranwale cites what appear to be specific attacks on Sikhism, but again the perpetrators are not sharply defined; they remain a vague, shadowy force of evil. 'The Guru Granth [scripture] has been buried in cowdung and thrown on the roadside', Bhindranwale informs his followers. 'That is your Father, your Guru, that they treat so.'[17] On another occasion he urges his followers to 'seek justice against those who have dishonored our sisters, drunk the blood of innocent persons, and insulted Satguru Granth Sahib'.[18] But the 'they' and the 'those' are not identified.

Occasionally, however, the enemy is more clearly specified: they are 'Hindus', 'the government', 'the press', the Prime Minister – whom he calls that 'lady born to a house of Brahmins'[19] – and perhaps most frequently Sikhs themselves who have fallen from the path. This somewhat rambling passage indicates these diverse enemies and the passionate hatred that Bhindranwale feels towards them:

> I cannot really understand how it is that, in the presence of Sikhs, Hindus are able to insult the [scriptures]. I don't know how these Sikhs were born to mothers and why they were not born to animals: to cats and to bitches .... Whoever insults the Guru Granth Sahib should be killed then and there .... Some youths complain that if they do such deeds then nobody harbours them. Well, no place is holier than this one [the Golden Temple] .... I will take care of the man who comes to me after lynching the murderer of the Guru Granth Sahib; I'll fight for his case. What else do you want? That things have come to such a pass is in any event all your own weakness .... The man whose sister is molested and does nothing about it, whose Guru is insulted and who keeps on talking and doing nothing, has he got any right to be known as the son of the Guru? Just think for yourselves![20]

And in a similar vein:

> Talk is not enough against injustice. We have to act. Here you raise your swords but tomorrow you may wipe the dust from the sandals of sister Indira .... We have the right to be Sikhs .... The dearest thing to any Sikh should be the honor of the Guru .... Those foes – the government and Hindus – are not dangerous. Rather one has to be wary of those who profess Sikhism yet do not behave as Sikhs.[21]

As important as Bhindranwale feels the immediate struggle is, he reminds his followers that the Sikh tradition has always been filled with conflict, and that the current battles are simply the most recent chapters in a long ongoing war with the enemies of the faith. The foes of today are connected with those from the legendary past. Indira Gandhi, for instance, is implicitly compared with the Moghul emperors: 'The rulers [the Congress party leaders] should keep in mind that in the past many like them did try in vain to annihilate the Gurus.'[22] In other speeches, Bhindranwale frequently looks to the past for guidance in dealing with current situations. When Sikhs who had sided with government policies come to him for forgiveness, for instance, he refuses. 'I asked that man', explains Bhindranwale, 'had he ever read a page of our history? Was the man who tortured Guru Arjun pardoned?'[23]

Occasionally Bhindranwale refers to some of the specific political, economic and social demands made by more moderate Sikh leaders. He supports these demands, but they are not his primary concern. In fact, the targets of these demands are often characterized simply as 'injustices', illustrations of the fact that the Sikh community is abused and under attack.[24] Since the larger struggle is the more important matter, these specific difficulties are of no great concern to Bhindranwale; they change from time to time. And it is of no use to win on one or two points and fail on others. Compromise is impossible; only complete victory will signal that the tide has turned. For that reason Bhindranwale scolds the Akali leaders for seeking a compromise settlement of the political demands made by Sikh leaders at Anandpur Sahib in 1973. 'Either full implementation of the Anandpur Sahib resolution', Bhindranwale demands, 'or their heads'.[25]

In a sense, then, Bhindranwale feels that individual Sikh demands can never really be met, because the ultimate struggle of which they are a part is much greater than the contestation between political parties and factional points of view. It is a vast cosmic struggle, and only such an awesome encounter is capable of giving profound meaning to the motivations of those who fight for Sikh causes. Such people are not just fighting for water rights and political boundaries, they are fighting for truth itself.

Clearly the religious language of Sikh militants like Bhindranwale is the language of ulitmate struggle. But two related matters are not so obvious: why is this language attached to the more mundane issues of human politics and economics? and why is it linked with violent acts?

A Pause for Definitions: Violence and Religion

Before we turn to these questions,, however, it might be useful to pause for a moment for definitions. Since I want to look at issues having to do with the general relation between violence and religion, not merely those that affect the Sikhs, it might be useful if I describe what I mean by these terms.

I will restrict my use of the word violence to actions that are aimed at taking human life – that intend to, and do, kill. Moreover, I mean especially abnormal, illegal, shocking acts of destruction. All acts of killing are violent, of course, but warfare and capital punishment have an aura of normalcy and do not violate our sensibilities in the same way as actions that seem deliberately designed to elicit feelings of revulsion and anger from those who witness them.[26] By speaking of violence in this restricted way, I mean to highlight the characteristics that we usually associate with terrorist acts.

The term religion is more difficult to define. I have been impressed with the recent attempts of several sociologists to find a definition that is not specific to any cultural region or historical period, and is appropriate for thinking about the phenomenon in modern as well as traditional societies. Clifford Geertz, for instance, sees religion as the effort to integrate everyday reality into a pattern of coherence that takes shape on a deeper level.[27] Robert Bellah also thinks of religion as the attempt to reach beyond ordinary reality in the 'risk of faith' that allows people to act 'in the face of uncertainty and unpredictability'.[28] Peter Berger specifies that such faith is an affirmation of the sacred, which acts as a doorway to a different kind of reality.[29] Louis Dupré' prefers to avoid the term 'sacred', but integrates elements of both Berger's and Bellah's definition in his description of religion as 'a commitment to the transcendent as to *another* reality'.[30]

What all of these definitions have in common is their emphasis on a certain kind of experience that people share with others in particular communities. It is an experience of another reality, or of a deeper stratum of the reality that we know in everyday life. As Durkheim, whose thought is fundamental to each of these thinkers, was adamant in observing, religion has a more encompassing force than can be suggested by any dichotomization of the sacred and the profane. To Durkheim, the religious point of view includes both the notion that there is such a dichotomy, and that the sacred aspects of it will always, ultimately, reign supreme.[31] Summarizing Durkheim's and the others' definitions of religion, I think it might be described as the perception that there is a tension between reality as it appears and as it really is (or has been, or will be).

This definition helps us think of religion as the subjective experience of those who use religious language, and in fact it is easier with this definition to speak of religious language, or a religious way of looking at the world, than to speak of religion in a more reified sense.[32] When we talk of the various 'religions', then, we mean the communities that have a tradition of sharing a particular religious point of view, a world view in which there is an essential conflict between appearance and a deeper reality. There is the hint, in this definition, that the deeper reality holds a degree of permanence and order quite unobtainable by ordinary means, as religious people affirm. The conflict between the two is what religion is about: religious language contains images both of grave disorder and tranquil order, and often holds out the hope that despite appearances to the contrary, order eventually will triumph, and disorder will be contained.

Why Does Religion Need Violence?

There is nothing in this definition that requires religion to be violent, but it does lead one to expect religious language to make sense of violence and to incorporate it in some way into the world view it expresses. Violence, after all, shocks one's sense of order and has the potential for causing the ultimate disorder in any person's life: physical destruction and death. Since religious language is about the tension between order and disorder, it is frequently about violence.

The symbols and mythology of Sikhism, for instance, are full of violence. The most common visual symbol of Sikhism is the two-edged sword (*khanda*), supported by two scabbards and surrounded by a circle. Sikhs often interpret the two edges of this sword as symbolizing spiritual and worldly foes,[33] and they say that a battle sword (*kirpan*) is included among the five objects that Sikhs are supposed to wear at all times to symbolize an awareness of these same enemies.[34] Unlike the Bible, the sacred scriptures of the Sikhs – known collectively as the *Guru Granth Sahib* – do not contain accounts of wars and savage acts, but the stories of the Sikhs' historical past are bloody indeed. In fact, these stories have taken on a canonical character within Sikhism, and they more vividly capture the imagination than the devotional and theological sentiments of the scriptures themselves. The calendar art so prominent in most Sikh homes portrays a mystical Guru Nanak, of course, but alongside him there are pictures of Sikh military heroes and scenes from great battles. Bloody images also leap from brightly-colored oil paintings in the Sikh Museum housed in the Golden Temple. There are as many depictions of martyrs in their wretched final moments as of victors radiant in conquest.

Because the violence is so prominent in Sikh art and legend, and because many symbols of the faith are martial, one might think that Sikhs as a people are more violent than their counterparts in other areas of India. But if one leaves aside the unrest of the past several years, I do not think this can be demonstrated. It would be convenient to say that the prestige of violent symbols in the Sikh religion has increased Sikhs' propensity for violent action, or that the Sikh religion is violent because Sikhs as a people are violent, but I do not think either of these arguments can be made very convincingly.

The fact is that the symbols and mythology of most religious traditions are filled with violent images, and their histories leave trails of blood. One wonders that familiarity can prevent Christians from being repulsed by the violent images portrayed by hymns such as 'Onward Christian Soldiers', 'The Old Rugged Cross', 'Washed in the Blood of the Lamb', and 'There is a Fountain Flowing with Blood'. Or perhaps familiarity is not the issue at all. The central symbol of Christianity is an execution device – a cross – from which, at least in the Roman tradition, the dying body still hangs. From a non-Christian point of view, the most sacred of Christian rituals, the eucharist, looks like ritual cannabalism, where the devout eat the flesh and drink the blood of their departed leader. At a certain level, in fact, this interpretation is accurate; yet few would argue that the violent acts perpetrated by Christians over the centuries are the result of their being subjected to such messages.

The ubiquity of violent images in religion and the fact that some of the most ancient religious practices involve the sacrificial slaughter of animals have led to speculation about why religion and violence are so intimately bound together. Some of these speculators are among the best known modern theorists. Karl Marx, for instance, saw religious symbols as the expression of real social oppression, and religious wars as the result of tension among economic classes.[35] Sigmund Freud saw in religious rituals vestiges of a primal oedipal act that when ritually reenacted provide a symbolic resolution of feelings of sexual and physical aggression.[36] More recently, Rene Girard has revived the Freudian thesis but given it a social rather than psychological coloration. Girard sees the violent images of religion as a symbolic displacement of violence from one's own communal fellowship to a scapegoat foe.[37]

What these thinkers have in common is that they see religious violence as a symptom of and symbol for something else: social hostility, in the case of Marx; sexual and physical aggression, in the case of Freud; social competition, in the case of Girard. They may be right: religion and other cultural forms may have been generated out of basic personal and social needs. Yet it seems to me that even without these explanations the internal logic of religion requires that religious symbols and myths express violent meanings.

Religion deals with the ultimate tension between order and disorder, and disorder is inherently violent, so it is understandable that the chaotic, dangerous character of life is represented in religious images. Of course, the religious promise is that order conquers chaos; so it is also understandable that the violence religion portrays is in some way limited or tamed. In Christianity, for example, the very normalcy with which the blood-filled hymns are sung and the eucharist is eaten indicates their domestication. In ritual, violence is symbolically transferred. The blood of the eucharistic wine is ingested by the supplicant and becomes part of living tissue; it brings new life. In song a similarly calming transformation occurs. For, as Christian theology explains, in Christ violence has been corralled. Christ died in order for death to be defeated, and his blood is that of the sacrifical lamb who atones for our sins so that we will not have to undergo a punishment as gruesome as his.

In the Sikh tradition violent images are also domesticated. The symbol of the two-edged sword has become an emblem to be worn on lockets and proudly emblazened on shops and garden gates. It is at the forefront of the worship center in Sikh *gurudwaras* where it is treated as reverently as Christians treat their own emblem of destruction, the cross. And the gory wounds of the martyrs bleed on in calendar art. As I have suggested, Sikh theologians and writers are no more hesitant to allegorize the meaning of such symbols and stories than their Christian counterparts. They point toward the war between good and evil that rages in each person's soul.

The symbols of violence in religion, therefore, are symbols of a violence conquered, or at least put in place, by the larger framework of order that religious language provides. But one must ask how these symbolic presentations of violence are related to real violence. One might think that they should prevent violent acts by allowing violent feelings to be channelled into the harmless dramas of ritual, yet we know that the opposite is sometimes the case. The violence of religion can be savagely real.

Why Does Violence Need Religion?

A reason often given to explain why religious symbols are associated with acts of real violence is that religion is exploited by violent people. This explanation, making religion the pure and innocent victim of the darker forces of human nature, is undoubtedly too easy; yet it contains some truth. Religion in fact is sometimes exploited, and it is important to understand why people who are engaged in potentially violent struggles do at times turn to the language of religion. In the case of the Sikhs, this means asking why the sort of people who were exercised over the economic, political and social issues explored at the beginning of this article turned to preachers like Bhindranwale for leadership.

One answer is that by sacralizing these concerns the political activists gave them an aura of legitimacy that they did not previously possess. The problem with this answer is that most of the concerns we mentioned – the inadequacy of Sikh political representation, for instance, and the inequity of agricultural prices – were perfectly legitimate, and did not need the additional moral weight of religion to give them respectability. And in fact, the people who were primarily occupied with these issues – Sikh businessmen and political leaders – were not early supporters of Bhindranwale. Even when they became drawn into his campaign, their relation with him remained ambivalent at best.

There was one political demand, however, that desperately needed all the legitimization that it could get. This was the demand for Khalistan, a separate Sikh nation. Separatist leaders such as Jagjit Singh Chauhan were greatly buoyed by such words of Bhindranwale as these:

> We are religiously separate. But why do we have to emphasize this? It is only because we are losing our identity. Out of selfish interests our Sikh leaders who have only the success of their farms and their industries at heart have started saying that there is no difference between Sikh and Hindu. Hence the danger of assimilation has increased.[38]

> When they say the Sikhs are not separate we'll demand separate identity – even if it demands sacrifice.[39]

Bhindranwale himself, interestingly, never came out in support of Khalistan. 'We are not in favor of Khalistan nor are we against it', he said, adding that 'we wish to live in India', but would settle for a separate state if the Sikhs did not receive what he regarded as their just respect.[40] Whatever his own reservations about the Khalistan issue, however, his appeal to sacrifice made his rhetoric attractive to the separatists. It also raised another, potentially more powerful aspect of the sacralization of political demands: the prospect that religion could give moral sanction to violence.

By indentifying a temporal social struggle with the cosmic struggle of order and disorder, truth and evil, political actors are able to avail themselves of a way of thinking that justifies the use of violent means. Ordinarily only the state has the moral right to take life – for purposes either of military defense, police protection or punishment – and the codes of ethics established by religious traditions support this position. Virtually every religious tradition, including the Sikhs', applauds non-violence and proscribes the taking of human life.[41] The only exception to this rule is the one we have given: most ethical codes allow the state to kill for reasons of punishment and protection.[42]

Those who want moral sanction for their use of violence, and who do not have the approval of an officially recognized government, find it helpful to have access to a higher source: the meta-morality that religion provides. By elevating a temporal struggle to the level of the cosmic, they can bypass the usual moral restrictions on killing. If a battle of the spirit is thought to exist, then it is not ordinary morality but the rules of war that apply. It is interesting that the best-known incidents of religious violence throughout the contemporary world have occurred in places where there is difficulty in defining the character of a nation state. Palestine and Ireland are the most obvious examples, but the revolution in Iran also concerned itself with what the state should be like, and what elements of society should lead it. Religion provided the basis for a new national consensus and a new kind of leadership.

There are some aspects of social revolution in the Punjab situation as well. It is not the established leaders of the Akali party who have resorted to violence, but a second level of leadership – a younger, more marginal group for whom the use of violence is enormously empowering. The power that comes from the barrel of a gun, as Mao is said to have remarked, has a very direct effect. But there is a psychological dimension to this power that may be even more effective. As Frantz Fanon argued in the context of the Algerian revolution some years ago even a small display of violence can have immense symbolic power: the power to jolt the masses into an awareness of their potency.[43]

It can be debated whether or not the masses in the Punjab have been jolted into an awareness of their own capabilities, but the violent actions of the militants among them have certainly made the masses more aware of the militants' powers. They have attained a status of authority rivalling what police and other government officials possess. One of the problems in the Punjab today is the unwillingness of many villagers in the so-called terrorist zones around Batala and Taran Tarn to report terrorist activities to the authorities. The radical youth are even said to have established an alternative government.

By being dangerous the young Sikh radicals have gained a certain notoriety, and by clothing their actions in the moral garb of religion they have given their actions legitimacy. Because their actions are morally sanctioned by religion, they are fundamentally political actions: they break the state's monopoly on morally-sanctioned killing. By putting the right to kill in their own hands, the perpetrators of religious violence are also making a daring claim of political independence.

Even though Bhindranwale was not an outspoken supporter of Khalistan, he often spoke of the Sikhs' separate identity as that of a religious community with national characterisics. The term he used for religious community, *quam*, is an Urdu term that has overtones of nationhood. It is the term the Muslims used earlier in this century in defending their right to have a separate nation, and it is the term that Untouchables used in the Punjab in the 1920s when they attempted to be recognized as a separate social and political entity.[44] Another term that is important to Bhindranwale is *miri-piri*, the notion that spiritual and temporal power are linked.[45] It is this concept that is symbolically represented by the two-edged sword and that justified Sikh support for an independent political party. Young Sikh activists are buttressed in their own aspirations to leadership by the belief that acts that they conceive as being heroic and sacrificial – even those that involve taking the lives of others – have both spiritual and political significance. They are risking their lives for God and the Sikh community.

Not all of the Sikh community appreciates their efforts, however, and the speeches of Bhindranwale make clear that disagreements and rivalries within the community were one of his major concerns. Some of Bhindranwale's harshest words were reserved for Sikhs who he felt showed weakness and a tendency to make easy compromises. In one speech, after quoting a great martyr in Sikh history as having said, 'even if I have to give my head, may I never lose my love for the Sikh Faith', Bhindranwale railed against Sikh bureaucrats and modernized youth who could not make that sacrifice, and ended with a little joke:

> I am sorry to note that many people who hanker after a government position say instead, 'even if I lose my Faith, may I never lose my position'. And our younger generation has started saying this: 'even if I lose my Faith, may a beard never grow on my face'. ... If you find the beard too heavy, pray to God saying ... 'we do not like this Sikhism and manhood. Have mercy on us. Make us into women ....'[46]

But most Sikhs in Bhindranwale's audience, including the youth, were not the sort who would be tempted to cut their hair; and few, especially in the villages where Bhindranwale had been popular, were in a position to 'hanker after a governmental position'. People, such as the Akali leaders whom Bhindranwale castigated for making compromises for the sake of personal gain, were no doubt objects of contempt in the villages long before Bhindranwale came along, and by singling them out, Bhindranwale identified familiar objects of derision – scapegoats – that humbled those who had succeeded in worldly affairs and heightened the sense of unity among those who had not.

Bhindranwale made a great plea for unity. 'Our misfortune is disunity', he told his audiences. 'We try to throw mud at each other. Why don't we give up thinking of mud and in close embrace with each other work with determination to attain our goals.'[47] Those who eventually opposed him, including the more moderate Akali leader, Sant Harchand Singh Longowal, regarded Bhindranwale as a prime obstacle to the very unity he preached. During the dark days immediately preceding Operation Bluestar in June 1984, the two set up rival camps in the Golden Temple and allegedly killed each other's lieutenants. It is no wonder that many of Bhindranwale's followers, convinced the Indian army had a collaborator inside the Golden Temple, were suspicious when Bhindranwale was murdered in the raid and Longowal was led off safely under arrest. No wonder also that many regarded Longowal's assassination a year later as revenge for Bhindranwale's.

While he was alive, Bhindranwale continued to preach unity, but it was clear that what he wanted was for everyone else to unite around him. He and his supporters wished to give the impression that they were at the center, following the norm of Sikh belief and behavior, and that the community should therefore group around them. This message had a particular appeal to those who were socially marginal to the Sikh community, including lower-caste people and Sikhs who had taken up residence abroad. Some of the most fanatical of Bhindranwale's followers, including Beant Singh, the assassin of Indira Gandhi, came from the Untouchable castes (Beant Singh was from the lowest caste of Untouchables, the Sweepers), and a considerable amount of money and moral support for the Punjab militants came from Sikhs living in such far-away places as London, Houston, and Yuba City, California.

These groups gained from their indentification with Bhindranwale a sense of belonging, and the large Sikh communities in England, Canada and America were especially sensitive to his message that the Sikhs needed to be strong, united and defensive of their tradition. Many of Bhindranwale's supporters in the Punjab, however, received a more tangible benefit from associating with his cause: politically active village youth and small-time clergy were able to gain support from many who were not politically mobilized before. In that sense Bhindranwale was fomenting something of a political revolution, and the constituency was not unlike the one the Ayatollah Khomeini was able to gather in Iran. In so far as Bhindranwale's message was taken as an endorsement of the killings that some of these fundamentalist youth committed, the instrument of religious violence gave power to those who had little power before.

When Does Cosmic Struggle Lead to Real Violence?

The pattern of religious violence of the Sikhs could be that of Irish Catholics, or Shi'ite Muslims in Palestine, or fundamentalist Christian bombers of abortion clinics in the United States. There are a great many communities in which the language of cosmic struggle justifies acts of violence. But those who are engaged in them, including the Sikhs, would be offended if we concluded from the above discussion that their actions were purely for social or political gain. They argue that they act out of religious conviction, and surely they are to some degree right. Destruction is a part of the logic of religion, and virtually every religious tradition carries with it images of chaos and terror. But symbolic violence does not lead in every instance to real bloodshed, and even the eagerness of political actors to exploit religious symbols is not in all cases sufficient to turn religion towards a violent end. Yet some forms of religion do seem to propel the faithful rather easily into militant confrontation: which ones, and why?

The current resurgence of religious violence around the world has given an urgency to attempts to answer these questions, and to identify which characteristics of religion are conducive to violence. The efforts of social scientists have been directed primarily to the social and political aspects of the problem, but at least a few of them have tried to trace the patterns in religion's own logic. David C. Rapoport, for instance, has identified several features of messianic movements that he believes lead to violence, most of which are characterized by a desire for an antinomian liberation from oppression.[48]

My own list of characteristics comes directly from our discussion of the religious language of cosmic struggle. It is informed by my understanding of what has happened in the Sikh tradition, but it seems to me that the following tenets of religious commitment are found whenever acts of religious violence occur.

1. The Cosmic Struggle is Played Out in History

To begin with, it seems to me that if religion is to lead to violence it is essential for the devout to believe that the cosmic struggle is realizable in human terms. If the war between good and evil, order and chaos, is conceived as taking place in historical time, in a real geographical location, and among actual social contestants, it is more likely that those who are prone to violent acts will associate religion with their struggles. This may seem to be an obvious point, yet we have some evidence that it is not always true.

In the Hindu tradition, for instance, the mythical battles in the Mahabharata and Ramayana epics are as frequently used as metaphors for present-day struggles as are the actual battles in Sikh and Islamic history and in biblical Judaism and Christianity. Like members of these traditions, Hindus characterize their worldly foes by associating them with the enemies of the good in their legendary battles. The main difference between the Hindus and the others is that their enemies are mythical – that is, they seem mythical to us. To many pious Hindus, however, the stories in the epics are no less real than those recorded in the Bible or in the Sikh legends. A believing Hindu will be able to show you where the great war of the Mahabharata was actually fought, and where the gods actually lived. Moreover, the Hindu cycles of time allow for a cosmic destruction to take place in this world, at the end of the present dark age. So the Hindu tradition is not as devoid of images of divine intervention in worldly struggles as outsiders sometimes assume.[49]

The major tradition that appears to lack the notion that the cosmic struggle is played out on a social plane is Buddhism. But this is an exception that proves the rule, for it is a tradition that is characteristically devoid of religiously sanctioned violence. There are instances in Thai history that provide Buddhist justifications for warfare, but these are rare for the tradition as a whole. In general, Buddhism has no need for actual battles in which the pious can prove their mettle.

2. Believers Identify Personally with the Struggle

The Buddhist tradition does affirm that there is a spiritual conflict, however: it is the clash between the perception that this imperfect and illusory world is real and a higher consciousness that surmounts worldly perception altogether. And in a sense, the struggle takes place in this world, in that it takes place in the minds of worldly persons. This kind of internalization of the cosmic struggle does not in itself lead to violence, and Buddhists are not ordinarily prone to violent deeds. Nor are Sufis, the Islamic mystics who have reconceived the Muslim notion of *jihad*. To many Sufis, the greater *jihad* is not the one involving worldly warfare, but the one within: the conflict between good and evil within one's own soul.[50]

This talk about the cosmic struggle as something inside the self would seem to be easily distinguishable from external violence, but in Sikh theology, including the rhetoric of Bhindranwale, they go hand in hand. 'The weakness is in us', Bhindranwale was fond of telling his followers. 'We are the sinners of this house of our Guru.'[51] Militant Shi'ite Muslims are similarly racked with a sense of personal responsibility for the moral decadence of the world, and once again their tendency toward internalization does not necessarily shield them from acts of external violence. The key to the connection, it seems to me, is that at the same time that the cosmic struggle is understood to impinge about the inner recesses of an individual person, it must be understood as occurring on a worldy, social plane. Neither of these notions is by itself sufficient to motivate a person to religious violence. If one believes that the cosmic struggle is largely a matter of large continuing social forces, one is not likely to become personally identified with the struggle; and if one is convinced that the struggle is solely interior there is no reason to look for it outside. But when the two ideas coexist, they are a volatile concoction.

Thus when Bhindranwale spoke about the warfare in the soul his listeners knew that however burdensome that conflict is, they need not bear it alone. They may band together with their comrades and continue the struggle in the external arena, where the foes are more vulnerable, and victories more tangible. And their own internal struggles impel them to become involved in the worldly conflict: their identification with the overall struggle makes them morally responsible, in part, for its outcome. 'We ourselves are ruining Sikhism', Bhindranwale once told his congregation.[52] On another occasion he told the story of how, when Guru Gobind Singh asked an army of 80,000 to sacrifice their heads for the faith, only five assented. Bhindranwale implied that the opportunity was still at hand to make the choice of whether they were to be one of the five or the 79,995.[53] He reminded them that even though the cosmic war was still being waged, and that the evil within them and outside them had not yet been purged, their choice could still make a difference.

Sikhism is not the only tradition in which this link is forged between the external and internal arenas of the cosmic struggle. Shi'ite Muslims bear a great weight of communal guilt for not having defended one of the founders of their tradition, Husain, when he was attacked and martyred by the vicious Yazid. During the Iranian revolution some of them relived that conflict by identifying specific foes – the Shah and President Jimmy Carter – as Yazids returned. There was no doubt that such people should be attacked. Radical Shi'ites in Iran were not about to compound their guilt and miss an historical opportunity of righting an ancient wrong.

The same sort of logic has propelled many Christians into a vicious anti-Semitism. It is a mark of good Christian piety for individuals to bear the responsibility for the crucifiction of Jesus: the theme of Christians taking part in the denial and betrayal of Jesus is the stuff of many a hymn and sermon. Some Christians believe that the foes to whom they allowed Jesus to be delivered were the Jews. Attacks on the present-day Jewish community, therefore, help to lighten their sense of culpability.

3. The Cosmic Struggle Continues in the Present

What makes these actions of Sikhs, Shi'ites and anti-Semitic Christians spritually defensible is the conviction that the sacred struggle has not ended in some earlier period, but that it continues in some form today. It is a conviction that also excites the members of the Gush Emunim, a militant movement in present-day Israel, who have taken Israel's victory in the Six Day War as a sign that the age of messianic redemption has finally begun.[54]

Not all Israelis respond to this sign with the same enthusiasm, however, just as not all Christians or Shi'ite Muslims are convinced that the apocalyptic conflict prophesied by their tradition is really at hand. Many of the faithful assent to the notion that the struggle exists within, for what person of faith has not felt the internal tension between belief and disbelief, affirmation and denial, order and chaos? But they often have to be persuaded that the conflict currently rages on a social plane, especially if the social world seems orderly and benign.

Bhindranwale took this challenge as one of the primary tasks of his ministry. He said that one of his main missions was to alert his people that they were oppressed, even if they did not know it. He ended one of his sermons with this fervent plea: 'I implore all of you in this congregation. Go to the villages and make every child, every mother, every Singh realise we are slaves and we have to shake off this slavery in order to survive.'[55]

In Bhindranwale's mind the appearances of normal social order simply illustrated how successful the forces of evil had become in hiding their demonic agenda. His logic compelled him to believe that Punjabi society was racked in a great struggle, even if it showed no indication of it. Long before the Punjab was torn apart by its most recent round of violence, Bhindranwale claimed that an even fiercer form of violence reigned: the appearance of normal order was merely a demonic deception. Bhindranwale hated the veil of calm that seemed to cover his community and recognized that his own followers were often perplexed about what he said: 'Many of our brothers, fresh from the villages, ask, "Sant Ji, we don't know about enslavement." For that reason, I have to tell you why you are slaves.'[56]

The evidence that Bhindranwale gave for the oppression of Sikhs was largely limited to examples of police hostility that arose after the spiral of violence in the Punjab began to grow. Some of his allegations, such as the account he gave of the treatment meted out to followers who hijacked Indian airplanes, have a peculiar ring:

> If a Sikh protests in behalf of his Guru by hijacking a plane, he is put to death .... None of the Sikhs in these three hijackings attacked any passenger nor did they damage the planes. But the rule is that for a fellow with a turban, there is the bullet ... . For a person who says 'Hare Krishna, Hare Krishna, Hare Rama', there is a government appointment. Sikh brothers, this is a sign of slavery.[57]

Those who attempted to combat Bhindranwale could not win against such logic. If they responded to Sikh violence they would be seen as oppressors. If they did not respond, the violence would escalate. And even if there was neither violence nor repression, the absence of the overt signs of conflict would be an indication to Bhindranwale of a demonical calm.

4. The Struggle is at a Point of Crisis

On a number of occasions, in referring to the immediacy of the struggle, Bhindranwale seemed to indicate that the outcome was in doubt. His perception of the enormity of the evil he faced and of the torpor of the Sikh response made his prognosis a dismal one. Sometimes he felt that the best efforts of a few faithful Sikhs were doomed: 'today', he darkly proclaimed, 'the Sikh community is under threat'.[58] But on other occasions he seemed to hold out a measure of hope. Things were coming to a head, he implied, and the struggle was about to enter 'the decisive phase'.[59]

What is interesting about this apocalyptic rhetoric is its uncertainty. If the outcome were less in doubt there would be little reason for violent action. If one knew that the foe would win, there would be no reason to want to fight back. Weston LaBarre describes the terrible circumstances surrounding the advent of the Ghost Dance religion of the Plains Indians: knowing that they faced overwhelming odds and almost certain defeat, the tribe diverted their concerns from worldly conflict to spiritual conflict, and entertained the notion that a ritual dance would conjure up sufficient spiritual force to destroy the alien cavalry.[60]

LaBarre concludes that sheer desperation caused them to turn to religion and away from efforts to defend themselves. But by the same token, if they knew that the battle could be won without a struggle, there also would be little reason for engagement. The passive pacifism of what William James calles 'healthy-souled religion' – mainstream Protestant churches, for example, that regard social progess as inevitable – comes from just such optimism.[61] Other pacifist movements, however, have been directly engaged in conflict. Menno Simons, the Anabaptist for whom the Mennonite church is named, and Mohandas Gandhi are examples of pacifist leaders who at times narrowly skirted the edges of violence, propelled by a conviction that without human effort the outcome they desired could not be won. In that sense Gandhi and Bhindranwale were more alike than one might suspect. Both saw the world in terms of cosmic struggle, both regarded their cause as being poised on a delicate balance between oppression and opportunity, and both believed that human action could tip the scales. The issue that divided them, of course, was violence.

5. Acts of Violence Have a Cosmic Meaning

The human action in the Sikh case is certainly not pacifist, for Bhindranwale held that there would be 'no deliverance without weapons.'[62] He was careful, however, to let the world know that these weapons were not to be used indiscriminately: 'It is a sin for a Sikh to keep weapons to hurt an innocent person, to rob anyone's home, to dishonor anyone or to oppress anyone. But there is no greater sin for a Sikh than keeping weapons and not using them to protect his faith.'[63] Contrariwise, there is no greater valor for a Sikh than to use weapons in defense of the faith. Bhindranwale himself was armed to the teeth, and although he never publically admitted to any of the killings that were pinned on him personally, Bhindranwale expressed his desire to 'die fighting', a wish that was fulfilled within months of being uttered.[64]

According to Bhindranwale, those who committed acts of religiously sanctioned violence were to be regarded as heroes and more. Although he usually referred to himself as a 'humble servant, and an 'uneducated fallible person',[65] Bhindranwale would occasionally identify himself with one of the legendary Sikh saints, Baba Deep Singh, who continued to battle with Moghul foes even after his head had been severed from his body. He carried it manfully under his arm.[66] In Bhindranwale's mind, he too seemed destined for martyrdom.

To many Sikhs today, that is precisely what Bhindranwale achieved. Whatever excesses he may have committed during his lifetime are excused, as one would excuse a lethal but heroic soldier in a glorious war. Even Beant Singh, the bodyguard of Indira Gandhi who turned on her, is held to be a saintly hero. Perhaps this has to be: if Indira was such a demonic foe, her assassin must be similarly exalted.

Even those who value the sense of order that religion provides sometimes cheer those who throw themselves into the arena of religious violence. Such people are, after all, struggling for good, and for that reason their actions are seen as ultimately producing order. But until such recognition of their mission can be achieved among the more conservative rank and file, such activists are forced, as prophets and agents of a higher order of truth, to engage in deeds that necessarily startle. Their purpose is to awaken good folk, mobilize their community, insult the evil forces, and perhaps even to demonstrate dramatically to God himself that there are those who are willing to fight and die on his side, and to deliver his judgement of death. The great promise of cosmic struggle is that order will prevail over chaos; the great irony is that many must die in order for certain visions of that victory to prevail and their awful dramas be brought to an end.

NOTES

Support for this project has come from the Woodrow Wilson International Center for Scholars. I greatly appreciate the kindness of the staff of the Center, the collegiality of the Fellows, the diligence of my research assistant, Jonathan Hornstein, and the critical judgment of my collegues, Sucheng Chan and Jack Hawley, who have read this paper in draft form and helped me to improve its flow of thought. I have also benefited from discussions of some of these ideas in a Dupont Circle sub-group of the World Affairs Council in Washington, DC, a discussion group at the World Bank, and a faculty and student gathering at Amherst College.

1. For general background on the Punjab crisis in the 1980s and a chronicle of events leading up to it, see Mark Tully and Satish Jacob, *Amritsar: Mrs Gandhi's Last Battle* (London: Cape, 1985), Amarjit Kaur, *et al.*, *The Punjab Story* (New Delhi: Roli Books International, 1984), and Kuldip Nayar and Khushwant Singh, *Tragedy of Punjab: Operation Bluestar and After* (New Delhi: Vision Books, 1984).
2. Indira Gandhi, 'Don't Shed Blood, Shed Hatred', All India Radio, 2 June 1984, reprinted in V.D. Chopra, R.K. Mishra and Nirmal Singh, *Agony of Punjab* (New Delhi: Patriot Publishers, 1984), p.189. Indian government officials seemed to be genuinely caught off-guard by the Sikh militancy. I remember once in the summer of 1984 when the Indian Consul General in San Francisco turned to me after we had been on a radio talk show and said, 'I haven't a clue; can you tell me why in the devil the Sikhs are behaving like this?'
3. The demand for a Khalistan – a Sikh state similar to Pakistan – was raised by a small number of Sikh militants, including a former cabinet minister of the Punjab, Jagjit Singh Chauhan, who set up a movement in exile in London. It was not, however, a significant or strongly supported demand among Sikhs in the Punjab until after Operation Bluestar in June 1984. The Indian government's account of Chauhan's movement is detailed in a report prepared by the Home Ministry, 'Sikh Agitation for Khalistan', reprinted in Nayar and Singh, *Tragedy of Punjab*, pp.142–55.
4. The Anandpur Resolution supported by leaders of the Akali Dal focused primarily on economic issues. For an analysis of the Punjab crisis from an economic perspective, see Chopra, Mishra and Singh, *Agony of Punjab*.

5. The fear of the absorption of Sikhism into Hinduism is the frequent refrain of Khushwant Singh; see, for instance, the final chapter of his *History of the Sikhs*, Vol.2 (Princeton, NJ: Princeton University Press, 1966). He attributes the cause of many of the problems in the Punjab in the mid-1980s to this fear as well; see his *Tragedy of Punjab*, pp.19–21.

6. For an interesting analysis of the general pattern of religious fundamentalism in South Asia of which the Hindu and Sikh movements are a part, see Robert Eric Frykenberg, 'Revivalism and Fundamentalism: Some Critical Observations with Special Reference to Politics in South Asia', in James W. Bjorkman (ed.), *Fundamentalism, Revivalists and Violence in South Asia* (Riverdale, MD: Riverdale, 1986).

7. I am grateful to Professor Ranbir Singh Sandhu, Department of Civil Engineering, Ohio State University, for providing me with several hours of tape-recorded speeches of Sant Jamail Singh Bhindranwale. Professor Sandhu has translated some of these speeches, and I appreciate his sharing these translations with me. For this article I am relying primarily on the words of Bhindranwale. They are found in the following sources: 'Sant Jamail Bhindranwale's Address to the Sikh Congregation', a transcript of a sermon given in the Golden Temple in November 1983, translated by Ranbir Singh Sandhu, April 1985, and distributed by the Sikh Religious and Educational Trust, Columbus, Ohio; excerpts of Bhindranwale's speeches, translated into English, that appear in Joyce Pettigrew, 'In Search of a New Kingdom of Lahore', *Pacific Affairs*, Vol. 60, No. 1 (Spring 1987) (forthcoming), and interviews with Bhindranwale found in various issues of *India Today* and other publications.

8. The spiritual leader of the Nirankaris, Baba Gurbachan Singh, was assassinated at his home in Delhi on 24 May 1980. Bhindranwale was implicated in the murder, but was never brought to trial. Kuldip Nayar claims that Zail Singh, who became President of India, came to Bhindranwale's defense at that time (Nayar and Singh, *Tragedy of Punjab*, p.37).

9. It is said that Bhindranwale was first brought into the political arena in 1977 by Mrs Gandhi's son, Sanjay, who hoped that Bhindranwale's popularity would undercut the political support of the Akali party (Nayar and Singh, *Tragedy of Punjab*, p.31, and Tully, *Amritsar*, p.57–61).

10. Bhindranwale, 'Address to the Sikh Congregation', pp.10–11.

11. Bhindranwale, excerpt from a speech, in Pettigrew.

12. Ibid., p.15.

13. Ibid.

14. Bhindranwale, 'Address to the Sikh Congregation', p.1.

15. Ibid.

16. Bhindranwale, excerpt from a speech, in Pettigrew.

17. Ibid.

18. Bhindranwale, 'Address to the Sikh Congregation', p.10.

19. Ibid., p.2.

20. Bhindranwale, excerpt from a speech, in Pettigrew.

21. Ibid.

22. Ibid.

23. Ibid.

24. Bhindranwale, 'Address to the Sikh Congregation', pp.1–5, and ibid., p.14.

25. Bhindranwale, excerpt from a speech, in Pettigrew.

26. For an interesting discussion of the definition of violence and terror in political contexts see Thomas Perry Thornton, 'Terrorism as a Weapon of Political Agitation', in Harry Eckstein (ed.), *Internal War: Problems and Approaches* (New York: The Free Press, 1964); and David C. Rapoport, 'The Politics of Atrocity', in Y. Alexander and S. Finger (eds.), *Terrorism: Interdisciplinary Perspectives* (New York: John Jay, 1977).

27. Clifford Geertz defines religion as 'a system of symbols which acts to establish powerful, pervasive and long-lasting moods and motivations in men by formulating conceptions of a general order of existence and clothing these conceptions with such an aura of factuality that the moods and motivations seem uniquely realistic' ('Religion as a Cultural System', reprinted in William A. Lessa and Evon Z. Vogt, (eds.), *Reader in*

Comparative Religion: An Anthropological Approach (New York: Harper & Row, 3rd ed., 1972), p.168).

28. Robert Bellah, 'Transcendence in Contemporary Piety', in Donald R. Cutler, *The Religious Situation: 1969* (Boston: Beacon Press, 1969), p.907.

29. Peter Berger, *The Heretical Imperative* (New York: Doubleday, 1980), p.38. See also his *Sacred Canopy: Elements of a Sociological Theory of Religion* (Garden City, NY: Doubleday, 1967).

30. Louis Dupré, *Transcendent Selfhood: The Loss and Re-discovery of the Inner Life* (New York: Seabury Press, 1976), p.26. For a discussion of Berger and Dupré's definitions, see Mary Douglas, 'The Effects of Modernization on Religious Change', *Daedalus*, Vol.III, No.1 (Winter 1982), pp.1–19.

31. Durkheim describes the dichotomy of sacred and profane in religion in the following way: 'In all the history of human thought there exists no other example of two categories of things so profoundly differentiated or so radically opposed to one another .... The sacred and the profane have always and everywhere been conceived by the human mind as two distinct classes, as two worlds between which there is nothing in common .... In different religions, this opposition has been conceived in different ways'. Emile Durkheim, *The Elementary Forms of the Religious Life*, trans. by Joseph Ward Swain (London: George Allen & Unwin, 1976) (originally published in 1915), pp.38–9. Durkheim goes on to talk about the sacred things that religions encompass; but the first thing he says about the religious view is the perception that there is this dichotomy. From a theological perspective it seems to me that Paul Tillich is saying something of the same thing in arguing for the necessary connection between faith and doubt (see, for example, the first chapter of his *Dynamics of Faith*).

32. On this point I am in agreement with Wilfred Cantwell Smith who suggested some years ago that the noun 'religion' might well be banished from our vocabulary, and that we restrict ourselves to using the adjective 'religious' (*The Meaning and End of Religion: A New Approach to the Religious Traditions of Mankind* (New York: Macmillan, 1962), pp.119–53).

33. For the significance of the two-edged sword symbol and its links with the Devi cult revered by people, such as Jats, who have traditionally inhabited the foothills of the Himalayas adjacent to the Punjab, see W.H. McLeod, *The Evolution of the Sikh Community* (Oxford: Clarendon Press, 1976), p.13.

34. Ibid, pp.15–17, 51–2. These five objects are known as the five K's, since the name for each of them in Punjabi begins with the letter 'k'. The other four are uncut hair, a wooden comb, a metal bangle and cotton breeches. See also W. Owen Cole and Piara Singh Sambhi, *The Sikhs: Their Religious Beliefs and Practices* (London: Routledge & Kegan Paul, 1978), p.36.

35. Karl Marx, 'Contribution to the Critique of Hegel's Philosophy of Right', reprinted in Karl Marx and Friedrich Engels, *On Religion* (New York: Schocken Books), p.42; see also Engels' class analysis of a religious revolt, 'The Peasant War in Germany' in the same volume, pp.97–118.

36. Sigmund Freud, *Totem and Taboo*, trans. by James Strachey (New York: W.W. Norton, 1950).

37. Rene Girard, *Violence and the Sacred*, trans. by Patrick Gregory (Baltimore and London: Johns Hopkins University Press, 1977); see especially Chapters 7 and 8. What is not clear in this book is how symbolic violence leads to real acts of violence; this link is made in a subsequent study of Girard's, *Scapegoat*, trans. by Patrick Gregory (Baltimore and London: Johns Hopkins University Press, 1986).

38. Bhindranwale, excerpt from a speech, in Pettigrew.

39. Ibid.

40. Bhindranwale, 'Address to the Sikh Congregation', p.9.

41. See my article, 'Nonviolence', in Mircea Eliade (ed.), *The Encyclopedia of Religion* (New York: Macmillan, 1987). For the ethic of non-violence in Sikhism see Cole and Sambhi, *The Sikhs*, p.138. For Sikh ethical attitudes in general see Avtar Singh, *Ethics of the Sikhs* (Patiala, India: Punjabi University Press); and S.S. Kohli, *Sikh Ethics* (New Delhi: Munshiram Manoharlal, 1975).

42. An excellent anthology of statements of Christian theologians on the ethical justification for war is Albert Marrin (ed.), *War and the Christian Conscience: From Augustine to Martin Luther King, Jr.* (Chicago: Henry Regnery, 1971). On the development of the just war doctrine in Christianity, with its secular parallels, see James Turner Johnson, *Ideology, Reason, and the Limitation of War: Religious and Secular Concepts, 1200–1740* (Princeton: Princeton University Press, 1975).
43. Frantz Fanon, *The Wretched of the Earth* (New York: Grove Press, 1963).
44. For a discussion of the term *qaum* in the Untouchable movements, see my *Religion as Social Vision* (Berkeley and London: University of California Press, 1982), p.45.
45. Joyce Pettigrew argues that the *miri-piri* concept 'gave legitimacy to the political action organized from within the Golden Temple' (Pettigrew, op. cit.). This 'political action' was the establishment of an armed camp of which Bhindranwale was the commander; it was to rout this camp that the Indian army entered the Golden Temple on 5 June 1984, in Operation Bluestar.
46. Bhindranwale, 'Address to the Sikh Congregation', p.13.
47. Ibid., p.8.
48. David C. Rapoport, 'Why does Messianism Produce Terror?' paper delivered at the 81st Annual Meeting of the American Political Science Association, New Orleans, 27 August – 1 September 1985. Although I find Rapoport's conclusions helpful, and in many ways compatible with my own, his emphasis on messianic movements seems unnecessary. The notion of messianism is largely alien to the Asian religious traditions, and much of what he says about it could be said of religion in general. See also his 'Fear and Trembling: Terrorism in Three Religious Traditions', *American Political Science Review* 78:3 (Sept. 1984), pp.658–77, which includes case studies of the Thugs, Assassins and Zealots and the essays in David C. Rapoport and Y. Alexander (eds.), *The Morality of Terrorism: Religious and Secular Justifications* (New York: Pergamon, 1982).
49. There are also examples in other cultures where mythic battles are thought to have had a historical effect. At a recent presentation at the Wilson Center, for instance, Professor Billie Jean Isbell described the influence of the notion of cosmic cycles of order and chaos in traditional Andean cosmology on the propensity for violence of the Sendero Luminoso tribal people of Peru ('The Faces and Voices of Terrorism', Politics and Religion Seminar, Wilson Center, 8 May 1986).
50. The term *jihad* is derived from the word for striving from something, and implies 'the struggle against one's bad inclinations' as well as what it has come to mean in the popular Western mind, holy war (Rudolph Peters, *Islam and Colonialism: The Doctrine of Jihad in Modern History*, The Hague: Mouton Publishers, 1979, p.118).
51. Bhindranwale, 'Address to the Sikh Congregation', p.7.
52. Bhindranwale, excerpt from a speech, in Pettigrew.
53. Bhindranwale, 'Address to the Sikh Congregation', p.13.
54. For an interesting analysis of the Gush Emunim, see Ehud Sprinzak's essay in this volume.
55. Bhindranwale, 'Address to the Sikh Congregation', p.8.
56. Ibid., p.2.
57. Ibid., p.3.
58. Bhindranwale, excerpt from a speech, in Pettigrew.
59. Ibid.
60. Weston LaBarre, *The Ghost Dance: Origins of Religion* (London: Allen & Unwin, 1972).
61. William James, *The Varieties of Religious Experience* (Cambridge, MA: Harvard University Press, 1985) (originally published in 1902), pp.71–108.
62. Bhindranwale, 'Address to the Sikh Congregation', p.10.
63. Ibid., p.10.
64. Bhindranwale, excerpt from a speech, in Pettigrew.
65. Bhindranwale, 'Address to the Sikh Congregation', p.14.
66. Bhindranwale, excerpt from a speech, in Pettigrew.

From Messianic Pioneering to Vigilante Terrorism: The Case of the Gush Emunim Underground

Ehud Sprinzak

Introduction

This study is part of a larger attempt to understand and explain the radicalization processes that have taken place within democratic societies in the last 25 years, and that led non-violent political movements to embark upon a violent course that finally produced terrorism. The study emerged from a specific interest in the radicalization of Gush Emunim (the block of the faithful), an Israeli messianic movement committed to establishing Jewish settlements in the West Bank (biblical Judea and Samaria). It was especially triggered by the exposure and arrest, in April 1984, of a terror group composed of highly respected members of the movement, who since 1980 had committed several stunning acts of anti-Arab terror in the West Bank. The fact that the 'underground' – as it was named in the press – had also developed a very elaborate plan to blow up the Muslim Dome of the Rock on Jerusalem's Temple Mount, for ideological-religious reasons, was of special significance. It showed that some prominent members of Gush Emunim, who started their careers as peaceful, idealistic settlers, had become extremely millenarian, radicalized to the point of considering catastrophe a means of achieving national and religious redemption.

The present article focuses on the tension that has existed within Gush Emunim, since its establishment. One is the pragmatic political desire to settle the West Bank in order to keep it Israeli, and, the other is the messianic aspiration *to redeem* the nation through an act of un-precedented national regeneration. The main purpose of the article is to show how the constraints of political reality – the non-messianic policy of the Israeli government and the local Arab resistance – have brought this tension to its peak and finally produced terrorism.

I will discuss five topics in the following order:

(1) The conditions under which Gush Emunim was established;
(2) The radicalization of the Gush Emunim;
(3) The ideological predicaments of Gush Emunim, which made it possible for some members to consider violence as a necessary and legitimate means;
(4) The formation of the underground and the nature of the process by which young and idealistic members became committed terrorists;

(5) The activities of the underground and how terror was perceived and justified by the members of the group to themselves, and to the rabbinical authorities within Gush Emunim.

History

The Emergence of Gush Emunim

Gush Emunim was officially born in 1974 as a reaction to the Yom Kippur War. But the spiritual inspiration for the new movement came directly out of the events of Israel's previous conflict, the Six Day War of 1967. Israel's swift victory, which brought about the reunification of Jerusalem, the return to Israel of biblical Judea and Samaria (the West Bank), the conquest of Sinai and the take-over of the Golan Heights, was perceived by many Israelis as an unworldly event. They simply could not believe it was all real. Zionist religious Jews were especially stunned. The new event did not square with the non-messianic, pragmatic stand they had maintained for years. It must have been a miracle. The God of Israel had once again showed his might. He came to the rescue of his people in their worst moment of fear and anxiety, and, as in the days of old (from Exodus to the Macabee revolt), turned an unbearable situation upside down. In one strike he placed the whole traditional *Eretz Yisrael* – the object of prayers and yearnings of thousands of years – in the hands of his loyal servants.

But while most of the nation, including the religious community, was still shocked and overwhelmed, there was one small religious school that was not. This school centered around Yeshivat *Merkaz ha-Rav*, in Jerusalem, and around the theology of the Kook family. The head of the Yeshiva, Rabbi Zvi Yehuda Kook, who succeeded the founder of the school (his revered father, Rabbi Avraham Yitzhak ha-Cohen Kook), was intensely preoccupied with the incorporation of the entire *Eretz Yisrael* into the state of Israel. His dreams were widely shared with his devoted students and were discussed in many courses and *halakhic* deliberations.[1] Following the teaching of his father, and the belief that ours is a messianic age in which the Land of Israel, in its entirety, is to be reunited, Rabbi Zvi Yehuda Kook left no doubt in the hearts of his students that in their lifetimes they were to see the great event. Distinct from the rest of the religious community, the student body of Merkaz ha-Rav was mentally and intellectually ready to absorb the consequences of the Six Day War – but not before witnessing a unique, seemingly miraculous event.

On the eve of Independence Day in May 1967, graduates of the Yeshiva met at Merkaz ha-Rav for an alumni reunion. As was his custom, Rabbi Zvi Yehuda Kook delivered a festive sermon, in the midst of which his quiet voice suddenly rose and he bewailed the partition of historic *Eretz Yisrael*.[2] His faithful students were led to believe that this situation was intolerable and must not last. When three weeks later, in June 1967, they found themselves citizens of an enlarged state of Israel, the graduates of

Merkaz ha-Rav were convinced that a genuine spirit of prophecy had come over their rabbi on that Independence Day.

In one stroke a flame had been lit and the conditions made ripe for imparting the political ideology of *Eretz Yisrael* to a wider religious public, especially young Zionist religious Jews. The disciples of Rabbi Kook became missionaries equipped with unshakeable confidence in the divine authority of their cause. They consequently transformed a wide religious community into a radical political constituency. According to the new ideo-theology, the entire historic Land of Israel would have to be annexed, immediately, to the state of Israel, whether by military action or by settlement and the legal extension of Israeli sovereignty.

The new theology of *Eretz Yisrael*, and the political spirit associated with it, had one problem. The secular government of Israel did not share its convictions and its messianic interpretation of politics. Pragmatic considerations prevailed, Judea and Samaria were not annexed, and Jewish settlement in the new territories was hesitant and slow. A core group of the future Gush Emunim, *Elon Moreh* – whose founders first formulated the settlement operational ideology – was preparing itself diligently to settle in the midst of Arab-populated Samaria.[3] Otherwise, little was taking place. The successful establishment of Kiryat Arba, a Jewish city adjacent to Hebron, was started illicitly and then authorized by the government. This strategy clearly showed the direction to follow. However, not until after the 1973 Yom Kippur War did these people feel a need to organize politically. Amid the gloomy public mood occasioned by the first territorial concessions in the Sinai Peninsula (required by the disengagement agreement with Egypt), the founders of Gush Emunim determined to oppose further territorial concessions and promote the extension of Israeli sovereignty over the occupied territories.

The founding meeting of Gush Emunim took place in March 1974 at Kfar Etzion, a West Bank Kibbutz that had been seized by the Arabs in the War of Independence and recovered by Israel in the Six Day War. This meeting had been preceded by informal discussions in which leading roles had been played by former students of Rabbi Zvi Yehuda Kook. At first, Gush Emunim was a faction within the National Religious Party (NRP), which at that time was a partner in the labor coalition government. Distrustful of the NRP's position concerning the future of Judea and Samaria, the Gush people soon left the party and declared their movement's independence. Since then, they have refused to identify with any political party and have gained a unique political status, a combination of pioneering settlement organization, powerful pressure group, and wild extraparliamentary movement. This combination of inner and outer systematic operation proved highly effective and fruitful.[4]

Under the Labor-led government of Yitzhak Rabin (1974–77), Gush Emunim pursued three types of activity: it protested the interim agreements with Egypt and Syria; it staged demonstrations in Judea and Samaria to underscore the Jewish attachment to those parts of *Eretz*

Yisrael (the Land of Israel, or biblical Palestine); and it carried out settlement operations in the occupied territories.

The most controversial issue pursued by Gush Emunim was the demand to settle the densely populated Arab Samaria. Basing its claim on God's promise to Abraham some 5,000 years earlier, Gush Emunim challenged the government's pragmatic Allon plan to avoid Jewish settlement in Samaria at all costs. The result was a political power struggle which ended, surprisingly, with Emunim's success. Through countless illicit settlement efforts, and street demonstrations, the young pioneers of Gush Emunim got what they wanted: several semi-official settlements in Samaria, the heartland of historic *Eretz Yisrael*.

The Likud victory in the elections of May 1977 and the declaration of the prime minister designate, Menachem Begin, that 'we will have many more Elon Morehs' induced Gush Emunim leaders to believe in all sincerity that their extra-legal period was over.[5] And indeed, the new regime accorded them full legitimacy. They were allowed to settle Samaria. Their settlement organization, *Amana*, was legitimized as an official settlement movement. Many of them welcomed this official acceptance and were happy to shed their extremist image.

But Gush Emunim did not rejoice for long. Despite the Gush's expectations, the government did not come up with a large-scale settlement program. The constraints of daily policy-making, Begin's failing health, and especially the pressures of the American government all began to leave their mark on the cabinet. The government was still sympathetic – Minister of Agriculture Ariel Sharon did not conceal his affection for Gush Emunim – but it gradually became clear that even under a Likud administration it might have to use the extra-legal tactics it had devised during the Rabin regime.

The Emergence of the Underground

17 September 1978 was the lowest point in the short history of Gush Emunim. Menachem Begin, Israel's prime minister, signed the Camp David Accords with Egypt and the United States, leaving Emunim's people stunned and in disbelief. His agreement to return all of Sinai to the Egyptians, as well as his initiation of the Autonomy Plan (for the Palestinians of the West Bank and Gaza) was inconceivable to them. For many years, these people had led themselves to believe that Begin, the great champion of undivided *Eretz Yisrael*, was their best insurance against territorial compromise with the Arabs. Most of them were not Begin's traditional supporters, but came to identify with him politically. His commitments to have 'many more Elon Morehs' had for them a special appeal.

The Camp David Accords presented to Gush Emunim a challenge of unprecedented magnitude. The accords signified a human (Begin's) error capable of stopping, or at least halting, an inevitable divine process, the process of redemption. How were they, members of a young and inexperienced political movement, to respond? Even their elderly rabbis were not sure, and most of the reactions indicated despair and confusion.[6] For a while it looked as if Gush Emunim would fold.

The most extreme reaction to the Camp David Accords was not known until the April 1984 arrest of the members of the Gush Emunim underground. When it was first apprehended, and a long time after the beginning of its trial, the group was considered an *ad hoc* terror team aimed at avenging PLO terrorism. However, it is now established that the first contacts of the leaders of the group took place late in 1978 and had nothing to do with revenge against Arab terrorism. The only issue on their agenda was blowing up what they called the *abomination* – the Muslim Dome of the Rock.[7] The idea was brought up by two remarkable individuals, Yeshua Ben Shoshan and Yehuda Etzion. Both men, although closely affiliated with Gush Emunim and its settlement drive, were nevertheless not typical members. More than most of their collegues they were intensely preoccupied with the mysteries of the process of regeneration that was about to bring the Jewish People – perhaps in their own lifetime – to its redemption.

The Kabbalistic Ben Shoshan and the Zealot Etzion brought the disappointment of Gush Emunim from the Camp David Accords to its peak. Literally messianic, the two convinced themselves that the historical set-back must have had a deeper cause than Begin's simple weakness. It was a direct signal from Heaven that a major national offence was committed, a sin that was responsible for the political disaster and its immense spiritual consequences. Only one prominent act of desecration could match the magnitude of the set-back: the presence of the Muslims and their shrine on Temple Mount, the holiest Jewish site, the sacred place of the First, Second and Third (future) Temples.

It is not precisely clear when the group was seriously solidified by the two and under what conditions. But the most important development in those early years certainly took place in Yehuda Etzion's mind. This energetic young man discovered the writings of an unknown ultra-nationalist thinker, Shabtai Ben Dov. Ben Dov, who for years was an unimportant official in Israel's Ministry of Industry and Commerce, developed in total isolation a grand theory of active national redemption. Among other notions, the new theory brought life into such ideas as the resumption of the biblical kingdom of Israel and the building of the Third Temple. The man wrote about territorial expansion, national moral expurgation, and the establishment of Jewish law in Israel. Drawing on the almost forgotten tradition of ultra-nationalist poet Uri Zvi Grinberg, but with a post-1967 religious enthusiasm, Ben Dov dared to think the unthinkable – a total and *concrete* transformation of the nation into a sacred people and a holy state. No one, including Gush Emunim rabbis, had done it before. Etzion, who only slowly absorbed his new discovery of the writings of Ben Dov, decided to devote himself completely to their publication.[9] By 1979, Ben Dov was dead, after a long illness. But in the mind of Yehuda Etzion, his ideas were very much alive.

Some time early in 1980, a secret meeting was convened by Yehuda

Etzion and his friend Menachem Livni. The meeting was attended by eight men.[10] This was the first time in which the Temple Mount operation was spelled out in great detail. The main speaker was Yehuda Etzion, who presented his new redemption theology in its grand contours. Etzion told the group that the removal of the Muslim mosques would spark a new light in the nation and would trigger a major spiritual revolution in the direction of intense religiosity and commitment to redemption. He appeared convinced that the operation would solve once and for all the problems of the people of Israel. His tone and spirit were prophetic and messianic.[11] The other speakers were more cautious. They raised technical as well as substantial political questions. Some did not believe the job could be tackled operationally, and others worried about the political and international consequences. Menachem Livni, a Hebron engineer and captain in the reserves who emerged as the operational head of the group and the most considerate and balanced person, agreed with Etzion in principle. He was, however, apprehensive about the immense consequences. Livni's conclusion, accepted by the rest of the group, was that concrete preparations for blowing up the Dome of the Rock could start immediately, irrespective of a final operative decision. There are so many details to be worked out that the question of a final decision to strike was irrelevant.[12]

May of 1980 was a critical month for the evolution of the Jewish underground. On Friday, 3 May, a group of Yeshiva students returning to Hadassah House in Hebron from a sabbath prayer, was fired upon by Arabs at close range. Six students died instantly and several others were wounded. The attack was not an isolated case. It came against the background of growing anti-Jewish violence in Hebron and in other parts of Judea and Samaria. The settler community was certain that the attack was masterminded by the Palestinian National Guidance Committee in Judea and Samaria, an unofficial PLO front organization which was allowed by Defense Minister Ezer Weizman to operate almost freely. It was generally felt that only a massive settler retaliation could put things back in order. Following two unofficial meetings in Kiryat Arba, attended by the communal rabbis, it was decided to act. Menachem Livni, a local resident, knew whom to contact – his friend and partner in the planned operation at the Temple Mount, Yehuda Etzion.[13] Instead of committing a retaliatory mass murder, in the custom of Arab terrorists, the two decided to strike at the top. The cars of five Arab leaders most active in the National Guidance Committee were to be blown up. The plan was to injure these people severely without killing them. The invalid leaders were to remain a living symbol for a long time to come.

The 'mayors affair' was crowned with partial success. Two of the leaders involved, Mayor Bassam Shakaa of Nablus and Mayor Karim Khalef of Ramalla, were instantly crippled. Two others were saved when the demolition teams failed to wire their cars. The fifth case ended with an Israeli tragedy. The mayor of El Bireh, whose garage was also set up to explode, was not at home. A police demolition expert rushed to the place mistakenly activated the explosive device. He was seriously wounded and blinded.

While the 'mayors affair' had no direct relation to the paradigmatic idea of the group, the Temple Mount plot, it apparently boosted the spirits of the plotters, for the settlers in Judea and Samaria applauded it overwhelmingly. The group thus resumed preparations for its assault on the Dome of the Rock. Indeed, Etzion, who masterminded the plan, and Livni, an expert on explosives, studied the Temple Mount and the Dome of the Rock in minute detail for two years. Following dozens of surveillance hikes to the Mount, a careful construction study of the mosque, and the theft of a huge quantity of explosives from a military camp in the Golan Heights, a full attack plan was worked out. Twenty-eight precision bombs were manufactured to destroy the Dome without causing any damage to its surroundings. The architects of the operation planned to approach the place silently, but were ready to kill the guards if necessary. For that purpose they purchased special Uzi silencers and gas canisters. More than 20 people were to take part in the operation.[14] Since the time of the final Israeli evacuation of the Jewish settlements in Sinai, agreed upon in the peace treaty, was approaching rapidly, the operation, which could prevent it, was to take place no later than early 1982.

The underground suffered, however, from one major drawback. None of the individuals involved, including Etzion, Livni, and Ben Shoshan, was an authoritative rabbi. The question of a rabbinical authority had already come up in the first meeting in 1980. Most of the members of the group made it clear that they could not operate without the blessing of a recognized rabbi. But all the rabbis the group had approached, including Gush Emunim's mentor, Rabbi Zvi Yehuda Kook, refused to grant their blessings. It is not clear how much of the planned strike had been spelled out to the authorities. But Livni, who needed the rabbinical approval, was left with no doubt. He *did not* have a green light. When the final date of decision arrived it was patently clear that only two individuals were ready to proceed, the originators of the idea, Etzion and Ben Shoshan. The grand plan had to be shelved.

The indefinite postponement in 1982 of the Temple Mount operation signified a major break in the short history of the Gush Emunim underground. It meant, for all practical purposes, the removal of the millenarian part of the plan – the aspect so attractive and dear to Etzion and Ben Shoshan – from the agenda. It is therefore not surprising that when the underground struck again, in July 1983, the two played minor roles. The operation took place in the Islamic college of Hebron in response to the murder of a Yeshiva student. It was deadly. Following an open attack on the school, just after its noon break, three students were killed and 33 wounded. While logistical support was provided by former group members, the operation itself was carried out by three men who were not involved in the 'mayors affair'. All three were extremist settlers in Hebron recruited by Menachem Livni (who masterminded the action). The attack was not as sophisticated as the first but otherwise followed the same logic. It was waged in response to a growing wave of anti-Jewish violence, culminating in the murder of a Yeshiva student in broad daylight. It expressed fatalism and a growing frustration with the government's inability to defend the settlers and it was approved by rabbinical authorities.[15] It was followed by some smaller acts of terrorism.

The emerging Hebronite fatalism was most visible in the last major operation of the group, the one meant to be the most devastating. In a response to a new wave of Arab terrorism – this time not in Hebron but in Jerusalem and near Ashkelon – Shaul Nir, the most aggressive member of the underground, became impatient. This young man considered the earlier attack on the Islamic college a great success. Determined to make it a model operation, he managed to convince the local rabbis that another decisive strike was needed.[16] Armed with their authority he prevailed over the unsure Livni and made him plan an unprecedentedly brutal act. Five Arab buses full of passengers were to be blown up in revenge for similar attacks on Israeli buses by Palestinian terrorists. The buses were to explode on Friday at 4.30 p.m., at a time and place Jews were not expected to be on the road.

The explosive devices were placed under the buses' fuel tanks to cause maximum damage and casualties.[17] Every detail was taken care of ... except one. By 1984 the Israeli Secret Service had finally spotted the Hebron group. Immediately after the completion of the wiring, the whole group was arrested, bringing the secretive part of the story of the first Gush Emunim underground to its end. The open part of the tale continues. Ever since the exposure of the group, a fierce debate about its legitimacy and its significance has been conducted continuously within Gush Emunim.

Ideology

Gush Emunim: Between Messianism and Fundamentalism

A thorough examination of the spiritual world of Gush Emunim, which includes its theology, political ideology, and modes of behavior, suggests that the movement is both messianic[18] and fundamentalist.[19] It is messianic because it maintains that ours is a messianic age in which redemption is a relevant concept and a possible historical event. It is fundamentalist because it reads the entire historical reality of our time, including the indications for redemption, through the sacred scriptures of the Torah and the Halakha, and prescribes on this basis a proper mode of behavior for its members and for the nation.

The relation between the messianic component of Gush Emunim and the fundamentalist element in the movement may well be illuminated by comparing the theologies of the two spiritual founding fathers of the movement, Rabbi Avraham Yitzhak ha-Cohen Kook – the man who before his death in 1935 established Yeshivat Mercaz ha-Rav – and his son Rabbi Zvi Yehuda Kook, who succeeded him in the Yeshiva and lived long enough to usher in Gush Emunim as a political and social movement. Rabbi Kook the father, by far the more original thinker of the two, believed that the era of redemption of the Jewish people had already begun. It was, he said, marked by the rise of modern Zionism, the Balfour Declaration, and the growing Zionist enterprise in Palestine.[20] Kook's interpretation of redemption was original and daring. It signified an immense deviation from the traditional Jewish belief that the messiah could only come through the single meta-historical appearance of an individual redeemer. And there were clearly some elements of heresy in the new interpretation, for it assigned a holy and redemptive status to the secular Zionists – the modern, non-observing, Jews. Kook's argument that the lay Zionists were unknowingly God's true emissaries, did not win him much support. This distinguished man, the first chief Rabbi of the Jewish community in Palestine, was constantly castigated by the anti-Zionist ultra-orthodoxy.

But Kook, the father, never advocated political fundamentalism or 'operative messianism'. Writing in the 1920s and 1930s, he wholly supported the vision of the secular Zionist movement, one of slow and prudent progress towards independence. He did not establish a political movement and did not call for a policy-making process based on a daily reading of the Torah. The theology that was studied for years in Yeshivat Mercaz ha-Rav had no immediate consequences and made no exclusivist political demands.

Israel's victory in the Six Day War, which miraculously placed the holiest places of the nation back in Jewish hands, transformed the status of Kook's theology. Suddenly it became clear to his students that they were indeed living in the messianic age. Ordinary reality assumed a sacred aspect; every event possessed theological meaning and was part of the meta-historical process of redemption.[21] Though shared by many religious authorities, the view was most effectively expounded by Kook's son, Rabbi Zvi Yehuda. This man who, before 1967, was only an unknown interpreter of his father's writings, became a leader of a fundamentalist movement. He defined the state of Israel as the halakhic kingdom of Israel, and the kingdom of Israel as the kingdom of heaven on earth.[22] Every Jew living in Israel was holy; all phenomena, even the secular, were imbued with holiness.[23] Not only Kook's students but the rest of the nation was expected to recognize the immense transformation and to behave accordingly. The government of Israel was counted upon to conduct its affairs, or at least part of them, according to Maimonides' 'rules of kings' and to be judged by these rules and by Torah prescriptions.[24]

The single most important conclusion of the new theology had to do with *Eretz Yisrael*, the land of Israel. The land – every grain of its soil – was declared holy in a fundamental sense. The conquered territories of Judea and Samaria had become inalienable and non-negotiable, not as a result of political or security reasoning, but because God had promised them to Abraham 5,000 years earlier and because the identity of the nation was shaped by this promise.[25] Redemption could only take place in the context of greater *Eretz Yisrael*, and territorial withdrawal meant forfeiting redemption. The ideologists of Gush Emunim ruled that the Gush had to become a settlement movement because settling Judea and

Samaria was the most meaningful act of human participation in the process of redemption.

The messianic enthusiasm of Gush Emunim, and the conviction of the spiritual heads of the movement that redemption was at hand, greatly shaped the operative theology of the movement. In fact, it shaped the lack of such idelogy. The heads of the movement, mostly rabbis, were very excited about the government of Israel that had commanded the army to its greatest victory ever. Following Rabbi Kook's theology, they were certain that the government was the legitimate representative of the kingdom of Israel in the making.[26] Their job, according to this interpretation, was not to contest the government but to settle Judea and Samaria and to make sure that on the critical issue of the territories, the nation did not go astray. That is the reason why Gush Emunim was, for many years, equivocal and unclear on three critical political issues: *the Arabs, democracy*, and the *rule of law*. However, over the years the members of the movement discovered, to their great dismay, that the rest of the world was not as enthusiastic about their prescriptions. There were too many Palestinians in the West Bank who were not thrilled about becoming passive observers of the Jewish regeneration in 'Judea and Samaria'. There were too many Israelis who were happier with their imperfect democracy than with the mystical and unclear vision of halakhic redemption. And most important of all, there was an officially elected government whose heads were either not enthusiastic about settling all the West Bank, or, even if they were, felt greatly bound by the law of the land and by Israel's international obligations.

The result of the encounter of Gush Emunim with the political reality of the world had been a very confused and unsystematic operative ideology. While the leaders of the Gush wanted to maintain the constructive and altruistic posture they started with, they realized that redemption could not be reached without pain. They furthermore discovered that their fundamentalist nature required that they draw their political inspiration not from the experience of the democratic West but from the tradition of the Torah and the twelfth century luminary Maimonides. The results have been very significant. The Palestinian Arabs, according to Gush Emunim, do not constitute a nation and are not entitled to collective political rights in *Eretz Yisrael*. The land is not theirs. The best they can hope for is to get the individual rights of what the Torah calls 'Stranger alien', the alien who fully recognizes the hegemony of the Jewish nation, and is consequently allowed to have full individual residence rights. But if the Jewish hegemony is not recognized and upheld chapter and verse, then the Palestinians have to be treated *today* as the *Canaanites* were treated in the old days: either be subdued and subjected in *Eretz Yisrael* or be evicted.[27]

Gush Emunim's position on democracy and the rule of law is equally equivocal. In principle, democracy is bound to given way to halakha theocracy, but this does not have to take place now. If the government of Israel fulfils its prescribed duties – settling all the land and making no territorial concessions to the Arabs – then democracy and the prevailing legal system may be allowed to function. But if conflict between democracy and Zionism (à la Gush Emunim) erupts, then Zionism takes precedence and extra-legal action becomes legitimate. The modern state of Israel was not established, according to Emunim's ideologists, in order to have another legal democracy under the sun. Two thousand years after its desruction it was revived for only one purpose, to redeem the nation and eventually the world. The prescription for this redemption is not written in the charter of the United Nations, it is writ large in the Torah, the book of books.[28]

Yehuda Etzion and the Theology of Active Redemption

One topic that never was on the agenda of Gush Emunim was the destruction of *Harem El Sharif*, the Muslim Dome of the Rock. While many members of this movement were greatly disturbed by the 'desecrating' presence of the Muslims – on the holy place to which even most Jews were not allowed to enter – almost none of them thought of blowing up the shrine. The feeling of unease was a product of the paradoxical situation created in 1967. While the reunification of Jerusalem signified the nation's return to its holiest place after 2,000 years, it also ruined, for religious Jews, much of this achievement. The government of Israel, acting out of its sovereign will, decided that Temple Mount must remain, for reasons of political prudence, in Muslim hands.

The fundamentalist members of Gush Emunim managed to live with the paradox because of their 'Kookist' theology. They believed that the lay government of Israel was legitmate and holy, that, despite its many mistakes, it had a bright future. Under the guidance of God, they felt, it was bound to change in time and lead the nation to redemption, just as it had in the Six Day War. There was a point in struggling against the government on the simple and clear issue of settling Judea and Samaria but there was no sense in disobeying it on such a sensitive issue as Temple Mount. The matter had to be left to God and to his mysterious ways of directing the world.

It was on the issue of Temple Mount that the underground deviated sharply from Gush Emunim, and the person who solidified the challenge to the official theology was Yehuda Etzion. This young man, 27 years old when he first developed his revolutionary theory, was a typical product of the movement. While he himself did not study in Mercaz ha-Rav, his rabbi in Yeshivat Alon Shvut was Yoel Ben Nun, one of the most influential graduates of 'Mercaz'.[29] But something happened to Etzion in 1978. Probably as a result of the crisis of Camp David and because of his immense interest in the mystery of redemption, he discovered a whole new world, the ultra-nationalist tradition worked out by the poet Uri Zvi Grinberg in the 1930s, the tradition of the 'Kingdom of Israel'.

The unique feature of this vision (which in Etzion's case was redeveloped by the unknown thinker Shabtai Ben Dov) was that it spelled out the notion of *active redemption*. According to Ben Dov, there was no need to wait for another miracle. All the conditions for concrete redemption were already present; one had merely to act. The revolutionary element in Ben Dov's ideology was his concept of redemption. He spoke about building the Third Temple and the institutionalization of Jewish theocracy on earth. He envisioned a system governed by Torah law and run by a supreme rabbinical court and a Sanhedrin (the council of the 70 wise men). None of the leaders and ideologists of Gush Emunim had ever spoken in such concrete terms. None of them dared press the issue.[30]

It is not clear whether Etzion would have followed the ideology of Ben Dov had the débâcle of Camp David not taken place. But in 1978 he started to develop a thorough intellectual critique of Gush Emunim and the ideology of Rabbi Zvi Yehuda Kook. Etzion's new theology was only written down and published after he was sent to prison in 1984, but there is no doubt that this is the system that inspired his activity within the underground.

The main thrust of the new theory is directed against Kook's sub-servience to the lay government of Israel. Etzion could not understand why Gush Emunim, which had identified the messianic quality of the present time, should wait until the secular politicians reach the same conclusion. He refused to grant a full legitimacy to 'erroneous' rulers who were commiting outrageous mistakes. Attacking the spirit of Mercaz ha-Rav, the fountainhead of Emunim's ideology, he wrote,

> ... the sense of criticism – which is a primary condition for any correction – perished here entirely. The State of Israel was granted in Mercaz ha-Rav, an unlimited and independent credit. Its operations – even those that stand in contrast to the model of Israel's Torah – are conceived of as 'God's will', or a revelation of his grace. There is no doubt that had the state announced its sovereignty in our holy mountain, driving thereby the Waqf out and removing the Dome of the Rock – it would have won a full religious backing. The voice coming from the school would have said 'strengthen Israel in greatness and crown Israel with glory'. But now that the state does nothing, what do we hear? That these acts are prohibited because it is not allowed. Moreover, letting the Arabs stay is a grace of God since we are, anyway, not allowed into the mount.[31]

Yeshivat Mercaz ha-Rav, and by implication Gush Emunim itself, has become a support system of secular Zionism according to Etzion. Narrowing its perspectives down to settlement only, it does not think in grand terms, does not challenge the inactive government of Israel, and fails to do what God wishes it to do.

What, then, is to be done? What direction should the misled Gush Emunim have taken had its rabbis read the Torah 'correctly'? Following Ben Dov and the ultra-nationalist School of the 'kingdom of Israel', Etzion maintains emphatically that the Torah portrays the 'deserved model' of life as a nation. This is,

> ... the proper kingdom of Israel that we have to establish here between the two rivers [the Euphrates and the Nile – E.S.]. This

kingdom will be directed by the Supreme Court which is bound to sit
on the place, chosen by God to emit His inspiration, a site which will
have a temple, an altar, and a king chosen by God. All the people of
Israel will inherit the land to labor and to keep.[32]

Etzion's deviation from the standard theology of Gush Emunim is thus
very clear. By his thinking, it is fully legitimate to portray *now* the contours
of the final stage of redemption, including a *theocratic government*
centered on Temple Mount and a country that controls, in addition to
present-day Israel, the Sinai, Jordan, Syria, and parts of Lebanon and
Iraq. Moreover, it is mandatory to strive *now* for the fulfilment of this
vision, and Gush Emunim or another devoted movement should take the
lead in the forthcoming struggle.

Why did Etzion focus on Temple Mount? How did he justify an
operation more incredible and dangerous than any anti-Arab plan ever
conceived of in Israel since the beginning of Zionism in the nineteenth
century? How does the Temple Mount operation fit into Etzion's general
theory of redemption? In a unique monograph, *Temple Mount*, published
while in jail, Etzion explained,

David's property in Temple Mount is therefore a real and eternal
property in the name of all Israel. It was never invalidated and never
will be. No legality, or ownership claim, which are not made in the
name of Israel and for the need of rebuilding the temple, are valid.[33]

The expurgation of Temple Mount will prepare the hearts for the
understanding and further advancing of our full redemption. The
purified Mount shall be – if God wishes – the ground and the anvil for
the future process of promoting the next holy elevation.[34]

The redemption of the nation was stopped, according to Etzion, on
Temple Mount. Not until its expurgation – a step that had to be taken by
the government of Israel but was not – could the grand process be
renewed. And since 'this horrible state of affairs' was not corrected by the
government but was rather backed by it, the task had to be fulfilled by the
most devoted and dedicated.

But how did Etzion, a very intelligent and educated man, believe that
Israel could go unharmed with the destruction of the Dome of the Rock?
How could it conquer Jordan, Syria, parts of Egypt, Iraq and Lebanon and
transform itself, in front of the rest of the world, into a Khomeini-like
theocracy? What did Etzion think about the constraints of political
reality?

Reading Etzion, and talking to him, reveals a unique combination of an
other-worldly messianic spirit and a very logical mind, a man who talks
and thinks in the language of this world but totally lives in another.
Etzion's response to these questions is based on the only intellectual
explanatory construct possible: a distinction between the *laws of existence*
and *the laws of destiny*.

> Securing and preserving life or its preservation is an 'utmost norm' for all the living nature, for humanity in general – and for us, *Israel*, too. This is indeed a norm that dictates laws, and in the name of which, people go to war. But as for ourselves 'our God is not theirs'. Not only is our existential experience different from theirs but also from their very definition. For the Gentiles, life is mainly a *life of existence*, while ours is a *life of destiny*, the life of a kingdom of priests and a holy people. We exist in the world in order to actualize destiny.[35]

The question about the constraints of political reality is relevant only to those who live by the laws of existence. But,

> Once adopting the laws of destiny instead of the laws of existence, Israel will be no more an ordinary state, one whose eyes are rolled from hour to hour ... she will become the kingdom of Israel by its very essence.

> It is therefore impossible to 'stick' to the present state some 'good advices', regarding its specific behavior in an isolated 'local' situation in the name of the laws of destiny. The stage of this change will take place, inevitably, in the immense comprehensive move of the transformation from the state of Israel to the kingdom of Israel.[36]

Operation Temple Mount was bound, according to Etzion, to trigger the transformation of the state of Israel from one system of laws to another. It was meant to elevate the nation *now* to the status of the kingdom of Israel, a kingdom of priests capable of actualizing the laws of destiny and of changing the nature of the world.

Terrorism

A close study of the underground suggests that while it was mainly shaped by the millenarian theology of Yehuda Etzion, it ended up with rugged vigilante terrorism. This internal evolution, which left Etzion himself isolated and disappointed, is a revealing exercise. It shows the course through which *idealistic dreams* produce *idealistic terrorism* and the way in which idealistic terrorism is *routinized* into *professional terrorism*. While the Jewish underground was caught before its evolution into a professional organization of killers, it had all the potential ingredients within it.

Towards Millenarian Terrorism: The Operation That Did Not Take Place

There is little question that the fundamental psycho-political framework for the emergence of the underground was formed within Gush Emunim long before the pact among Etzion and his friends. This framework was constructed with the ideology of Rabbi Yehuda Kook, who created within his followers immense expectations. Many observers of Gush Emunim have not failed to identify its behavioral messianic craze, that extranormal quality of intense excitement and hypernomian behavior[37] that produced within many members of the movement constant expectations of progress toward redemption.[38] David C. Rapoport, who studied the affinity between terrorism and messianism, recently observed that: 'Once a messianic advent is seen as imminent, particular elements of a messianic doctrine become critical in pulling a believer in the direction of terror.'[39] Rapoport argued convincinly that, messianism – once it becomes operational – and terrorism imply extra-normal behavior, a pattern of action and orientation which is predicated on the conviction that the traditional conventions of morality and conduct are not binding.

Under certain conditions that usually imply a failure of an expected redemption to materialize, it is possible, according to Rapoport, for messianic people to resort to extra-normal acts of violence. Either because they want to prove to themselves that redemption remains relevant, or because they want to convince God that this is the case, they may opt for exceptional catastrophe.[40] Menachem Livni, the operational 'commander' of the underground, described to his investigators how it was all born.

> Shortly after President Sadat's visit of Israel, I was approached by a friend who showed me the picture of the Dome of the Rock on Temple Mount – to which I shall heretofore refer as the 'abomination'. My friend argued that the existence of the abomination on Temple Mount, our holiest place, was the root cause of all the spiritual errors of our generation and the basis of Ishmael [that is, the Arabs – E.S.] hold in Eretz Yisrael. In this first meeting I did not clearly understand my friend and more meetings were held to which an additional friend joined.[41]

What apparently happened after the crisis of Camp David is that most of the members of Gush Emunim, who were also shocked by the postponement of redemption, were able to follow old Rabbi Kook's instruction to maintain their allegiance to the Israeli government and to its legal system, but a few were not. They gathered around Yehuda Etzion, Yeshua Ben Shoshan and Menachem Livni, who all believed they had a better response to the disaster, an act that would alleviate the misery in a single strike.

The spiritual and mysterious nature of the project was described in great detail by many members of the underground. Long before they started to discuss operational matters, such as explosives and guns, they immersed themselves in halakhic issues and kabbalistic spiritual deliberations. Chaim Ben David, who attended the meetings since 1978, described how he was recruited and in what terms operations were discussed.

> In about 1977 or 1978, I was approached by Gilaad Peli from Moshav Keshet in the Golan Heights, a man I have known since 1975 and his activity within Gush Emunim. He told me to come to Yeshua Ben Shoshan with whom I had a previous learning experience in Torah subjects. Following the learning part, Yeshua and Gilaad discussed

with me a plan to remove the Dome of the Rock on Temple Mount – a
plan meant to be part of a spiritual redemption of the people of
Israel. The great innovation for me was that this was a 'physical
operation' capable of generating a spiritual operation.

I agreed to join the group and participate in its project. Then came
the stages of the meetings and conferences in Yeshua's house as well
as in an isolated house ... owned by Ben Shoshan's releatives. There
were many sessions and I am sure I did not attend them all because of
my physical distance. The meetings were attended by Menachem
Livni, Yehuda Etzion, Yeshua Ben Shoshan, Gilaad Peli and
myself. There were several sessions in Yeshua's house without his
personal presence ... . In the sessions the spiritual side of the idea
was discussed as well as questions relating to the posible acceptance
of, and resonse to, the act by the people of Israel. Then they started
to discuss operational matters. The first idea was to bomb [the place]
from the air – we had a pilot in our group – but it is not clear whether it
was serious or just a joke. Finally, it was decided to blow up the
Mosque by explosives.[42]

As we have already seen, Operation Temple Mount never took place.
Despite three years of intense preparations and planning that far
exceeded anything else done by the group, the project was finally
abandoned by Menachem Livni, the 'commander'. Only two men, Etzion
and Ben Shoshan, wanted to go ahead[43] when none of Gush Emunim's
main rabbis was willing to cooperate. But in his final word on the issue,
Livni did not appear disappointed or beaten:

In retrospect it appears to me that the honor of Temple Mount and
the Temple itself, as well as the dignity of the people of Israel
instructs us that this operation should be carried out by a united
nation and its government. We, on our behalf, did our best in front of
heaven and earth, as if it was like 'open for me a niche needle wide',
and I pray that we shall be blessed to see the building of the Temple in
our time. And comments that were made on Rabbi Akiva are true
and relevant to all the events and all members involved, 'Bless thee
Rabbi Akiva for being caught following the Torah'.[44]

A close reading of Livni's statement suggests a mystical approach.
Paradoxically, the statement epitomizes the entire millenarian nature of
the underground. Livni does not only speak to his interrogators, he also
appeals to God. While somewhat apologetic, he is nevertheless proud and
hopeful. He seems to believe that although he and his collegues did not
remove the Dome of the Rock, nor did they shun their apocalyptic
mission. In fact, he argues, they did all they could. They identified the
national spiritual malaise, they singled out the 'abomination' as the root
cause of it, they delved into the problem, studied it, and prayed about it,
and finally they went all the way to preparing to act. Only inches away
from the operation, they did not get God's final signal, his ultimate O.K.

God, he felt, should know how devoted they were and how serious their mission was. He should be aware of the 'needle wide' niche they opened. Perhaps he would move the government and the nation to concrete action.

From Settler Extralegalism to Vigilante Terrorism

The underground of Gush Emunim became a terror organization on 2 June 1980. It was on that night and under the command of Menachem Livni and Yehuda Etzion, that the group blew up the cars of two Arab West Bank mayors held responsible for anti-Jewish terrorism. The act that provoked the attack was the brutal murder of six Yeshiva students near Beit Hadassah in Hebron. The 'mayors affair' was welcomed by the settler community in Judea and Samaria as well as by many segments of the Israeli society. It opened the way to several additional terror plans and operations that took place between 1982 and 1984. The most brutal among these operations was the attack, on 26 July 1983, on the Islamic College of Hebron. The attackers, who responded to another murder of a Yeshiva student in Hebron, killed three Muslim students and wounded 33. In 1984 the group drew up a plan to bomb the men's dormitory of Bir Zeit University in Ramala. When the operation was postponed, because of a governmental shutdown of the university, it was replaced by a more comprehensive one – an attempt to blow up five Arab buses full of passengers. Every detail of this plan was perfectly worked out, including the final wiring of the buses on 27 April 1984. But at the last moment, the whole conspiracy was exposed and the bombs were defused in time. The arrest that followed ended up the career of the most daring Jewish terror underground in 40 years.

A review of the confessions and testimony of all the members of the undergound, and especially of Livni's and Etzion's, the leaders, suggests that the issue at stake was not religious and that it had only slight relation to redemption or messianism. The name of the game was revenge. The only association between the Dome of the Rock plan and the acts of terror that actually took place was the identity of the perpetrators. The group that blew up the mayors' cars, and some of those who continued to operate until 1984, were the same people who started to prepare themselves, morally and spiritually, to expurgate Temple Mount. But the motivations and the thinking were totally different. Discussing his participation in the 'mayors affair' in relation to his main concern, Temple Mount, Yehuda Etzion told the court:

> Planning and executing the attack on the murder chieftains took only one month of my life, one month that started with the assassination night of six boys in Hebron, and ended up in conducting this operation. I insist that this operation was right. So right in fact, that to the best of my understanding ... even the law that prevails in the state of Israel could recognize its justice or ought to have recognized it as a pure act of self defense .... It is unquestionable that in our present reality ... the reality of the sovereign state of Israel ... the

> defense forces of the state had to take care of this matter, quickly,
> neatly and effectively, so that nobody could have, in his right mind,
> thought about such operation, I, furthermore, do not deny that it was
> a clear case of undue excess. But the situation at stake was a case in
> which the 'policeman' responsible for the matter, not only stepped
> aside ... not only ignored the gravity of the case, and the fact that the
> murderers were allowed to act freely ... but developed with them a
> friendly relationship .... This situation Sirs, was a case of no choice,
> a condition that created a need to act in the full sense of the word, for
> the very sake of the word, for the very sake of the preservation of
> life.[45]

No reader familiar with the literature on vigilante movements could fail
to detect in Etzion's speech the classical logic of the *vigilante mind*. What
Etzion so eloquently told the court was that he took one month of his life, a
life otherwise devoted to the approximation of redemption, to become a
vigilante terrorist. A vigilante movement, we should recall, never sees
itself in a state of principled conflict, either with the government or with
the prevailing *concept* of law. It is not revolutionary and does not try to
bring down authority. Rather, what characterizes the vigilante state of
mind is the profound conviction that the government, or some of its
agencies, have failed to enforce their *own* laws or to establish their *own*
order in an area under their jurisdiction.[46] Backed by the fundamental
norm of self-defense and speaking in the name of what they believe to be
the valid law of the land, vigilantes, in effect, enforce the law and execute
justice. 'Due process of law' is the least of their concerns.[47] When Yehuda
Etzion responded in May 1980 to Menachem Livni's request for help in
avenging the blood of six Yeshiva students murdered in Hebron, he was
not thinking of messianism but of vigilantism. He took a short leave of
absence from his main concern to take care of an altogether different
business.

But how did Etzion, the messianic dreamer, suddenly become a rough
vigilante? What was the psycho-social mechanism that made it possible
for him – and also for his millenarian followers in the underground – to
switch from their *other-worldly* lofty concern about redemption to the
this-worldly mundane concern about revenge and law and order? And
why was the vigilante terrorism of the members of the underground
legitimized by the rabbis of Gush Emunim who refused to support the
millenarian terrorism on Temple Mount?

The answer to these questions, without which a full understanding of
the undergound is bound to be incomplete, has very little to do with either
the teaching of Rav Kook or the intellectual climate of Gush Emunim. It
concerns, instead, another facet of Gush Emunim, which until now was
not elaborated upon, *the existential extra-legalism of the movement* as a
'frontier' operation in the West Bank. Gush Emunim, as Goldberg and
Ben Zadok so well remind us, did not produce only strange messianic
types, true believers that would walk the hills of Judea and Samaria

expecting redemption to be delivered. It equally created a breed of *doers*, rugged frontier men who started their career as illicit political settlers and sustained it through a growing friction with their neighboring Arabs.[48]

While the extra-legal nature of Gush Emunim was a typical feature of the movment since its inception, its vigilante side was not recognized until the early 1980s. Rumors about settler violence against Arabs prevailed, but with no proof. However, in 1982, a committee headed by Yehudit Carp, the state Deputy Attorney-General, studied 70 cases of Jewish anti-Arab violent acts involving killings, woundings, physical assaults, property damage and the application of armed and unarmed threats. It found that 53 out of 70 cases ended in no action. Forty-three of the files were closed because a suspect could not be found, seven because of the non-existence of official complaints, and three because of a lack of public interest to justify prosecution.[49]

The vigilante nature of the settler community was examined in a comprehensive pioneering study conducted by David Weisburd, a young American Ph.D. candidate in 1983.[50] Weisburd found that 28 per cent of the male settlers and five per cent of the female settlers, out of a sample of 500, admitted to having participated in some type of vigilante activity. Sixty-eight per cent of Weisburd's respondents agreed with the statement that 'it is necessary for the settlers to respond quickly and independently to Arab harassments of settlers and settlements'. Following another finding, that only 13 per cent of those questioned disapproved of vigilantism, Weisburd concluded:

> The vigilantism of Gush Emunim settlers is part of an organized strategy of social control calculated to maintain order in the West Bank. Though a minority of settlers actually participate in vigilante acts, they are not isolated deviant figures in this settlement movement. Rather, those vigilantes are agents of the Gush Emunim community as a whole. They carry out a strategy of control that is broadly discussed and supported.[51]

Weisburd's study of the vigilantism of the settler community, as well as the Carp report and other documented studies,[52] were written and published before the exposure of the Gush Emunim underground. They nevertheless provide us with useful factual and analytical perspectives to comprehend the actual terrorism of the group. They tell us that the communal leaders of Kiryat Arba – the Jewish city adjacent to Hebron – who convened after the Beit Hadassah murder of six students, were not strangers to communal conflict, anti-Arab violence or vigilante justice. Extremist rabbis, soldiers and military reserve officers and rugged settlers – all were used to the idea of communal reprisal. They also knew, as we are told by Weisburd, that the price for previous vigilante acts, was very low.[53]

The convergence point, between the millenarian orientation of the underground and the vigilante spirit of the settlers, that actually produced terrorism, was described in some detail by Menachem Livni. Livni told his interrogators that immediately following the Beit Hadassah murder, it was decided in Kiryat Arba to respond. A special action committee was assigned the job, but its members did not have the 'adhesive spirit necessary to act'. Livni then approached Rabbi Levinger, the leading authority in the city, and told him that 'for these purposes we have to choose pure people, highly observant and sinless, people with no shred of violence in them and who are disinclined to reckless action'.[54] Levinger apparently approved and it was at that point that Livni asked Yehuda Etzion, not a resident of Kiryat Arba, to help him. Only then did the two decide to moblize the entire group, which until that time was preoccupied with preliminary deliberations about Temple Mount. The group members were perceived by their leaders to be pure and devoted. They were not terrorists but rather God's emissaries. Their immense commitment and dedication to God and nation qualified them for the merciless task.

A key to the understanding of the operations that did and did not take place is the issue of the *rabbinical authority*. A careful reading of the confessions and testimonies of the members of the underground does not clarify how much of the *operational* part of the conspiracy was shared by the leading rabbis of Kiryat Arba. But it makes clear that none of the operations that took place was opposed by the rabbis and that all of these acts were, in fact, blessed by these authorities. The first operation, the 'mayors affair', was opposed by Rabbi Levinger, but the reason for the objection was that Levinger preferred extreme action and recommended an indiscriminate act of mass violence. Rabbi Eliezer Waldman, a prominent Gush Emunim rabbi and, since 1981, a Knesset member, even volunteered, according to Livni, to participate in the first operation. Two other Hebron and Kiryat Arba rabbis were instrumental in inducing Livni to commit the last two operations that involved indiscriminate terrorism.[55] Shaul Nir, the man who conducted the murderous attack on the Islamic College in Hebron, told his interrogators:

> I would like to add that in the time span of three years, I discussed the issue with four rabbis, all of whom expressed their support for warning operations within the Arab public .... I also heard the names of an additional three rabbis who stated their support in different stages of the operation.[56]

The rabbinical backing given to the terrorism of the underground gets its full meaning in view of the rabbinical *refusal* to support the operation on Temple Mount and the resulting cancellation of that operation. Both approval and disapproval indicate how critical was the rabbinical authorization. We learn, in fact, that despite the rather spontaneous organization of the group and its relative marginality, its terrorism could never have taken place without the participation of key Gush Emunim leaders. Another way of saying the same thing is that *the radicalization process that finally produced terrorism within Gush Emunim was not marginal but central. It was a structural Gush Emunim phenomenon.*

Conclusion: The Radicalization of a Messianic Movement and the Evolution of Terrorism

What do we learn from the story of the Jewish underground? What lesson is to be drawn from the internal radicalization that took place within Gush Emunim and which led some of its most idealistic members to engage in terrorism, an extra-normal and totally unconventional activity, and one they could not even dream about before embarking on this course?

It appears to me that the main lesson to be derived from this terrorism-producing sequence of events has to do with the special vulnerability of messianic movements to extreme violence and their built-in orientation towards abrupt historical short-cuts. The present case lends strong support to David Rapoport's proposition that there is an internal logical and pyschological link between messianism and terrorism.[57] Messiansim and messianic movements *do not have* to produce terrorism but they are much more inclined to do so than other social movements faced with the same political conflicts. Under circumstances that imply uncertainty, doubts, political crisis and especially some hostile violence, they are likely to resort to excessive violence and eventually to terrorism. If the movement in question is not violent by its very nature but rather naive, idealistic and moralistic, the chance that all its leaders and members, or even the majority of them, will embark on a terroristic course is very slim. But it is highly probable that some of these people will, usually a small minority. Certain elements within the messianic movement, the most idealistic, action-oriented and preoccupied with the mystery of redemption, would become impatient with the ordinary procedures, the boring rules of conventional conflict-management and with all the other barriers. Facing hostility, sometimes aggression, but especially *unbearable delays in the process of redemption*, they will be drawn to violence and to terrorism.

It is thus possible to conclude that the *combination of messianic belief in national redemption coupled with a situation of endemic national conflict has within it a built-in propensity for incremental violence − extra-legalism, vigilantism, selective terrorism and finally ... indiscriminate terrorism. A 'majestic' act of 'holy' terrorism may well fit into this scheme.* As for the Gush Emunim underground it may be suggested that had its operations not been stopped in 1984, by Israel's intelligence services, it would likely have become a professional group of killers, a Jewish IRA.

NOTES

Research for this study was supported by the Harry Frank Guggenheim Foundation and completed under a fellowship at the Woodrow Wilson International Center for Scholars.

1. Zvi Ranaan, *Gush Emunim* (Tel Aviv: Sifriyat Poalim, 1980), Ch. 4; Danny Rubinstein, *On the Lord's Side: Gush Emunim* (Hebrew) (Tel Aviv: Hakibutz Hameuchad, 1982), pp.18–28; E. Sprinzak, 'Gush Emunim: The Iceberg Model of

Political Extremism' (Hebrew), *Medina, Mimshal Vehechasim Beinleumiim* 17 (1981), pp.29–30.

2. *Nequda* (The Magazine of the Settlers in Judea, Samaria and Ghaza), 86, pp.6–7 (Hebrew).
3. *Nequda*, 69, pp.5–7.
4. Sprinzak, op. cit., pp.23–4.
5. Ibid., p.26.
6. Rubinstein, op. cit., pp.147–56.
7. Menachem Livni, *Interrogation* (court documents) 5/18/1987.
8. Interview with Etzion 9/9/1985.
9. Ibid.
10. Itzhak Ganiram, *Interrogation* (court documents) 5/5/1984.
11. Uri Meir, *Interrogation* (court documents) 4/30/1984.
12. Livni, *Interrogation*, 5/18/1984.
13. Ibid.
14. Etzion, interview, 9/9/1984.
15. Livni, *Interrogation*, 5/18/1985.
16. Ibid.
17. Licht's Report (court documents) 5/22/1984.
18. For a definition of messianism see Hans Kohn, 'Messianism', *Encyclopedia of the Social Sciences* (New York: Macmillan, 1935); R.J. Zvi Werblovsky, 'Messiah and Messianic Movements', *The New Encyclopedia Britannica Macropedia*, Vol.11 (Chicago: Encyclopedia Britannica, 1981).
19. For a systematic treatment of the concept of Fundamentalism see Robert E. Frykenberg, 'Revivalism and Fundamentalism: Some Critical Observations with Special Reference to Politics in South Asia' in James W. Bjorkman, *Fundamentalism, Revivalism and Violence in South Asia* (Riverdale, forthcoming), pp.1–5; Robert E. Frykenberg, 'On the Comparative Study of Fundamentalist Movements: An Approach to Conceptual Clarity and Definition', Working Paper, Woodrow Wilson Center, Spring 1986.
20. Cf. Sprinzak, 1981, op. cit., pp.29–30.
21. Cf. Zvi Yaron, *The Teaching of Rav Kook* (Hebrew) (Jerusalem, 1979). Raanan, op. cit., pp.28–30; Charles S. Liebman and Eliezer Don-Yehigy, *Religion and Politics in Israel* (Bloomington, IN: Indiana University Press, 1984), pp.70–74.
22. Raanan, op. cit., pp.64–7.
23. Cf. Uriel Tal, 'Foundations of a Political Messianic Trend in Israel', *The Jerusalem Quarterly* 35 (1985).
24. Cf. Rav Zvi Yehuda Kook, 'Honest We Shall Be: In the Land and in the Torah' (Hebrew), in Y. Shaviv, *A Land of Settlement* (Jerusalem, 1977), pp.106–10.
25. Sprinzak, 1981, op. cit., p.30; Uriel Tal, op. cit., pp.39–41.
26. Sprinzak, op. cit., pp.32–3.
27. Cf. E. Sprinzak, 'Gush Emunim: The Politics of Zionist Fundamentalism in Israel', *Research Paper* (New York: The American Jewish Committee, 1986), pp.11–13.
28. Ibid.
29. Interview with Yoel Ben Nun, 3/10/1985.
30. Shabtai Ben Dov, *The Redemption of Israel in the Crisis of the State* (Hebrew) (Safad: Hamatmid, 1960); *Prophesy and Tradition in Redemption* (Tel Aviv: Yair Publications, 1979).
31. Y. Etzion, 'From the Flag of Jerusalem to the Redemption Movement' (Hebrew), *Nequda* 94 (1985), p.28.
32. Ibid., p.22.
33. Y. Etzion, *Temple Mount* (Hebrew) (Jerusalem: E. Caspi, 1985).
34. Ibid., p.4.
35. Y. Etzion, 'To Fly, At Last, The Flag of Jerusalem' (Hebrew), *Nequda* 93 (1985), p.23.
36. Y. Etzion, 'From the Laws of Existence to the Laws of Destiny' (Hebrew), *Nequda* 75 (1984), p.26.
37. David C. Rapoport defines 'hypernomion behavior' as 'asceticism, excessive self-

discipline and a stringent observation of rules which comprehend every aspect of the individual's life' in 'Why Does Messianism Produce Terrorism?', unpublished paper read at the Eighty-First Meeting of the American Political Science Association, New Orleans, August 1985, p.8.

38. Cf. Raanan, op. cit., Ch.3.
39. Rapoport, op. cit. (abstract).
40. Ibid., pp.16–18.
41. Livni, *Interrogation*, 5/18/1984.
42. Chaim Ben David, *Interrogation*, 4/30/1984.
43. Interview with Yehuda Etzion, 9/11/1985.
44. Livni, *Interrogation*, 5/18/1984.
45. Y. Etzion, 'I felt an Obligation to Expurgate Temple Mount' (Hebrew), *Nequda* 88 (1985), pp.24–5.
46. Cf. Richard Maxwell Brown, 'The American Vigilante Tradition' in H. Graham and T. Gurr (eds.), *Violence in America*, (New York: Signet Books, 1969), pp.144–6; John H. Rosenbaum and Peter C. Sederberg, 'Vigilantism: An Analysis of Establishment Violence', *Comparative Politics* 6 (1974).
47. Richard Maxwell Brown, 'Legal and Behavioral Perspectives on American Vigilantism', *Perspectives in American History* 5 (1971), pp.95–6.
48. Giora Goldberg and Ephraim Ben Zadok, 'Regionalism and Territorial Cleavage in Formation: Jewish Settlements in the Administered Territories' (Hebrew), *Medina, Mimshal Vechechasim Beinleumiim* 21 (1983).
49. Judith Carp, 'Investigation of Suspicions Against Israelis in Judea and Samaria', *A Report of the Follow Up Committee*, 23 May 1982.
50. David Weisburd with Vered Vinitzky, 'Vigilantism as Rational Social Control: The Case of Gush Emunim Settlers' in M. Aronoff (ed.), *Cross Currents in Israeli Culture and Politics, Political Anthropology*, Vol.4 (New Brunswick: Transaction Books, 1984).
51. Ibid., p.82.
52. Cf. Meron Benvenisti, *The West Bank Data Project* (Washington: American Enterprise Institute, 1984), pp.41–3; Dedi Zuker, 'A Study of Human Rights in the Territories Administered by the IDF, 1979–1983', *Interim Report*, International Institute for Peace in the Middle East, 1983.
53. Weisburd and Vinitzky, op. cit., pp.80–82.
54. Livni, *Interrogation*, 5/18/1984.
55. Ibid.
56. Shaul Nir, *Interrogation*, 5/9/1984.
57. Cf. Rapoport, op. cit.

Cultural Narrative and the Motivation of the Terrorist

Khachig Tololyan

Political science seems all too eager for a model, or at best a few models, that will enable generalizations suitable to its empirical discourse and instrumental aims. Understanding terrorism primarily as a form of opposition to the State and to the rule of Law,[1] political science aspires to a schematic and exhaustive typology of terrorism. However, terrorism is in fact such a complex conjunction of socio-cultural, psychological and political factors that a conceptually satisfying schema of terrorism is likely to remain elusive, at least for the time being. One way to begin is to address questions of the terrorist's self-image and motivation, because the difficulties that confront us as we grapple with these elements of the phenomenon are instructive: they reveal the persistence and inadequacy of the ethnocentric Western will to generalize from notions of ego-psychology implicit in current analyses. For example, Joseph Margolin's dismissal of crude beliefs that 'the terrorist is a psychotic' or a 'highly irrational individual' rejects some common pitfalls, only to revert to the search for a generalizing behaviorist model: 'It must be assumed that the terrorist is human. Whether rational or irrational, he is governed as we all are by the same laws of behavior.'[2] I would not dispute that terrorists are human. They are; they are socially produced, out of a specific cultural context; consequently, their behavior can not be understood by the crude – or even by the careful – application of pseudo-scientific laws of general behavior. We need to examine the specific mediating factors that lead some societies under pressure, among many, to produce the kinds of violent acts that we call terrorist. A universalizing model may in fact be applicable to the factors that belong in the explicitly political realm, but I shall be dealing with culturally specific factors which resist such generalization.[3]

Whereas the imperative of a cultural analysis is frequently acknowledged, the acknowledgment too often takes the form of lip-service. Walter Laqueur speaks eloquently against 'generalizations about the terrorist personality', which he deems of 'little validity', and insists on the importance of 'the historical and cultural context'[4] of terrorism. He then proceeds to do two things: he lists dozens of different organizations and instances of terrorism, and then, the gesture towards heterogeneity completed, he moves on in one mighty leap to make those general statements and analyses of terrorism for which his work is best known. This pattern is very widespread. Elsewhere, an analyst of wholly different background and attitudes, H.H. Cooper, remarks that 'terrorism is not a discrete topic that might be conveniently examined apart from the political, social and economic context in which it takes place .... Terrorism is a creature of its own time and place.'[5] That is exactly right, and leads immediately to considerable difficulties all too easily evaded by most students of the topic, including Cooper. The *time* relevant to a particular terrorist act or group might be the day, the month, the decade or the century previous to the event. What is more, it can be the time that is embedded in the historiography, traditional narratives, legends and myths with which a society constitutes itself as a temporal entity.

The specific forms of narrative for which I shall be making large claims are the projective narrative and the regulative biography.[6] The precise meaning of these terms will emerge as I turn my attention to an analysis of Armenian terrorism. For the present, a projective narrative is one that not only tells a story of the past, but also maps out future actions that can imbue the time of individual lives with transcendent collective values. In a sense, then, projective narratives plot out how ideal selves must live lives; they dictate biographies and autobiographies to come. They tell individuals how they would ideally have to live and die in order to contribute properly to their collectivity and its future. They prescribe not static roles but dynamic shapes of the time of our lives.

Similarly, the 'place' of terrorism that is, in Cooper's terms, a 'creature of time and place', is no simple geographical locale. It is not simply the 'rabbit warrens' that Casper Weinberger sees in Shi'ite Beirut, or the mist-shrouded pastures of Ireland. It can be the Promised Land of Zion and of all covenantal theology – the American Puritans, the South African Boers. It can be the revanchist's vision of a land that he has never seen or the aspiration of the alienated ecologist seeking a land unmarked by society. Not only the time and place that are, but absent times and places, as well as projected times and places, provide that context which is the domain in which a cultural vision can produce terrorists.

I take as my point of departure Professor Paul Wilkinson's brief survey, 'Armenian Terrorism', which begins by contrasting the Baader–Meinhof gang, among others, with Armenian terrorists, among others. He is especially concerned with terrorists who 'claim to be authentic champions of a whole ethnic community'. Wilkinson cites the Irish, Croatians and Armenians as having produced such terrorists, who are said to secure 'a broader and more loyal base of political sympathy and support'[7] than groups like the Baader–Meinhof. The way in which Wilkinson establishes authenticity is directly relevant to my argument: he cites historical precedents. Whereas there are no roots of valid grievance and reactive terrorism reaching down into the German past, he points out, the Armenians have a history of both: oppression, pogrom, genocide and then terrorism as a response to them are said to be 'part of a very long tradition' of Armenian history; as a result, the 'well-springs of ... terrorist violence' lie 'deep in national psyches and traditions'.[8] Committed as I am to notions of the social construction of individual motivation through narrative, I find a great deal that is appealing in this respect for history and tradition. It is therefore all the more disappointing to find Professor Wilkinson writing, two pages later, that 'the roots of modern Armenian terrorism lie in ... tragic events of sixty-eight years ago', namely in the genocide, and in the examples provided by earlier terrorism. 'Young Armenians are ready to go on suicide missions', he writes, because they have both a grievance and an exemplar of terrorism as a proper response to that grievance.[9]

What seems striking about both Professor Wilkinson's otherwise very good analysis and several less creditable discussions of the same topic is the disciplinary rush to the politicization of terrorism. By 'politicization' I mean that the profession of political science seems powerfully impelled to turn enormously complex events into mere, or only, or just *political* facts that can then be seen as motivating other political acts, including terrorism. This reduction happens despite frequent genuflection in the direction of the complexity of social phenomena. The history of certain nations is seen as a series of basically political events which, as though moving through a vacuum of social life, become links in a chain of other politico-diplomatic events, and eventually stretch across the decades to cause yet more political events. Whether the causes be genocide, loss of sovereignty or loss of land, when they result in terrorism the model is the same at its core: one set of events, described as political, functions as a 'cause', creating among its victims a set of agents who are motivated either by politics or by pathology to commit another set of acts described as terrorist.

What is crucially lacking in such a model is the concept of *mediation*, or a serious consideration of the possibility that past events, including the rare purely political events, are perpetuated, disseminated and experienced in a particular culture not as political events but as narratives that transcribe historical facts into moral or immoral acts, vehicles of social values. Such acts sometimes become symbols, models or paradigms of behavior, especially when they are internalized, when the narratives no longer exist 'out there' in the culture, to be sampled occasionally, but in the minds of individuals, as part of the mental equipment with which they are raised to perceive the meaning of events, to interpret them, and to launch new ones. Whether we are speaking of the tale of the 47 masterless samurai made so popular in inter-war Japan, or of the Armenian projective narratives I shall be discussing shortly, we can venture one relatively safe generalization: *terrorism with an authentically popular base is never a purely political phenomenon.* A few other commentators have said this in general terms. Moshe Amon, significantly a professor of religion writing as an outsider for an audience of political scientists, suggests that 'the legitimacy of terrorist movements may stem from a mythological model adopted by the terrorists and endorsed by large segments of society'.[10] All too often in writings on terrorism, the word 'mythology' lacks the complex meaning implied in Amon's sentence; rather, it comes to refer to that set of mystifying beliefs which happens to provide the underpinnings of national liberation movements that employ terrorism. To one reading through the professional literature with the outsider's eye, it sometimes seems that the entire question of cultural difference or specificity is handled by the ritual invocation of the tired truism that 'one man's terrorist is another man's freedom fighter'. Under the aegis of this cliché, the whole set of questions that I want to consider is then overlooked, shunted aside.

One explanation for the inability of commentators to carry through with the insight that they need to evaluate culturally specific accounts of terrorism is the potency of the analytic model which was developed in the study of, and found its early illustrations in, groups close to home, like the Baader–Meinhof gang. The vocabulary and categories with which such terrorists are described in the literature are remarkably consistent. The pivotal terms are ideology, alienation and pathology. Such terrorists are correctly said to be better educated than the average Western citizen, with greater access to abstract theory and ideology. They are said to suffer from 'biographical deficits'[11] and psychopathologies ranging from sadism to 'a desire to express hate and revenge, to smash, to kill and to disrupt – or simply to feel big'.[12] Finally, they are seen as estranged from the mainstream of their society, forced to find shelter, for a time, among relatively alienated populations of student radicals, and in time to lose even that base of passive support. It is not my intention to dispute this characterization, which may be adequate in many contexts. But it too often persists even when the analysis moves on to consider groups like the Irish or Armenian terrorists. Endowing these movements with more authentic, perhaps even legitimate, grievances is something that the more thoughtful analysts, like Professor Wilkinson, are willing to do. But the model of personality, of relations with the rest of society, and therefore of motivation, which is grafted on to the descriptions of terrorists in these movements, remains unchanged. The persistence of the model of the individual terrorist as an alienated Western youth is remarkable, and not without serious consequence. It disables any effort to give a culturally specific description of the way in which different societies maintain their vision of their collective selves with different projective narratives, and so produce different terrorisms and different terrorists. The act of terrorism may well continue to have identical legal status in the courts of Western governments (although even this can be disputed to some degree). Yet if our aim as scholars is not merely to dismiss the complexity of an act by reference to its legal classification, but rather to understand it, we must acknowledge the ways in which cultural meanings and culturally inscribed motives are relatively autonomous of legal codes.

At this point, I must invoke Clifford Geertz's well-known phrase, 'thick description', and move from my more general theoretical critique to a case study that will illustrate what I see as the promise of an alternative mode of inquiry. I will take my examples from the terrorist group whose writings are in the native language I know best, and who are products of Middle-Eastern Armenian society. I mean to lay equal stress on both elements, writings and society. It is not enough to know the dates of pogroms and genocide, or to scan the English-language communiqués of the rather prolific terrorist groups, especially the ASALA, the Armenian Secret Army for the Liberation of Armenia. Their vehement, error-laden English and French, or Arabic and occasionally even Turkish broadsides allow an observer to develop a fairly clear sense of their programs and activities, and of the extent to which the PLO, say, or Kurdish guerrillas and oddly interpreted traditions of Marxism-Leninism have influenced them. But their Armenian writings do not merely recapitulate this material. They also reveal minds steeped in a recognizable Armenian idiom that has roots, not in a 68-year old genocide, but in 15 centuries of both learned and popular discourse, in ecclesiastical ritual and popular narrative, and, perhaps most importantly, in living song. Alone among the commentators I have read, Professor Wilkinson acknowledges, in one sentence, the importance of literature and religion to the tradition of Armenian resistance;[13] I want not only to confirm that, but also to enlarge greatly the claims that may be made about their significance.

The traditions and texts that constitute Armenian social discourse cannot simply be mutely juxtaposed against the ideological pamphlets of terrorists; nor can the terrorists simply be seen as being in opposition to Armenian society, as alienated, fringe elements of their culture. The Armenian writings of terrorists' pamphlets are thoroughly intertextual, in the sense of being explicitly allusive to and continuous with mainstream Armenian social discourse. This stands in sharp contrast to the texts and situations which have thus far provided the models for the study of terrorists' self-image and motivation. It is easy to mock and dismiss the turgid theoretical pronouncements of groups like the Baader–Meinhof gang by pointing to the chasm that separates them from the discourse of ordinary life and ordinary Germans. Reinhard Rupprecht, for example, has observed that German terrorists often 'retreat from family and the ordinary way of life' as a prelude to coming under the influence of ideologies.[14] The Armenian situation very nearly requires that we reverse this observation. Armenian youth in the post-genocide diaspora, when they retreat from family, tend to do so in the direction of assimilation; they do not become terrorists. Those who *do*, speak in the accents of parents and grandparents, in the language of sermons and of the dominant political party, even when furiously rejecting the latter's more cautious platforms. The 'biographical deficits' of Armenian terrorists are usually the slaughter of most of their grandparents' generation, an event conveyed to them vividly through detailed narrative. Yet such memory is never by itself enough to cause terrorism. There are always more grievances than guerrillas, revolutionaries or terrorists. The catalyst here is the coupling of the vivid collective memory of injustice with traditional and valued paradigms for action, paradigms embodied in projective narratives. To be an Armenian in an 'ordinary' way in many Middle Eastern communities means, first, that one understands the present experience of injustice in terms of familial stories and national narratives that are deeply intertwined. Second, one anticipates any confrontation with such injustice in terms of narratives of earlier resistance. These are projected upon both the present and the future as morally privileged patterns for action and for interpretation of that action; hence the term 'projective narrative'.

Before I give an account of the ways in which diaspora culture is shaped by the master-narratives involved, and of their effect on Armenian terrorism, I must further qualify certain of my terms. In an Armenian diaspora that numbers nearly 1.5 million people in some 30 countries, a typical Armenian is a fiction, not unlike that of the typical international terrorist. Not all diaspora Armenians are relevant to a discussion of terrorism. Only one Armenian terrorist captured or otherwise identified is American-born; another is French-born; the remainder were all born in Lebanon, Iran, Syria or Turkey. Both the ordinary Armenian and the terrorist of my analysis come from a certain stratum of Middle-Eastern Armenian communities, a stratum that makes up a minority of the Armenian population of Iran, possibly a plurality in Syria and probably a majority in Lebanon. In most of these cases, the terrorist and the relevant stratum both live in a common cultural reality. The foundations of this cultural reality are not just endogamy or cuisine; they are religious, linguistic, rhetorical and mythic. This primarily verbal and narrative reality is maintained through a network of churches, schools, athletic unions, youth and student groups. Obviously, none of these institutions have the production of terrorism as their aim: their purpose is to reproduce and perpetuate a certain culture in a diaspora under the pressure of assimilation. Of the elements which give that Armenian cultural tradition its cohesion and shape, perhaps the most central is a ubiquitous cluster of stories. Among those I shall turn now to, two are part of the cultural experience of every Armenian in the diaspora; others are specific to the strata mentioned above.

The first of these is the story of the genocide, which is always articulated at two levels, the national and the familial. On each level one encounters both a story of traumatizing events and an invocation of place. The first story is of the planned slaughter of a Nation and the appropriation of a Fatherland; the other is the tale of how family members died and a reminiscence of the ancestral village or town. Those familiar with older Armenians anywhere in the diaspora and with Armenian life in the relevant Middle Eastern communities will know the importance of compatriotic associations and of the frequent question 'where are you from?', which always has a double import: where in the diaspora are you from, and where in the lost Fatherland were your grandparents from? This concern is reinforced by a resurgent practice of naming children after lost places and landmarks: Ani and Ararat, Van and Masis, Daron and Nareg.

The second ubiquitous narrative dates from the second half of the fifth century AD, and is the story of Vartan and the martyrs, whose memory is commemorated by a Saints' Day in the calendar of the Armenian Apostolic Church. Armenian children encounter their story at Church, in Sunday school, in kindergarten and elementary school. More advanced students in the parochial school systems of the Middle East encounter it in extended narrative form, usually in contemporary Armenian but sometimes even in the classical Armenian in which it was written down by the cleric Yeghishe. This narrative has been ably translated and controversially edited by the Harvard scholar, Robert Thomson,[15] who believes that the historically accurate residue in the narrative is small, and that the model for the heroic resistance and martyrdom of Vartan and his men derives more from the Biblical books of the Maccabees than from reality. However, the debate about the historical accuracy of the work is beside the point here. The invocation of the model of the Maccabees only serves to underscore the ways in which the Vartan story enables and sanctions certain kinds of resistance, endowing it with a mantle of traditional and religious authority. While this religious dimension was vital in the period extending from the fifth to the nineteenth centuries, it has steadily become less so since. In the nineteenth century, the increase of literacy, the revival of Armenian literature and the accessibility of secular education combined to spawn a dozen versions of the tale. The first important Armenian romantic poet composed one of his most important poems about the battlefield where Vartan and his followers fell in battle against the Sassanid Persians. Two of the most important early romantic historical novels authored by Raffi, the Armenian equivalent of Victor Hugo, invoke Vartan as model, while a third takes related figures from the same era for its heroes and villains. In the process of secularization of the tale and proliferation of its versions, two words have remained in play: *martyros*, from the Greek martyr, and *nahadag*, its Armenian synonym. In many recountings of the tale, in speeches, sermons, laments and funeral orations, the formulaic line most frequently invoked is *mah imatzyal anmahootyun e*, that is, 'death knowingly grasped is immortality'. The line is pivotal to Yeghishe's text, and refers to the willingness of Vartan and his followers to risk all in defense of Armenian Christianity, conceived then (as now) as a crucial component of national identity.

The crisis which provoked the remark was brought on by the Persian Empire's insistence, in AD 450/1, on converting the Armenians, who had been Christian since AD 301, to militant Zoroastrianism. Defiant Armenian princes and clergy were summoned to Ctesiphon, the capital of the Sassanid empire, submitted to coerced conversion, and upon their return to Armenia vacillated about imposing a similar conversion on the mass of their subjects until events took matters out of their hands. Proselytizing Persian priests forcibly converted altars to fire-altars. They were attacked by enraged Armenians led by a priest, and the conflagration spread. The Persian army invaded; Vartan (the hereditary commander of the Armenian armies) and his troops met it in unequal battle. He and 1,036 of his followers fell, and 30 years of passive resistance punctuated by minor uprisings followed until AD 484, when Vartan's nephew obtained a favorable treaty of peace and autonomy from an otherwise embattled Persian empire. Such are the bare bones of the story. What matters to my analysis is the way in which what was originally a struggle for religious tolerance, local autonomy and feudal privilege became an exemplary narrative of virtuous action, in defense of national identity and personal honor, simultaneously. Today, it retains the most potent aspects of martyrology without any longer being a tale that inspires religious piety as such; it has been reinterpreted, through its many nineteenth-century retellings, as primarily a struggle for national identity. Its exemplary status can be made clearer by comparison with a medieval parallel. As Christ's life, narated in sermons and pictured on cathedral windows, constituted an invitation to *imitatio Christi*, an exemplar revealing the way by which to live one's life so that it conformed to the highest ideals of the community as embodied in the New Testament narratives, so also Vartan's life and death are endlessly narrated with a passion that establishes them as models of exemplary courage and virtue. Today, even in Sunday schools in the USA, the grandchildren of pacific third-generation Armenian-Americans still learn to recite a rhyme that declares: *Hye em yes, hye em yes/Kach Vartanin torn em yes*, namely, 'I am Armenian, I am Armenian/ the grandchild of valiant Vartan'. The first and second statements are equal, and they imply a regulative auto-biography: to be Armenian is to acknowledge Vartan as ancestor. To acknowledge as ancestor one who is not a blood relative is to acknowledge his moral and symbolic authority. In an ethnically pluralist America, the lines and the tradition may have no further import. In the Middle East, where Armenians are less assimilated and much beset, the statement and the Vartan stories as a whole come into play as projective narratives.

The omnipresent narratives of the genocide and of Vartan provide a frame for a series of more specific narratives of Armenian heroism and sacrifice. The most popular form in which these are embodied is song, learned in early childhood in schools and clubs, and in formal and informal public occasions where they are spontaneously sung. In the US, where the music of Elvis Presley is sometimes relegated to 'oldies' radio programs, it is difficult to imagine the musical practice of a culture in which disco music coexists with songs composed mostly in the period 1890–1920 in honor of executed revolutionaries and guerrillas fallen in combat. In the US, of course, only a very small portion of Armenian-Americans retain this musical and narrative culture; Western records, cassettes, television and video dominate both musical and non-musical narrative, for Armenians as for other ethnic groups. But in the Middle East, in the countries whence most Armenian terrorists have come, at least a plurality of the people retained this traditional culture until very recently. In Lebanon, confessional warfare is temporarily reviving its fading vitality. Armenian bookstores still sell songbooks containing such songs. Of these, one has the status of a national anthem. The quatrain inevitably included in all versions ends with the lines: *Amenayn degh mahe me e/Mart me ankam bid merni/Paytz yerani oom ir azki/Azadootyan ge zohvi* – 'Death is the same everywhere/and a man dies only once/ Lucky is he/ who dies for the freedom of his nation'. Another, composed in 1896, honors the revolutionaries who occupied the Franco-Turkish Banque Ottomane in

Istanbul. They held hostages and demanded access to the European powers and press in the hope of publicizing the plight of the Armenians during a moment of persecution and pogrom particularly vicious even by the Sultan Abdul Hamid's high standards. Nearly a century later, the song is still sung spontaneously, with something of the ease with which an American might put a golden oldie on the turntable as a party winds down. Of course, this and other songs do not explicitly affirm the legitimacy of terrorism. Their sentimental melodies and depictions of suffering, daring, rare partial success and heroic death constitute projective narratives which serve to establish the willingness to act against very high odds, and to accept violent death, as essential elements of the character of those who would honorably live out lives that are socially approved precisely because their paradigm is represented in projective narratives. Literally dozens of other songs from this period celebrate small victories and large, heroic defeats that testify to Armenian endurance in what Wilkinson calls their 'very long tradition of resistance'.[16] This tradition is alive in the web of culture, not just a matter for the learned, the books, the museums. It is inscribed into the minds of a certain proportion of diaspora Armenians as they grow up; it partially but importantly constitutes their Armenianness.

The final cluster of traditional narratives that should be mentioned consists of stories of the Armenian assassins who, in 1921–23, after the genocide, struck down several members of the Young Turk junta responsible for its organization, chief among them Talaat Pasha. Other stories concern the killing of Armenian traitors, or even particularly oppressive Tzarist officials in Eastern Armenia. These stories have been restricted to a more narrow audience, because they are not enshrined in song. Still, they are familiar to many. They were invoked in countless discussions and articles in the first few years of the revival of Armenian terrorism, which began with Kourken Yanikian's revenge-killing of two Turkish officials in Santa Barbara, California, in 1973. Of course, to a detached observer, there is a clear sense in which the earlier assassinations do not provide appropriate models for thinking about terrorism directed against officials whose guilt could only be established after extended moral and philosophical argument, if at all. Direct participation in a genocide is a different order of crime from working for the civil service of the contemporary Turkish state, however much that state continues to benefit from the crimes of the Young Turks while distorting the historical record. The fact that phrases like 'the avenging arm of Talaat's assassins can strike again' were used to discuss such complex issues provides one measure of the saturation of Armenian culture by this narrative idiom of persecution and revenge. The persecution has been very real, of course, and revenge is not to be easily dismissed as a value or motive; what must be underscored is that they are not political facts that are politically institutionalized in Armenian life, but complex cultural and psychological phenomena woven as narratives into the matrix of what passes for ordinary life in certain Middle Eastern societies.

Since my aim has been to depoliticize the discussion of terrorism, that is, to counter the tendency of political science to reduce terrorist acts to mere disturbances of the political order caused by political motives, I have so far avoided the exposition of Armenian political realities. By no means all, but certainly much, of the maintenance of the narrative traditions has been the work of intellectuals, teachers, artists, organizers and activists who are or were, at one time or another, under the influence of the *Hye Heghapokhaganneri Dashnagtzootyun*, the Federation of Armenian Revolutionaries, founded in 1890, in the Tzarist Empire, as a confederation of existing student radical groups heavily influenced by the Narodniki. In the diaspora, since the Sovietization of the short-lived independent Armenian Republic, this party, known in English by the acronym ARF, has struggled for dominance, which it achieved in Lebanon, Syria and Iran to a considerable degree in the 1920s and then again between 1948 and 1967. There are very few card-carrying 'Dashnags' in the diaspora; there are tens of thousands of sympathizers and many ex-Dashnags. As with members of the Roman Catholic Church, so with Dashnags the imprint of its political culture is not easily removed, even from those in rebellion against its dogma. That dogma has been a rhetorically potent but politically ineffective declaration of the rights of the Armenian people to a restored homeland, not accompanied by action. It has been difficult, for Armenians scattered in a diaspora, to conceive of a course of action likely to result in the recognition of genocide, let alone the restoration of their lost homeland.

The gap between rhetoric and action has been all the more underscored by the nature and origins of ARF culture. Since it was the dominant party in the resistance against Turkish persecution from 1890 on, a very large proportion of the songs, tales, memoirs and formal literary narratives from this period are about its cadres and heroes. It is not an exaggeration to say that the political entity called the Dashnag party in the diaspora has been, above all else, a cultural institution, even as it has exercised a serious measure of political power in the Armenian quarters of Beirut. Almost everywhere, its prestige and capital have been its past achievements and defeats, as commemorated in the narratives discussed. From Papken Suny at the Banque Ottomane to Kevork Chavoush, Aghpyoor Serop and his wife Soseh, and to Antranig Pasha, the larger-than-life heroes of Armenian projective narratives, men and women both, have been predominantly members or former members of the ARF. Until 1973, its cultural institutions were the chief custodians of the projective narratives I have described. Ironically, the first generation of terrorists spoke insistently of the bankruptcy of ARF rhetoric and of its failure to live up to its own narrative traditions as a motive for the formation of their own units. Many of these terrorists had broken away from ARF-dominated youth groups after being saturated by their unacted projective narratives. The frequency of indignant or ironic citation of these heroic models in the early pamphlets of the ASALA is readily apparent to anyone familiar with the relevant strata of Armenian culture.

My argument rests, of course, on several interdependent claims. One is that it is reductive and finally inadequate to think of terrorist acts as only a political response to political facts, past or present. Neither political nor psychological explanations can compensate for a lack of analysis of the cultural milieu that provides the medium in which political facts are interpreted and engender new acts. Discussions of motivation and self-image that depend primarily on the manipulation of psychological and behavioristic categories inevitably trivialize the cultural matrix. Second, I have made narrative the major conceptual category of my analysis, suggesting that in cultures like the Armenian, terrorism is not the product of a particular individual's alienation, but the manifestation of a desire to give one's individual life an iconic centrality in the eyes of the community, which professes to value certain forms of behavior articulated in narratives. I say 'professes' because, of course, only a very tiny proportion of people sentimentally moved by either popular or high-cultural fictions are actually tempted to enact them. Life imitates art and other fictions only rarely; but imitate it does.

I have given a detailed account of the dominant narratives and the socio-political structures that mutually sustain each other in the Armenian diaspora because these narratives animate 'the example[s] set by predecessors' which Martha Crenshaw sees, in another context, as 'contribut[ing] to make the terrorists' purpose salient'.[17] It remains to demonstrate that a direct link exists between the narratives, on the one hand, and the terrorists and their diaspora audience, on the other.

Such a demonstration requires textual analysis of Armenian writings by the terrorists, by the sympathetic interpreters of their words and deeds, and even by their critics. Over the past five years, I have read some 4,000 pages of such texts. Clear evidence of the links we seek is abundant in them. Limitations of space require that I limit myself to only a few examples. These were obtained by my *random* scanning of five issues of the ASALA periodical, *Hayasdan*, and of one not-randomly selected ARF publication.

The genocide is massively present everywhere. It is constantly referred to as the double crime of mass murder and dispossession that can justify any terrorist act, which is inevitably seen as minor in comparison with this crime. The genocide is denounced as the reason why the diaspora exists and why assimilation can ravage most Armenian communities. Known as 'white massacre', assimilation is portrayed as inevitable in the diaspora, and as the completion of the genocide, which is invoked by photographs that stud many texts whose actual content is not the genocide. Thus, a communiqué about a terrrorist operation, or a theoretical piece on Third World Marxism, can be 'illustrated' by reduced and poorly reproduced photographs of Armenian dead from the genocide. Typically, no more direct relation need be established, because internalized social discourse can be counted upon to do that work. The cover of one issue of ASALA's periodical features a photograph of a pile of skulls and a caption (in French) that translates as: 'that the 24th of April may become a day of struggle'.[18] That date, in 1915, marks the day when mass arrests of

Armenian intellectuals in Istanbul 'officially' launched a genocide already begun in late March in the plains of Anatolia. The thought is elaborated in a longer Arabic caption and embroidered upon elsewhere in this as in all issues. Killings of Kurdish civilians and guerrillas in south-eastern Turkey are viewed as a continuation of the Armenian genocide and as part of the age-old dream of Turkification; this is perhaps true, but hardly argued carefully by means of ordinary evidence. All is told as part of the narrative of an ongoing genocide: first the Armenians, then the assimilative cultural genocide of the diaspora, then Kurdicide. The implication is that we know this story, and we know its awful outcome, and we also know what must be done in response to it. All this does not remain at the level of the generalized story; there are practical details which reinforce it. Whereas an American military operation might be named Rolling Thunder, the ASALA often names its attacks after lost comrades and also after lost territories. The attack on Ankara Airport was named Garin, the Armenian name of the city of Erzerum; other 'commando groups' bear the names of the old and new heroes of projective narratives: 'Antranig Pasha', say, or 'Yanikian'. It is as if the terrorists' actions are responses to the double question I alluded to earlier: whom did you lose and what place did you lose?

The Vartan narrative is not as ubiquitous, but is present in ways direct and indirect in the periodicals examined. The ASALA publications are illustrated with the photographs of fallen terrorists; the captions include an incongruous coupling of the Christian and the Marxist: all the dead are *nahadag-ungers*, that is, martyr-comrades. One issue[19] has a paragraph describing the death of a terrorist that reads, in part (in my own translation): '*Fedayee* Megerdich Madurian completed his mission before he exploded a grenade he carried attached to his waist, thus showing that the Secret Army is determined to continue in the path of "death knowingly grasped" – of "*imatzyal mah*"' – cited in the original classical Armenian from Yeghishe's Vartan narrative. Such an explicit identification of ASALA cadres in 1983 with the Vartan of AD451 constitutes a rejection of the simplifying Western notion of a suicide mission. Vartan and his men did not commit suicide; they went to do battle against large odds that in fact proved deadly to some of them, but their act was not suicidal in motive, their defeat did not lead to extermination, and the word suicide is not associated with their action. This is the narrative logic applied even to acts that are, in fact, inevitably fatal to the perpetrators when carried out in Turkey proper. Yet they are represented as standing and fighting to the death for Armenia.

Even opponents and critics of the terrorists, who (whatever the impression given by the popular press) are legion in the Armenian community, invoke the Vartan narrative. Khachig Pilikian, an artist living in London, recently privately published his own critique of terrorism in which he attacks terrorists who refuse the challenge of enduring creatively as a diaspora and instead resort to violence. In doing so, he refers to ASALA cadres as 'new *fedayeen*, little lefties of brave Vartan'.[20] The clause is incoherent but significant. The ASALA terrorists are dismissed, but precisely in the terms they proudly claim for themselves: as leftists, as heirs of the Armenian *fedayees* of the pre-genocide resistance, as descendants of Vartan, as youthful and therefore daring (and therefore unwise, according to Pilikian).

The terrorists of the Secret Army see themselves as the heirs of the 'abandoned' and even 'betrayed' traditions of the early ARF; they neglect the historical context in which the ARF organized resistance against Turkish oppression of Anatolian Armenians who then were living on their ancestral territories, not scattered in a diaspora. Thanks to the very narratives they have inherited from ARF-dominated culture, they find it possible to shoulder the goals of ARF rhetoric without examining too closely why those goals remained unfulfilled. The logic of ASALA analysis in the end owes more to the logic of the dominant narratives of Armenian culture, to the employment of sacrifice on the altar of national identity, than to Marighella or Lenin or George Habash. Despite the radical changes in that historical context over the centuries, the projective narrative that dictates the logic of action and projects that action and its agents into the future retains its stubborn structure, inherited from textualizations of history that begin in the Vartan narratives and have continued since. Thus, the blinding by an accidental bomb explosion of ASALA leader Yenikomshian is compared to the death, under similar circumstances but a full 75 years earlier, of Krisdapor Mikayelian, a member of the founding trinity of the ARF.[21] This comparison recurs throughout the early 1980s publications of the ASALA, even in some of the most vituperative essays attacking the contemporary ARF. The deep structure of such discourse has its own pre-analytic logic. It resembles most what scholars of literature and religion call typological-prefigurative narrative, in which historical and contextual changes intervening between two events do not necessarily create a discontinuity of meaning-making, of interpretative procedure. Just as Abraham sacrificing his son Isaac prefigures God sacrificing his son Christ, so also the whole of the Old Testament prefigures the New, and the book of Apocalypse the end of the world in nuclear holocaust, all proclaimed by persons who think with the same narrative 'logic' as the ASALA.

Regulative biographies are retrospective manifestations of a similar logic. Kourken Yanikian's killing of two Turkish diplomats in 1973 was the isolated act of a solitary individual, a classic example of the work of the lone assassin. ASALA became active in early 1975, and from the beginning it appropriated Yanikian's action as something it was not, and has reinscribed it within the narratives of continuity and repetition as an instance of 'rebirth'. That this can be done to an action that has no relation to organized terrorism either early or late is testimony to the belief that the master-narratives have on collective thought. Thus, the April 1981 issue of *Hayasdan*[22] features a photograph of Yanikian. The caption reads: '*verkerov li jan fedayee*' – a nearly untranslatable address to the *fedayee* bleeding, like Christ or Saint Sebastian, from many wounds, but more importantly a quotation from the first line of a famous song of the early 1900s. Although he was neither wounded nor a *fedayee*, Yanikian is nevertheless not understood in the context of his life, of his real biography, or even in the context of the brief autobiography we can glean from his utterances. He is assigned a regulative biography, and understood through it.

What the ASALA does in this instance with Yanikian, it often does with its own cadres. After the fact of the terrorist act, cadres are depicted in regulative biographies that interpret their actions in terms of past narratives and of the values the living tradition assigns to actions in those narratives. Even in more general essays about their own actions, they represent the design of their political project in terms of these narratives. Thus, an article occasioned by Shahan Natali's death, in the August 1983 issue of *Hayasdan*,[23] eulogizes this long-ago expelled member of the ARF as 'the first Armenian Nemesis' along with other famed avengers from the same organization – Tehlirian, Torlakian, Yerganian – who assassinated Talaat Pasha, Behaeddin Shakir and Jemal Azmi, three architects of the genocide. These names are intoned together with Yanikian's and to them is added the phrase 'the martyrs and imprisoned warriors of the ASALA', all enlisted in a resonating roll-call that blurs history, context and nuance. All become actors of the same master-narrative. The device of the roll-call that erases individual motives and historical detail is not, of course, unique to the Armenian situation. To glance for a moment outside my purview, at a context where my approach might be relevant in the hands of a seasoned observer of Irish culture, let me cite what seems to me the most Armenian of Willian Butler Yeats's poems, 'Easter 1916'. He ends that famed poem with a similar short list:

> And what if excess of love
> burdened them til they died?
> I write it out in a verse-
> MacDonough and MacBride
> and Connolly and Pearce,
> Now and in time to be
> wherever green is worn
> are changed, changed utterly:
> a terrible beauty is born.

We might endlessly debate the terrible beauty of the events referred to, but the potency of the intoned list is indisputable. The list enlists; it tells us little about the different individuals and their different motives, but rather inscribes them in a past and future narrative, valid wherever green is worn, wherever, the poem implies, the sacrifice and resurrection of Christ which we celebrate at Easter are known as narratives of salvation. This is what it is to be a martyr or a *martyros* or a *nahadag-unger*, a martyr-comrade whose death is always represented as a choice of enlistment in the narrative of national salvation, which requires the individual's death as the price of the national collectivity's resurrection.

To cap this brief sampling of the intertextuality that obtains between terrorist discourse and the master-narratives of the culture in question, let me glance at the ways in which other Armenians have interpreted Armenian terrorism. One of the best-known acts of recent years was the seizure of the Turkish embassy in Lisbon by Armenian Revolutionary Army, or ARA, terrorists. It ended when an explosion killed all five terrorists. Some believe an accident caused the detonation of explosives brought in by the ARA cadres; others believe it was a group suicide committed when the terrorists realized they were about to be captured by Portuguese commandos reputed to be well-trained by Britain's SAS. While the facts are in dispute, the interpretation of it by a segment of ARF-dominated Armenian society is not. Throughout that part of the community, the reach of regulative narrative is unchallenged. What is more impressive, even to a scholar accustomed to its power, is a poem composed in Soviet Armenia, by a poet who was born and recently died there, in the USSR, and who most probably knew of the terrorism only through Voice of America broadcasts and tourists' stories. He wrote a celebration of the heroism of the Lisbon Five, as they are generally known, in which the refrain is:

> *Hishek, Hyer, inchbess Tizbon*
> *Yereg Tizbon, aysor Lisbon ...*

and continues with:

> *Yeg, vor Vartann Avarayri*
> *Anedzk tarna Turkin vayri.*

In Armenian, Tizbon is the pronunciation of Ctesiphon, the capital of the Sassanid Empire where Vartan and others were forced into a conversion they later renounced. The rhyme with Lisbon ushers in the whole Vartan-narrative in the lines which mean, translated loosely (as they must be): 'Come, Armenians, [and recall] how it was in Tizbon/Yesterday Tizbon, today Lisbon'. To make his point even more unmistakable, the poet writes in the latter lines: 'Come, let the Vartan of Avarayr/Become the curse of the savage Turk'. This poem is found reprinted in an Armenian-language weekly published in Canada,[24] read entirely by recent immigrants from the Middle East, who can be counted upon to see the logic of narrative: the Sassanid empire is dead, Ctesiphon is a heap of ruins that some tourists to Baghdad may visit, but the struggle is the same. The narrative of 451 still applies in 1985.

At a certain level of analytical abstraction, there is a sense to the logic. Armenians continue to struggle for cultural identity, which is perceived by them, and by so many other ethnics, as a self-evident value in its own right. That culture was produced by centuries of resistance in unequal struggle. Given the presence of some 'political' factors beyond the range of this analysis, such a culture, I have been trying to suggest, is able to produce and sustain a certain level of terrorist activity, even in diaspora conditions, perhaps especially in diaspora conditions. For the Armenians in the diaspora, there is no state that can conduct their political life for them, that can challenge, for example, Turkish misrepresentations of Armenian history, or claim the legitimate use of force. The absence of a state and a country means that there is no possibility in the diaspora for enacting a classical narrative of social revolution on either the Marxist or another model: neither Angolan revolution nor Afghan guerrilla war is possible. Under such circumstances and in the conditions that have prevailed in the Middle East since 1967, the dominant cultural narratives overdetermine conditions that help to produce terrorism and are in turn reanimated by it. Such terrorism produces new heroes for old stories. It would be a mistake for analysts to delude themselves into believing, as the terrorists themselves have, that the true audience and target of Armenian terrorism is Turkey and its NATO allies. Neither of those is likely to be moved; at most, a few nations might express a desire to set the record straight on the genocide. But the true audience of Armenian terrorism remains the Armenian diaspora, whose fraying culture is constituted to a remarkable degree by old stories, and who see in contemporary terrorists Vartan's refusal to abandon cultural identity and national rights.

NOTES

I am grateful to Professors Martha Crenshaw of Wesleyan University and David C. Rapoport of UCLA for inviting me, a humanist, to contribute to the deliberations of an APSA panel where the first version of this article was given, and for providing me with references to relevant work. My thanks also to Professor Ellen Rooney of Brown University for her careful reading of earlier drafts.

1. For example, Richard Clutterbuck, *Guerrillas and Terrorists* (London: Faber, 1977), p.11.
2. Joseph Margolin, 'Psychological Perspectives in Terrorism', in Y. Alexander and S. Finger (eds.), *Terrorism: Interdisciplinary Perspectives* (New York: John Jay Press, 1977), p.271.
3. To resist such universalization is not, of course, to devalue the political realm, which remains indispensable to the study of terrorism. However, as I argue in the body of this article (which is part of a book on Armenian terrorism in progress), certain terrorist movements cannot be understood by political analysis alone, or even *primarily* by standard methods of such analysis, no matter how nuanced. It is necessary to distinguish between – and for purposes of analysis, temporarily to separate – the political ideology and behavior of terrorist movements from the larger and more innocuous political culture of the ethnic group from which the terrorists originate. Finally, political ideology and political culture both must in turn be situated in the larger culture. The core assumption of my argument is that Armenian terrorism in particular (along with some other terrorisms emanating from ethnic populations), can never be fully understood simply by reference to the objectives it announces and the antagonists it identifies. One must always take into account its embeddedness in the political culture from which it emanates and which it seeks to renew or transform by action.
4. Walter Laqueur, *Terrorism* (Boston: Little, Brown, 1977), p.120.
5. H.H.A. Cooper, 'Voices from Troy: What Are We Hearing?' *Outthinking the Terrorist: An International Challenge*, Proceedings of the Tenth Annual Symposium

on the Role of Behavioral Science in Physical Security, Defense Nuclear Agency, Washington, DC, 1985, p.95.

6. I derive the latter term from 'regulative psycho-biography', a locution I encountered in Professor G.C. Spivak's 'The Political Economy of Women as Seen by a Literary Critic', unpublished. It has a somewhat different meaning in her work than that given to it here.

7. Paul Wilkinson, 'Armenian Terrorism', *The World Today* (Sept., 1983), p.344.

8. Ibid.

9. Wilkinson, p.346.

10. Moshe Amon, 'Religion and Terrorism: A Romantic Model of Secular Gnosticism', in D.C. Rapoport and Y. Alexander (eds.), *The Rationalization of Terrorism* (Frederick, MD: University Publications of America), p.82.

11. Reinhard Rupprecht, 'Terrorism and Counterterrorism in the Federal Republic of Germany', *Outthinking the Terrorist*, op. cit., p.73.

12. Clutterbuck, op. cit., p.94.

13. Wilkinson, op. cit., p.344.

14. Rupprecht, op. cit., p.73.

15. Robert Thomson, tr. and comm. Yeghishe, *History of Vartan and the Armenian War* (Cambridge, MA: Harvard University Press, 1982).

16. Wilkinson, op. cit., p.344.

17. Martha Crenshaw, 'Incentives for Terrorism', *Outthinking the Terrorist*, op. cit., p.18.

18. *Hayasdan* (*Armenia*, in Armenian), 24 April 1981 (Special Issue).

19. *Hayasdan*, 16 June 1983, p.47.

20. Khachig Pilikian, *Refuting Terrorism: Seven Epistles from the Diaspora* (London: Heritage of Armenian Culture Publications, 1984), p.21.

21. *Hayasdan*, Dec. 1980, p.16.

22. *Hayasdan*, April 1981.

23. *Hayasdan*, Aug. 1983, p.14.

24. Hovhanness Shiraz, 'Lisboni Voghchageznerin' (poem in Armenian), *Horizon* (Montreal, Canada), 29 July 1984, p.6.

III. CONCLUDING SEQUEL

Terror as an Instrument of Foreign Policy

Grant Wardlaw

There is little disagreement that sovereign states are involved in the planning, financing and execution of many acts of international terrorism.[1] Just what is defined as international terrorism, what constitutes state sponsorship of it, what strategic, domestic or foreign policy goals are intended to be pursued by such sponsorship, and which states may be classified as terrorist sponsors are, however, the subject of acrimonious debate.[2] As with so many issues in the field of terrorism, the questions surrounding state-sponsored terrorism reflect a good deal more ideology and wishful thinking than scholarly analysis and weighing of the available evidence. In essence, the lack of a universally-accepted definition of terrorism and the combative and manipulative nature of international relations conspire to ensure that state-sponsored terrorism embraces a wide range of actions committed only by one's enemies. The assertion that this or that state is a sponsor of international terrorism increasingly is being wielded as a propaganda weapon and as a foreign policy tool itself.

This preoccupation with state involvement in international terrorism is no mere academic side-show. Increasingly, the issue is assuming major importance on foreign policy agendas, and sometimes dominates them.[3] Public opinion polls show that state-sponsored terrorism is considered to be one of the major threats to international stability.[4] This perceived threat from and importance of state involvement in terrorism is magnified with each new terrorist incident and the subsequent demonstration of the difficulties target states experience in responding effectively. When it is a superpower which is 'humiliated' in this fashion the issue becomes critical as means are sought to redress the balance.

It is primarily because the United States has seen itself as the major target of state-sponsored terrorism in recent times that the issue has assumed such major importance. Immediately upon taking office in 1981 the Reagan Administration raised the issue of state-sponsored terrorism to a position of prominence on its list of foreign policy priorities. Initially the focus was on the Soviet Union, with Secretary of State Alexander Haig claiming that the USSR was the major instigator of international terrorism.[5] This theme has been continued by other officials in the ensuing years[6] and has been reflected in a growing literature arguing the merits of the case for Soviet involvement in terrorism.[7]

Over the past five years, however, both events and a growing explicitly-politicised use of the concept of state-sponsored terrorism have resulted in a wide range of nations being identified as terrorist sponsors, with the spotlight moving away from the Soviet Union. The latter is now portrayed as providing 'heavy financial and material support to countries that sponsor international terrorism'.[8] However, it is other states which are claimed to be the direct supporters. The list of such countries continually grows and changes, with the changes often appearing to be related directly to the political needs of the United States government. Thus, Syria was identified as a direct supporter of terrorism in an official statement of March 1985,[9] but was conspicuously absent from those identified in President Reagan's speech of July 1985. This speech followed the release, facilitated by Syria, of American hostages taken during the hijacking of TWA Flight 847 in June 1985.[10] However, Syria again resumed its high profile on America's list of terrorist sponsors following Great Britain's call for action against Syria as a result of evidence of continuing Syrian involvement in acts of international terrorism.[11]

The case of Syria illustrates how the concept of state-sponsored terrorism, and evidence for it, lacks clarity and is used politically. In June 1986, United States officials concluded that 'although Syria's involvement in terrorism may be "much more professional, much more deadly" than Libya's, the evidence remains murky about Syria's direct links to recent acts of violence'.[12] Yet only five months later the State Department was confident enough of the evidence to release a list of 46 terrorist incidents claimed to have links to Syria.[13] In an accompanying statement, the Department said that the list was 'not intended to be all-inclusive but is illustrative of Syria's involvement in and support for terrorism and terrorist groups'.[14]

At various times, most of the Western leaders in the so-called 'fight against state-sponsored terrorism' have shown extreme reluctance to name Syria as a sponsor state in spite of the obvious connections in many instances. This reluctance is explained by the necessity of eliciting Syrian assistance in negotiating the release of United States, British and French citizens being held hostage by various terrorist groups in the Middle East and is a recognition of the vital role Syria has to play in any peace settlement in the area. Thus, British Prime Minister Margaret Thatcher claimed in May 1986 that Britain 'at the moment has no such evidence against Syria of state-sponsored terrorism of anything like that that obtains in the case of Libya'.[15] The French government, even after being confronted with convincing evidence of direct Syrian involvement in the attempted bombing of an El Al airliner at Heathrow Airport, London in April 1986,[16] refused to acknowleldge Syria's role because it was involved in negotiations, involving Syria, to obtain the release of French hostages held in Beirut[17] and, it has been suggested, as part of an effort to curb a bombing campaign in Paris which many believe also has Syrian connections.[18]

The reluctance of states to name others as terrorist sponsors seems to be related not to the unavailability of solid evidence with which to back up suspicions, but to other, more political, factors. For the past few years, Libya, under the leadership of Colonel Mu'ammar Gadhafi has consistently been named by a number of countries as a sponsor of international terrorism. The identification of Libya as sponsor reached a crescendo in 1986 and culminated in the US bombing raid on Tripoli and Benghazi in retaliation for Libyan complicity in a bomb attack on a discothèque in Berlin in which an American serviceman was killed and numerous others were wounded. For our purposes, what is noteworthy is that, for those terrorist acts which might reasonably be thought of as having major implications for international relations, the evidence for Libyan involvement is generally not of a significantly better quality than that available for, say, Syrian sponsorship. That is, it is based on similarities, known connections between individuals and organizations, reasonable assumptions, and an informed opinion about what the sponsor would hope to gain by the act. By the very nature of such information, assertions based on it are liable to one of two errors of interpretation. Either the evidence is downplayed because of the difficulty of proving the connections and of the difficult political consequences which may ensue (the accusation, for example, of proponents of the Soviet-sponsorship argument such as Claire Sterling) or it is overplayed as every possible inference and hint of conspiracy is given full rein (the accusation of those who see the search for state sponsors as a sort of contemporary international McCarthyism). What seems to determine towards which end of the spectrum evaluation of the evidence will go is a complex combination of the presumed political fall-out of determining sponsor status and the ease and relative safety with which an accuser can take action against an accused. Thus in the cases of Syria and Libya one might conclude that there are fewer impediments to interpreting events as evidence for Libyan sponsorship than for Syrian. Syria is seen as more critical to the resolution of Middle East problems, as an agent of influence whose offices are essential to successful negotiations affecting outside powers (for example, negotiations concerning release of foreign hostages), as having powerful support for both economic and political reasons both inside and outside the region, and as being less vulnerable to attack and better able to defend itself.[19] In short, there are more reasons to be careful in making assertions about Syrian sponsorship than Libyan, and in acting upon those assertions. The costs of accusing Syria of terrorist sponsorship and of seeking to act firmly to stop it are much greater than those attaching to accusing and acting against Libya. The same argument applies to a comparison of the costs of responding to Iran *versus* Libya.

It is these costs which lead to a situation of great confusion over what constitutes evidence of sponsorship, what indeed is sponsorship, and what can be done about it. Thus we can have the Director of the CIA state that 'probably more blood has been shed by Iranian-sponsored terrorists during the last few years than by all other terrorists combined',[20] yet it is Libya, not Iran, which is subsequently the focus of accusations of sponsoring terrorism and of retaliatory action. Indeed, within months of the latter event evidence is leaked implicating the United States in concluding a secret deal with Iran in which arms are sold in exchange for the release of American hostages.[21] This in spite of official acknowledgement of Iranian (and Syrian) complicity in a number of major terrorist attacks on American facilities and personnel.[22] It seems, on the face of it, that what distinguished Libya in American eyes was its foolhardy bragging about support of terrorism,[23] but in fact it was its relative weakness which made it the ideal sponsor of which to make an example by taking reprisals against it. None of this is, of course, to deny the seriousness of Libyan involvement in terrorism or to excuse or minimize the seriousness of such behavior. Rather, it is to demonstrate how the realities of international relations do not sit well with a strong, moralistic approach to the issue of state sponsorship.

There is little doubt that Gadhafi's regime has sponsored many acts of international terrorism. In recent years Libya's oil revenues have allowed it to finance a wide range of terrorist organizations in many parts of the world. Libyan Peoples' Bureaux (diplomatic missions) in a number of countries have been identified as conduits for terrorist arms and money. Many terrorists have been trained at camps in Libya. Clearly, Libya is a potent ingredient in the international terrorist mixture and it is entirely appropriate that its role should be identified and attempts made to modify its behavior.

In deciding on how to deal with the behavior of states such as Libya, however, prudent nations should take great care to analyze the type and degree of threat posed, the extent to which Libya (and similar states) is involved in acts which threaten *vital national interests*, and the likely consequences of various retaliatory options. Central to deliberation of these issues is the nature of the concept of 'state-sponsored terrorism' and the uses to which this concept are put. The boundaries, first of the term 'terrorism', and now of the sub-species 'state-sponsored terrorism' have proved to be infinitely flexible. In general, they can be expanded to encompass almost any act of violence or threat of violence which suits the purpose of the proposer or, alternatively, can be limited and skewed to take in only those acts with whose perpetrators or aims the proposer is at odds.[24] Thus Western nations look for a state sponsor behind almost all acts of terrorism but deny that there is any remote similarity in their aiding revolutionary movements or repressive regimes in other parts of the world. The growing list of states identified as terrorist sponsors by the West argue similarly about their behavior, claiming the legitimacy of support for 'national liberation movements' and accusing Western nations of sponsoring terrorism against their interests. If there is to be any coherent strategy developed at the international level to combat terrorism it is essential, then, that some basic agreement be reached on the nature and dimensions of state-sponsored terrorism. Is it a unitary phenomenon or is it a collection of state behaviors which must be dealt with differentially? What is the nature of the threat posed by state-sponsored terrorism (or its constituents) and what policies might be adopted to deal with the threat?

The case of Libya is illustrative of the importance of answering these questions. The facile labelling of various terrorist acts as having been

Libyan-sponsored has allowed the development of an image in the public consciousness of a coherent, efficient and deadly policy whose consequences pose real threats to the vital interests of many countries. When the phrase 'state-sponsored terrorism' is bandied about with increasing regularity in referring to various behaviors associated with a large number of communist and Middle East states, the impression is created of a dangerous new monster stalking the globe. In an effort to encourage support for action against Libya (presumably as a demonstration of what would happen to more important, but more difficult to punish, states if they did not modify their ways) the United States government, in particular, mounted a concerted campaign to identify and publicize Libyan links to terrorism. The result of this campaign was to leave the impression that Libya was behind a significant proportion of international terrorism and that it was a real threat to Western nations.[25] In the final analysis, it was this build-up which either assisted or propelled the Administration towards exercising the retaliatory option against Libya. This impression, however, is inconsistent both with reality and with previous US Administration statements (on the basis of which one would expect to see Syria, Iran and the Soviet Union as those held most responsible for terrorist activities).

In fact the raid on Libya seemed designed both to punish Libyan-sponsored terrorism and, more importantly, to act as a warning to other, more important sponsors, that the United States would not just sit back and let them go on unhindered. By invoking the overarching concept of a battle with state-sponsored terrorism more generally, the United States provided further justification for its actions. The concern about the dangers of state-sponsored terrorism raises a number of questions, however. First, there is the question of what sort of threat Libyan-sponsored terrorism poses, and to whom. Thus far, it is Libyan dissidents abroad, not the vital national interests of the Western democracies, who have borne the brunt of Libyan terrorism.[26] It is, of course, a matter of great seriousness that the murders and bombings that these assaults on Libyans have entailed have taken place on British, French, West German, Cypriot, Austrian, Greek and other territory. But inflating the spectre of state-sponsored terrorism has created the impression that these acts somehow threaten the vital interests of the states within whose borders they take place. For the most part they threaten only public order, not the survival of the state. This is certainly no argument for inaction. Clearly states have a right to maintain public security within their borders and must take action. It is obvious that the Colonel Gadhafi's of the world will not be persuaded merely by reasonable argument to relinquish their support of terrorism. But equally the employment of options such as major military action should be reserved for retaliation against acts which clearly threaten the retaliating nation.

This brings us to the question of the purpose of the particular form of retaliation and its effectiveness. Stripped of its political verbiage, the US action in bombing Libya appears to have been aimed at least as much at effecting domestic political purposes as at diminishing international terrorism. The Reagan Administration is very much a prisoner not only of its own ideological outlook but of the public's expectations about the manner in which a 'strong' US government should respond to terrorism.[27] These expectations have been created partially by the Administration's stressing of the importance and threat of state-sponsored terrorism. Emphasizing that these attacks are part of an emerging pattern of 'low-intensity warfare' being directed at the United States and Western interests, officials have set the scene for a military response. The fact that many official statements, particularly those of President Reagan and Secretary Shultz, threatened decisive and harsh action following attacks involving American victims, but eventuated in nothing more than words, raised the pressure on the Administration. Both the public in general and conservative critics in particular clamored for decisive action. The exercise of the military option thus became almost inevitable.

What, though, did the raids achieve? Certainly, there was no real expectation that international terrorism would be seriously affected by that action alone.[28] Although some officials have recently claimed there has been a lull since the reprisal, the incidence of international terrorism does not, in fact, appear to have diminished. Whether or not Libya's behavior itself has been modified is difficult to discern. US State Department figures show five possible incidents with Libyan connections in the period October 1985 to 15 April 1986 and five in the post-raid period of 15 April to 1 July 1986.[29] These figures indicate anything but cessation of presumed Libyan-backed terrorism. There is also the problem of the accuracy of any statistics on such matters. The revelation in October 1986 that the US Administration had launched an elaborate disinformation campaign against Libya which included false claims of renewed Libyan backing for terrorism[30] served totally to undermine confidence in US government assertions about evidence for state-sponsored terrorism.[31] It is little wonder that when a State Department official subsequently announced at a conference that there was evidence of Libyan preparation for further terrorism,[32] scepticism was expressed in some quarters.

Comfort has been taken by some that after the raid Colonel Gadhafi seems to have had problems asserting control over elements within the Libyan leadership and had moderated his behavior somewhat. While he seemed initially to be more circumspect in his public utterances about terrorism, as time passed he again showed signs of the bombastic posturing which provide the fuel for the characterizations of him as 'crazy' and a 'barbarian'.[33] Indeed, in the theatre of terrorism Gadhafi seems intent on delivering to his enemies the evidence for their charges. But it is evidence of a sort which feeds propaganda campaigns and not the sort upon which opposing nations should base a sound counter-terrorist campaign.

Since images and expectations are as important a part of the terrorist scenario as are the operational and political realities, it is essential that those nations which set the agenda for the counter-terrorism policy debate pay particular attention to the psychological climate they create by their own statements and policies. I believe that Western governments in general, and the United States government in particular, have overplayed both the dangers of most forms of terrorism and the possibilities of controlling it. They have done this largely by claiming that insurgent terrorism poses a real threat to the *existence* of democratic societies and, increasingly, as international terrorism has been shown to have links to sovereign states, that state-sponsored terrorism is a new and more deadly form of low-intensity warfare which threatens the vital national interests of target states and the functioning of the international system. In reality, whilst insurgent or domestic terrorism poses or has posed severe problems of public security in some countries (such as Italy, West Germany, or France) there is a strong case for the argument that it cannot *fundamentally* threaten a democracy (unless it be by forcing the state to betray its own values by overreacting).[34] Similarly, with state-sponsored terrorism the nature of the phenomenon and the type and degree of threat have been misinterpreted. As will be argued below, by refusing to take an historical perspective, by reserving the attribution of state sponsorship only to acts committed by one's enemies or opponents and by using the concept to fight moral and ideological battles, states of many political persuasions have both undermined the credibility of atempts to understand and cope with the very real problem of state sponsorship to terrorism which *do* exist and have inflated some of the dangers far beyond their actual potential for harm.

Of course it is acknowledged that determining the level and nature of threat posed by terrorism and coping with it are both extremely difficult and complex enterprises. However, it is vital to be accurate in assessment and balanced in response. We must not lose sight of the fact that two of the foremost aims of terrorists are to induce widespread fear in the population and to force the authorities to overreact and undermine their own legitimacy. For all types of terrorism but, in the current circumstances, particularly in the case of state-sponsored terrorism, the tone of much of the discussion about the problem is of a nature such as may well aid rather than hinder the aims of the terrorists. Alarmist and inaccurate estimates of the type of threat facing a society or parts of the international community can cause public apprehension far in excess of that warranted by an objective assessment. Such apprehension can lead to personal fear, changes in business and other practices which are unnecessary and damaging to economic or social life and, eventually, to government actions which may undermine democratic institutions or the balance of international relations.

It seems, in fact, that state-sponsored terrorism entails three real dangers. The first is what Laqueur has called the 'Sarajevo Complex'[35] – terrorist activities which escalate into war between two or more small countries, drawing the global powers to intervene. The second is that a major power, feeling (probably unnecessarily) that its vital interests are threatened or (probably inevitably) that its national prestige can take no further assaults, takes unilateral military action which destabilizes international relations or causes significant escalatory violence (either by the sponsor state or by another state acting on its behalf). The third is when the terrorist's strategy of provocation succeeds in fundamentally altering the nature of democracies, either internally or in the manner in which they execute foreign policy.

All this does not imply that terrorism is not a serious problem or that military or other coercive responses are always inappropriate. Whilst there are dangers in overplaying the threat of state-sponsored terrorism, there are also grave dangers in ignoring its reality and in failing to predict and understand, at least in broad terms, the types of attacks which may confront us and the consequences of their occurrence. Failure in this area will inevitably lead to being unprepared for this sort of terrorist attack, to being incapable of responding to it in the most appropriate and effective manner available, to a collapse of public confidence in the government of the victim state, to foreign or other policy changes being made under duress and, almost inevitably, to eventual counter-violence (often motivated as much by simple frustration as by a proper consideration of the response options available).

Given the complexities of definition, threat assessment, and response policies, what is required is a much more discriminating and sophisticated approach to the problem of state-sponsored terrorism than is evident at present. Inevitably this need must focus initially on the tone and content of official statements on state-sponsored terrorism and the assumption and definitions which underlie them. Because of the expectations created by the media, politicians, security officials and others,[36] much of the discussion of counter-terrorism policy seems to be predicated on the assumptions that state-sponsored terrorism is something unique to the present time and poses a new and more powerful threat than anything short of war which may have preceded it, that such terrorism can be defeated (that is, reduced to a low enough level so as not to occasion much national or international concern), and that, given the will (manifested by adequate security measures and the ability and willingness to project military counter-terrorist power), any country can reduce the probability of attack against it to a very low level. In fact, these assumptions are unrealistic. Worse, they are dangerously unrealistic.

The danger is that accepting them can lead to an accompanying uncritical acceptance of excessive levels of security domestically, and military measures internationally, which may themselves be counter-productive, destabilizing, and contribute to further terrorism. The reality that, whatever we do, terrorism will be part of the international landscape for the forseeable future and that no country can prevent all acts of terrorism, must be accepted as a basis for a rational threat assessment and discussion of appropriate counter-terrorist policy and machinery.

The foregoing discussion underlines the importance of understanding in more detail the phenomenon of state-sponsored terrorism and how it relates to other forms of conflict between states. The task is made particularly difficult by the confusion (both accidental and deliberate) over terms and concepts, by the basic dishonesty which governs many relations between states and the consequent propagandistic use of charges of state-sponsorship, and by a one-sided morality which allows states to condemn behavior as terroristic which in other circumstances (that is, when they themselves support it) they label as something positive (for example, freedom fighting, overthrowing the yoke of tyranny, etc).

In determining the threat posed by state-sponsored terrorism one has first to ask why it is that states view the occurrence of this form of violence with such seriousness? After all, in terms of lives lost (however horrific it may be), the toll of international terrorism pales into insignificance beside the toll of many other evils (for example, war, violent crime, famine, traffic accidents, the violence directed at their own populations by some governments). Even acknowledging the impact of the psychological dimension of terrorism (which is, of course, the element which gives it such power), it is hard to see, on the face of it, why *states* should feel so intimidated by an act of international terrorism. This is particularly so given that those who seem most concerned about terrorism are amongst the most powerful states. One convincing argument is that terrorism, especially when it occurs in the international arena, violates the monopoly of power, and especially of violence, which states have sought to assign to themselves as the international system has evolved. Terrorism is guilty, particularly, of ignoring the restrictions placed on the right to wage war. These restrictions are: (i) that the right is confined to states; (ii) that there are certain conventions which should be observed on the way in which war is conducted (for example, the 'rules of war', arguably more honoured in the breach than the observance, but standards to which states can be held in some circumstances nevertheless); (iii) that attempts are made to restrict the geographic spread of wars that have broken out by the invocation of laws of neutrality and laying down the rights and duties of neutrals and belligerents in relation to each other; and (iv) that limitations are placed on the reasons or causes for which a state can legitimately resort to war.[37]

It may be true that these restrictions, in combination with other factors, have reduced many of the excesses of warfare (or at least limited the excesses which are now possible with modern weaponry) but it is also apparent that they favor large over small states. The order which has been brought to international affairs in the last hundred years or so is an order which, in political and strategic terms, benefits the major powers most. What many states seem to fear most is a reversal of the process, a decentralization of forces which places coercive power in the hands of smaller units. This may go hand in hand with the coexistence of different modes of warfare which could erode the boundaries between forms of political violence. Thus, in looking to the future, Jenkins sees a world in which:

> Warfare will cease to be finite. The distinction between war and peace will dissolve .... Nominal peace will be filled with continuing

confrontations and crises .... Fighting may involve conventional armies, guerrilla bands, independent and state-directed terrorists groups, specialized antiterrorist units, and private militias .... With such continuous, sporadic, armed conflict, blurred in time and space, waged on several levels by a large array of national and subnational forces, warfare in the last quarter of the twentieth century may come to resemble that waged before the emergence of national armies.[38]

Moving towards this state of affairs may, however, be an inevitable consequence of the over-control (or over-dominance) of the international system by the major powers. As Jenkins recognizes in his scenario of warring states, mini-states and non-state actors, war waged with the authority of a public body (the state) is a relatively recent concept, the outcome of a process of limitation or confinement of violence, and a concept which may not survive in its present form. Bull reminds us that: 'We are accustomed, in the modern world, to contrast war between states with peace between states; but the historical alternative to war between states was more ubiquitous violence.'[39] A principal reason for a possible return to a situation of 'more ubiquitous violence' is that the monopolization of the right and ability to use violence has not just been attempted by states over non-states, but by powerful over weak states. In particular, the two superpowers, the United States and the Soviet Union, see themselves as the 'policeman' having the right and being responsible for maintaining order in their areas of perceived strategic interest (which in some parts of the world overlap and are in conflict). For the United States this role leads to particular difficulties. It is perceived by states which do not share its world view as domineering and dictatorial and as interfering in and limiting their pursuit of what they see as their national interests. In view of the massive imbalance between their power (measured in terms of military or economic influence) and that of the United States, such states may feel that the conventional (in the modern sense) forms of coercion used so readily and so effectively by the major powers are not viable options for them. Some then turn to various forms of sponsorship of violence short of acknowledged warfare as a method which may increase their influence. The Soviet Union faces less problems in this regard for two reasons. First, unlike the United States, it is prepared to routinely and brutally repress any indication of deviance by states within its direct orbit (Eastern Europe).[40] Thus, as its internal repression means it has less of a problem with domestic terrorism, so its degree of control over large parts of its sphere of influence means it faces less terrorism there. Of more importance though is simply that whereas the United States is generally a status quo power, the Soviet Union more often supports those who seek to disrupt the status quo – and these, by extension, are more likely to be the forces seeking to use unconventional means to challenge the power of a state and/or its protectors.[41,42] A further source of threat for the United States is simply that its global reach and, hence, its availability as a potential target, is greater than that of the USSR. It might be argued, then, that major states in general and major Western states in particular have been so successful in ordering the international system into a hierarchy of power that those who have been disempowered have inevitably turned to means which avoid meeting those states on their terms. With the monopoly of conventional power in the hands of the major states, it will seem logical to some less important states and to non-state actors to seek other means to effect their foreign policy goals. High on the list of such means will be the use of terrorism as a lever to influence the behavior of powerful opponents.

The current fascination with terrorism in the councils of state, however, tends to obscure the historical continuity of state-sponsored violence. By referring to terrorism as a new and particularly virulent form of threat to national interests and by calling for its recognition as an important new form of low-intensity *warfare* we ignore the fact that states have always employed deniable and clandestine tactics to effect changes in the policies of other nations, and we fail to give due emphasis to the political nature of warfare and the even more political nature of terrorism. This is not to deny that state-sponsored terrorism cannot be and is not used as a form of warfare. But placing the emphasis on this aspect as a way of focusing attention on the problems of *responding* to terrorism results in a rather too narrow concept both of the nature of the phenomenon and of the possible solutions. Labelling terrorism as a form of low-intensity warfare leads to military analyses and military solutions (both of which are sometimes appropriate but which in general provide only part of the analysis) and inappropriately sets terrorism apart from those many acts of state-sponsored violence which have long existed.

The fact that we can confuse the essential nature of state-sponsored terrorism by concentrating on its categorisation as warfare was recognized by some of the earlier writings on the topic, but is becoming lost in a fog of emotion as strident calls for its recognition as low-intensity warfare have mounted.[43] For example, in 1976 the Rand Corporation organized a discussion on future low-intensity conflict at which several participants argued that all forms of conflict which tend to be lumped together as low-intensity conflict should be more clearly categorized. It was pointed out that they do not constitute a single type of conflict. Some of the experts argued that international terrorism should be seen as a State Department problem and should not be included conceptually with crises that may involve the more immediate use of military force.[44]

At another Rand Corporation conference some years later, Ambassador Antony Quainton (then head of the Office for Combating Terrorism, in the State Department) reminded the audience of the necessity of asking whether there are significant differences between international terrorism and other forms of low-level political conflict and violence. As the Ambassador warned: 'Far too often the terms "international terrorism" and "terrorist groups" are used as nothing more than convenient grab bags into which to stuff all forms of violent small-scale political dissent and conflict *of which we disapprove*[45] (my emphasis).

Whilst recognizing the importance of coming to grips with the problems of state-sponsored terrorism, we must be wary of oversimplification, especially when we view the activities of some states as being a form of 'surrogate warfare' in the eventual interests of states at yet a further remove. It is this line of reasoning, when accepted uncritically and applied to any act of violence which it seems even remotely possible to classify as state-sponsored terrorism, which has led to the propagandistic and often dishonest use of the concept. It is this line of reasoning which has led to the simple-minded Soviet-culprit theories of sponsorship, giving way without explanation to Libya-culprit or Iran-culprit or Syria-culprit theories dependent merely on the latest incident or the current political fashions. Clearly all of these nations have had an important part to play in the spread of terrorism, as have many others – including many not normally named as sponsors. The difficulty with the way we view their activities lies in the intense spotlight placed on particular states at particular times – an examination which often reflects pressures other than the actual importance or extent of sponsorship as it impacts upon the vital interests of those who protest the loudest. The fact that these pressures change independently of the level of actual sponsorship so that a nation recently and repeatedly vilified can, for reasons of international politics, be suddenly freed from the press of accusations whilst not seeming to change its behavior, totally undermines the credibility of the accuser state. Thus, in the case of the United States, the list of countries named as terrorist sponsors has varied so much over such short periods of time (without any evidence of corresponding fundamental changes in the behavior of the states concerned) that it must be regarded as essentially a political rather than an analytical enterprise. The additional fact that the list is such a partial one, excluding acts carried out by 'friendly' forces which would clearly be labelled terrorist if carried out by 'hostile' forces, further unbalances the analysis and underlines the political use of terrorist terminology.

The problem of oversimplification of the issue of state-sponsored terrorism, that is, of failing to distinguish adequately between different forms and levels of sponsorship, has its greatest impact on the assessment of the threat posed by international terrorism. The problem is compounded by the ahistorical view that terrorism as state-sponsored behavior is a unique feature of the contemporary international landscape. This latter view ignores the wealth of historical examples of state-supported violence, intimidation and coercion short of warfare.[46] Thus the condemnation of the abuse of diplomatic facilities to aid or conceal terrorist activities which has become the focus of much recent discussion has a long lineage. Indeed, as Bull points out, the

> principle that ambassadors should not interfere in the politics of the receiving country, now so central, was not established in the early

days of resident diplomacy, but emerged only as interference by ambassadors was challenged by the receiving government .... . Even in the eighteenth century there were numerous cases of fomentation of resistance and revolt by ambassadors.[47]

Assassination has also had a long history directly in the service of foreign policy. During the Reformation assassination was a 'conventional instrument' of states.[48] But as with the wider category of state-sponsored terrorism, the threat posed by assassinations can be vastly overestimated. In his review of the history and theory of assassination and terrorism, David C. Rapoport concludes that a government which cannot pursue foreign policy by conventional means is also likely to be one 'so vulnerable that its weapons perform like boomerangs in the hands of the inexperienced'.[49] As with all forms of 'unconventional' intervention in the affairs of other states, the effects are hard to control or to predict. Rapoport's analysis of assassinations, however, does lead to some distinctions which might make more conceptual sense of the notion of state-sponsored terrorism. He argues that whereas assassination is an incident, terrorism is a process. What sets terrorism apart is the element of continuing fear.[50] This analysis suggests a distinction between state-sponsored terrorism as terrorism and as low-intensity warfare. It may be classified as the latter when it involves discrete targets and is thus more akin to assassination. It may not involve continuing fear unless the target state 'talks up' the issue and by this means creates an ongoing climate of fear. This distinction also points up a real problem facing target states – if they do not by their own actions (or, usually, words) create a fearful situation they may find it difficult to justify some of the responses they may feel are appropriate. This applies particularly to military responses. On the other hand, if they amplify the fear too much they succeed mainly in doing the terrorists' job for them.

The dangers of mistakenly (or deliberately) overestimating the level of threat posed by state-sponsored terrorism are also noted by Zeigler in his analysis of the nature of international politics. He reminds us that 'there is no reason to seize on every challenge to [the nation-state] and elevate a potential development into an accomplished fact'.[51] There are significant differences between domestic and international terrorism, but many of the lessons learnt in combatting the former can be readily adapted to the latter. Notable among these is the lesson of not overreacting to terrorism. States should indeed acknowledge the challenge posed by state-sponsored terrorism, but must be wary of overestimating or overstating it. Some measures against terrorism, especially those attempting to mould opinion and build support for particular counter-terrorist policies, can easily have the unintended consequence of strengthening the credibility and power of the *terrorists* if not handled carefully.

These words of caution do not appear to affect many of those who now write on the topic of state-sponsored terrorism. For many of these authors the analysis is simple and the preferred solutions seemingly even simpler.

The definitions used are either non-existent, so wide as to incorporate almost anything, or so partial as to seriously limit their applicability (or honest use). The evidence used is fragmentary and often unconvincing. This may reflect the clandestine nature of the operations, in which case at least a sophisticated attempt must be made to provide a convincing strategic rationale for each state's use of the tactic. On the whole this is conspicuously absent. The analysis is often more journalistic than academic. This is not to belittle the journalistic style, but to point out that the analysis often collapses categories, asserts without supporting argument and generally glosses over gaps, inconsistencies and difficulties in the interpretation of the inevitably unsatisfactory evidence. It has about it the tone of a crusade or a witchhunt, not of sober weighing of evidence and an honest pondering of alternative strategies of response. Indeed, while Willian Casey, the Director of the US Central Intelligence Agency, claims that 'international terrorism has become a perpetual war without borders'[52] it might more accurately be referred to as a war without *perceptual* borders.

Typical of contemporary opinions are those expressed by such authors as Neil Livingstone, Ray Cline and Yonah Alexander. Livingstone's works are littered with throw-away lines such as 'Terrorism is war without limits, and as such, virtually anyone or anything is fair game as a terrorist target'[53] and 'Terrorism is "clandestine and undeclared" warfare against the West and, therefore, must be recognized as a clear and present danger both to the individual and collective security of the United States and its allies'.[54] Such statements are not however dissected to lay out for the reader the various types of sponsorship and their impact upon particular state interests. We are merely told, and told again, that the West fails to understand the danger terrorism poses. Thus Livingstone and Arnold agree with the proposition that

> ... World War III has already begun ... although it is strategic warfare on the cheap, *its stakes are no less significant or meaningful to the United States and the other nations of the West than a direct clash between the two superpowers* (emphasis added).[55]

Bald claims of extreme threat are made in a similar vein by Cline and Alexander who believe that state-sponsored terrorism 'endanger[s] domestic security, political stability, and military defense almost as much, or sometimes as much, as if a declared state of war existed'.[56] What follows, however, is mainly more rhetoric. There is no real analysis of how terrorism achieves such an impact or what vital interests it harms in what ways. Instead we are merely confronted with further exhortations to understand the seriousness of the situation. Thus, for example, state-sponsored terrorists are said to be 'one of the most disruptive elements in the fabric of civilized order on the face of the earth'.[57] Absent is any analysis other than in moralistic/ideological terms which tries to justify this assertion. Absent also is any serious attempt to compare terrorism with other evils or ills which might allow one to judge its relative disruptive potential.

Underlying the deficiencies of approachs such as Cline and Alexander's is an unwillingness to define the phenomenon precisely, to differentiate between different types of sponsorship and to apply the concept even-handedly to those of *any* persuasion who employ the tactic. Even terms such as 'patron' or 'sponsor', often used to describe states in some way involved in terrorism, are problematic. The too easy use of these terms and their imprecise meaning carry, in the context within which they are used, connotations of a strategic plan, of direction of operations for specific foreign policy goals, and so forth. That these connotations may sometimes reflect reality is not in question, but more often what is involved is little more than financial or moral support of those espousing like-minded ideologies. This may be serious enough and may indeed foster terrorism, but the implications for threat assessment and for the determination of appropriate international counter-terrorist policies are surely different than in the case of direct involvement of a state in the planning and control of terrorism *for its own foreign policy goals*. It is thus vital at the analytical level to distinguish between providing support, training and finance to terrorist groups and setting up and directing them for specific state policy purposes. Even those terrorist groups closely associated with particular states may operate according to their own agenda part of the time, and sometimes this will not be in the direct interest of their sponsor state.

The conflict between the goals of sponsor and sponsored may have quite significant implications for threat assessment. There are particular dangers when a state pursues a vigorous counter-terrorist policy against another without appreciating the distinction between influence and control. In general terms, the strength of the argument for considering state-sponsored terrorism to be a particularly serious contemporary threat lies precisely in the presumed dependence of the terrorists on their backers. Thus, because we believe that a particular terrorist group is so heavily dependent on a state sponsor for finance, arms, logistical support, intelligence, etc, we tend to accept uncritically that their strategic goals, and possibly their targets, will be determined by their sponsors. At the very least, we believe that they will coincide with those of their sponsors. The firmer we believe the control by the sponsor to be, the greater the threat posed by particular incidents will be assessed – largely because of its link to conflicts between the sponsor state and other nations.

Accurate threat assessment, therefore, is dependent on an accurate appraisal of the degree of influence exerted by the sponsor on a terrorist group's *operational* decison-making. It is not enough to assert that support entails control, regardless of the level of support. The critical job for intelligence agencies is to demonstrate the degree of contol. States must remain aware that sponsor nations do not always exert the control they desire or even believe they do and that there may well be a significant divergence between the goals of the groups and their sponsors. In particular, it must be remembered that the relationship between sponsor and sponsored is often a dynamic and uncertain one, so that a degree of coincidence of views, or even sponsor control of general direction, which exists at one time, may not persist. Thus, accurate threat assessment also depends on a continuous assessment of the degree of contol and must not be based on the assumption that a demonstrated high level of control at one point necessarily translates into a similar situation some time later (or vice versa).

The dangers of failing to understand (or acknowledge) the tensions between sponsor and sponsored can be illustrated by both historical and contemporary examples. The most striking example perhaps is the belief held by Austria in 1914 that Gavrilo Princip and his Young Bosnian co-conspirators were backed directly by Serbia in their successful assassination plot against the Archduke Franz Ferdinand. In fact, of course, the backing came from a Serbian nationalistic organization, the Union of Death (better known as the Black Hand), whose members included a number of important Serbian army officers. The Union was not, however, a creature of the Serbian government and, indeed, 'A silent struggle went on for a time between the government and the Black Hand'.[58] Fuelled by 'popular demand for a grand pattern of international intrigue to account for such events'[59] and by their own misunderstanding of the nature of the Serbian links to the Bosnian terrorists, Austria issued its harsh and unacceptable ultimatum to Serbia. It is perhaps not going too far to say that rather than the assassination at Sarajevo precipitating the First World War, it was the pursuit of the belief that the act was one of state-sponsored terrorism that was the precipitant.

Those who see the hand of a state behind most significant acts of terrorism ought to reflect upon the dangers and limitations inherent in state direction and control of terrorism for both the state and the terrorists. For the terrorists there is the problem of ensuring that such sponsorship does not lead to splits within their own organization over whose goals are being pursued. This sort of problem was identified by an unnamed participant in a conference on terrorism held in Tel Aviv in 1979 who, discussing the problems of the PLO, noted that 'The more it becomes identified with a foreign power and with a foreign propaganda arm, the more difficult it becomes for it to establish a really firm basis'.[60] Where more than one sponsor is involved, as is often the case, the problems mulitply. Thus, as another participant at the Tel Aviv conference commented, again in relation to the PLO:

> Despite the fact that the Palestinians have so much strength, they still need unity and have yet to set up common headquarters. One of the reasons for this is multiplicity of support. They are dependent on a number of Arab countries and some of the factions or organizations within the PLO represent an extension of the country which they depend on.[61]

Sponsorship also carries potential costs for the sponsor state. The Soviet

Union, as discussed earlier, is mentioned frequently not merely as a supplier of terrorist arms and trainer of terrorist personnel, but also as a planner and director of terrorist acts. For the most part, however, the Soviets are unwilling to support avowed terrorist groups openly. Their support has to be disguised and channelled through middlemen, often in complex and multi-chained arrangements. The consequence, however, as Laquer points out, is that:

> ... they cannot have full control over the terrorists; the gunmen may land them in situations that were not planned and which may be politically harmful. To engage in international terrorism is to play with a fire that is difficult to control.[62]

Thus, we may accept that some states will sometimes seek to control substantially the direction of a particular group's activities. We should remember, however, the dangers to states of so doing, dangers of which those determining the state's perilous foreign policy course will be well aware. The reality of the dangers can reasonably be expected to reduce the incidence of attempts at control to the minimum considered essential. I believe that minimum is well below the incidence of control claimed by those who see state sponsorship of terrorism as one of the contemporary world's most pressing problems.

A more detailed analysis of why this should be so is given by Gregory Foster in his examination of the principles governing intervention by a state in the affairs of another.[63] Foster points to the problems of dependence on a third party to execute the desired act in a timely and competent manner and to the considerable dangers of failure: '... where failure eventuates, the fragile facade of deniability is likely to be turned on its head by aggressive propagandists who will be quick to point out the failed sponsorship ...'.[64] According to Foster, four conditions must be satisfied before any proxy relationship can be effective.[65] First, the interests and objectives of the two parties must be compatible in large measure. Second, the sponsor must be able to exert leverage and control over the surrogate by virtue of the condition of dependence or inter-dependence that exists. Third,

> ... a subtle form of manipulation, sometimes bordering on duplicity, may have to be applied by the sponsor so as to allow the surrogate nation [or, in the present case, terrorist group] to function under the illusion that it is not a puppet – and thereby retain its self-respect – or to believe that the instrumental benefits of the relationship outweigh the costs sufficiently to make it worthwile.[66]

And, fourth, the group being sponsored must be powerful enough to succeed in its mission without the intervention of the sponsor. Clearly, the number of situations in which these conditions will be met is limited. One might reasonably conclude, therefore, that sponsorship involving significant control by states of the activities of terrorist groups is not as common as many believe. It might be added parenthetically that the conditions necessary for successful proxy relationships (from the sponsor's point of view) may provide additional pressure points which might be exploited in a counter-terrorist strategy precisely to prevent sponsorship arrangements being reached.

In terms of deciding on the response appropriate to each incident then, it is important to distinguish between various levels of state involvement (ranging from an independent act by a group which has had some state support to an act planned and directed by a state). It is equally important to attempt to discern the precise motives of policy objectives behind each type and instance of state involvement, for example, destabilization, internationalization of revolution, forcing policy changes, revenge, tying down military resources, causing loss of face, preventing access to raw materials or other strategic supplies, disrupting negotiations or alliances, undermining the influence of another state, projecting power, etc. One has to look very hard to find amongst the burgeoning literature on state-sponsored terrorism works which seriously attempt such an analysis. It is rare to find an article or book listing and condemning state sponsorship which tries to analyze the strategic goals of such support.

The lack of discrimination in the field extends to other areas also. Most authors fail to distinguish between state-sponsored attacks directed against the internal foes of the sponsor and against the interests of another state. There is sometimes a confusion between institutionally- and individually-motivated state terror which reveals a shallowness in analysis. Thus, Livingstone and Arnold are typical of those who are able to view Libyan terrorism as totally irrational because of their view of the influence of a leader they cannot understand.[67] They, therefore, see no need to attempt to analyze strategic ojectives. Syria, on the other hand, seems to them less in the grip of a forceful personality and its terrorism seems more institutionalized, so they at least mention some strategic rationales for its sponsorship of terrorism. Once again, there can be no argument with the proposition that in some states the personality of the leader may be more important than in others as a determinant of the style and course of methods used to pursue state ends. It will be rarely, if ever, however, that strategic considerations and analyses of goals will ever be irrelevant. What often appears to occur is that if something is so different from the prevailing norm that we cannot explain it in our own terms of reference, there is a tendency to simplify it so that we can feel 'comfortable' by having thereby 'understood' it. Thus we can explain what appears to be 'irrational' (that is, not within normally accepted bounds) state behavior by attributing it to the influence of a 'mad' leader. Clearly this is not sufficient. What we must do is to come to grips with the complexity which confronts us.

These difficulties indicate that we have far to go in analyzing and understanding state-sponsored terrorism. The first task is to clearly define our terms and to attempt to distinguish various types of state involvement.[68] This can then be used as a basis for setting out possible strategic rationales for the employment of state-sponsored terrorism and, eventually, for determining the level of threat presented to vital national interests by various acts of terrorism.[69] If the concept is to have meaning it will also have to apply to acts falling within the definition regardless of who carries them out. Thus, support for groups using terrorism must be clearly noted as instances of state-sponsorship of terrorism whether it be by friend or foe. Until these conditions are met the idea of state-sponsored terrorism will be little more than a propaganda weapon used by each side to condemn the (often similar) behavior of the other in a dispute. The dangers of some forms of state-sponsorship are too real to let the false images undermine such international will as does exist to do something concerted and constructive to address them. Those who have argued that we need to reassess our concept of warfare, our military doctrines and theories, and the structure of our response capabilities are right to have done so.[70] But these reassessments must have a sound analytical basis which is currently lacking. Above all, we should remember that both analysis and history tell us that lack of confidence and over-reaction in the face of terrorist attack are at least as dangerous as many of the attacks themselves. As Walter Laquer has said: 'There is a tendency to magnify the importance of terrorism in modern society: society is vulnerable to attack, but it is also astonishingly resilient.'[71] Reminding ourselves that this is true may ensure that the debate about state-sponsored terrorism rises above the mire of ideological cant.

NOTES

The views expressed in this article are the author's and do not necessarily reflect those of the Australian Institute of Criminology. My thanks to Peter Grabosky for his critique of this manuscript.

1. Harry H. Almond, Jr, 'The Use of Organized Groups by States as Vehicles to Promote their Foreign Policy', in Henry Hyunwook Han (ed.), *Terrorism, Political Violence and World Order* (Lanham, MD: University Press of America, 1984), pp.229–66; Ray S. Cline and Yonah Alexander, *Terrorism as State-Sponsored Covert Warfare* (Fairfax, VA: Hero Books, 1986); Neil C. Livingstone and Terrell E. Arnold (eds.), *Fighting Back. Winning the War Against Terrorism* (Lexington, MA: Lexington Books, 1986); James Berry Motley, 'International Terrorism. A New Mode of Warfare', *International Security Review* 6 (Spring 1981), 93–123; Jeffrey W. Wright, 'Terrorism: A Mode of Warfare', *Military Review* (Oct. 1984), 35–45.
2. Edward Herman, *The Real Terror Network* (Boston: South End Press, 1982); Jeane Kirkpatrick, 'Defining Terrorism', *Catholicism in Crisis* (Sept. 1984), 41–4; Walter Laqueur, 'Reflections on Terrorism', *Foreign Affairs* 65 (Fall 1986), 86–100; Michael Stohl, 'National Interests and State Terrorism in International Affairs', *Political Science* 36 (July 1984), 37–52; Michael Stohl, 'International Dimensions of State Terrorism' in Michael Stohl and George A. Lopez (eds), *The State As Terrorist* (Westport, CT: Greenwood Press, 1984), pp.43–58; Paul Wilkinson, 'State-Sponsored International Terrorism: The Problems of Response', *The World Today* (July 1984), 292–8.
3. For example, state sponsorship of terrorism was one of the two major issues which dominated discussions between the leaders of the seven major Western industrialized countries held in Tokyo in May 1986 (the 'Tokyo Summit'). The other issue was nuclear

safety in the aftermath of the explosion at the nuclear power plant at Chernobyl in the Soviet Union.

4. For example, a CBS News Poll released on 11 April 1986 showed that more Americans name terrorism as the most important problem facing the country than name any other specific problem, and that concern appears to be increasing. These figures were collected in the aftermath of several well-publicized terrorist acts generally portrayed as having been instigated by particular nation states.

5. United States Department of State, Current Policy No.258, Alexander Haig, News Conference, 28 Jan. 1981.

6. See, for example, William Casey (Director of Central Intelligence), 'The International Linkages – What Do We Know?' in Uri Ra'anan, Robert L. Pfaltzgraff, Jr., Richard H. Shultz, Ernst Halperin and Igor Lukes (eds.), *Hydra of Carnage* (Lexington, MA: Lexington Books, 1986), pp.5–15.

7. The arguments for Soviet sponsorship are made most forcefully by Ray S. Cline and Yonah Alexander, *Terrorism: The Soviet Connection* (New York: Crane Russak, 1984); Roberta Goren, *The Soviet Union and Terrorism* (London: George Allen & Unwin, 1984); Claire Sterling, *The Terror Network* (London: Weidenfeld & Nicolson, 1981). For critical reviews of this line of reasoning see Herman (1982), op. cit., note 2; Michael Stohl, 'Review Essay: The International Network of Terrorism', *Journal of Peace Research* 20 (1983), 87–94; Grant Wardlaw, 'A Terror Network?', *Quadrant* 30 (July/Aug. 1986), 131–3.

8. United States Department of State. Gist. International Terrorism. Sept. 1984.

9. United States Department of State. Combatting International Terrorism. Current Policy No.667. 5 March 1985.

10. President Ronald Reagan, Address delivered to the Convention of the American Bar Association, Washington, DC, 8 July 1985.

11. 'US Takes Steps to Isolate Syria', *Sydney Morning Herald* (Sydney, Australia), 29 Oct. 1986.

12. 'US Lacks Evidence of Syrian Terror', *Sydney Morning Herald*, 6 June 1986.

13. 'List Links Syria to Worldwide Terrorism', *Canberra Times* (Canberra, Australia), 17 Nov. 1986.

14. Ibid.

15. 'Thatcher: Evidence on Syria Falls Short', *Washington Post*, 24 May 1986.

16. The evidence came out in the trial of Nezar Hindawi in London in October 1986 and in official British government statements. See statement of Britain's Secretary of State for Foreign and Commonwealth Affairs, Sir Geoffrey Howe, to the House of Commons, 24 Oct. 1986.

17. Indeed shortly after Britain severed diplomatic relations with Syria in the aftermath of the Hindawi trial, two of the French hostages were released in Damascus in what was seen widely as a gesture of thanks to France for helping to minimize subsequent European Community sanctions against Syria. 'French Hostages Freed in Syrian Goodwill Deal', *Australian Financial Review* (Sydney, Australia), 13 Nov. 1986.

18. 'Paris Said to Seek Deal With Syrians to Curb Terrorism', *New York Times*, 30 Oct. 1986.

19. To be fair, it must also be acknowledged that Syria is often said to be more skilful in concealing direct evidence of its links to terrorism. While this may in part be true, it is not always a convincing argument. At least part of the evidence against Libya is the impression created by claims made by Gadhafi about support for 'freedom fighters' and threats such as those to kill the US President. This may give confidence to analysts in their interpretations of events but it adds little to the quality of much of the evidence itself.

20. William J. Casey, remarks before the Annual Conference of the National Security Studies Program at the Fletcher School of Law and Diplomacy, 17 April 1985.

21. 'McFarlane Calls Sending Arms to Iran a "Mistake"', *Washington Post*, 20 Nov. 1986.

22. 'Terrorism: A War Without Rules, Without Frontiers', USIA interview with Terrell Arnold, US State Department (Canberra, Australia: US Information Service, 18 Jan. 1984).

23. Secretary of State George Shultz, interview on the NBC 'Today Show', 13 May 1986.
24. For a general discussion of the problems of defining terrorism see, Grant Wardlaw, *Political Terrorism: Theory, Tactics, and Counter-Measures* (Cambridge: Cambridge University Press, 1982), Ch.1.
25. A CBS News Poll, 'Responses to Terrorism', released on 8 Feb. 1986 showed that Libya was the most frequently named country thought to be involved in planning and financing terrorist acts. Libya is consistently identified by the public as the probable backer of many individual terrorist attacks; see, for example, CBS News Poll, 'Response to Libya', released 16 April 1986; 'Poll Says Americans Favor Action Against Terror', *Washington Post*, 10 Sept. 1986.
26. For example, the majority of acts listed in a recent British government briefing on Libyan terrorism involved anti-dissident activities; see Background Brief, 'Libyan State Terrorism' (London: Foreign and Commonwealth Office, April 1986). Similarly, a much more extensive list published by the US State Department includes a high proportion of acts against Libyan dissidents abroad, see Backgrounder, 'Chronology of Libyan Support for Terrorism' (Canberra: US Information Service, 21 Aug. 1986). What is noteworthy about this latter chronology is the expansive interpretation given to the concept of state support for terrorism. Included on the list are such items as 'Libya uses civil aircraft to send troops to aid Uganda's Idi Amin'; 'U.S. Embassy in Tripoli burned'; 'After being fired upon, two F-14 fighters from the aircraft carrier USS Nimitz down two Soviet-built Libyan Sukhoi-22 fighters over the Gulf of Sidra'; 'Libya provides material support to coup in Burkina Faso'; etc. These may arguably be evidence of Libya's aggressive line on foreign policy or unwarranted interference in the affairs of other states, but they are clearly not what most people think of as involvement in acts of terrorism. However, by combining together a multitude of violent or manipulative acts under the heading of state terrorism, a false impression of a coherent and dangerous threat is presented.
27. For example, a Washington Post-ABC News Poll taken following the hijacking of a Pan Am aircraft in Karachi in September 1986 found that 74 per cent of those interviewed thought the US should take military action against any Middle Eastern nation found to be aiding terrorist acts against Americans. In a similar poll taken after incidents a year earlier, only about half favored such use of force, see 'Poll Says Americans Favor Action Against Terror', *Washington Post*, 19 Sept. 1986. These options may be contrasted with those revealed in British and Australian polls in which less than 30 per cent of respondents supported such action, see Market and Opinion Research International Poll, *The Times* (of London) 15–16 April 1986, and Age Poll, 'Snub for Reagan Line on Terror', *The Age* (Melbourne, Australia), 14 June 1986.
28. Although President Reagan's 'Adress to the Nation' on 14 April 1986 did indicate his belief that it would impact signifieantly on Gadhafi.
29. Cited in Michael Stohl, 'Terrorism, States and State Terrorism: The Reagan Administration in the Middle East', paper presented at a seminar on 'Terrorism and the Middle East: Context and Interpretations', Center for. Contemporary Arab Studies, Georgetown University, Washington, DC, 11 Sept. 1986.
30. 'Gadhafi Target of Secret U.S. Deception Plan', *Washington Post*, 2 Oct. 1986.
31. 'Reagan's Credibility Seen Hurt by Anti-Kadafi Effort', *Los Angeles Times*, 4 Oct. 1986.
32. 'Libya is Gearing Up for Terror, Says US', *Canberra Times*, 25 Nov. 1986.
33. 'Gadhafi Denounces Nonaligned; Vows to Lead Anti-Imperialist Army', *Washington Post*, 5 Sept. 1986; 'Irish to Break Ties With Libya?', *The Herald* (Melbourne, Australia), 30 Oct. 1986; 'Freedom Fighters Avenged US Bombing', *The Australian*, 4 Nov. 1986.
34. See, for example, the arguments in Andrew Mack, 'The Utility of Terrorism', *Australian and New Zealand Journal of Criminology* 14 (Dec. 1981), 197–224.
35. 'Terrorism Held Overreported and Overrated', *New York City Tribute*, 9 June 1986.
36. The others most significantly feature the rapidly expanding army of academics who have climbed onto the terrorism bandwagon. Many of the contributions of these opportunistic analysts have made the literature on terrorism, in general, one of the

most superficial around.

37. Hedley Bull, *The Anarchical Society. A Study of Order in World Politics* (London: Macmillan, 1977), p.188.
38. Brian Michael Jenkins, 'New Modes of Conflict', *Orbis* 28 (Spring 1984), 15–16.
39. Bull, op. cit., p.185.
40. The United States may be prepared to intervene militarily in another country's affairs, as it has on a number of occasions in Central America, but this is quite different in nature from the routine, total, direct and continuing repression of national expression by the Soviet Union in Eastern Europe. In my view, most of the American actions deserve to be condemned, but the Soviet crime is of a significantly greater magnitude.
41. In this case, the difference between the two superpowers is principally one of degree rather than kind. Both support, directly or indirectly, various forms of insurgencies which seek in part to undermine the interests of the other. The Soviet Union, however, does so more frequently because it is not the status quo power. However, the United States frequently supports actions to shore up incumbent regimes, these actions being of a nature which it would classify as terrorist if carried out by the insurgents. See Michael Stohl, 'States, Terrorism and State Terrorism: The Role of the Superpowers' in Robert Slater and Michael Stohl (eds.), *Current Perspectives on International Terrorism* (London: Macmillan and New York: St Martin's Press, 1987), for arguments on the roles of the two superpowers as supporters of terrorism.
42. It should be noted that the presumption that those forces, usually relatively weak in military terms, which try to usurp entrenched state power will be amongst those most likely to employ conventional means, excludes consideration of terrorism in the service of the state as a means of internal control. Of course, it is state terrorism employed against the state's own people which is statistically the most important form of terrorism – see generally Michael Stohl and George A. Lopez (eds.), *Government Violence and Repression. An Agenda for Research* (Westport, CT: Greenwood Press, 1986).
43. Examples of arguments in favor of categorizing terrorism as low intensity warfare include Alvin H. Bernstein, 'Iran's Low-Intensity War Against the United States', *Orbis* 30 (Spring 1986), 149–67; Ray Cline and Yonah Alexander, *Terrorism as State-Sponsored Covert Warfare* (Fairfax, VA: Hero Books, 1986); James Berry Motley, 'International Terrorism: A New Mode of Warfare', *International Security Review* 6 (Spring 1981), 93–123; Neil Livingstone and Terrell Arnold (eds.), *Fighting Back. Winning the War Against Terrorism* (Lexington, MA: Lexington Books, 1986); Jeffrey W. Wright, 'Terrorism: A Mode of Warfare', *Military Review* (Oct. 1984), 35–45.
44. George K. Tanham, Brian Jenkins, Eleanor S. Wainstein and Gerald Sullivan, 'United States Preparation for Future Low-Level Conflict', *Conflict* 1 (1978), 1–20.
45. Opening address by Ambassador Antony Quainton in Brian M. Jenkins (ed.), *Terrorism and Beyond. An International Conference on Terrorism and Low-Level Conflict* (Santa Monica, CA: Rand Corporation, 1982), p.31.
46. Not only state-sponsored terrorism, but also, of course, the insurgent variety has a long history. Thus, as Hedley Bull points out in *The Anarchical Society* (op. cit.): 'Private international violence ... is not new or unprecedented; all that is clearly new is the global scale on which it takes place' (p.269).
47. Bull, *The Anarchical Society*, op. cit., p.168.
48. David C. Rapoport, *Assassination and Terrorism* (Toronto: Canadian Broadcasting Corporation, 1971), p.33.
49. Ibid., p.34.
50. Ibid., pp.37–8.
51. David W. Ziegler, *War, Peace, and International Politics*, 2nd ed. (Boston: Little, Brown, 1981).
52. Casey, 'The International Linkages – What Do We Know?', op. cit., p.5.
53. Neil Livingstone, *The War Against Terrorism* (Lexington, MA: Lexington Books, 1982), p.125.
54. Ibid., p.28.
55. Neil C. Livingstone and Terrell E. Arnold, 'Democracy Under Attack' in N.C.

Livingstone and T.E. Arnold (eds.), *Fighting Back. Winning the War Against Terrorism* (Lexington, MA: Lexington Books, 1986), pp.2–3.

56. Cline and Alexander, *Terrorism As State-Sponsored Covert Warfare*, op. cit., p.1.
57. Ibid., p.8.
58. Feliks Gross, 'Political Violence and Terror in 19th and 20th Century Russia and Eastern Europe' in J.F. Kirkham, S. Levy and W.J. Crotty, *Assassination and Political Violence*. A Report to the National Commission on the Causes and Prevention of Violence (Washington, DC: USGPO, 1969), p.450.
59. Franklin L. Ford, *Political Murder. From Tyrannicide to Terrorism* (Cambridge, MA: Harvard University Press, 1985), p.247.
60. Discussion of paper by M. Asa, 'Forms of State Support to Terrorism and the Possibility of Combating Terrorism by Retaliating Against Supporting States', in Ariel Merari (ed.), *On Terrorism and Combating Terrorism* (Frederick, MD: University Publications of America, 1985), p.130.
61. Ibid.
62. Walter Laqueur, 'Reflections on Terrorism', *Foreign Affairs* 65 (Fall 1986), p.96.
63. Gregory D. Foster, 'On Selective Intervention', *Strategic Review* 11 (Fall 1983), pp.48–63.
64. Ibid., p.59.
65. Ibid. The arguments Foster advances are in relation to the employment of states as surrogates. The principles seem to apply equally, however, to the sponsorship of terrorist groups.
66. Ibid.
67. Livingstone and Arnold, *Fighting Back*, op. cit.
68. One of the few analyses which attempts to categorize state involvement in terrorism is found in Michael Stohl, 'States, Terrorism and State Terrorism: The Role of the Superpowers', op. cit.
69. Of course these 'vital national interests' also need to be carefully defined.
70. See, for example, General Edward C. Meyer, 'Low-Level Conflict: An Overview', in Brian Jenkins (ed.), *Terrorism and Beyond*, op. cit., pp.38–42.
71. Walter Laqueur, 'Reflections on Terrorism', op. cit.

'Leaderless Resistance'

Jeffrey Kaplan

Pray for victory and not an end to slaughter [Joseph Tommasi]

Don't follow leaders, Watch your parking meters [Bob Dylan]

More a mark of despair than a revolutionary strategy, leaderless resistance as it was formulated and disseminated to the far right faithful sought to make a virtue of weakness and political isolation. Leaderless resistance may be defined as a kind of lone wolf operation in which an individual, or a very small, highly cohesive group, engage in acts of anti-state violence independent of any movement, leader or network of support. This violence may take the form of attacks on state institutions or operatives, or it may take the form of random targets of opportunity selected on the basis of their perceived vulnerability and their symbolic importance.[1] Thus acts of leaderless resistance may be aimed at targets as diverse as inter-racial couples, gay book stores or clubs, or indeed, at government agents or buildings.

The leaderless resistance concept was popularized in the late 1980s as a last gasp of defiance by the American radical right which was then at the nadir of its already bleak fortunes. This article will examine the historical context which gave birth to leaderless resistance, follow it through its National Socialist, Christian Identity and neo-pagan Odinist formulations, and will close with a speculative consideration of Timothy McVeigh as a possible case study of the strategy of leaderless resistance.

The internal debates which produced the leaderless resistance strategy did not begin the 1980s. Rather, they are of considerable vintage and reflect a long standing division in the far right. On the one hand, there has always been a conservative majority of the movement who saw – correctly as it happens – that to engage prematurely in revolutionary violence against a vastly more powerful state would be foolhardy at best, suicidal at worst. The political strategy of choice was thus to utilize propaganda and legal demonstrations so as to build a 'revolutionary majority'.[2] This approach in National Socialist circles came to be known as the theory of mass action.

All but the most idealistic adherent of National Socialist mass action theory realized full well that the American masses were hardly likely to flock to the swastika banner short of some catastrophic turn of events. Thus, throughout the 1960s and 1970s, the literature of American National Socialism blended prognostications of the deleterious impact of integration and school-busing to achieve racial balance, lurid crime stories with a racial slant that would have done the supermarket tabloids proud, and hopeful speculations of impending cataclysm, economic collapse and urban mayhem.³ In one of the great ironies of American National Socialism, George Lincoln Rockwell, the sole charismatic figure produced by the post-war movement, was himself one of the architects of the mass action strategy. Yet at the same time, Rockwell would continually decry as the ruination of the movement the 'hobbyists' (i.e. part-time Nazis) that such a strategy could not help but attract.⁴

Following the assassination of Rockwell in 1967, the party began to fragment. Matt Koehl succeeded the Commander, soon renamed the American Nazi Party the National Socialist White People's Party (NSWPP) and initiated the endless round of purges that would soon cost the Party its bare handful of capable adherents. Two victims of these purges and angry resignations, William Pierce and Joseph Tommasi, figure prominently in the development of the leaderless resistance concept.

Of Pierce much more will be said later. Joseph Tommasi concerns us first. Tommasi ironically was a Koehl loyalist almost to the day he was unceremoniously purged from the NSWPP and subsequently murdered by an NSWPP member in 1975.⁵ Tommasi was one of the young West Coast party members whose radicalism thrilled a few and appalled the majority of American National Socialists. Addressing the Second Party Congress in 1970, his ringing call for revolutionary action NOW brought him to the attention of William Pierce – then in the throes of his own bitter dispute with Matt Koehl.⁶ Tommasi, like Pierce, was acutely aware of the bold actions undertaken by the Weathermen and the Symbionese Liberation Army to name but two of the left wing combatant organizations of the day. They were determined to create a campus-based revolutionary movement of the right on the same model. Thus was born the National Socialist Liberation Front (NSLF).

In 1973 or 1974, Tommasi published his now famous poster, 'THE FUTURE BELONGS TO THE FEW OF US WILLING TO GET OUR HANDS DIRTY. POLITICAL TERROR: It's the only thing they understand', and his seminal pamphlet, *Building the Revolutionary Party*, to announce the formation of the NSLF. The NSLF's revolutionary ideology was based on the rejection of the conservative theory of mass action which Tommasi correctly believed was paralyzing the NS movement. For Tommasi, the mass action doctrine meant in reality that no serious anti-state actions were possible given the patent impossibility of creating a mass based National Socialist party in the US.

Tommasi gathered some 43 adherents to the foundational meeting of the NSLF in El Monte, California on 2 March 1974. But this number is somewhat deceiving. Few of these young National Socialists were sufficiently suicidal to act on Tomassi's rhetoric.⁷ In the end, only four NSLF 'members' undertook revolutionary action: Tommasi, Karl Hand, David Rust and James Mason (Mason had not officially joined the group, only receiving his membership card after Tommasi's assassination). As James Mason recalls:

> Yes, the N.S.L.F. of Tommasi had four persons who carried out the illegal activities. The remainder, the majority, weren't that much

different from the N.S.W.P.P. members except they were a lot more forward thinking.[8]

The NSLF soldiered on at least in name for another decade. In that time, however, Tommasi was murdered, Hand and Rust were incarcerated for acts of racially motivated violence and firearms charges, and James Mason found a new avatar in Charles Manson. But the NSLF's contribution to the leaderless resistance concept is incalculable.[9] The NSLF was the first to act on the theory that, regardless of the dearth of public support, a blow could be struck against the hated state, provided that the determined revolutionary was prepared to act resolutely and alone. Tommasi was among the first to grasp fully the truth of the strategic situation – in the milieu of the radical right, no one is to be trusted, anyone could be (and probably is) an informer either for the government or for one of the many watchdog organizations monitoring radical right wing activity, and short of divine intervention, public support would not be forthcoming no matter what tactical approach the movement was to adopt. Yet in this state of weakness, there is ultimate strength. With nothing left to lose, a man is totally free to act as he will. For while the state had proven over and over again that it could effortlessly penetrate any right-wing organization, it had yet to develop the capability to thwart the will of one man acting alone!

This revelation would do the NSLF little good. The group actually died with Tommasi.[10] The actions of Hand and Rust were in reality pathetic outbursts of pointless violence which succeeded only in bringing them into the care of the state's prison system. But the example, once proffered, could not be erased. Although it had yet to be given a name, leaderless resistance was born.

At the same time, it is important to remember that the conservative majority of the far right did not approve of the unauthorized actions of leaderless resistors. Their well grounded fear was of precisely the sort of pointless and undisciplined actions which landed the tiny NSLF combatant cadre in prison. Rather, between impotent dreams of mass action and the antinomian reality of leaderless resistance, there was a third path which would become a model for the more extreme fringes of the present day militia movement. Borrowed from Leninist theory, the cell structure under a centralized command was the mark of the 1960s era Minutemen under the leadership of Robert Bolivar DePugh. R. N. Taylor recalls of these days:

> The Minutemen never advocated leaderless resistance 'per se'. In fact where such did occur, where an individual or small group, did in fact take some action on their own, it was generally a cause for concern and created trouble for the National organization. We did our very best to maintain a certain discipline among the members.
>
> Originally the structure of organization was in 'bands' [that] pretty well conformed to the classic guerrilla band of from 6 to 12 people. Later for security reasons, we began to reorganize along the lines of 'cells' of three people. When all the members, in a geographical

proximity to one another had been made a part of a cell, then we instituted a dispersed cell system for members who lived at too great a distance from other members. Where three people from 500 or more miles apart would be members of a dispersed team. This was on the understanding that, if directed to do so, they would all meet at a given time and place. When they had fulfilled whatever function they were called upon to accomplish, they all would then return to their respective locations. Only one of the three would even know the identity of the other two members, and that party would be the only one directly in touch with the National Organization. This is like an underground or resistance war type of structure. In addition to these modes of organization, the national organization had what they termed the 'Defense Survival Force'. The DSF was a group of inner core members who had expertise and training in such skills as surreptitious entry, lock-picking, electronic eavesdropping and proficiency in weapons, tactics and all else that might apply to specialized para-military operations. The DSF to my knowledge never consisted of more than 50 members. This small sector were of course under control of the National Organization. There was nothing spontaneous or thrill of the moment about this inner corps' activities. So, from the very beginning the Minuteman Organization was always attempting to maintain leadership and some sense of discipline and restraint among its members.[11]

The decade which followed Tommasi's death and the fall of the NSLF were, from the perspective of the far right, both eventful and deeply disheartening. Most notable, a true revolutionary movement, the Silent Brotherhood, more popularly known as the Order, under the leadership of Robert Mathews arose and after a brief but incandescent revolutionary career, was smashed by the state. It was not until the Order was nearing its inglorious end that many in the radical right were able to accept that the group could be anything other than a diabolically clever federal entrapment scheme.[12]

The death of Robert Mathews in a shoot-out with the FBI was thus traumatic to the movement, but far worse was to come. The 1989 Fort Smith, Arkansas sedition trial brought into the dock a virtual 'who's who' of the radical right. Louis Beam, the author of the original 'Leaderless Resistance' tract was there. So were surviving members of the Order. And so too were such venerable movement patriarchs as Richard Butler of the Aryan Nations and the ever jovial Robert Miles.[13] The defendants were in the end found innocent of all charges, but not before a parade of their erstwhile allies, men such as the head of the Covenant, Sword and Arm of the Lord Identity compound James Ellison and the Church of Israel's Dan Gayman betrayed the movement by appearing as witnesses for the prosecution. Little wonder in such a bleak situation that the power of the federal government, and of what was seen as its Jewish puppeteers personified as the Anti-Defamation League of B'nai B'rith, were reified into

ZOG, the all-powerful Zionist Occupation Government (ZOG) now seen as the masters of the nation and, indeed, of the world.

The ZOG discourse offered a form of comfort and an ironic sense of security for the faithful. Against so all-pervading a foe, what could be done but to withdraw and wait and seek to persevere? Movement discourse thus in the late 1980s became increasingly chiliastic. The mass action theories of the previous generation were discarded as hopeless dreams. And so things may have stayed had two searing events not galvanized the movement. In 1992, a heretofore obscure Identity adherent, Randy Weaver, became an unlikely movement icon when, in the wake of a botched federal government sting operation, Weaver's wife, young son and family dog were killed in a siege which took the life of a federal agent as well.[14] Then the next year – in the midst of the Weaver trial as it happened – there was the massacre at Waco.[15] Suddenly, previously isolated voices calling for individual acts of violent resistance to state tyranny began to be heard and to a limited degree heeded by a few in the milieu of the far right wing. No better symbol of this new found credibility can be posited than the inclusion of Louis R. Beam's original 'Leaderless Resistance' essay in pastor Pete Peters' published report on a meeting of Identity Christians which was convened to discuss the Randy Weaver drama.[16] Suddenly, leaderless resistance was no longer an isolated theory. It was seen as a matter of survival in the face of a government now determined to eradicate the righteous remnant of the patriot community once and for all. With this brief historical context, it is time to examine the texts which gave form and substance to the Leaderless Resistance strategy. These texts were, in chronological order, William Pierce's sad sequel to the *Turner Diaries*, *Hunter*; Richard Kelly Hoskins' foray into imagined history, *Vigilantes of Christendom*; Louis Beam's seminal essay 'Leaderless Resistance'; and David Lane's reprise of the theory in Viking garb, 'Wotan is Coming'.[17]

William Pierce, a confidant of George Lincoln Rockwell, was the spiritual father of the NSLF and the ghost in the machine whenever serious acts of radical right wing violence are contemplated or undertaken. His *Turner Diaries*, soon to be released in a mass market edition, was said to be a major source of inspiration for both the Order and for Timothy McVeigh, the convicted Oklahoma City bomber.[18] Yet Pierce himself has kept cautiously in the background, carefully building his National Alliance organization cum book distributorship and living the life of a gentleman farmer on his West Virginia estate.

For all the attention given to the *Turner Diaries*, however, his long awaited follow up, *Hunter*,[19] is a dispirited affair which has garnered little public attention. Yet *Hunter*, like its more famous predecessor, well reflects the ethos of the time in which it was written. *Hunter* is the story of one Oscar Yeagar, a character closely modeled on the real-life prototype of the lone wolf killer, James Vaughn, a.k.a. Joseph Franklin, to whom the book is dedicated.[20] *Hunter's* hero, stoically accepting the hopeless situation of the right in the wake of the fall of the Order, the Fort Smith fiasco and the perceived ever present reality of Jewish control of the nation and the world, sheds his attachments to family and friends, to career and creature comforts, and provides a fictional model of the lone wolf assassin, stalking the enemies of the white race. The ultimate goal is to demonstrate the weakness of the system and eventually to ignite a race war. But unlike the exuberant *Turner Diaries* in which the protagonist, Earl Turner, helps to unleash a revolution that changes the very face of the planet, *Hunter* ends not with a bang but with a resigned sigh:

> He sighed. Well, he would be very busy during the next few days discharging responsibilities he had already incurred. But after that it would be time to do some more hunting.[21]

Where *Hunter* offered a plausible if rather unpromising model for action, Richard Kelly Hoskins offered the Christian Identity faithful something better; a safe but deeply satisfying dream. Hoskins' 1990 magnum opus, *The Vigilantes of Christendom*, offered the dispirited faithful the age-old dream of supernatural succor as personified by a timeless band of selfless avengers, the Phineas Priesthood (Num. 23:6–13; Ps. 106:29–31).[22] The Phineas Priests in the pages of *Vigilantes of Christendom* are presented as a Templar-like order of assassins whose sacred role is to cull from the pure flock of Christ those wayward sheep who through race mixing or other transgressions, would do the work of Satan and his earthly servants, the Jews. The Phineas Priesthood came with a catchy motto,

> As the Kamikaze is to the Japanese
> As the Shiite is to Islam
> As the Zionist is to the Jew
> So the Phineas Priest is to Christendom[23]

And who are the Phineas Priests? A long list of claimants to the title are on offer. Robin Hood, St. George, Beowulf, King Arthur, John Wilkes Booth, Jesse James, Gordon Kahl, Robert Mathews and Doug Sheets (accused of murdering homosexuals) are but a few of the worthies in Hoskins' elaborate fantasy.

The Phineas Priesthood was, in the context of the times, a fantasy so alluring that it was only a matter of time before a few brave or deranged individuals would take up for themselves the title and set out in search of God's enemies. Given the fanciful nature of the Phineas Priesthood, such a quest must unambiguously qualify as an act of leaderless resistance. And indeed, a few did style themselves Phineas priests, not only in the radical right, but in the most radical fringes of the pro-life rescue movement as well.[24]

Clearly the most important text to emerge concerning leaderless resistance is Louis R. Beam's eponymous essay on the subject. Beam, a Klansman with close ties to Richard Butler's Christian Identity Aryan Nations compound, has for many years been at the cutting edge of movement theory. It was Beam who early on realized the Klan's marginality and sought manfully, but ultimately unsuccessfully, to bring the organization into the twentieth century. It was Beam too who was the first to propose –

and attempt to institute – the use of computers as a tool of radical right communication and recruitment.[25] Beam was quick to comprehend the dire strategic situation of the far right at the end of the 1980s, and to seek some way to keep the flame of violent opposition alive.

Louis Beam's writings take a serious interest in history and evince an academic's care to identify his sources. Thus, Beam takes no credit for coining either the concept or the term 'leaderless resistance'. Rather, he traces its origin to one Col. Ulius Louis Amoss, the founder of the Baltimore based International Service of Information Incorporated, who published an essay titled 'Leaderless Resistance' on 17 April 1962.[26] Col. Amoss was suggesting guerrilla tactics in case of communist invasion and conquest of America, but in the event, the scenario did not eventuate and the essay was eventually forgotten. Such might have been the fate of Beam's essay as well had it not been written a mere few months before the events of Ruby Ridge, Idaho. As noted above, Beam's essay was included in Pete Peters' report on the Weaver tragedy, and suddenly the term leaderless resistance was on everyone's lips. The movement, seeing in Ruby Ridge and far more so in Waco, evidence of a long feared government plot to eliminate the patriot community, and understanding full well the weakness and isolation of the movement, began to see leaderless resistance as the only hope of striking a last despairing blow before inevitable defeat. The watchdog community too seized on the concept as evidence of a resurgence of radical right wing violence. And the government appears, in the wake of Waco, to have undergone some paralysis as it sought to understand what had gone wrong and, with the sudden rise of the militias across America in response to Waco, where such wide spread anti-state anger could have come from so suddenly.

In this supercharged atmosphere, Beam's essay seems somewhat discordant, given its despairing tone and limited expectations for success. The essay, however, perfectly reflected the mood of the late 1980s and the pre-Waco 1990s. Beam begins:

> In the hope that, somehow, America can still produce the brave sons and daughters necessary to fight off ever increasing persecution and oppression, this essay is offered. Frankly, it is too close to call at this point. Those who love liberty, and believe in freedom enough to fight for it are rare today, but within the bosom of every once great nation, there remains secreted, the pearls of former greatness. They are there. I have looked into their sparking eyes; sharing a brief moment in time with them as I passed through this life. Relished their friendship, endured their pain, and they mine. We are a band of brothers, native to the soil gaining strength one from another as we have rushed head long into a battle that all the weaker, timid men, say we can not win. Perhaps...but then again, perhaps we can. It's not over till the last freedom fighter is buried or imprisoned...[27]

Hardly the words of a man confident of victory. But following a discourse on other seemingly doomed causes that somehow turned out well in the end, Beam offers his tactical suggestions:

> The concept of Leaderless Resistance is nothing less than a fundamental departure in theories of organization. The orthodox scheme of organization is diagrammatically represented by the pyramid, with the mass at the bottom and the leader at the top... The Constitution of the United States, in the wisdom of the Founders, tried to sublimate the essential dictatorial nature of pyramidal organization by dividing authority into three: executive, legislative and judicial. But the pyramid remains essentially untouched.
>
> This scheme of organization, the pyramid, is however, not only useless, but extremely dangerous for the participants when it is utilized in a resistance movement against state tyranny. Especially is this so in technologically advanced societies where electronic surveillance can often penetrate the structure revealing its chain of command. Experience has revealed over and over again that anti-state, political organizations utilizing this method of command and control are easy prey for government infiltration, entrapment, and destruction of the personnel involved. This has been seen repeatedly in the United States where pro-government infiltrators or agent provocateurs weasel their way into patriotic groups and destroy them from within...
>
> An alternative to the pyramid type of organization is the cell system. In the past, many political groups (both right and left) have used the cell system to further their objectives...
>
> The efficient and effective operation of a cell system after the Communist model, is of course, dependent upon central direction, which means impressive organization, funding from the top, and outside support, all of which the Communists had. Obviously, American patriots have none of these things...
>
> Since the entire purpose of Leaderless Resistance is to defeat state tyranny (at least insofar as this essay is concerned), all members of phantom cells or individuals will tend to react to objective events in the same way through usual tactics of resistance. Organs of information distribution such as newspapers, leaflets, computers, etc., which are widely available to all, keep each person informed of events, allowing for a planned response that will take many variations. No one need issue an order to anyone. Those idealists truly committed to the cause of freedom will act when they feel the time is ripe, or will take their cue from others who precede them...[28]

With Beam's formulation, the theory of leaderless resistance was essentially complete. All that remained was to adapt and disseminate it to ever wider constituencies of the far right wing. One of the more interesting of these hermeneutical endeavors was that of imprisoned Order veteran David Lane. Lane, an Odinist and an icon in the racialist wing of that

movement, juxtaposed the leaderless resistance strategy with the Phineas
Priest concept and arrived at the dread Wotan, a man alone – a true beserker
– who will carry on the battle against impossible odds until the day of
Ragnarök.

> So, let's go on to strategy. Resistance to tyranny within an occupied
> country necessarily forms into certain structures. Most basic is the
> division between the political or legal arm, and the armed party which
> I prefer to call Wotan as it is an excellent anagram [sic] for the will of
> the Aryan nation. The political arm is distinctly and rigidly separated
> from Wotan. The political arm will always be subjected to
> surveillance, scrutiny, harassment, and attempted infiltration by the
> system. Therefore the political arm must remain scrupulously legal
> within the parameters allowed by the occupying power. The function
> of the political arm is above all else to disseminate propaganda. The
> nature of effective propaganda is magnificently detailed in *Mein
> Kampf*, and condensed in Lane's *88 Precepts*. The political arm is a
> network and loose confederation of like minded individuals sharing a
> common goal.
>
> Wotan draws recruits from those educated by the political arm.
> When a Wotan 'goes active' he severs all apparent or provable ties
> with the political arm. If he has been so foolish as to obtain
> 'membership' in such an organization, all records of such association
> must be destroyed or resignation submitted.
>
> The goal of Wotan is clear. He must hasten the demise of the system
> before it totally destroys our gene pool. Some of his weapons are fire,
> bombs, guns, terror, disruption, and destruction. Weak points in the
> infrastructure of an industrialized society are primary targets.
> Individuals who perform valuable service for the system are primary
> targets. Special attention and merciless terror is visited upon those
> white men who commit race treason. Wotan has a totally
> revolutionary mentality. He has no loyalty to anyone or anything
> except his cause. Those who do not share his cause are expendable
> and those who oppose his cause are targets. Wotan is mature, capable,
> ruthless, self-motivated, silent, deadly, and able to blend into the
> masses. Wotan receives no recognition for his labors for if the folk
> knows his identity then soon the enemy will also. Wotan are small
> autonomous cells, one man cells if possible. No one, not wife,
> brother, parent or friend, knows the identity or actions of Wotan.[29]

Conclusion

By its very nature, leaderless resistance is an act undertaken through
individual initiative. How then to determine with certainty whether a crime
was committed as an act of leaderless resistance, or as an impulsive act of
opportunity? Certainly Joseph Franklin, Karl Hand and David Rust would
appear to have been engaged in leaderless resistance, although it is most

unlikely that they either read Col. Amoss' 1962 essay or believed that their actions would have much of an effect on the government or on the course of the nation.

Illustrative of this problem of interpretation is the Oklahoma City bombing. Certainly, by any objective analysis, Timothy McVeigh would appear to be the veritable paradigm of the leaderless resistance concept. Estranged from any right wing group, rejected by the militia movement for whom his angry words appeared to be either the ravings of a madman or, more likely, a federal plot, McVeigh with the help of one or two close friends planned and executed the most destructive act of domestic terror in American history. Moreover, McVeigh was very much a denizen of the cultic milieu of the radical right, giving him access to a vast array of conspiratorial and hate literature. It is not at all unlikely that McVeigh was familiar with Beam's essay. Indeed, given his widely reported fondness for the *Turner Diaries*, it is almost inconceivable that he would be unfamiliar with *Hunter*. But as is usual in the world of the American radical right, things are not so simple, and McVeigh is not inclined to discuss the subject.

When McVeigh was arrested, he was carrying patriot literature in his car. Subsequent publicity brought forward McVeigh friends and associates who offered further literature distributed by McVeigh, as well as his personal letters. This article will close with a brief consideration of some of these documents and letters in the context of McVeigh's possible intention to act on the leaderless resistance concept.[30]

First, it must be emphasized that nothing found in McVeigh's possession in any way indicated an interest in, or a knowledge of, any of the texts dealing with leaderless resistance theory. In McVeigh's car at the time of his arrest an envelope was found containing fragments of what appear to be several articles culled from various unnamed patriot publications. These documents deal with the question of when a citizen has the right and duty to resist a tyrannical government. Most notable among these documents are a series of quotations from such luminaries as Thomas Jefferson, Alexander Solzhenitsyn and John Locke on the subject. The last is of particular note in that McVeigh writes this on the papers in his own hand, and the same quote recurs several times in McVeigh's effects:

> I have no reason to suppose that he who would take away my liberty would not when he had me in his power, take away everything else; and therefore, it is lawful for me to treat him as one who has put himself into a 'state of war' against me; and kill him if I can, for to that hazard does he justly expose himself, whoever introduces a state of war and is aggressor in it.
>
> John Locke, *Second Treatise of Government*

Leaderless Resistance envisions an individual battle against hopeless odds in which the long range strategic objective appears to be little more hopeful than perseverance. There is scant hope that the American masses will rise against a state that the fighter sees as the embodiment of evil. The patriot literature found with and distributed by McVeigh, however, suggests no such suicidal course of action. Rather, exhortations to awaken, to organize and to resist are formulated here in terms of the creation of a mass movement which will call America back to the ideals of the Founding Fathers. Thus, one article, 'The American Response to Tyranny', juxtaposes Waco with the American Revolution and urges the faithful: 'Don't Get Discouraged'.

Other articles, 'US Government Initiates Open Warfare Against American People', and 'Waco Shootout Evokes Memory of Warsaw '43', decry government actions, but stop well short of urging violent reprisals. Rounding out McVeigh's traveling collection is that staple of every patriot home and automobile, a copy of the Declaration of Independence and the Bill of Rights.

Through the years, McVeigh sent a number of documents to his sister, Jennifer. These appear to be little different from those found in his car on the day of his arrest save for one typewritten sheet titled 'Constitutional Defenders'. Apparently written by McVeigh himself, the last line of the undated text has been widely quoted – sans context – in the news media. The brief text bears directly on our concern with the leaderless resistance concept, and so should be quoted in full.

Constitutional Defenders

We members of the citizen's militias do not bear our arms to overthrow the Constitution, but to overthrow those who PERVERT the Constitution; if and when they once again, draw first blood (many believe the Waco incident was 'first blood').

Many of our members are veterans who still hold true to their sworn oath to defend the Constitution against ALL enemies, foreign AND DOMESTIC. As John Locke once wrote 'I have no reason to suppose that he who would take away my liberty, would not, when he had me in his power, take away everything else; and therefore, it is lawful for me to treat him as one who has put himself into a 'state of war' against me, and kill him if I can, for to that hazard does he justly expose himself, whoever introduces a state of war, and is aggressor in it'. The (B)ATF are one such fascist federal group who are infamous for depriving Americans of their liberties, as well as other Constitutionally-guaranteed and INALIENABLE rights, such as one's right to self defense and one's very LIFE. One need only look at such incidences as Randy Weaver, Gordon Kahl, Waco, Donald Scott, (et ILL [sic]), to see that not only are the ATF a bunch of fascist tyrants, but their counterparts at the USMS [sic], FBI, and DEA (to name a few), are, as well.

Citizen's militias will hopefully ensure that violations of the Constitution by these power-hungry stormtroopers of the federal government will not succeed again. After all, who else would come to the rescue of those innocent women and children at Waco?!? Surely not the local sheriff or the state police! Nor the Army – whom are used overseas to 'restore democracy', while at home, are used to

DESTROY it (in full violation of the Posse Comitatus Act), at places like Waco.

One last question that every American should ask themselves: Did not the British also keep track of the locations of munitions stored by the colonists; just as the ATF has admitted to doing? Why???...Does anyone even STUDY history anymore???

ATF,

All you tyrannical motherfuckers will swing in the wind one day, for your treasonous actions against the Constitution and the United States. Remember the Nuremburg War Trials 'But..but..but...I was only following orders!'......

Die, you spineless, cowardice (sic) bastards!

Finally, McVeigh corresponded with a Michigan woman who made the material available to the FBI after the bombing. There is in this material a considerable quantity of patriot articles expressing rage at government actions at Waco:

The people of this nation should have flocked to Waco with their guns and opened fire on the bastards! The streets of Waco should have run red with the blood of the tyrants, oppressors and traitors that have slaughtered our people. Every person responsible for this massacre deserves nothing less than to die. If we want to live in peace, then sometimes we must go to war...

If this is too extreme for you, then bow down, lick the hand of your master like a willing, complacent whore and shut your mouth. Take whatever is dealt to you and your children and do not dare to complain to me about your fate. I do not have the patience to listen to the whining of cowards.

There will be future massacres because we allow them to occur.[31]

Angry words to be sure. But once again, the thrust of this and all of the other articles sent to the Michigan woman by McVeigh is for a mass uprising, not lone wolf actions. Yet in a letter to her dated 30 April 1995, other thoughts emerge. Writing from a lonely desert encampment, McVeigh expresses themes of loneliness, isolation, fear of aging, frustrated sexual desire and, most of all, a new found sense of personal mission. Noting that passing out literature is proving to be a futile gesture of defiance against the power of the state, and taking as a model the example of those revolutionaries of a previous day who risked all to sign the Declaration of Independence, McVeigh notes that while he is today at the peak of his mental and physical prowess, it will not be long before time dulls his lethal edge. Thus:

Hell, you only live once, and I *know*. You know it's better to burn out, then...rot away in some nursing home. My philosophy is the same – in only a short 1–2 years my body will slowly start giving away – first maybe knee pains, or back pains, or whatever. But I will not be 'peaked' anymore. Might as well do some good while I can be 100% effective!

In short, if a popular revolution is not on the horizon, what is left but the despairing bravado of the lone wolf assassin?

NOTES

1. Ehud Sprinzak, 'Right-Wing Terrorism in Comparative Perspective: The Case of Delegitimation', *Terrorism and Political Violence* (hereafter *TPV*) 7/1 (Spring 1995) pp.17–43. The essay is reprinted in Tore Bjørgo (ed.), *Terror from the Extreme Right* (London: Frank Cass 1995).
2. This theory is best articulated by the author of the most influential tract on leaderless resistance, Louis R. Beam, Jr. See Louis R. Beam, 'Revolutionary Majorities', e-text available from the Aryan Crusader's Library <http://www.io.com/~wlp/aryan-page>. The original essay was published in Beam's 'On Revolutionary Majorities', *Inter-Klan Newsletter and Survival Alert* 4 (1984).
3. A good flavor of the era's NS agitprop may be found in *The Best of Attack!: Revolutionary Voice of the National Alliance* (Hillsboro, WV: National Vanguard Books 1984, 1992), which features the work of the erstwhile propagandist of George Lincoln Rockwell's American Nazi Party, William Pierce. For the best of the era's histrionic style, see George Lincoln Rockwell, *This Time the World* (Arlington, VA: Parliament House 1963); and idem., *White Power* (n.p.: 1967, 1977). The latter volume offers pictorial evidence of the 'decline of Western civilization'.
4. George Lincoln Rockwell, *This Time the World* (note 3), p.193.
5. Interview with James Mason, 28 Nov. 1996.
6. Ibid.
7. On the meeting, and for reprints of Tommasi's writings, see James Mason, *Siege* (Denver, CO: Storm Books 1992). On the formation of the NSLF, letter from James Mason, 16 Dec. 1996.
8. Letter from James Mason, 16 Dec. 1996. Mason was responding to the suggestion that this core/peripheral membership was at the root of differing claims by Tommasi of the level that NSLF support was either more than 40 or only 4.
9. One such contribution is provided by the special double issue of the NSLF's newsletter which offered a 'how to' manual for those seeking to organize their own NS combatant organizations. See Karl Hand, 'Special Double Issue: How to Organize a Local Unit', *National Socialist Observer* (Feb. & March 1985) pp.1–12.
10. James Mason, *Siege* (note 7), p.104. Interview with James Mason, 28 Nov. 1996.
11. Interview with R.N. Taylor, 11 June 1997. Even today, however, Taylor does not completely discount the utility of the leaderless resistance concept, given the unlikely possibility that the right person may emerge to carry on the fight:

    As for its [leaderless resistance's] effect on 'demonstrating resistance-however doomed it might appear'. This might be the case, and perhaps the only case in which something effective would be accomplished. It brings to mind the Catalan, Francisco Sabater, who conducted a one-man guerrilla war against Franco's government, for decades. He became something of a mythic Robin Hood figure in Spain. I'm sure his activities and the publicity generated by them, helped to serve as a sort of torch or beacon... What made Sabater the legend he was? I'm sure it was based on his daring, his determination and flair. He wasn't a madman, he wasn't a pervert – he was an idealistic patriot and nationalist of the highest order. So, if someone like that were to conduct some one man war, it might well capture the popular imagination. But nothing less than that.

12. On the Order, see Kevin Flynn and Gary Gerhardt, *The Silent Brotherhood* (New York: Signet 1990). On the movement's suspicion of the Order as a federal government sting operation see Rick Cooper, 'Warning', *NSV Report* (July/Sept. 1984) p.6. Too late, Cooper would realize his mistake and publish a eulogy to the Order. See *NSV Report* (April/June 1985) pp.1–5.
13. Robert Miles, *From the Mountain* (March-April 1987–March-April 1988). The Ft. Smith coverage filled all the issues in the given months.

14. Jess Walter, *Every Knee Shall Bow: The Truth and Tragedy of Ruby Ridge and Randy Weaver Family* (New York: Regan Books 1995).
15. Stuart Wright (ed.), *Armageddon at Waco* (Chicago, IL: University of Chicago Press 1995).
16. Pete Peters, *Special Report on the Meeting of Christian Men Held in Estes Park, Colorado October 23, 24, 25, 1992 Concerning the Killing of Vickie and Samuel Weaver by the United States Government* (Laporte, CO: Scriptures for America, n.d.).
17. All of these texts are considered in a more general context in Jeffrey Kaplan, *Radical Religion in America: Millenarian Movements from the Far Right to the Children of Noah* (Syracuse, NY: Syracuse University Press 1997).
18. Andrew Macdonald [William Pierce], *The Turner Diaries* (Arlington, VA: National Vanguard Books 1978). Such is the influence of this text that CNN broadcast an interview with Pierce on 1 June 1997, and offered an interactive forum with the author on its web site on the same day.
19. Andrew Macdonald [William Pierce], *Hunter* (Arlington, VA: National Vanguard Books 1989).
20. Franklin is currently serving a life term in Utah for the murder of two mixed race couples. He is suspected of several more racially motivated murders. A former member of the NSWPP, Franklin was apparently much affected by the 1969 Mobilization against the War in Vietnam and, breaking with the conservative majority of the NSWPP, single-handedly attacked the New Mobe headquarters with gas bombs. For a laudatory review of Franklin's life and works, see James Mason, *Siege* (note 7), pp.194–9. Mason helpfully includes an entire section on the movement's lone wolves in this text.
21. Andrew Macdonald [William Pierce], *Hunter* (note 19), p.259.
22. Richard Kelly Hoskins, *Vigilantes of Christendom* (Lynchburg, VA: Virginia Publishing Co. 1990). For a discussion of the importance of this text to the world of the radical right, see my review in *Syzygy* 1/3 (Summer 1992).
23. Ibid., front cover.
24. In the rescue world, Paul Hill, currently on death row in Florida for killing an abortionist and his bodyguard, cites the example of Phineas to justify his act. See Paul J. Hill, 'Should We Defend Born and Unborn Children With Force?' *Prayer + Action Weekly News* 28, e-text, no page numbers. For a case in Spokane, Wahington, that suggests some Identity/rescue cross-over, see Nicholas K. Geranios, 'Three Bomb Suspects Nabbed', *Associated Press*, 10 Oct. 1996; and James Brook, 'Arrests Add to Idaho's Reputation as Supremacists' Haven', *New York Times*, 27 Oct. 1996.
25. Beam's writings are both voluminous and engaging. For his early analysis of the ZOG discourse, see his untitled article, Louis Beam, *The Seditionist* 1 (Winter 1988). On his earlier attempts to bring the Ku Klux Klan into what he called the 'Fifth Era', see John C. Calhoun and Louis R. Beam, 'The Perfected Order of the Klan', *Inter-Klan Newsletter and Survival Alert* 5 (1984), the letters cited had no page numbers. On computers, see idem., 'Computers and Patriots', *The Seditionist* 10 (Summer 1991) p.8.
26. Louis R. Beam, 'Leaderless Resistance', *The Seditionist* 12 (Feb. 1992). Beam's text is available today through a number of web sites.
27. Louis R. Beam, 'Leaderless Resistance'.
28. Ibid.
29. David Lane, 'Wotan Is Coming', WAR (April 1993), e-text, no page numbers. Cf. Jeffrey Kaplan, *Radical Religion in America* (note 17), pp.95–6.
30. This material was made available to potential witnesses for the defense in the penalty phase of the McVeigh trial. All references below are to these documents.
31. This is drawn from a fragment of an essay printed by the Keystone Second Amendment Association of Curwensville, PA. McVeigh writes on page 47 of the piece 'Read all – start here, just "catch up" – subject Waco'.